CHRISTOPHER MARLOWE

CHRISTOPHER MARLOWE

A BIOGRAPHICAL AND CRITICAL STUDY

BY

FREDERICK S. BOAS

M.A. (Oxon.); Hon. LL.D. (St. Andrews);
Hon. D.Lit. (Belfast); F.R.S.L.

OXFORD
AT THE CLARENDON PRESS

Oxford University Press, Amen House, London E.C.4

GLASGOW NEW YORK TORONTO MELBOURNE WELLINGTON
BOMBAY CALCUTTA MADRAS KARACHI KUALA LUMPUR
CAPE TOWN IBADAN NAIROBI ACCRA

FIRST PUBLISHED 1940

REPRINTED LITHOGRAPHICALLY IN GREAT BRITAIN
AT THE UNIVERSITY PRESS, OXFORD
FROM CORRECTED SHEETS OF THE FIRST EDITION, 1946
WITH THE ADDITION OF A SUPPLEMENTARY NOTE, 1953
1960

PREFACE

THE author of a recent brilliant work on Sir Thomas More states in his preface that he has striven to imitate More's early biographers, who 'brooded for twenty or thirty years before writing the life of their hero'. I doubt whether I have the philosophic capacity to brood, but I have been engaged in the study of Marlowe's life and writings for over forty years. And since 1920 I have had to record annually in the English Association's *The Year's Work in English Studies* the new contributions to Marlovian scholarship.

In 1929, in *Marlowe and his Circle*, I tried to sum up the biographical results achieved in the era that had been opened by Professor J. Leslie Hotson's *The Death of Christopher Marlowe* (1925). The completion, in 1933, of the six-volume edition of Marlowe's *Life and Works*, under the general editorship of Professor R. H. Case, to which I contributed *Doctor Faustus*, suggested to me that it would be opportune to attempt a comprehensive study from both the biographical and the critical angles. Various causes, including two visits to the U.S.A., have delayed the fulfilment of this plan till now, but I have thus been enabled to refer to the chief recent additions to Marlovian research. These include the documents relating to the Marlowe and Baines families printed by Professor C. F. Tucker Brooke in his *Life* of Marlowe in the six-volume edition; the new facts about Robert Poley supplied in articles by Miss Ethel Seaton and Miss E. de Kalb; the new light thrown from the Middlesex Guildhall archives by Mr. Mark Eccles on Marlowe's London life; the details about the Coroner's jury gathered from their wills by my lamented friend, Edgar Vine Hall; and the results of the researches by Mr. John Bakeless in the archives preserved at Canterbury and at Corpus Christi College, Cambridge.

Twenty years ago Professor G. C. Moore Smith drew

valuable new information about Marlowe's Cambridge career from the Corpus Christi College Account books. To Mr. Bakeless we are now indebted for disclosing a fresh source in the College Buttery books recording Kit's expenditure from week to week, of which he gave a few details in his recent volume, *Christopher Marlowe*. By the kindness of the Estates Bursar of Corpus Christi College, Mr. T. R. B. Sanders, I have been able to examine the Buttery books and to draw conclusions from the evidence that they supply, compared with that of the scholarship payments in the Account books, about the periods of Marlowe's residence at the College. The Estates Bursar has also allowed me to reproduce part of a leaf from the Buttery book that contains Marlowe's first item of expenditure. Other documents here reproduced in facsimile, so far as I know, for the first time are the inquisition returned by the Coroner on Marlowe's death[1] and parts of Richard Baines's original 'Note'.

While not attempting to fill in the background of the Elizabethan 'scene' or theatre I have tried to follow up all clues concerning Marlowe himself and such related figures as Poley, Frizer, and Baines. Here I have incorporated parts of *Marlowe and his Circle*, with the requisite additions and modifications. Every piece of new evidence gives greater significance to Poley's career and brings Richard Baines into clearer view. It will be seen that the picture here presented of Marlowe differs in considerable degree from the traditional conception of him as 'unhappy in his life and end', though an enigmatic element remains.

In my critical interpretation of the plays and poems special attention has been given to two aspects. Recent investigation has proved that, however revolutionary otherwise, Marlowe was remarkably faithful to his sources. I have therefore entered into a detailed analysis of his plots in relation to these sources, and I have

---

[1] The pardon granted to Frizer, incorporating almost all the inquisition, is facsimiled in Dr. Hotson's *The Death of Christopher Marlowe*.

suggested that the texts of *Doctor Faustus* and *The Massacre at Paris*, though undoubtedly imperfect, preserve more of the dramatist's original work than is usually allowed. The other aspect which I have emphasized is the extent and the quality of classical influence on Marlowe, not only in the translations and *Dido*, but throughout his work. In the light of these and other aspects of his dramatic technique I have approached the perplexing problems raised by *The First Part of the Contention* and *The True Tragedy*, and have stated a case for Marlowe's authorship of *Arden of Feversham*. The quotations from the plays and poems are given with modernized spelling and punctuation. A reprint with these in their original form, as in Professor Tucker Brooke's Oxford edition, is indispensable for textual criticism. But for the purposes of a more general study there is a balance of gain over loss in adopting the familiar form of presentation. Quotations from documents, on the other hand, are, as a rule, in the original spelling, though contractions have been silently expanded. References to these documents will be mainly found in the list that follows the last chapter, while those to later, including contemporary, authorities are given (without courtesy prefixes) in the footnotes, though some duplication has been unavoidable.

Besides the obligations acknowledged above, I have to thank Mr. H. H. Cox, Librarian of Lincoln College, Oxford, for kindly allowing me to reproduce the title-page of the recently discovered copy in the College library of the long unknown 1628 edition of *Doctor Faustus*. My brother-in-law, Dr. S. G. Owen, has given me helpful information about the early editions of Ovid's *Amores*. My wife, with whom, as a lover of Marlowe, I would associate this volume, has lent her aid in the preparation of the Index. I am once again greatly indebted to the vigilance of the lynx-eyed Clarendon Press Readers. Finally, I wish to thank the Delegates of the Press for proceeding with the publication of this work amidst war's alarms. Yet it is perhaps not inappropriate that this study of Marlowe should appear at a time when we are witnesses of double-crossing and megalomaniac fury as rampant as in *The Jew of Malta* and *Tamburlaine*. Will they be material for some Marlowe of the future?

WIMBLEDON   F. S. B.
January, 1940

CONTENTS

LIST OF ILLUSTRATIONS

SUPPLEMENTARY NOTE

SINCE 1945 there has been a constant flow of Marlovian research and scholarship. The relevant books and articles have been noted, as they appeared, in successive volumes of *The Year's Work in English Studies*. The most important of them are here grouped under their respective headings.

I and II Tamburlaine

In a letter to *The Times Literary Supplement* (22 Sept. 1945) Percy Simpson drew attention to a curious reference to the passage in *II Tamburlaine*, Act IV, iii, beginning, 'Holla, ye pampered Iades of Asia!' The authorities of Bridewell made its inmates scavenge the city. An unidentified R. M. in *Micrologia* (1629) quotes some lines on 'the terror of the new law':

> That (yoakt in Carts) they now must purge the streets
> While, as they passe, the people scoffing say,
> 'Holla, ye pampered Iades of Asia!'

This is testimony that the notorious line must still have been current coin more than thirty years after the play's first performance.

Francis R. Johnson, in *A Journal of English Literary History* (March 1945), stated that in Renaissance astronomy the *coelum empyreum* or empyrical heaven was the immovable heaven lying just beyond the *primum mobile*. He therefore rejects the modernized spelling 'imperial' for 'emperiall', adopted by Una Ellis-Fermor where the epithet is prefixed to 'heaven' in *I and II Tamburlaine*, and by myself similarly in *Doctor Faustus*. The right rendering is 'empyreal'.

J. C. Maxwell in *The Times Literary Supplement* (4 Jan. 1947) made an attractive conjectural emendation of the keyword in *II Tamburlaine*, v. iii. 91–92, which reads:

> Besides, my love, this day is critical,
> Dangerous to those whose crisis is as yours.

Maxwell holds that this is tautological, and that in l. 92 we should read 'crasis', i.e. temperament, though there is no record of the word in this sense till 1616.

Lynette and Evelyn Feasey in a series of articles in *Notes and*

Queries between 7 January and 30 September 1950 pointed out parallels between passages in *I and II Tamburlaine* and the Homilies and Biblical Prophetic Books, and suggested that the audiences sensed the ironic humour of the parallels.

There was a successful revival of both parts of *Tamburlaine* in a condensed form at the Old Vic theatre in September 1951, with Donald Wolfit in the titular part.

The Jew of Malta

Leo Kirschbaum in *Modern Language Quarterly* (March 1946) made a contribution to the debate, outlined in my appendix to Chapter IX, pp. 148–50, whether the Friar scenes in Act IV, ii and iii are by Marlowe or were added by Thomas Heywood. Kirschbaum holds that when Aaron in *Titus Andronicus* declares:

> Oft have I dig'd up dead men from their graves;
> And set them upright at their deare friends dore,

he has in mind the episode in *The Jew of Malta*, where Barabas and Ithamore set the dead friar Bernadine upright against the door. In that case the scenes belong to the original version of the play.

The Massacre at Paris

In an appendix to Chapter X of *Christopher Marlowe* I printed 'the Collier Leaf' and noted the defence of its authenticity by J. Quincy Adams (pp. 168–71). His view has now received additional support from J. M. Nosworthy in an article in *The Library* (Sept.–Dec. 1945), who gives reasons for doubting that Collier could have forged the leaf, and who points to the parallelism between some distinctive words and phrases in it and in Marlowe's undoubted works. Nosworthy further argues that it is probably in Marlowe's own hand.

In Chapter X, p. 153, in accordance with A. H. Bullen and H. S. Bennett in their editions of the play, I mentioned as the source of the earlier scenes Book X of *Commentaries of the Civill Warres* in France by Jean de Serres translated by Thomas Timme. But Paul H. Kocher pointed out in *P.M.L.A.* June, 1941, that while Books I–IX and XI–XII of the *Commentaries* are by de Serres, Book X, with a separate heading and pagination, is a reprint of an English version (probably by Timme) of *De Furoribus Gallicis* by 'Ernest Varamund of Freseland', a pseudonym for a Huguenot lawyer, François Hotman. Furthermore, in *Modern Language Quarterly* (June 1947) he stated that as sources for the later scenes he examined some fifty contemporary pamphlets and concluded that the villainies of Guise were traceable to anti-Catholic diatribes circulating in England and France.

Doctor Faustus

The Catalogue of English Poetry in the National Book League Exhibition, April, 1947, compiled by John Hayward, included an unrecorded copy of the 1609 quarto of *Doctor Faustus* in the library of Lord Leconfield at Petworth, which makes the third of the known copies of this edition. The controversy about the date of the first publication of the play has continued, with Paul H. Kocher being the chief defender of the traditional 1589 date. On the other hand, Sir Walter Greg in his authoritative edition of the parallel texts, 1604 and 1616, of the play (Clarendon Press, 1950) has placed it within the last year of Marlowe's life not only because its main source is P. F.'s version of the German *Historia* of Doctor Faustus, published about May 1592, but because in its finest parts it reaches a spiritual level far in advance of *Tamburlaine*. In general accordance with the views of Percy Simpson and myself, Sir Walter has given precedence to the 1616 text, supported by quotations from *The Taming of a Shrew*. But in parallel passages, as is proved by common mistakes and misprints, this text was largely dependent on the earlier bad quarto, though not on its 1604 but its 1611 issue. On the basis of his examination of the parallel texts Sir Walter has also in a small volume given a conjectural reconstruction of the play.

The comic scenes at the Papal and Imperial Courts in the 1616 text appear to have been based on a manuscript, in which Samuel Rowley had a hand. Leslie M. Oliver in an article in *Modern Language Notes* (June 1945) pointed out that the episode in Act III. i. 89–95 concerning the Emperor and his candidate 'Saxon Bruno' for the Papal Chair was derived from Foxe's *Actes and Monuments*, though Rowley changed the names and other details.

Leo Kirschbaum in *The Review of English Studies* (July 1945) wrote further in support of his view, set forth *ibid*. (July 1942) that Mephistophilis first rose in the shape of a stage-property dragon through a trap-door, and that the illustration on the 1616 title-page represents this.

Francis R. Johnson in a further article on Marlowe's astronomy in the *Journal of English Literary History* (Dec. 1946) threw light on the system expounded by Mephistophilis in Act II. ii. It is an unorthodox modification of the current Ptolemaic astronomy, which accepted only eight instead of ten moving spheres within the motionless empyreal heaven. This view was derived directly or indirectly from a treatise by Augustinus Ricius.

Sir Walter Greg in the *Modern Language Review* (April 1946) emphasized that throughout the play 'Spirit' means devil, and that when the Bad Angel tells Faustus, 'Thou art a spirit; God cannot pity thee', it is implied that through his bargain he has taken on the infernal nature. Greg further suggested that when Helen appears it is as a 'spirit', and that in making her his paramour Faustus commits the sin of demonialty, bodily intercourse with a demon.

Translations of *Doctor Faustus* have appeared in or about 1949 by Adolf Seebass in German, N. D'Agostino in Italian, and A. de O. Cabral in Portuguese.

'*I walked along a stream for pureness rare.*' A fragment, so beginning, of 24 lines in *ottava rima* was attributed to Marlowe by Robert Allott in his anthology, *England's Parnassus* (1600). The lines seemed characteristic of his poetic style, and were partly quoted by me (*Christopher Marlowe*, pp. 222–3). In *The Times Literary Supplement* (4 Jan. 1947) John Crow showed that they come from a rare elegy by Gervase Markham, entitled *Devereux*. On 11 Jan. (*ibid.*) Peter Davies suggested that the source of the stanzas by Markham was a fourth-century Latin poem by Tiberianus, *Amnis ibat inter arva*, &c.

General

In *The Times Literary Supplement* (16 Sept. 1949), starting from information by Dr. L. Antheunis of Louvain in a Flemish periodical, I suggested a possible new identification of Richard Baines, the informer against Marlowe. A man of that name entered the English seminary at Rheims in the spring or summer of 1581, became a priest, and formed a plan of revealing Roman Catholic plots against Elizabeth. A confederate disclosed his design, and he suffered confinement till 13 May 1583, when he signed a full confession. If he got back later to England he was the type of man who might have delivered the Note against the dramatist. In any case the coincidence of his name with the Richard Baines of the Inner Temple, to whom the Note has been attributed (*Christopher Marlowe*, pp. 245–52) is striking.

The Note occupies a predominant place in Paul H. Kocher's

Marlowe: A Study of his Thought, Learning, and Character (Chapel Hill, 1946). He has found in it 'the master-key to the mind of Marlowe'. Kocher regards Marlowe as a highly subjective writer, whose chief preoccupation was not drama but religion, and whose 'utterances represent a carefully designed attack on Christian drama'. From contemporary treatises Kocher throws some useful light on Marlowe's astronomical knowledge and his allusions to the art of war. But his study, as a whole, though scholarly, presents Marlowe in a wrong perspective. This may also be said of his article from a similar standpoint on Marlowe as an individualist in *The University of Toronto Quarterly* (Jan. 1948).

An Italian volume on the dramatist by N. D'Agostino (Rome, 1950) included an earlier article by him on Marlowe's 'Ideologia', and two new studies of his plot-construction and his versification. These were followed by a full bibliography, including a special section on Italian translations and critical works.

Tucker Brooke in his posthumously published volume on *Shakespeare and other Elizabethans* paid a last tribute to Marlowe, in which, besides one or two more doubtful claims, he stated that he 'taught drama the splendour of romance', had the rare Elizabethan virtue of a sense of form, and a hatred of religious intolerance which gained him the reputation of atheism.

A helpful and well-written introduction to the dramatist's career and works has been supplied by Philip Henderson in his *Christopher Marlowe* in the 'Men and Books' series (Longmans, 1952).

December, 1952

I

CANTERBURY

I

THE MARLOWE FAMILY

AS the fifteenth century was nearing its close there
was born in the Bavarian medieval city of Nuremberg,
on 5 November 1494, the cobbler-poet, Hans Sachs. His
life, divided, as has been said, between his last and his lyre,
was prolonged for what was at that time an unusual
span, till 1576. By 1567, according to his own computa-
tion, he had written over 4,000 *Meisterlieder*, 1,700 tales
and poems, and over 200 dramas, mainly dialogue-pieces
or Shrovetide farces. Three years before this date, in the
English medieval city of Canterbury, there was born to
another shoemaker, John Marlowe, a son, Christopher,
whose life's measure was to be little more than a third of
that of Sachs, and who, leaving behind him less than a
dozen plays and poems has through them brought im-
perishable reflected glory to the paternal 'gentle craft'.

It is not, however, as shoemakers that Marlowes first
appear in the Canterbury city records. The name had
even more than the normal quota of variant spellings—
Marlowe, Marlow, Marloe, Marlo, Marlen, Marlin, Mar-
lyne, Marlinge, Merlin, Marley, Marlye, Morley, Morle.
In 1414 William Morle, a fuller, became a freeman of the
city by redemption, on payment of ten shillings. In 1438
Simon Morle, a vintner, was similarly admitted. In 1459
Thomas Morle, son of William, and also a fuller, gained the
privilege without payment by virtue of his birth. In 1478
Thomas Marlow, roper, was admitted by redemption.

A fuller, a vintner, and a roper have little in common
with a shoemaker, but John Marley, a tanner, admitted
a freeman by redemption in 1467, introduces into the
record of the Canterbury Marlowes a closely allied trade.
John was followed both as a tanner and a freeman by his

son Richard, who died in 1521, leaving a detailed will mainly in favour of his only son Christopher, then a minor. Richard was a man of substance, for the property which he devised included the tanhouse, the 'principal tenement' in which he dwelt, three messuages in North-lane, and twenty acres of land leased from 'Sir John Ffyneux, Knight'.[1] There is further evidence at a later date of connexion between the Marlowe and the Phineaux families.[2]

Christopher Marley, the first bearer of the name, died in 1540, leaving one daughter and his wife, Joan, with an unborn child who, if a 'man child', was to inherit his dwelling-house and the adjoining 'Old Hall' with the land belonging to it, while the widow was to have the twenty leased acres and, presumably, the tanhouse. There is no documentary evidence, but it is a reasonable supposition that the unborn child of Christopher Marley's will was John Marley, or Marlowe, who was to be father of the second Christopher, the dramatist, and also of a daughter, Joan, thus carrying on the names of both grandparents. Moreover, 'the dates of John Marlowe's marriage, business career, and death agree well with the assumption that he was born in 1540'.[3]

If the speculation concerning John Marlowe's genealogy is correct, it might have been anticipated that he would continue the trade of tanning in which the family had been profitably engaged for three generations. But he took up the allied trade of shoemaking, the tanners and shoemakers being associated in Canterbury in the same guild. A recent discovery by John Bakeless proves that John Marley was enrolled by Gerard Richardson, shoe-maker and freeman of Canterbury, as an apprentice in 1559-60.[4]

The usual period of apprenticeship was seven years, but

---

[1] The will is printed in full in C. F. Tucker Brooke's *Life of Marlowe* (1930), pp. 83-9.
[2] See below, p. 110.   [3] Tucker Brooke, op. cit., p. 6 *n*.
[4] 'Marlowe and his Father', in *T.L.S.*, 2 Jan. 1937.

John Marlyn, shoemaker, was admitted as a freeman in 1564, on payment of 4*s*. 1*d*. While still an apprentice he married on 22 May 1561, in the church of St. George the Martyr, Catherine Arthur, who seems to have been the daughter of the Reverend Christopher Arthur, rector of St. Peter's, Canterbury, 1550–2. According to local tradition he brought his bride to a house still standing, though much renovated, at the corner of St. George's Street and St. George's Lane.

Children were born of the marriage in rapid succession, and the entries of their baptisms in the St. George's Church register and the archdeacon's transcripts illustrate some of the various spellings of the family name.

> May 21, 1562. Mary, the daughter of John Marlowe.
> Feb. 26, 1563/4. Christofer, the son of John Marlow.
> Dec. 11, 1565. Margarit, the daughter of John Marloe.[1]
> Oct. 31, 1568. —, the son of John Marlow.
> Aug. 20, 1569. John, the son of John Marlow.[2]
> July 26, 1570. Thomas, son of John Marle.
> July 14, 1571. An, daughter of John Marle.
> Oct. 18, 1573. Daretye, daughter of John Marlye.

The register also records the early death of three of these children. An unnamed daughter of John Marlow, buried on 28 August 1568, was probably Mary; an unnamed son, buried on 5 November 1568, was apparently the child christened on the previous 31 October; and Thomas, also dying in infancy, was buried on 7 August 1570. Six years later the name Thomas was revived in the family for another son, baptized apparently on 8 April 1576 in St. Andrew's Church.[3] For between the births of Dorothy and this second Thomas their father

---

[1] Entered in the transcript, with a difference of date, as 'Dec. 18, 1566. Marget, daughter of John Marlo'.

[2] Tucker Brooke (op. cit., p. 8) suggests that this is a clerical error for Jane or Joan, as the baptism of Joan Marlowe (see below, p. 4) is not recorded, and there is no other mention of a son, John.

[3] This is the date in the archdeacon's transcript. The St. Andrew's Church register has 5 Nov. 1567, which must be wrong.

had moved his household from St. George's to a more central position in St. Andrew's parish.

Even with the loss of three children, John Marlowe had six dependent upon him, including four daughters. Presumably after the manner of Canterbury Marlowes he prospered in business. But all that is known about him as a shoemaker is that he was able successively to enrol at least four apprentices whose names are on record. The first, in 1567–8, was Richard Umbarffeld. Two others were Elias Martyn and William Hewes, who, having been apprentices to John Marlowe, presumably for the normal seven years, became freemen respectively on 3 July 1583 and 26 April 1594. On 23 December 1594 Hewes was succeeded in the apprenticeship by Thomas Mychell.[1]

John Marlowe did not follow the proverbial maxim which bids a shoemaker stick to his last. From 1579 onwards he is found acting, according to an Elizabethan practice, as a professional bondsman on behalf of couples seeking marriage licences. On 28 April 1579 John Marley of St. Andrew's, Cant., shoemaker, became security for no less a sum than £100.[2] He next appears as a bondsman on 8 February 1588, and thenceforward nearly once a year till 11 August 1604.

But John Marlowe's connexion with marriages was not merely professional. His second surviving daughter, Jane or Joan (if the baptismal entry of 20 August 1569 refers to her), was only thirteen when she was married in St. Andrew's Church on 22 April 1582 to John Moore, a shoemaker.[3] At a later date the Marlowe family again moved, to a house in the neighbouring parish of St. Mary Bredman. Here the church register records the marriages

[1] See the particulars given by John Bakeless in *T.L.S.*, 2 Jan. 1937.
[2] J. M. Cowper, *Canterbury Marriage Licences*, 1st series, 1568–1618, col. 365.
[3] This is the date in the Church register. In the city roster of freemen admitted by marriage there are two entries relating to the union of John Moore and Jane or Joan, dated respectively 1583 and 1585. Tucker Brooke suggests (op. cit., p. 9) that the first entry may have been invalid owing to the youthfulness of the couple.

of the three other daughters. On 15 June 1590 Margaret took to husband John Jordan, a tailor. On 10 June 1593 Ann followed the example of Jane by marrying John Crawford, a shoemaker. On 19 June 1594 the youngest daughter, Dorothy, revived an old Marlowe association by wedding Thomas Cradwell, or Gradwell, a vintner.

Her place in the household was partly taken by her cousin, Dorothy Arthur, sole survivor when the plague in August and September 1593 carried off both her parents and four of their children. She had then come under her aunt Catherine Marlowe's roof, and she showed her gratitude when shortly before her death on 26 August 1597 she left all her goods to this paternal aunt, to the exclusion of an aunt by her mother's side.

In his later years, with lighter family responsibilities, John Marlowe found time for parochial duties. In the entry of his burial, 26 January 1604/5, in the register of St. George's Church, he is called 'clerk of St. Maries'. How long he had held this office is not known. But a recent discovery shows that in 1591–2 he had signed the register of St. Mary Bredman, in the capacity of church-warden, as 'Iohn Marley'.[1] It is therefore evident that the mark which takes the place of a signature to his will was not due to illiteracy. This will, drawn up on 23 January 1604/5, is a remarkably brief document. He directs that he should be buried in the churchyard of St. George's parish, where his earlier married life had been spent, and he leaves all his 'temporall goods' to his wife whom he appoints his sole executrix. In striking contrast are the detailed provisions of Catherine Marlowe's own will, fourteen months later, made on 17 March 1605/6.[2]

Among other legacies she bequeaths to her eldest sur-viving daughter, Margaret Jordan, 'the greatest golde ringe'; to Ann Crawford 'a golde ringe' and 'an other siluer ringe'; to Dorothy Cradwell 'ye ringe wth ye double

---

[1] John Bakeless in *T.L.S.*, loc. cit.

[2] The wills of John Marlowe and of his wife are printed by Tucker Brooke, op. cit., pp. 93–6.

posye'. Similarly, the spoons, including the six 'greatest siluer spoones', are divided among her daughters and their children. The daughters are also each to have two cushions and to have the use between them of her 'Christeninge linnen'. Jane, who had married so early, must have been dead, for she is not mentioned, but her husband, John Moore, is left forty shillings and 'the ioyne presse that standeth in the greate chamber where I lye'. John Crawford, the senior son-in-law, is appointed residuary legatee and executor.

As Catherine Marlowe lingers so solicitously over the bestowal of her gold and silver rings, her greatest silver spoons, her taffeta cushions and the rest, is it fanciful to conjecture that Christopher may in part have inherited from his mother his eye for 'seld-seen precious stones', for the dazzling blaze and colours of the world? It is permissible to catch at even such a slight clue to the sudden flowering from a prosperous, well-ordered tradesman stock of a revolutionary poetic genius—as inexplicable a sport of nature as the emergence in a later age of a Shelley or a Swinburne from an equally conventional, though far higher, social environment.

II

THE KING'S SCHOOL

But of Christopher's home life not the faintest echo remains either in tradition or in his writings. The one institution that links him with Canterbury is the King's School, where he entered as a scholar on 14 January 1578/9. This ancient foundation, from time immemorial attached to the Cathedral, was put on a new basis by Henry VIII when in 1541 he instituted a collegiate body to take the place of the monks of Canterbury as controllers of the Cathedral. The capitular statutes contained very precise regulations concerning the school. There were to be 'two public teachers of the boys in Grammar', i.e. Latin grammar. Their pupils were to be 'fifty poor boys, both destitute of the help of friends, and endowed with minds apt for learning, who shall be called scholars of the grammar school, and shall be sustained out of the funds of our Church'. These boys were not to be admitted till they had learnt to read and write and were moderately versed in the first rudiments of grammar. They were to be maintained for four, or at most five, years 'until they have obtained a moderate acquaintance with the Latin grammar, and have learned to speak in Latin and write in Latin'. The age-limits for election were fixed at nine and fifteen respectively.

It is curious that Christopher was not elected till he was within a few weeks of the upward limit of age. He certainly had a mind apt for learning, and though the son of John Marlowe was not destitute of the help of friends, the designation of 'poor boy' was given a very elastic interpretation. Each of the scholars received a yearly stipend of £1. 8s. 4d., together with allowances for commons and for a new gown every Christmas, the total annual payment being £4. These payments were recorded in the accounts of the Treasurer of the Cathedral, which have been preserved for 1578–9. Here appear the names of the fifty boys who received the quarterly allowance of one pound.[1] 'Christopher Marley' is not found among them in the first quarter, but in the second he fills a vacancy caused by the departure of John Emtley. His place is 47th in the Treasurer's list, and in the third and fourth terms 48th and 45th respectively. The Treasurer's accounts for 1579–80 are missing, but Christopher must have continued to attend the school and make good use of his time till near the close of the Michaelmas term 1580, when he went up to Corpus Christi College, Cambridge, and was soon afterwards elected to a scholarship on Archbishop Parker's foundation.[2]

[1] Facsimile in J. H. Ingram's *Christopher Marlowe and his Associates* (1904), p. 33. Alphabetical list of scholars in Tucker Brooke, op. cit., pp. 19–20.   [2] See below, p. 10.

Marlowe thus spent just under two years at the King's School. But on a boy of his exceptional gifts and interests, in the formative period between fifteen and seventeen, they must have had a highly important influence. The curriculum of the school, as has been seen, was fashioned according to the Renaissance pedagogic ideals, and its chief aim was to train the scholars to speak and write Latin fluently. It is one of the purposes of the pages that follow in this volume to illustrate, more fully than has yet been attempted, the extent of the classical influences upon Marlowe's work. The foundation of his familiarity with Latin literature and with the mythology of Greece and Rome must have been laid at the King's School in 1579–80.

A favourite Renaissance method of teaching boys to speak Latin intelligently was training them to act in classical or neo-classical plays. Anthony Rushe, head-master of the King's School, 1561–5, received from the Cathedral Chapter £14. 6s. 8d. in 1562–3 for 'setting out of his plays at Christmas'.[1] In the light of the school's curriculum some at least of these may be presumed to have been in Latin. There is no documentary record of performances under Christopher's two headmasters, John Gresshop (1566–80) and Nicholas Goldsborough (1580–4), nor indeed till the reign of Charles I. But whether or not there was acting by the King's scholars in 1579–80, it must have counted for something in Christopher's development that his school had a tradition of theatrical production which was favoured by the authorities of the Cathedral.

Otherwise the Cathedral, and all that it stood for, seems to have left strangely little impression on him. The revelation of beauty came to him through the channel of classical antiquity and not by the way of gothic medieval-ism. Here again he is linked with Shelley and Swinburne, both worshippers at the shrines of Greece and Rome, but the one scorning York Minster as a 'huge erection of

[1] C. E. Woodruff and H. J. Cape, *Schola Regia Cantuariensis*, pp. 79–80.

unreason',[1] the other deaf to the enchantment whispered from Oxford's towers.

Thus when Christopher left Canterbury for Cambridge towards the end of 1580 there is nothing to show that he ever returned. Recently discovered evidence shows that he was resident in college when his sister Jane was married on 22 April 1582.[2] By his native townsmen it might have been said of him, when he took his leave, with the change of the place-name to Canterbury, that he

> came, as most men deem'd, to little good,
> But came to Oxford and his friends no more.[3]

[1] E. Dowden, *Life of Shelley*, p. 89.

[2] John Bakeless, *Christopher Marlowe*, p. 26 (1938).

[3] The statement that there is nothing to show that Marlowe ever returned to Canterbury now needs correction. Among documents discovered in 1939 by Mr. F. W. Tyler in the Canterbury Public Record Office is the Will of Catherine Benchkyn of Canterbury which was attested in the autumn of 1585 by four witnesses including Christopher Marlowe and his father (see John Bakeless, *The Tragicall History of Christopher Marlowe*, vol. i, pp. 25-6 and 74-5 (1942)).

CAMBRIDGE

I

ARCHBISHOP PARKER'S SCHOLAR

THE first documentary evidence of Christopher Marlowe's residence in Cambridge, recently discovered,
is the entry in the Buttery books of Corpus Christi College
of a charge to 'Marlen' of 1*d*. in 'septimana 10ᵃ post
Michael', i.e. the second week of December 1580.[1] It
was a paradoxical academic initiation for one whose
imagination was hereafter to be filled with 'infinite riches
in a little room'. In the following three weeks he was
more prodigal, and made a number of disbursements in
sums varying from 15*d*. to ½*d*.

Marlowe was, therefore, in residence at Corpus Christi
during the last four weeks of the first (Michaelmas) term
of the academic year 1580–1. He did not formally
matriculate till near the end of the second (Lent) term, on
17 March 1580/1, when the entry 'Coll. Corp. Xr.
Chrōf. Marlen' appears in the University Matriculation
Registry in the *convictus secundus*, i.e. students intermedi-
ate between fellow-commoners and sizars. In the College
Registrum Parvum or Admission Book 'Marlin' in the
second term 1580–1 is listed among the *Pensionarii*, being
last but one among the twenty-eight entries during the
year ending 24 March 1580/1.

It is not till the third (Easter) term that there is found
among entries in the *Registrum Parvum*, dated between
7 and 11 May 1581, relating to scholarships at the College,
'Marlin electus et admissus in locum domini Pashly'.
Marlowe thus officially became a scholarship-holder and
paid the customary fixed fee on his election, for the
Corpus Christi accounts record, 'Pro introitu in Con-

---

[1] John Bakeless, op. cit., p. 72.

Part of a leaf of the Corpus Christi College, Cambridge, Buttery Book for the tenth week after Michaelmas, 1580, containing the item of 1*d.* spent by 'Marlen', which is the first documentary record of Marlowe's residence at Cambridge

victum Magistri et Sociorum et Scholarium . . . Marlin iij^s iiij$^{d'}$. These accounts also record the payment to 'Marlin' of twelve shillings in the Lent term, and he must therefore have been counted as a scholar previous to his formal election.[1]

The researches of G. C. Moore Smith, supplemented by those of later investigators, have established the precise character of Marlowe's scholarship and the conditions on which it was held. The learned Matthew Parker, Archbishop of Canterbury (1558–75), was a generous benefactor to Corpus Christi College, of which he had been successively Scholar, Fellow, and Master. In 1567 he founded three scholarships tenable at the College by boys from Norwich, and in 1569 five for boys from Canterbury School, followed by two additional Norwich scholarships. Finally, by his will made on 5 April 1575, Parker founded three further scholarships of the value of £3. 6s. 8d. annually:

'Quorum scholasticorum primum electum volo per successores meos in Scholâ *Cantuar.* & in ea urbe oriundum: Secundum electum volo è Scholâ de *Aylesham* & tertium è Scholâ de *Wymondham*: In hiis duabus villis oriundos.'

The Archbishop died on 17 May and effect was immediately given to the above provision in his will, for in the College accounts for 1575–6 the names are given of the three scholars elected in accordance with its terms, Thexton, Poynter, and Pashley, of whom the third was the one from the King's School, Canterbury. In an indenture made in April 1580 between the Archbishop's son, John Parker, and the college authorities, the conditions governing the award of the scholarship were more

---

[1] May he also have been so counted during the previous Michaelmas term or part of it? G. C. Moore Smith who first printed the entries in the C.C.C. account books (*M.L.R.*, Jan. 1909) noted that 'Marlin' had been entered among the scholars in the first quarter of 1580–1, but had been crossed out and 'Pashlye' written above. As the Buttery book now proves that Marlowe was in residence in Dec. 1580, may not the original entry be correct?

closely defined and John Parker expressly reserved the
nomination to himself.[1] He has not yet received due
recognition of his discriminating choice of Christopher
Marlowe, though he had been only two years in the
King's School, to fill the vacancy caused by the retirement
of the first Canterbury scholar on that particular foundation, Christopher Pashley.

In 1580–1 Pashley had drawn his stipend for nearly
six years, and it would appear that, as in the case of the
Norwich scholars, those appointed under the terms of the
will were elected for three years or for six, if they intended
to be ordained.

The indenture specified that the scholars should have
certain musical qualifications and be well instructed in
their grammar, and 'if it may be such as can make a
verse'. Christopher could certainly satisfy the last condition, though the reference is to skill in Latin, not English,
prosody. The three scholars under the terms of the will
were to be lodged in a chamber formerly known as the
Storehouse which had been repaired by John Parker.
Strict regulations were made about residence. They were
not to be absent from college more than one month in
the year except upon College business or 'through some
notable sicknes'.

The Universities in the sixteenth century were far
from entertaining the modern conception of 'the Long
Vacation'. Even so it was found impossible to carry out
stringently Parker's regulations, though in any week that
a scholar was absent he forfeited his allowance of one
shilling. With a full attendance he would receive thirteen
shillings in each of the first three quarters, and fourteen
in the last.[2] The entries, therefore, in the college accounts,

---

[1] The indenture was discovered by John Bakeless in the Corpus Christi
College archives. See his *Christopher Marlowe*, pp. 47 and 335.

[2] It will be seen that the maximum yearly allowance was thus £2. 13s.,
though in his will Archbishop Parker had allowed £3. 6s. 6d. to each
scholar. The difference may be accounted for by the fact that the three
scholars had such privileges as 'their barber and laundry freely without
any thing paying therefor'.

as G. C. Moore Smith was the first to point out,[1] of the scholarship payments to Marlowe show how long he was in residence during each term.[2] The payments are, in tabular form, as follows:

	1ᵃ Trim.	2ᵃ Trim.	3ᵃ Trim.	4ᵃ Trim.
1580–1		Marlin xijˢ	Marlen xiijˢ	Marlen xijˢ
1581–2	Marlin xiijˢ	Marlin xiijˢ	Marlin xiijˢ	Marlin vijˢ
1582–3	Malyn xijˢ	Marlin xiijˢ	Marlin vjˢ	Marlin xiiijˢ
1583–4	D Marlyn xijˢ	D Marlyn xiijˢ	D Marlyn xiijˢ	D Marlin xjˢ vjᵈ
1584–5	Ds Marlin iijˢ	Ds Marlin vijˢ	Ds Marlin iiijˢ	Ds Marlin vˢ
1585–6 (Accounts missing)				
1586–7	Ds Marly ixˢ	Dˢ Marlye vˢ vjᵈ		

Marlowe was thus in virtually permanent residence from his arrival in Cambridge till the fourth term of his second academic year of which he appears to have missed exactly half. This is confirmed by the Buttery book, in which there are no entries of expenditure by him during the fourth term of 1581–2 in the second to the eighth weeks inclusive. Similarly, in the third term of his third year, 1582–3, he was absent about half of it. There are no entries against his name in the Buttery book from the fourth to the ninth weeks inclusive. In his fourth year, 1583–4, he was in almost constant attendance. During this year, in the second term, he took his B.A. degree. In the Buttery book for the sixth week after Christmas he is still merely 'Marlin'. From the seventh week after Christmas he becomes 'Dominus Marlin'. In the scholarship accounts he gets the prefix, by courtesy, from the beginning of the academic year.

The record of Marlowe's academic attendance for the first four years is, taken all in all, creditable, and compares favourably with the similar records of such fellow scholars as Thomas Lewgar, Thomas Munday, and William Cockman.[3] In his fifth year, 1584–5, the scholar-

[1] He reproduces, loc. cit., pp. 173–5, the payments to Marlowe and his companion scholars, 1580–1 to 1586–7. Similarly in Tucker Brooke, op. cit., pp. 27–8.

[2] See, however, p. 14.

[3] See the details of scholarship payments given by Moore Smith and Tucker Brooke, loc. cit.

ship payments suggest an abrupt change, but here they are not entirely confirmed by the Buttery book. In Michaelmas term Marlowe is paid only three shillings, but there are entries of expenditure by him in the second, third, fourth, seventh, tenth, eleventh, and twelfth weeks. In the second term he is paid seven shillings but has entries against him in nine weeks. In the third term the scholarship accounts and the Buttery book nearly tally, for there are no entries of expenditure by him from the fifth to the twelfth weeks inclusive; and in the fourth term they agree, for there are no entries against his name for nine of the fourteen weeks, from the fourth to the twelfth inclusive.

The scholarship accounts for 1585–6 are missing, but by good fortune the Buttery book for that year is preserved—the last extant till the middle of the eighteenth century. It proves that, except in the third term, Marlowe was in regular attendance throughout his last full academic year. In the Michaelmas term there are two weeks without entries and in the second term there are three weeks. In the third there is only one entry before the last two weeks of the term. On the other hand, somewhat surprisingly, he is shown in the fourth term to have been in attendance every one of the fourteen weeks, as also in the first three weeks of the Michaelmas term, 1586, after which the Buttery book fails us.

Presumably the Government service upon which Marlowe was for a time employed before taking his M.A. degree[1] was after he had become 'Dominus'. If so, on the evidence of the Buttery books his only lengthy periods of absence from Cambridge, if this was involved, were in the third or fourth terms of 1584–5, or the third of 1585–6. Otherwise, and this is more probable, the service must have been rendered after he had 'gone down' in or after the Lent term 1587.

Can it have any bearing on this question that Marlowe's weekly expenditure in 1585–6 seems to have been in excess of any previous period, items from xviii*d.* to xxi*d.*

[1] See below, pp. 22 ff.

being not infrequent, though even from the first he had by no means always kept within his scholarship allowance of one shilling and must have had it supplemented in some way? Though he began with the humble payment of 1*d*., his life at Corpus was far from one of penury.

In 1587 he had held his scholarship for the maximum period of six years, on the presumption, as it would seem, that he intended to take holy orders. He had complied in the normal way with the University regulations for students taking the course for the Bachelor of Arts degree. For this it was technically necessary to have completed a *quadrennium*, or four years' residence. But difficulties had arisen because candidates had to pass their final tests between Ash Wednesday and the Thursday after the fourth Sunday in Lent. Hence by a decree of 15 February 1578/9 it was ordained that any one who had been enrolled 'before, at, or upon the day when the ordinary sermon *ad clerum* is or ought to be made in the beginning of the Easter term, shall be reputed and accounted to have wholly and fully satisfied the statute, if he shall proceed in the fourth Lent next following the said sermon'.

On this interpretation of the statute Marlowe had complied with its requirements by Lent 1584, and his *supplicat* to be allowed to proceed to the degree is extant, certificated by Thomas Harris, a Fellow of Corpus.

'Supplicat Christopherus Marlin ut duodecim termini completi in quibus ordinarias lectiones audivit (licet non omnino secundum formam statuti) una cum omnibus oppositionibus responsionibus caeterisque exercitiis per statuta regia requisitis sufficiant ei ad respondendum quaestioni.'

His college tutor thus guaranteed that Marlowe had satisfactorily performed the public exercises in which he propounded certain philosophical theses and attacked others. In the University Grace Book 'Christof. Marlyn' appears second in a list of twelve Corpus Christi College undergraduates admitted to the degree, and in the 'Ordo Senioritatis' Marlowe is 199th among 231.

What were the 'ordinary lectures' attended by Marlowe, and what were his academic studies? There is only one piece of documentary evidence. In a list dated 29 October 1581 'Merling' is one of the Corpus Christi College undergraduates (among them being his fellow scholars Lewgar and Munday) in the class of 'Mr. Johnes, professor lecturae dialecticae'.[1] It was the combination of the ratiocinative and the imaginative faculties in Marlowe that was to be the distinctive note of his genius. He would, therefore, at any time have been a keen student of logic. But at this period the subject was exciting special interest and controversy in Cambridge, where the University was torn between the adherents of the traditional Aristotelian system and the followers of the heretical Parisian professor, Petrus Ramus. Echoes of these academic debates were to be strangely mingled in *The Massacre at Paris* with the cries of the victims on the eve of St. Bartholomew.[2] And in the opening scene of *Doctor Faustus* where the chief subjects of the curriculum are passed in review the definition of the aim of logic

Bene disserere est finis logices

is taken from the *Dialectica* of Ramus.[3]

In the Cambridge atmosphere of his day a student with so restlessly inquiring a mind as Marlowe would thus not have been content to 'live and die in Aristotle's works'. But that he was familiar with many of the Stagirite's writings, at any rate in their Latin dress, is shown by his references to the *Analytics* and the *Organon*, by his adapted quotations from other of his works and the allusion to the doctrine of ὂν καὶ μὴ ὄν.[4]

From metaphysical speculation it was a natural transition to the more concrete problems of cosmology. How

[1] See also below, p. 31.

[2] See below, pp. 159–60.

[3] Editions of this work had been published in London by T. Vautrollier in 1576 and by T. Thomas at Cambridge in 1584.

[4] In A. H. Bullen's convincing emendation of the 1604 quarto 'Oncaymaeon' in *Doctor Faustus*, I. i. 12.

'ravished' Marlowe was with these and how they come breaking, appropriately or otherwise, into his dramatic and poetic work will appear in the discussion of the plays and poems. Cosmology was allied on the one hand with astronomy, in its Ptolemaic phase, and on the other with geography as set forth in the *Theatrum Orbis Terrarum* of Ortelius which so profoundly influenced him.[1]

Of medical science he knew, at any rate, enough to be well versed in contemporary concepts of psychology and physiology.[2] Law is stigmatized by Faustus as a study fit only for 'a mercenary drudge', and though he need not here be speaking for Marlowe, his quotations from Justinian's *Institutes* are inaccurate, and there is a notable absence in his works of the legal phraseology so abundantly used by Shakespeare and other Elizabethan dramatists. On the other hand, detailed investigation into the sources of his plays has shown Marlowe to have been a diligent and close student of history, as he found it in the annals of Turkish and Scythian affairs and in French and English chronicles.[3]

But however ardently Marlowe's intellect roamed through other fields of study it was by classical poetry and legend that he was enthralled and inspired. They were the magic casements through which this young Englishman, a tradesman's son and a churchman's protégé, was to gaze upon the mundane spectacle and see it gloriously transfigured. And this was achieved, so far as can be judged, without his having direct access to the noblest and purest products of classical genius. Though 'Homer's Iliads' loom large before Marlowe, there is no clear evidence that he had read the Greek epics in the original,

[1] See below, pp. 88 and 91.

[2] See 'Marlowe and Elizabethan Psychology', by C. Camden, jr., *Phil. Quarterly*, Jan. 1629.

[3] See especially Una Ellis-Fermor's edition of *Tamburlaine*, pp. 26–50, and Ethel Seaton, 'Marlowe and his Authorities', *T.L.S.*, 16 June 1921, and 'Fresh Sources for Marlowe', *R.E.S.*, Oct. 1929. Bakeless, op. cit., pp. 60–4, discusses some of the books available to Marlowe in the University or C.C.C. libraries.

that he had made 'blind Homer sing to' him in his own majestic tones. Of the glories of Attic tragedy there is not the faintest echo throughout his work. And when he borrowed the theme of his *Hero and Leander* from a Greek versifier of the fifth century A.D., he probably made use of the Latin version which had opportunely appeared in 1587.[1] And even when Faustus quotes texts from St. Paul's and St. John's Epistles they are not in the Hellenistic Greek of the New Testament but in the Latin of 'Jerome's Bible', the Vulgate.[2]

Without denying that Marlowe during his six years' residence at Cambridge may have acquired the elements of Greek, there can be no doubt that to him as to nearly all English humanists of his time, except a select group of scholars and divines, the revelation of the antique world came through the literature of Rome. And to Marlowe the pre-eminent source of this revelation was Ovid—not only in the *Amores*, of which his translation may even have dated from his Cambridge days, but in such storehouses of myth and legend as the *Metamorphoses*, the *Fasti*, and the *Heroides*. The peculiar influence of Ovid on Marlowe is discussed later in detail.[3] Here it is enough to say that in the elegist who romanticized so much that was august or primitive in the mythology and annals of Greece and Rome the young English poet found a genius in many points akin to his own. Only second was the attraction for him of Virgil to whom his debt extends well beyond the confines of *Dido, Queen of Carthage*. And between the singer of the *Aeneid* and Lucan, whose first Book of the *De Bello Civili* Marlowe translated, there was for the humanists of his day no such gap as separates for us the poets of the golden and the silver ages of Latinity. Indeed, for him the corpus of Latin literature would include the medieval and neo-classic annalists and biographers who furnished him with materials for *Tambur-*

---

[1] See below, p. 227.

[2] *Doctor Faustus*, I. i. 38, 'Jerome's Bible, Faustus, view it well', and ll. 39-41.   [3] See below, pp. 29-42.

laine. And he himself, if we may rely on the reported testimony of a Kentish and (approximately) Cambridge contemporary, Simon Aldrich, practised the neo-classic poetic art. Aldrich, a member of a Canterbury family, matriculated at Trinity College about 1593, graduated B.A. in 1596–7, and later became a Fellow. He ultimately became a tenant and neighbour of Henry Oxinden, a collector of plays and writer of commonplace-books, near Canterbury. Oxinden notes on 10 February 1640 that 'Mr. Aldrich saies that Marloe . . . was a rare scholar and made excellent verses in Latin'.[1] But he has left nothing in that language which could be dated from his Cambridge days.

To what extent then or later Marlowe became familiar with the languages derived from Latin is difficult to say. Though 'Machiavel' speaks the prologue to *The Jew of Malta,* Marlowe's conception of his doctrines does not seem to be based upon the Florentine's own writings but on Gentillet's French counterblast *Contre N. Machiavel* (1576). The relation between *Orlando Furioso,* xxvii–xxix, and two scenes in *Tamburlaine,* Part II (III. iv and IV. ii), is not sufficiently intimate necessarily to imply first-hand knowledge of Ariosto's epic, of which Harington's translation was not published till 1591. In this episode and elsewhere Marlowe appears to have used Belleforest's *Cosmographie Universelle.* In Act II. i of *The Jew of Malta* two lines of Spanish are introduced (39 and 64), but of the Romance languages there is little doubt that it was French of which Marlowe had the best working knowledge.

But however wide the range of his studies in arts and

---

[1] Oxinden's memoranda about Marlowe are contained in his commonplace books, one of which is in the Folger Shakespeare Library in Washington, and the other in the British Museum (Add. MSS. 28012). They were also noted in the fly-leaf of a copy of the 1629 *Hero and Leander,* which was in the Heber Library, and were summarized by J. P. Collier before the sale of the library in 1834. Collier's evidence was suspect and the quarto has now disappeared. But the discovery of Oxinden's commonplace-books has established the genuineness of the memoranda. See 'Marlowe in Kentish Tradition,' by Mark Eccles, *N. & Q.,* 13, 20, 27 July, 24 Aug. 1935.

sciences Marlowe as a six-year scholar apparently destined
to take holy orders must have been supposed to give the
first place to divinity in his academic curriculum. For the
common use of his Norwich scholars Parker had provided
a number of books chained in one of the chambers set
apart for their residence.[1] These included, in addition
to classical lexicons and *thesauri* and a history of Cambridge,

Textus Bibliae cum Gloss. Lyrae in quatuor Voluminibus.
Novum Testamentum Graecum, cum Versionibus Vulgat. &
Erasmi.
Paraphrasis Erasmi super Novum Testament. in duobus Volu-
minibus Latinè.
Concordantiae Bibliorum.

This small and specialized chained library is sufficient
evidence of the direction in which the Archbishop intended that the studies not only of the Norwich but of
all his other scholars should mainly move. Even if Marlowe, like Faustus, was afterwards to bid 'divinity adieu',
it is surprising that there are not more echoes in his
writings of his long years of theological apprenticeship.
Apart from the quotations from the Vulgate in *Doctor
Faustus* they are almost entirely confined to some Scriptural references by Barabas, of which the most specific
is in *The Jew of Malta*, I. ii. 182–6, to the first chapter
of the Book of Job.

Thus, like many another youthful genius from his day to
ours, Marlowe gave his intellectual bent a free rein outside
the prescribed course of studies. Probably he did so increasingly after taking his B.A. degree. Yet in the three
years that followed he again fully satisfied the requirements of the academic authorities. His *supplicat* for the
M.A. degree is in the ordinary form and is signed by the
Master of his College as well as by a Fellow.

'Supplicat reverentijs vestris Christopherus Marley vt nouem
termini completi (post finalem eius determinationem) in quibus

[1] Moore Smith, loc. cit., p. 170, quoting from Strype's *Life of Parker*,
p. 291.

lectiones ordinarias audiuit (licet non omnino secundum formam statuti) vna cum omnibus oppositionibus, responsionibus ceterisque exercitijs per statuta regia requisitis sufficiant ei ad incipiendum in artibus.

Robertus Norgate
Henricus Ruse, praelector'.

The 'grace' was granted in respect of 'Chr. Marley', together with his fellow scholar Thomas Lewgar and five other members of Corpus Christi College, on 31 March 1587 and in the order of seniority 'Marley' ranks as 65th. Up to this date there is no evidence to suggest that Marlowe during his Cambridge career had given any offence to either the College or the University authorities. Any allegations that he had provoked them by mutinous conduct or subversive opinions are purely speculative and are inferences from later events. All seemed clear for him to take the M.A. degree at the 'Commencement' in July. But before that date strange things were to happen.

II

THE PRIVY COUNCIL'S CERTIFICATE

THE last scholarship payment to Marlowe, as has been seen, was in the Lent term 1586/7, when he drew vs. vjd. It would be natural for a successor to be appointed as soon as possible to the vacancy. But it is not till 10 November 1587 that the College *Registrum Parvum* has the entry 'Bridghman ele[c]tus et admissus in locum dominj Marley'. The College Order Book dates his election considerably later, on 27 April 1588:

'Jacobus Bridgman electus et admissus est discipulus hujus Collegij in locum Cantuariensis scholaris vacantem quia M. Parker secundum ordinationem Domini Archiepiscopi patris sui alium ad supplendum locum predictum tempore constituto ad collegium non miserit.'

There is a third discrepancy, because in the College accounts Bridgeman appears as paying the customary fee of iijs. iiijd. on election during the year ending

Michaelmas 1587. G. C. Moore Smith, who published these entries from the Corpus Christi archives in 1909,[1] therefore suggested that 1588 in the Order Book entry might be a mistake for 1587, though there would still be a discrepancy with the *Registrum Parvum*. But it seems unlikely that such an otherwise precise entry would be misdated by a year, and it looks as if the College had waited for some time to give John Parker his option of nominating to the vacancy. Moreover, there was a reason unknown to Moore Smith in 1909 which may have delayed the choice of a successor to Marlowe. But he pointed out that the Order Book entry omitted Marlowe's name, though in a formula of admission it was usual that the name of the last holder of the scholarship should be mentioned. And he shrewdly raised the question whether Marlowe when his successor was elected was in some way in bad odour with the College authorities.

To this question an unexpected answer was to be given in 1925 by Leslie Hotson when he drew attention to the following entry in the Privy Council Register under the date 29 June 1587, when the Archbishop of Canterbury, the Lord Chancellor, the Lord Treasurer (who was Chancellor of the University of Cambridge), the Lord Chamberlain, and 'Mr. Comptroler' were present:

'Whereas it was reported that Christopher Morley was determined to haue gone beyond the seas to Reames and there to remaine Their Lordships thought good to certefie that he had no such intent, but that in all his accions he had behaued him selfe orderlie and discreetlie wherebie he had done her Majestie good service, & deserued to be rewarded for his faithfull dealinge: Their Lordships request that the rumor thereof should be allaied by all possible meanes, and that he should be furthered in the degree he was to take this next Commencement: Because it was not her Majesties pleasure that anie one emploied as he had been in matters touching the benefitt of his Countrie should be defamed by those that are ignorant in th' affaires he went about.'[2]

[1] Loc. cit., pp. 175-6.
[2] See *The Death of Christopher Marlowe*, pp. 58-9.

If the Christopher Morley here mentioned was the Christopher Marley of the King's School and the later Cambridge entries, it is evident that he had got into trouble with the University authorities after the signing of his 'supplicat', and that the Privy Council's intervention was necessary to obtain permission for him to proceed to his M.A. If this be so, the Council's action had immediate results, for Marlowe took the degree in July.

The episode is so unusual and apparently out of relation to the dramatist's previous Cambridge career that Hotson's identification of this Christopher Morley has been questioned, and the problem has proved to be more complex than he thought. He knew of one other Cambridge Christopher Morley who had to be considered. This Morley was a scholar of Trinity, who took his B.A. in 1582/3. As, however, he proceeded to his M.A. in 1586 he cannot be the man on whose behalf the Privy Council intervened a year later.

It was natural for Hotson to conclude that this Christopher Morley of Trinity was the Christopher Marlor mentioned in a letter to the Privy Council by William Vaughan, written from Pisa on 14 July 1602, 'to forewarn the Council of certain caterpillars, I mean Jesuits and seminary priests, who are to be sent from the English seminary at Valladolid to pervert and withdraw her Majesty's loyal subjects from their due obedience to her. . . .

'In the said seminary there is one Christopher Marlor (as he will be called) but yet for certainty his name is Christopher, sometime master in arts of Trinity College in Cambridge, of very low stature, well set, of a black round beard, not yet priest, but to come over in the mission of the next year ensuing.'[1]

But in this identification Hotson, it has since been proved, was mistaken. There were two, not one, Christopher Morleys or Marlowes at Trinity, Cambridge, in the later years of Elizabeth's reign.

Sir Israel Gollancz, in a letter to *The Times*, 23 June

_____
[1] Hotson, op. cit., pp. 60–1.

1925, drew attention to the fact that, in a document then belonging to Messrs. Dobell, this seminarist Christopher Marlowe is mentioned. The document consists of twenty large folio sheets containing the original bills rendered by the keepers of the Gatehouse Prison, Westminster, for the diet and other necessaries of prisoners from 1596 to 1606. On the sheet containing the bills from 25 June 1604 to 23 Sept. 1604 the following entry is found:

Committed by my Lorde Chiefe Justice	Christopher Marlowe *alias* Mathews, a seminary preist owith for his dyet & lodging for 7 weeks, and two days being close prisoner at the rate of 14^s the weeke 5^{li} 2^s For washinge 2^s 4^d ... £5. 4^s 4^d.

Sir Israel was right in identifying this 'Marlowe *alias* Mathews' with the Marlor mentioned by Vaughan. But he was mistaken, as has been since proved, in going on to identify him also with the Christopher Morley 'in furtherance of whose degree, the Privy Council drew up the certificate in 1587'—in which case, of course, there would have been no question of its referring to Marlowe the dramatist. A month later, in a letter to *The Times*, 24 July, J. B. Whitmore from inquiries made at Valladolid was able to show that the seminarist could not have been alluded to in the Privy Council entry. The records of the English College show that on 30 May 1599 there was admitted to the college John Matthew (Mathews) *alias* Christopher Marler, aged twenty-seven, born and educated at Cambridge where he spent seven years at Trinity College, and had taken his B.A. and M.A. He was converted by Father Thomas Wright, and received into the Roman Catholic Church by Father Garnett, S.J., and had been imprisoned in the Clink for fifteen days before he left England.

From the University records it appears that this John Mathews came up to Trinity from Westminster School in Michaelmas 1588 (when he was about sixteen), took his B.A. in 1592/3 and his M.A. in 1596. He was therefore still at Westminster when the Privy Council certificate was issued. He was consecrated priest in September 1602, and was sent back to England in the spring of 1603. It was he who, as the documents concerning the Gatehouse Prison show, was arrested in the summer of 1604, and was afterwards deported.

Thus the progress of investigation since Hotson's book was published, while it has corrected details in his views, has gone far to confirm his main conclusion that the Christopher Morley on whose behalf the Privy Council intervened was the Morley or Marlowe of Corpus Christi College, and that he had been engaged on some government service, probably in the period between Lent and June 1587. For this service he had been 'defamed by those that are ignorant in th' affaires he went about'. This defamation Hotson interpreted vaguely, 'by turning the Council's language inside out', as a report that 'he was disorderly in his behaviour and indiscreet in his actions'. He here missed the full significance of part of his own discovery. The key is in the opening words of the entry in the Council's register: 'Whereas it was reported that Christopher Morley was determined to haue gone beyond the seas to Reames and there to remaine Their Lordships thought good to certefie that he had no such intent.' For 'busy tongues' to give out (in Hotson's paraphrase) that 'he was to go to Rheims for a protracted stay' is not on the face of it a damning allegation. But let us turn for illumination to Part I of *The Return from Parnassus*, v. iii. 1585–6. Here the two Cambridge scholars, Studiosus and Philomusus, in despair of making a living at home decide to fly to foreign climes, 'to Rome or Rheims', apparently in the hope of being rewarded by the Roman Catholic Church as fugitives from England and likely converts. Was not this the sting in the allegation? Did not Marlowe's enemies suggest in 1587, as they did afterwards in 1593, that he had leanings towards Roman Catholicism, almost as deadly a charge at the time as the later alternative accusation against him of atheism?

Rheims and Rome had taken the place of Douai and Louvain as the head-quarters of English Roman Catholics on the Continent. The English College at Douai, founded by the Pope at his own expense, had been closed by the new governor of the city and province in March 1578, and its members had to take refuge at Rheims. The importance attached by the Holy See to the welfare of the college in its new home is shown in a letter from the Papal Secretary of State to the Nuncio in France, dated 19 May 1578. After mentioning the expulsion from Douai he continues:

'And whereas Dr. Allen, Rector of that College, a man most exemplary and good and learned, has thereby been constrained to withdraw with his comrades to the city of Reims in that realm, therefore it has seemed good to the Pope that they make their abode there to continue their work: and so, while providing them with money, he has warmly commended them to the Cardinal of Reims and the Chapter of the said church, that they may be accorded all needful aid and favour. And as it is feared that the pretended Queen of England who shows herself most ill disposed towards the said Dr. Allen will do her utmost with His Most Christian Majesty to procure his and his comrades' expulsion from the realm of France, even as they have been expelled from the province of Flanders, his Holiness has charged me to write to you bidding you to exhort and beseech his said Majesty not only to allow them to abide in the realm and in that city of Reims, but also to direct that they be well treated, and accorded the favour of residing there in security and peace of mind, whereby his Majesty, besides sharing in the merit of so worthy a wish, will do a thing in the last degree acceptable to the Pope.'[1]

The French King complied with the Pope's wishes and the College at Rheims became the head-quarters of the English Catholics who were constantly plotting the invasion of England and the dethronement of its 'pretended Queen'. A large number of Catholic scholars from Cambridge took refuge there between 1580 and 1592.[2] The

[1] *Calendar of State Papers relating to English affairs, preserved principally at Rome*, vol. ii, 1572–8, p. 435, ed. J. M. Rigg (1926).
[2] Interesting details of this migration are given by Austin K. Gray in

year 1587, which saw the execution of Mary, Queen of Scots, on 8 February, and the expedition of Drake to singe the King of Spain's beard in April, was a profoundly disturbed period at home and abroad. The government secret service was exceptionally active and some one in authority who had recognized Marlowe's remarkable powers entrusted him with some kind of confidential commission to which the Privy Council's letter studiously refers in vague terms. If it brought him, even by way of espionage, into contact with Catholic recusants the rumour might easily be spread and accepted that he was intending to join them in their principal continental centre. The career of Robert Poley shows how equivocal could be the position, in a tense and suspicious atmosphere, of a far more experienced government agent than Marlowe.

The College authorities may now also have been legitimately prejudiced against the scholar who had enjoyed the Archbishop's bounty for the full six years and was then turning his back upon the clerical career. A contemporary reference, that does not name the play but that seems to be otherwise decisive, establishes the fact that both Parts of *Tamburlaine the Great* had been written and produced by 10 November 1587 by the Lord Admiral's company in London.[1] Hence Marlowe, abandoning the pulpit for the stage, must have hurried, after his M.A. *supplicat* was signed, from Cambridge to the capital. And as part of his time before the end of June seems to have been occupied in the Queen's service he must have written the two *Tamburlaine* plays rapidly. Indeed, he may have begun the first Part while he was still in residence in Corpus Christi. We are thus brought up against the problem of how far, and in what fashion, Marlowe had 'commenced author' in his Cambridge days.

'Some Observations on Marlowe as a Government Agent,' in *Pub. Mod. Lang. Assoc. Amer.*, Sept. 1928.   But his views on the nature of Marlowe's service are highly speculative.

[1] See below, p. 71.

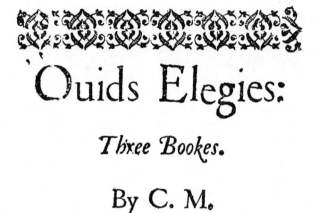

Ouids Elegies:

Three Bookes.

By C. M.

Epigrames by I. D.

At Middlebourgh.

III

CLASSICAL TRANSLATIONS

I

OVID'S ELEGIES

NO work bearing Marlowe's name was published, so far as is known, during his lifetime. The two Parts of *Tamburlaine* appeared anonymously in 1590 and 1592. *Edward II* was first published in 1594, and in the same year there was the only edition of *Dido, Queen of Carthage*. Marlowe's uncompleted *Hero and Leander* was issued in 1598 and was republished in the same year with Chapman's continuation. *The First Book of Lucan* appeared in 1600. The first extant edition of *Doctor Faustus* dates from 1604, and *The Jew of Malta* survives only in the 1633 quarto. *The Massacre at Paris* and the six editions of *Ovid's Elegies* are undated.

The publishers thus give little help in determining the chronology of Marlowe's writings. For some of them additional evidences of dates may be gathered from entries in the Stationers' Register or in Henslowe's *Diary*, from contemporary allusions or from internal references to historical events and indications of source. These will be discussed in connexion with the individual works. But for the poems, especially the translation of Ovid's *Amores*, we are dependent almost entirely upon the more impalpable evidences of style and metre.

Marlowe's translation of the *Amores* in all the editions is accompanied by Sir John Davies's *Epigrams*. The only mention of the work in the Stationers' Register is its inclusion among books to be publicly burnt by an order of the Archbishop of Canterbury and the Bishop of London on 1 June 1599.[1] The book was unlicensed and the imprint of Middleburgh (in Holland) on the title-pages as the place of publication was in all probability spurious.

[1] Arber, *Transcript of Stationers' Register*, iii, pp. 677–8.

Four of the editions contain *All Ovids Elegies: 3. Bookes.* (with the variant, *Ouids Elegies: Three Bookes.*). *By C. M. Epigram(e)s by I. (J.) D.* Two others, entitled *Epigrammes and Elegies, by I. (J.) D. and C. M.*, present *Certaine of Ovids Elegies*, with the full name, C. Marlow, on a second title-page. The selection contains Book I, i, ii, iii, v–xiii, xv; Book II, iv and x; Book III, vi and xiii, and was evidently designed to include a number of the more erotic among the Elegies.

It is to be presumed that copies of the offending volume (whether the selection or one containing the '3 Books') were burnt as soon as possible after publication. If so, Nashe must have seen the work, or part of it, in manu-script when in 1594, in *Jack Wilton*, he quoted two salacious lines, II. iii, ll. 3–4, in Marlowe's rendering. It is much more doubtful, I think, whether Shakespeare had read the line, 'The moon sleeps with Endymion every day', I. xiii, l. 43, when he makes Portia cry (*M. of Ven.*, v. i. 109–10):

> Peace, ho! The moon sleeps with Endymion,
> And would not be awaked.

The story of the love of Luna for Endymion was familiar, and the contexts of the two passages are entirely different. Portia bids the music cease not to disturb the goddess and her beloved. Ovid bids Aurora find a young partner for her bed like Endymion instead of the aged Tithonus.

In any case the references of Nashe and Shakespeare are both after Marlowe's death and do not help to date a work which it is natural to refer to an early period in his career. A translation of the *Amores* might well sug-gest itself to a Cambridge student with a natural gift for writing verse. The venture, as has often been pointed out, has defects of scholarship and style which are marks of immaturity. But, as I endeavour to show, its counter-balancing merits and its importance in Marlowe's develop-ment have not been sufficiently recognized.

It will be remembered that there is documentary evidence of Marlowe having been in October 1581, early in his second academical year, a member of a class in dialectic.[1] In the first play of the Cambridge 'Parnassus' trilogy, *The Pilgrimage to Parnassus*, acted in or near the Christmas season, 1598–9, a St. John's College dramatist represents the two students, Philomusus and Studiosus,[2] after passing through the lands of Logic and Rhetoric, as being beguiled by the voluptuary Amoretto to pervert poetry into the instrument of sensual passion. We are probably doing the youthful Marlowe no wrong when we find, in part, an illustration of a similar academic 'rake's progress' in his choice of the *Amores* for rendering into English verse. Ovid had already found gifted six-teenth-century translators. Arthur Golding's version of the first four Books of the *Metamorphoses* in 1565 had been followed in 1567 by the complete fifteen Books. In the latter year George Turberville had published his transla-tion of the *Heroides*, and in 1572 appeared Thomas Churchyard's version of the first three Books of the *Tristia*. The 'unbaptized rhymes' of Marlowe's rendering of the *Amores* were the offspring of a more frankly wanton Muse.

But it would be a mistake to over-emphasize this aspect and not to realize that the poem had many-sided attrac-tions for an enthusiastic lover of antiquity. In the dedicatory epistle to his translation of the *Heroides* Turberville speaks of 'the learned Poet Ovid'. And the epithet is equally applicable to him in respect of the *Amores*. The poem is no undiluted series of erotic imaginings. It is, in part, an antiquarian and mythological handbook. When Ovid bids his mistress visit his birth-place, Sulmo (II. xvi), he draws an attractive picture of a rural retreat, with its streams and olives and vines. When he accompanies her to a race-course (III. ii) he re-creates before our eyes the processional ritual and the fevered excitement of the contest between the charioteers. In III. x he deplores the abstinence paradoxically associ-ated with the festival of Ceres; and in III. xiii he lingers

[1] See above, p. 16.   [2] See above, p. 25.

lovingly over the details of the sacrifices and glittering pageant of Juno's festival.

Even in the more lusciously amatory elegies the pages overflow with mythological allusions that 'may make us less forlorn', and lift us out of the cloyingly sensuous atmosphere. In remorse that he has struck his mistress (i. vii) he bethinks himself of Ajax butchering the flocks and Orestes taking vengeance on his mother, and he likens the girl herself to Atalanta, Ariadne, or Cassandra. When she sets forth on a voyage (ii. xi) he bids her beware of the perils from Scylla and Charybdis and the Syrtes. When a snow-swollen stream bars his progress to her (iii. vi [v][1]) he reproaches it with a roll-call of rivers who have been victims of love. Her preference of a wealthy rival (iii. viii [vii]) recalls how Jove had to turn himself into a golden shower to win Danaë and how in the Saturnian age metals were still hidden in the earth.

And mythology is skilfully turned to another use when in the opening canto Ovid accuses Cupid of usurping the role of the Muses and forcing him to sing love-songs in elegiac couplets of six and five feet instead of sounding forth deeds of arms in hexameters. And similar imagery recurs when he tells his friend the epic poet Macer (ii. xviii) how the God of Love defeated his further attempt to become a writer of tragedy (ll. 13–16):

> Sceptra tamen sumpsi, curaque tragoedia nostra
> Crevit, et huic operi quamlibet aptus eram.
> Risit Amor pallamque meam pictosque cothurnos
> Sceptraque privata tam cito sumpta manu.

Yet the successful writer of verse in any form—(i. xv) from Homer and Hesiod to Virgil and Tibullus—is assured of an immortality denied to the soldier, the lawyer, and the politician. Thus when the body of Tibullus (iii. ix [viii]) has ascended the funeral pyre, with Cupid as chief mourner, his spirit will abide in the Elysian vale. And so, as in his closing lines he bids his own elegies fare-

---

[1] Marlowe omits iii. iv. of modern texts and his numbering thus differs.

well, before undertaking graver themes, Ovid prays that
they may live on after he is no more.

Such reflections and aspirations must have stirred
responsive chords in the breast of the young English poet,
preparing to try his wings, and interested from the first
in metrical experiment. He too, before donning the robe
and buskin of tragedy, was dallying in this version of the
Amores with a more sportive muse. And he had at once
to decide how he could most fittingly reproduce Ovid's
elegiac couplets in the vernacular. Golding had given
himself some additional elbow-room by rendering the
hexameters of the *Metamorphoses* into 'fourteeners'.
Throughout the whole 12,000 lines he never deviated from
this jog-trot, lumbering metre.

Turberville took a freer hand in his translation of the
4,000 lines of the *Heroides*. Each line of the original, the
alternate hexameter and pentameter of the elegiac couplet,
is represented, as a rule, by two lines in his version. But
he varies his metres. Eighteen epistles are rendered into
four-line stanzas, rhyming in the second and fourth lines.
In six of these the lines contain alternately four and three
feet; in twelve the first, second, and fourth lines contain
three feet, and the third line has four. The other six of
the twenty-four epistles are turned into blank verse. Turberville is thus entitled to the credit of a metrical experi-
menter. Churchyard, on the other hand, in his version
of the *Tristia* returned to Golding's fourteeners, which,
though they might pass in the rendering of the hexameters
of the *Metamorphoses*, are in our eyes to-day singularly ill
suited to reproduce the elegiac couplet. But Golding,
Turberville, and Churchyard all hit the taste of their
own age, and before Marlowe left Cambridge three or
four editions of their several translations had appeared.

One or other of these may have fallen into Marlowe's
hands, but there is no evidence, as with Shakespeare's debt
to Golding,[1] to prove it. In any case he was not influenced

---

[1] See 'Ovid and Shakespeare's Sonnets,' in *Elizabethan and other Essays*,
by Sidney Lee.

by any of his predecessors when he decided to translate the *Amores* into five-foot rhyming couplets. They had all chosen metres which gave opportunity for expanding the original. Marlowe, on the other hand, replaced the eleven feet of the Latin elegiac couplet by ten, which was a handicap in translating from a synthetic into an analytic language.

In a curious epilogue to his version of the *Heroides* Turberville had warned 'the captious sort of sycophants' of the difficulties that confronted translators from Latin into English.

> For though the thing but slender be in sight,
> And vaine to viewe of curious carping skull,
> In mother tongue a forraine speeche to write:
> Yet he shall find he hath a Crow to pull
> That undertakes with well agreeing File
> Of English verse to rub the Romaine stile.

> Devises of the language divers are
> Well couched words and feately forged phrase,
> Eche string in tune, no ragged rime doth jarre,
> With figures fraught their bookes in every place:
> So that it is a worke of prayse to cause
> A Romaine borne to speake with English jawes.

How far does Marlowe's version of the *Amores* deserve the commendation of being 'a work of prayse'? It is a question that has been variously answered and that requires closer consideration than it has always received. In the first place it has to be noted that in an age when the translator had a much wider licence than to-day Marlowe sought conscientiously to render every line of the Latin text into its English equivalent. This fidelity to his original in what is presumably one of his earliest undertakings is significant for his whole career. For however revolutionary his opinions may have been, all recent investigation has helped to show that in his poetic and dramatic work he kept close to such sources as he used.

Thus in his edition of Marlowe's *Poems* published in 1931 L. C. Martin did a signal service to his reputation by proving that a large number of apparent mistranslations in *Ovid's Elegies* are renderings not of the modern text of the *Amores* but of readings in sixteenth-century editions. What seem in a considerable number of other instances to be inaccuracies are accounted for by changes in the meaning of words since the Elizabethan period. And the compression due to Marlowe's choice of the five-foot couplet, or the necessities of rhyming, produced inversions and other obscurities of phrasing and construction which are largely resolved when the English and the Latin texts are set side by side.

But when all this has been taken into account, can we, like Mr. Aldrich, acclaim Marlowe as 'a rare scholar'?[1] Not so, by modern standards, for he can be charged with several major and many more minor mistranslations. Yet when narrowly examined they do not, in my opinion, form a heavy indictment against the Cambridge graduate who was not a classical specialist. Two of his most notorious mistakes come from his falling into the trap (as many have done since) set by 'cān-' instead of the more familiar 'căn-'. Thus, 'Plena venit canis de grege praeda lupis' (1. viii. 56) means 'From the flock a full prey comes to the hoary wolves', but is rendered 'From dog-kept flocks come preys to wolves most grateful'. Here the dative plural of 'cānus' is confused with the genitive of 'cănis'. Similarly, in 'Ipse locus nemorum canebat frugibus Ide' (III. x (ix). 39), 'cānebat' means 'was white', but is translated as if it were 'cănebat,' 'did sing'—which is certainly forcible. More venial is the misunderstanding of the puzzling line, 'Carmine dissiliunt abruptis faucibus angues' (II. i. 25), i.e. 'Song bursts the serpents' jaws apart, and robs them of their fangs', which is translated, 'Snakes leap by verse from caves of broken mountains'. Less noticed but more of a 'howler' is the rendering of 'nisi vittatis quod erat Cassandra capillis' (1. vii. 17) as 'Cassandra ... Deflower'd except', where 'vittatis' (bound with chaplets) seems to be confused with 'vitiatis' (defiled).

[1] See above, p. 19.

Another, more evident, verbal confusion makes havoc of
the translation of II. ix. 22, 'Tutaque deposito poscitur
ense rudis', i.e. 'The harmless foil is claimed when the
sword has been laid aside', which is rendered as 'His
sword laid by, safe, though rude places yields', where
'rudis' (foil) is taken to be the epithet 'rudis'. But Marlowe's mistake here arose partly from his ignorance of
the fact that a Roman gladiator's discharge was marked
by the gift of a wooden foil. And similar antiquarian
ignorance accounts for other mistranslations. Thus in
I. viii. 100 'Sacra roganda Via est' means that inquiry
must be made in the Sacred Way, the shopping centre,
but it becomes pointless in the rendering, 'let him from
thee wend'. And in III. ii. 19, 'cogit nos linea jungi' does
not mean 'force conjoins us now' but that the 'linea', the
line which divided the seats of the spectators at the
chariot race, obliged Ovid and Corinna to sit close. No
such excuse, however, can be made in the same elegy
(l. 43) for distorting the familiar invocation, 'linguis
animisque favete', i.e. 'keep silence and attend', into
'themselves let all men cheer'. So in xiii (xii). 29, 'ore
favent populi' is turned into its exact opposite as 'loud
the people hollow'. One of the very few places where
Marlowe actually shirks a difficulty is in III. ix (viii). 33–4,
'quid nunc Aegyptia prosunt sistra?', which he omits
in his rendering. He evidently did not know that the
'sistrum' was a musical instrument used in the worship
of Isis.

These examples could be multiplied and they would
doubtless prevent Marlowe from scoring high marks in
a scholarship examination to-day. But when the 4,000
lines of the *Amores* are considered, and when we remember
how large a proportion of them are given a substantially
correct English equivalent in Marlowe's version, his
Latinity, whatever its imperfections, may be said, on the
whole, not to have been unequal to its aim.

But there are higher tests to be applied to Marlowe's
translation than that of verbal accuracy. How far does

it reproduce Ovid's distinctive technique and atmosphere, and to what degree does it bear the impress of Marlowe's own poetic genius? Here we may be helped by a comparison with Turberville's translation of the *Heroides*, allied to the *Amores* by its elegiac metre and its amatory themes. Turberville was a competent translator, who made few serious mistakes, and who carried out his task with unflagging zeal. As has been seen above, he chose verse-forms that allowed some expansion of the original Latin. He is at his happiest when he is expanding some of Ovid's descriptive passages with additional picturesque details.[1] Here his verse runs with a lusty vigour. But in his quest of liveliness he too often gives a free rein to colloquialisms, e.g. 'fist' for 'hand', 'jawes' for 'mouth', 'trull' for 'girl', 'brat' for 'child', 'smack' for 'kiss'. He is fond, too, of tasteless alliteration, and he makes little attempt to reproduce the effects of balance and antithesis which are the very essence of the elegiac metre. Thus Turberville, though born of an 'ancient and genteel family' and educated at Winchester, New College, and an Inn of Court, failed to catch in his version of the *Heroides*, in spite of its merits, Ovid's tone of sophistication and well-bred ease.

It is the outstanding merit, on the other hand, of Marlowe's translation of the *Amores*, that without Turberville's advantages of tradition behind him, he was able by instinctive artistry to reproduce in no slight measure the peculiar Ovidian atmosphere. He, too, makes use of colloquialisms, e.g. 'old trot' for 'beldame', 'to odds' for 'at variance', 'blab' for 'tattler', 'nags' for 'horses', 'tittle', and 'tut'. But they are not so frequent as with Turberville, and they have not the same disturbing effect. One important exception must, however, be made. Though the word may have undergone some deterioration since the Elizabethan period, it is unfortunate that Marlowe should almost uniformly use 'wench' for 'amica' or

[1] See Ovid's *The Heroycall Epistles*, translated by G. Turberville, ed. F. S. Boas (1928), pp. xviii–xx.

'puella'. It is ill suited to a 'society' world of elegant intrigue.

Otherwise Marlowe uses effectively a varied vocabulary. We find technical terms like 'knights of the post' and 'corps-du-guard'; rare words, like 'cadess' (jackdaw), 'rampir'd' (blocked-up), 'rivelled' (wrinkled), 'a-life' (dearly), 'corrive' (be a rival); and words used in unfamiliar fashion: 'shine' as an adjective, 'cling'd' as a transitive verb, 'stable' meaning 'to hold fast', and 'hoodwink'd' in a literal sense.

Another notable feature of his vocabulary as a translator is the number of compound epithets that he introduces: fair-tress'd sun, 'rain-doubled' floods, 'storm-mixed' snows, 'wave-moist' hands, 'coat-tucked' Diana, 'four-chariot' horses, 'self-angry' hands, 'star-spangled' towers. Not all these and other compounds are equally clear or felicitous, but in the main Marlowe gives the impression of handling words and phrases in his translation with skill and ease, and of preserving in his Elizabethan vernacular no small trace of the metropolitan accents of imperial Rome.

But in versification Marlowe was as yet in a more experimental stage, and here his workmanship has curious inequalities. Lines i. vii. 9–10:

> Et, vindex in matre patris, malus ultor, Orestes
> ausus in arcanas poscere tela deas

are, in his version:

> And he who on his mother veng'd his ire
> Against the Destinies durst sharp darts require.

In the second of these lines the dragging monosyllables and the excess of sibilants produce a harsh effect. Equally jarring for similar reasons is the translation of i. ix. 7–8, comparing the lover and the soldier:

> Pervigilant ambo; terra requiescit uterque—
> ille fores dominae servat, at ille ducis.

> Both of them watch: each on the hard earth sleeps.
> His mistress' doors this: that his captain's keeps.

Lines 29–30 of the same elegy

> Mars dubius nec certa Venus; victique resurgunt
> quosque neges unquam posse jacere, cadunt

are rendered:

> Doubtful is war and love; the vanquish'd rise,
> And who thou never think'st should fall, down lies.

Here the first line will pass, but the second exemplifies strikingly the two metrical defects already noted. Miss Ellis-Fermor has called attention to 'the jarring metre' of II. i. 20:

> Her shut gates greater lightning than thine brought.

Another example may be found in III. vi (v). 7–8,

> With snow thaw'd from the next hill now thou gushest,
> And in thy foul deep waters thick thou rushest.

Such examples could be multiplied, but they are sufficient to prove that Marlowe as a metrist had as yet imperfect control of his instrument. Nevertheless, there are signs in plenty that he was soon to be master of it. He refrains, as a rule, from the tasteless cumulative alliteration to which Elizabethan translators were fatally prone. He makes effective use of double rhymes both in single couplets and in such longer passages as I. vii. 21–8:

> But secretly her looks with checks did trounce me,
> Her tears, she silent, guilty did pronounce me.
> Would of mine arms my shoulders had been scanted,
> Better I could part of myself have wanted.
> To mine own self have I had strength so furious,
> And to myself could I be so injurious?
> Slaughter and mischief's instruments, no better,
> Deserved chains these cursed hands shall fetter.

Not infrequently a sonorous word gives a rhythmical effect that presages the 'mighty line', as in the following renderings:

I. ii. 8:

> Et possessa ferus pectora versat Amor.
> 'Tis cruel Love turmoils my captive heart.

I. ii. 28:

> Haec tibi magnificus pompa triumphus erit.
> So will thy triumph seem magnifical.

II. ix. 21:

> Longaque subductam celant navalia pinum.
> The dock inharbours ships drawn from the floods.

II. xvii. 27:

> Sunt mihi pro magno felicia carmina censu.
> For great revènues I good verses have.

And alone among Elizabethan translators of Ovid Marlowe succeeds in conveying the epigrammatic effect and antithetical poise of his original, though in an analytic language several words may have to take the place of one. The following are examples:

I. i. 29:

> Me miserum! certas habuit puer ille sagittas.
> O woe is me! he never shoots but hits.

I. vii. 15:

> . . . periuri promissaque velaque Thesei.
> Her perjur'd Theseus' flying vows and sails.

I. viii. 50:

> Et celer admissis labitur annus equis.
> And with swift horses the swift year soon leaves us.

II. vi. 60:

> Quo lapis exiguus par sibi carmen habet.
> The little stones these little verses have—

and another instance, where the change of meaning in 'witty' obscures the force of the line to our ears to-day:

III. viii (vii). 8:

> Turpiter huc illuc ingeniosus eo.
> I here and there go, witty with dishonour.

In addition to happily turned single lines or couplets there are longer passages where Marlowe's rendering, even if not faultless, is notably lucid and melodious. Most familiar of these is Elegy I. xv, on the immortality conferred by poetry, which Ben Jonson introduces into *The*

Poetaster, 1. i. 43–84, with emendations which, as a whole, are of little advantage. But an even better example of Marlowe's gifts in Book I is Elegy xiii, in which he appeals to Aurora to delay her coming, as in ll. 7–18:

> The air is cold, and sleep is sweetest now,
> And birds send forth shrill notes from every bough.
> Whither runn'st thou, that men and women love not?
> Hold in thy rosy horses that they move not.
> Ere thou rise, stars teach seamen where to sail,
> But when thou comest, they of their courses fail.
> Poor travellers though tir'd, rise at thy sight,
> And soldiers make them ready to the fight.
> The painful hind by thee to field is sent;
> Slow oxen early in the yoke are pent.
> Thou cozen'st boys of sleep, and dost betray them
> To pedants that with cruel lashes pay them.

In Book II, Elegy ix, bewailing the tyranny of Cupid, ll. 29–38 have the right poignant ring:

> Even as a headstrong courser bears away
> His rider vainly striving him to stay,
> Or as a sudden gale thrusts into sea
> The haven-touching bark now near the lea,
> So wavering Cupid brings me back amain,
> And purple Love resumes his darts again.
> Strike, boy, I offer thee my naked breast,
> Here thou hast strength, here thy right hand doth rest.
> Here of themselves thy shafts come, as if shot;
> Better than I their quiver knows them not.

In Book III, Elegy ii, the translation reproduces vividly the successive emotions and exclamations of the lover with his mistress at the chariot-race.

More tranquil is the rhythm of lines in III. viii (vii). 35–44, depicting an idyllic age in the past:

> Yet when old Saturn heaven's rule possest,
> All gain in darkness the deep earth supprest.
> Gold, silver, iron's heavy weight, and brass,
> In hell were harbour'd; here was found no mass.
> But better things it gave, corn without ploughs,
> Apples, and honey in oaks' hollow boughs.

With strong ploughshares no man the earth did cleave,
The ditcher no marks on the ground did leave,
Nor hanging oars the troubled seas did sweep,
Men kept the shore and sail'd not into deep.

Such are some of the passages that the author of *Tamburlaine* and *Doctor Faustus* and *Hero and Leander* had no cause to be slow in acknowledging. Indeed in *Hero and Leander* there are manifest echoes from the translation, and in *Faustus* the great closing soliloquy enshrines (v. ii. 146) the invocation in the original from I. xiii. 40, 'lente currite, noctis equi'. Most of the earlier Elizabethan writers of tragedy had graduated in the lurid rhetoric of the Senecan school. It was fortunate for Marlowe that his genius, in its plastic stage, went through the discipline involved in seeking to reproduce the technique of one of the most highly accomplished poetic craftsmen of the ancient world.

II

LUCAN'S FIRST BOOK

On 28 September 1593 there was entered to John Wolf in the Stationers' Register 'a booke intituled Lucans *first booke of the famous Civill warr betwixt* Pompey *and* Cesar Englished by Christopher Marlow'. Immediately below is the entry also to Wolf of *Hero and Leander*.

But Wolf does not seem to have exercised his right of publication of either work. The only known edition of *Lucan's First Book* is a quarto printed in 1600 by P. Short for Thomas Thorpe, who, in a dedicatory epistle to his friend, Edward Blount, speaks of 'your old right in it'. Blount in 1598 had published the incomplete *Hero and Leander*, and this was followed in the same year by Paul Linley's edition with Chapman's continuation.[1]

In 1600 John Flasket published a quarto entitled *Hero*

[1] See further, p. 224.

*and Leander: Begunne by Christopher Marloe: Whereunto
is added the first booke of Lucan translated line for line by
the same Author.* Though Chapman's continuation is
included, his name is not mentioned. On the other hand,
the *Lucan* is mentioned but not included.

Wolf must therefore have passed over his rights in
Lucan and *Hero and Leander* to Blount, though this is not
mentioned in the Stationers' Register, which however
records on 2 March 1597/8 Blount's assignment to Linley
of *Hero and Leander.* The right to the *Lucan* must also
have passed to Linley, though this is not stated, for when
on 26 June 1600 twenty-four works belonging to him
were transferred to Flasket, one of them is HERO AND
LEANDER *with the j booke of* LUCAN *by* MARLOWE. The
most plausible explanation of what followed has been
given by Tucker Brooke.[1]

'Flasket's original design may have been to produce an edition
of the Marlovian part of *Hero and Leander,* supplemented by the
Lucan. Such an intention may have preceded the arrangement with
Linley, and would naturally in that case have been altered when
the possession of Chapman's long continuation of *Hero and
Leander* rendered it unnecessary to eke out a thin volume by the
insertion of the *Lucan.* The latter work, being then of no immediate
consequence to Flasket, would seem to have been acquired and
at once printed by Thomas Thorpe. The Stationers' Register
contains no record, however, of the transfer of the piece from
Flasket to Thorpe or to any one else, and the question of the precise
origin of this single early edition of the poem is not easily soluble.'

For the dating of the *Lucan* there is nothing but internal evidence. The translation of a Book of the *De
Bello Civili,* line for line, would seem, like that of the
Amores, to be a more likely enterprise for the Cambridge
student than the London playwright. In their general
merits and defects the two versions have much in common.
And Lucan, as I try to show, may have supplied Marlowe
with hints for the background of *Tamburlaine.* On the
other hand, the metrical evidence of run-on lines and

[1] *Works of Marlowe,* p. 643.

feminine endings, and the closely knit texture of the phrasing, are marks of maturity.

But whether sooner or later, it seems, at first sight, a sharp descent when Marlowe passed from the *Amores* to the *De Bello Civili*, from the Augustan to the Neronian literary age. Ovid, with the instinct of a master of his craft, did not venture on the loftiest poetic heights. It is these heights that Lucan essayed to climb with his epic, but his place is among the great verse-rhetoricians and not among the great singers of imperial Rome. In the sphere of art he had far less than Ovid to teach a young English poet. But in its subject-matter and some of the broader features of its technique *the First Book of Lucan* formed a valuable complement to *Ovid's Elegies* for the training of a writer of tragedy.

Instead of the sighing of 'the low lutes of love' there rings the clang of

> Trumpets and drums, like deadly threat'ning other.

Rome is not seen as a gay, luxurious capital, the home of amusement, frivolity and vice, but as a city of terror, panic-stricken at the approach to its gates of foes of its own household. The leading figures are now not lovers and their mistresses, but 'the captains and the kings', a Caesar and a Pompey, and the stakes that they play for are not kisses and caresses but dictatorships and world-dominion. In the *Amores* a river in flood holds up Ovid on his way to his lady-love; in the *De Bello Civili* a similarly swollen river cannot stay Caesar on his march to Rome.

Lucan, by a bold innovation, had discarded the supernatural machinery hitherto traditional in the epic, and his poem is almost bare of the mythological brocade of which Ovid was so profuse. On the other hand, he let his eye range over the three continents, to the farthest limits where the legions had trod, and he poured forth a wealth of geographical and ethnographical detail which was not lost on the author of *Tamburlaine*. His gaze, too, at times swept the heavens, and here again he touched an answering chord in the Cambridge student of cosmology. Whether or not Marlowe ever meditated a translation of more than the First Book of Lucan, he found in its 700 lines congenial material.

The claim on the title-page of the quarto that the translation is 'line for line' is substantially justified, though two or three lines are omitted from the English version, and there is occasional variation in the order. Again Marlowe proves himself to be a conscientious translator, and there is no such glaring 'howler' as two or three in *Ovid's Elegies*, except l. 423,

> The Santons that rejoice in Caesar's love

for 'gaudetque amoto Santonus hoste', where, however, the text used may have had 'amato' instead of 'amoto'. An almost inspired blunder is 'tuneful planeting', with reference to the music of the spheres, in l. 640, for 'numerisque moventibus astra', i.e. calculations affecting the stars. Other mistakes spring from imperfect anti-quarian knowledge. Thus 'Latiare caput' (l. 535), the capital of Latium, Alba Longa, becomes 'the Capitol', Cybele (l. 600) is transformed into Sibylla, and the 'exiguum asylum' of Romulus (l. 97), a sanctuary for criminals, into 'a poor church'. A curious error of another kind is 'Nilus' mouth' (l. 20) for 'nascenti Nilo', and there are many other inaccuracies and some obscurities. Thus (ll. 348–9):

> Arma tenenti
> Omnia dat, qui justa negat

is scarcely recognizable in

> They that now thwart right
> In wars will yield to wrong.

Nor does 'chain'd troops' for (ll. 492–3)

> serieque haerentia longa
> Agmina

represent clearly the continuous rush of a mob.

But broadly considered, especially from an Elizabethan point of view, Marlowe's version is forcible and adequate. His vocabulary, allowing for the difference of subject-matter, has much in common with that in *Ovid's Elegies*. Without sacrifice of dignity or clearness he again frequently introduces colloquial or unusual words and phrases, e.g. 'garboils' (tumults), 'whist' (silent), 'brabbling' (talkative), 'cleyes' (claws), 'wallowed' (gushed), 'souse down' (knock down), 'shivered out' (divided), 'butting lands' (boundary lands), 'open slops' (loose trousers). There are striking double epithets, 'flame-bearing', 'death-presaging', 'thunder-hoof'd', 'dropping-ripe', though they are less frequent than in the translation from Ovid. At times Marlowe vivifies with detail the more generalized descriptions of Lucan. Thus 'errantes-que domos' of nomad tribes he turns into 'waggons and tents'; and 'tollens apicem', used of the Flamen, is elaborated into 'with net-work woollen veils'.

The rhyming couplet served better than the hexameter for reproducing epigrammatic antitheses, and here Lucan fared less well at Marlowe's hands than Ovid. The test case is the most famous line in the *De Bello Civili* (128),

> Victrix causa deis placuit, sed victa Catoni,

which is blunted into

> Caesar's cause
> The gods abetted, Cato lik'd the other.

The cynical terseness of the description of Pompey (l. 135),

> Stat magni nominis umbra,

loses its edge in

> And thought his name sufficient to uphold him.

Nor is the exact point caught of (ll. 175–6)

> Mensuraque juris
> Vis erat

in the translation,

> Force mastered right, the strongest govern'd all.

Yet at times Marlowe can hit the mark in the rendering of an aphorism, as in ll. 92–3:

>   omnisque potestas
>   Impatiens consortis erat

which he renders

>   Dominion cannot suffer partnership.

Here in a single line is illustrated what in longer passages are the cardinal virtues of Marlowe's translation, its verbal resonance and melodious rhythm. And it is to be noted that these are to be found especially when the epic rises above the tumult of the earthly conflicts of men into more elemental regions. Thus it is when Lucan pictures the ascent of Nero to heaven (ll. 47 ff.):

>   where thou wilt reign as king,
>   Or mount the Sun's flame-bearing chariot,
>   And with bright restless fire compass the earth,
>   Undaunted though her former guide be chang'd;
>   Nature and every power shall give thee place,
>   What god it please thee be, or where to sway—

or in this vision of the dissolution of the universe (73 ff.):

>   So when this world's compounded union breaks,
>   Time ends, and to old Chaos all things turn.
>   Confused stars shall meet, celestial fire
>   Fleet on the floods, the earth shoulder the sea,
>   Affording it no shore, and Phoebe's wain
>   Chase Phoebus, and enrag'd affect his place,
>   And strive to shine by day, and full of strife
>   Dissolve the engines of the broken world—

or in this description of a territory which is the prey of contending elements (410 ff.):

>   that uncertain shore
>   Which is nor sea nor land, but ofttimes both,
>   And changeth as the ocean ebbs and flows;
>   Whether the sea roll'd always from that point
>   Whence the wind blows, still forced to and fro;
>   Or that the wandering main follow the moon;
>   Or flaming Titan (feeding on the deep)
>   Pulls them aloft and makes the surge kiss heaven,

> Philosophers, look you; for unto me,
> Thou cause, whate'er thou be whom God assigns
> This great effect, art hid.

Here Marlowe, with his passionate interest in cosmology, may well have felt the appeal of the words, 'Quaerite, quos agitat mundi labor', which he translates, 'Philosophers, look you'. So, too, his speculative instinct must have been stirred by the description of what were to Lucan the paradoxical beliefs of the Druids (449 ff.):

> And only gods and heavenly powers you know,
> Or only know you nothing. For you hold
> That souls pass not to silent Erebus
> Or Pluto's bloodless kingdom, but elsewhere
> Resume a body; so (if truth you sing)
> Death brings long life.

'With Marlowe', as Caroline Spurgeon has said, 'images drawn from books, especially the classics, and from the sun, moon, planets, and heavens far outnumber all others'.[1] In the growth of such images the translation of Lucan's First Book played its part. And in three lines whose music is in an exceptionally soft key (443-5):

> And you, French Bardi, whose immortal pens
> Renown the valiant souls slain in your wars,
> Sit safe at home and chant sweet poesy—

may we not find a source and seed of the glorious rhapsody in *Tamburlaine*, Part I, v. ii, beginning:

> If all the pens that ever poets held, . . .

[1] *Shakespeare's Imagery*, p. 13. See also Chart II, illustrating the range and subjects of Marlowe's imagery.

IV

DIDO, QUEEN OF CARTHAGE

*T*HE *Tragedy of Dido, Queen of Carthage*, based upon
the earlier Books of the *Aeneid*, stands, whatever
their respective dates may have been, in intimate relation
with Marlowe's translations from Ovid and Lucan and
with his Cambridge studies. The play is preserved only in
a quarto edition, 1594, entitled *The* | *Tragedie of Dido* |
Queene of Carthage: | *Played by the Children of her* |
Maiesties Chappell. | *Written by Christopher Marlowe,*
and | *Thomas Nash. Gent.* | . . . *Printed, by the Widdowe*
Orwin, for Thomas Woodcocke. Though Woodcocke was
under-warden of the Stationers' Company the book was
not entered for copyright, and Tucker Brooke suggests
that it was probably published almost at the moment of
his death on 22 April 1594.[1]

When was *Dido* acted by the Children of the Chapel?
There is no record of any performance by this company
in London between 1584 and 1601. But during 1586–7,
towards the close of the academic careers of Marlowe
and Nashe, they visited Ipswich and Norwich,[2] and while
performing in the eastern counties they may have got
possession of a play written at Cambridge and produced
it, though it was not very suitable dramatic fare for a provincial audience. If so, the natural inference from the
title-page would be that Marlowe of Corpus Christi and
Nashe of St. John's had collaborated in their student
days in the work. But such intimacy as they had seems to

---

[1] *Dido*, ed. Tucker Brooke, pp. 118–19. Brooke points out that the
rights in *Dido* passed from Woodcocke to Linley, and that among Linley's
books transferred to Flasket (cf. above, p. 43) were *Cupydes Journey to*
hell with the tragedie of Dido.

[2] In the Ipswich 1586–7 accounts the payment of 20*s.* to 'the quenes
players being the children' is entered under 26 May [1587]; in the Norwich
accounts for the same period a similar payment 'to the children of the
Q. chapel' is not dated. See J. T. Murray, *English Dramatic Companies*, ii.
292 and 366.

belong to a later period, and there is little internal evidence of Nashe's hand in the play. It is more probable that he prepared it for publication after Marlowe's death. His own play, *Summer's Last Will and Testament*, had been acted in 1592 by a company of boys apparently before Archbishop Whitgift at Croydon.

Light might have been thrown on these points had any of the three known copies of the 1594 quarto contained the tribute by 'Tho. Nash in Carmine elegiaco tragoediae Didonis praefixo in obitum Christoph. Marlovii', mentioned by Thomas Tanner in his *Bibliotheca Britannico-Hibernica*, p. 512 (1748). Thomas Warton more than thirty years later assured Malone that he had seen a copy of *Dido* in 1754 in T. Osborne's shop with the elegy by Nash inserted immediately after the title-page.[1] But he let pass the chance of buying 'this rare piece' and it has disappeared from view. This is the more unfortunate in that the close investigations of Knutowski,[2] R. B. McKerrow,[3] and Tucker Brooke have revealed very little in *Dido* that there is reason to credit to Nashe. The lame Vulcan dancing (I. i. 32) has a parallel in *Summer's Last Will and Testament*, ll. 1933–8, and the reference to Ulysses stealing into the tent of Rhesus and intercepting Dolon (I. i. 70–3) is repeated in *The Unfortunate Traveller*. Some rare words, or with unusual meanings, found in Nashe but not elsewhere in Marlowe, occur in *Dido*. Among them are 'attract' = take in (I. i. 136), 'famoused' (I. ii. 21 and v. i. 275), 'shelves' = sandbanks (III. i. 107 and IV. iv. 58), 'hoising' (IV. iv. 15), and 'Getulian' (III. iii. 19) used contemptuously.[4] There may be traces here of some revision by Nashe, but the scenes in which these passages and phrases appear have, as a whole, the stamp of Marlowe. It will be simpler, therefore, to speak

---

[1] See Malone's note in the Bodleian copy of *Dido*, quoted by Tucker Brooke, op. cit., p. 122.

[2] *Das Dido-Drama von Marlowe und Nash* (1905).

[3] *Works of Thomas Nashe*, vol. ii (1904) and vol. iv (1908).

[4] See further notes *ad loc.* by McKerrow and Brooke.

of him as the author of *Dido* while recognizing that his
name may here and there cover that of Nashe.

The metrical evidences point to an early date for *Dido*.
The considerably larger proportion of rhymed couplets
than in any other of the plays links it with the translation
of the *Amores*. But it is curious that Marlowe, who had
there avoided the exaggerated alliteration of Turberville
and Churchyard, can in *Dido* repeatedly write lines like

> Triton, I know, hath fill'd his trump with Troy.
> And they so wrack'd and welter'd by the waves.
> And slice the sea with sable-colour'd ships.

On the other hand, except in a few passages inten-
tionally in a lighter vein, the occasionally jarring colloquialisms of the *Elegies* are absent.

The almost unbroken succession in *Dido* of end-stopped
lines may well have been influenced by Marlowe's translation of thousands of Ovidian couplets. But a monotonous
effect is largely averted by various metrical devices.
'Nine-syllable lines (in which the first foot is made up of
a single syllable) are freely used, and hexameters are not
uncommon, while trimeters, tetrameters, and syllabic
verse pauses are employed for definite effect.'[1] These
metrical characteristics are common to *Dido* and the two
Parts of *Tamburlaine*, and they have also many verbal
parallels.

But there are other parallels with later works. Dido's
cry (IV. iv. 123):

> And he'll make me immortal with a kiss

anticipates Faustus's invocation to Helen (v. i. 109), as
do also v. i. 146–8. And the line (II. i. 231),

> Threatening a thousand deaths at every glance

reappears unchanged in *Hero and Leander* (i. 382). There
are numerous, though less striking, parallels with *Edward II*, and Knutowski has conjectured that Marlowe
revised *Dido* while he was writing his historical play.[2]

---

[1] Tucker Brooke, op. cit., p. 116.
[2] Knutowski, op. cit., pp. 56–9.

Whatever the date was of his dramatization of the story of Dido Marlowe had at least three predecessors, who had all written in Latin. John Ritwise, headmaster of St. Paul's School (1522–31), had 'made the Tragedy of Dido out of Virgil and acted the same with the scholars of his school before Cardinal Wolsey with great applause'.[1] Edward Halliwell, a former Fellow of King's College, made another adaptation, for performance before Queen Elizabeth in the College chapel on 7 August 1564.[2] William Gager, of Christ Church, Oxford, wrote and produced a third adaptation in the College hall before Albertus Alasco, Prince Palatine of Siradia in Poland, on 12 June 1583.[3] The plays of Ritwise and Halliwell have disappeared. Gager's *Dido* was not printed, but is preserved in Christ Church Library in a manuscript which was probably 'the book of the play' prepared for the use of the Prince Palatine or the Chancellor of the University, the Earl of Leicester. It is very unlikely that Marlowe knew this unpublished play, which combined a Senecan structure with elaborate scenic effects, and which has curiously slight parallelism with *Dido, Queen of Carthage*, though both are quarried from the same source.[4]

Marlowe is more likely to have been influenced by the plays of Lyly dealing with classical subjects and acted by the Children of the Chapel and of Paul's. Sir Edmund Chambers has shown that the stage-setting of *Dido* is similar to that of Lyly's court-comedies.

'I think that one side of the stage was arranged *en pastorelle*, and represented the wood between the sea-shore and Carthage, where the shipwrecked Trojans land and where later Aeneas and Dido hunt. Here was the cave where they take shelter from the storm. . . . The other side of the stage represents Carthage. Possibly a

[1] A. Wood, *Athenae* (ed. Bliss), i. 35.

[2] F. S. Boas, *Univ. Drama in Tudor Age*, p. 94.

[3] Ibid., pp. 183–91, where an account is given of Gager's play, and it is compared with *Dido, Queen of Carthage*.

[4] An English play 'of dido & eneas' was performed by the Admiral's men on 8 January 1597/8. Henslowe's *Diary*, ed. Greg, ii. 189.

wall with a gate in it was built across the stage, dividing off the two regions.'[1]

What is certain is that Marlowe when basing a play upon so august a foundation as the earlier Books of the *Aeneid* felt himself free, as with the less sacrosanct *Hero and Leander* of Musaeus, to draw upon his general classical reading. Nothing could be farther from the decorous gravity of Virgilian epic than the opening scene of *Dido*, when 'the curtains draw' and 'there is discovered Jupiter dandling Ganymede upon his knee'. The half-line in the *Aeneid* glancing at 'rapti Ganymedis honores' as one of the causes of Juno's rage against Aeneas gives but a slight cue for this elaborate scene of dalliance between Jupiter and the 'female wanton boy' who is the 'darling' of his 'thoughts'. In such an episode Marlowe, who treats love between man and woman with so delicate a touch, may have given a handle to those who, like Richard Baines, charged him with abnormal vice.

To the pert complaint of the cup-bearer that Juno 'reach'd me such a rap for that I spill'd', Jupiter replies with an adjuration borrowed, so far as is known, from the *Iliad*, xv. 18 ff.

> I vow, if she but once frown on thee more,
> To hang her, meteor-like, 'twixt heaven and earth
> And bind her, hand and foot, with golden cords,
> As once I did for harming Hercules.

And there is an echo of the *Amores* (i. xiii. 40) when he reminds Ganymede how he has

> oft driven back the horses of the Night
> Whenas they would have hal'd thee from my sight.

From each of the Olympians in turn some treasure is to be rifled to adorn or gratify Jupiter's 'little love'—even Juno's gems worn on her marriage-day.

With the entry of Venus Virgil also first enters, though treated with scant ceremony, for the seventy lines telling of the wreck of Aeneas' fleet by Aeolus and his winds are

[1] *Eliz. Stage*, iii. 35–6.

cut down to a few, and are followed by variations in a strain of Ovidian fantasy on the theme (1. i. 64 ff.).:

> Poor Troy must now be sack'd upon the sea.

The voice of Virgil sounds again in Jupiter's speech assuring Venus that her 'Aeneas' wandering fate is firm', and that when his warfare is accomplished on Italian soil,

> poor Troy, so long suppress'd,
> From forth her ashes shall advance her head.

In the prophecy that follows of the fortunes of Rome it is bright Ascanius, Aeneas' son, not the Virgilian Augustus, who (1. i. 98–103)

> Shall build his throne amidst those starry bowers,
> That earth-born Atlas, groaning, underprops:
> No bounds but heaven shall bound his empery,
> Whose azur'd gates, enchasèd with his name,
> Shall make the morning haste her grey uprise,
> To feed her eyes with his engraven fame.

Again Marlowe draws upon cosmic imagery in lines that might have been written of Tamburlaine.

The change from heaven to earth is awkwardly managed, for Venus after her dialogue in Olympus with Jupiter, who departs with Ganymede, spies her son Aeneas and his companions landing on the Punic shore. In the address of Aeneas to his followers and in his interview with Venus disguised as a huntress Marlowe follows Virgil closely. But the playwright's instinct is shown in the omission of redundant material, and in the addition of such human touches as that of Ascanius fainting for want of food.

In the second scene there is the more significant addition of Iarbas listening to the story of Ilioneus and his fellows who have been separated from Aeneas. Virgil mentions Iarbas once among Libyan suitors rejected by Dido (*Aen.* iv. 36):

> despectus Iarbas
> Ductoresque alii, quos Africa terra triumphis
> Dives alit.

But it will be seen that it is a constant feature of Marlowe's technique to give a heroine in his dramas two

rival lovers, and Iarbas foreshadows the important part
that he is to play by welcoming the strangers to the court
in Dido's name.

At the beginning of Act II there is another notable
departure from the Virgilian source where Aeneas on
entering Carthage sees in the temple of Juno pictures
representing episodes from the Siege of Troy. In the
play these are replaced by a statue of Priam in stone,
about which Aeneas weaves fancies that are in Ovidian
rather than Virgilian vein (ii. i. 24 ff.):

> Achates, though mine eyes say this is stone,
> Yet thinks my mind that this is Priamus
>
> .   .   .   .
>
> Achates, see, King Priam wags his head!
> He is alive; Troy is not overcome.

When Dido appears and welcomes Aeneas to a banquet,
his reiterated refusal to sit beside her because of his mean
fortune is incongruous and has no suggestion in the epic.
As soon, however, as Aeneas responds to her persuasive plea
(ii. i. 106–9):

> May I entreat thee to discourse at large,
> And truly too, how Troy was overcome?
> For many tales go of that city's fall
> And scarcely do agree upon one point—

Marlowe rises, in the main, to the height of the great
argument. Gager in his Latin play had ingeniously
shirked the difficulty of introducing the long recital of the
downfall of Troy.[1] Marlowe compresses the 800 lines of
this recital in Book II of the *Aeneid* into 180 lines of vivid
narrative, broken at intervals by Dido's sympathetic out-
cries. Translating and adapting, omitting, transposing,
and adding, the dramatist retells the tragic story from the
drawing of the fatal horse within the walls till the flight
of Aeneas with his family to the ships. The horse's entry

----

[1] See *Univ. Drama in the Tudor Age*, pp. 184–5.

is marked by a roll of unmistakably Marlovian, not
Virgilian, music (ii. i. 172 ff.):

> O had it never enter'd, Troy had stood!
> But Priamus, impatient of delay,
> Enforc'd a wide breach in that rampir'd wall,
> Which thousand battering-rams could never pierce,
> And so came in this fatal instrument.
>
> .   .   .   .
>
> From out his entrails Neoptolemus,
> Setting his spear upon the ground, leapt forth,
> And after him a thousand Grecians more,
> In whose stern faces shin'd the quenchless fire
> That after burnt the pride of Asia.

It is Marlowe also, in cruder vein, not Virgil who gives
the details of the carnage in Troy and who adds lurid
details to the tragic fate of Priam's youngest son. Nor do
we recognize Virgil's Priam, buckling on his long-disused
armour and feebly grasping his sword, in the suppliant
king who pleads with Pyrrhus (ii. i. 233–9):

> Achilles' son, remember what I was,
> Father of fifty sons, but they are slain;
> Lord of my fortunes, but my fortune's turn'd;
> King of this city, but my Troy is fir'd;
> And now am neither father, lord, nor king:
> Yet who so wretched but desires to live?
> O let me live, great Neoptolemus!

In their artificial balance these lines have an Ovidian ring,
and it is *Metamorphoses*, xiii. 558 ff., that suggested Hecuba's use of her hands upon a murderer (ii. i. 244–6):

> At which the frantic queen leap'd on his face,
> And in his eyelids hanging by the nails,
> A little while prolong'd her husband's life.

But it is the dramatist alone who is responsible for the
lines that follow:

> At last the soldiers pull'd her by the heels,
> And swung her howling in the empty air,
> Which sent an echo to the wounded king:

Whereat he lifted up his bed-rid limbs,
And would have grappled with Achilles' son,
Forgetting both his want of strength and hands;
Which he disdaining, whisk'd his sword about,
And with the wind thereof the king fell down.
Then from the navel to the throat at once
He ripp'd old Priam.

They are unique in Marlowe's writings. Elsewhere in these there are passages of rhodomontade on the one hand and of bathos on the other, but there is nothing that is frankly absurd. I agree with Bullen and Tucker Brooke that it is this episode that is burlesqued in *Hamlet*, ii. ii. 420–82. In the play that was caviare to the general there was, says the Prince, 'one chief speech I chiefly loved; 'twas Aeneas' tale to Dido; and thereabout of it especially where he speaks of Priam's slaughter'. Gager, it has been seen, omitted this recital by Aeneas. Marlowe, on the other hand, reproduced as much of it as was possible, without breaking his dramatic framework. In it he gives a prominence to the episode of Pyrrhus and Priam that is quite out of proportion to its place in Virgil's narrative. Moreover, though the Pyrrhus of the *Aeneid* is ruthless and mad with slaughter, it is only such phrases as 'his harness dropping blood' (l. 213) and 'with Megæra's eyes star'd in their face' (l. 230) that can have suggested to Shakespeare 'from head to foot Now is he total gules' and 'with eyes like carbuncles'. So, too, when Shakespeare wrote:

Pyrrhus at Priam drives; in rage strikes wide
But with the whiff and wind of his fell sword,
The unnerved father falls

he must have had in mind

whisk'd his sword about,
And with the wind[1] thereof the king fell down.

And though the First Player's 'mobled queen' differs as much from Marlowe's frantic Hecuba as from the

[1] The quarto reads *wound*, of which Shakespeare is, in a sense, the first emendator.

venerable affrighted wife and mother in the *Aeneid*,
Shakespeare was thinking of the grisly details of Priam's
slaughter in *Dido* when he added the caricaturing touch:

> When she saw Pyrrhus make malicious sport
> In mincing with his sword her husband's limbs.

One thing, however, must be also said. The Shakespeare
of *Hamlet* was not the younger Shakespeare of *A Midsummer Night's Dream* who in 'Pyramus and Thisbe'
could write sheer burlesque. There are lines in the
Player's speech, e.g.

> So as a painted tyrant Pyrrhus stood,
> And like a neutral to his will and matter
> Did nothing

and

> Would have made milch the burning eyes of heaven
> And passion in the gods—

which Marlowe might have been glad to father at second
hand.

Aeneas' tale of his own escape, and of the loss of his
wife Creusa, is compressed into a few lines, though to add
further horror to the recital Marlowe makes him witness
the tragic fates of Cassandra and Polyxena. Dido can
bear no more—'I die with melting ruth: Aeneas, leave.'
The excited questions that burst from the other listeners
have true dramatic force, as has also Aeneas' appeal to
Achates to speak for him, 'sorrow hath tir'd me quite'.

When Dido leads off the company to cheer them with
some pleasing sport, Venus, 'entering with Cupid at another door, takes by the sleeve' Ascanius who is following
the others. In verses of lyrical charm that fall sweetly on
the ear after 'the tumult and the shouting' of Aeneas'
recital, the Goddess beguiles the child into her arms, and
after singing him asleep lays him in a 'grove', probably
outside the wall. With Cupid transformed into the likeness of Ascanius and nestling in her lap, Dido is no longer
a free agent. Thus when at the beginning of Act III she
is half inclined to lend a favouring ear to the suit of Iarbas,

the little love-god turns her heart to his brother Aeneas.
He finds an ally in Dido's sister Anna, whom the dramatist,
without any cue from Virgil, represents as a jealous rival
for Iarbas' love. And he is almost equally far from Virgil
when he turns Dido's burning passion 'to favour and to
prettiness' (III. i. 84–9):

> I'll make me bracelets of his golden hair;
> His glistering eyes shall be my looking-glass;
> His lips an altar, where I'll offer up
> As many kisses as the sea hath sands;
> Instead of music I will hear him speak;
> His looks shall be my only library.

In a similarly fanciful vein is her promise to repair the
Trojan ships, on condition that they bear away Achates,
not Aeneas (III. i. 115 ff.):

> I'll give thee tackling made of rivell'd gold,
> Wound on the barks of odoriferous trees;
> Oars of massy ivory, full of holes,
> Through which the water shall delight to play
>
> .   .   .   .
>
> The masts whereon thy swelling sails shall hang,
> Hollow pyramides of silver plate;
> The sails of folded lawn, where shall be wrought
> The wars of Troy—but not Troy's overthrow.

This sugared speech changes to an acid tone as she
exhibits to Aeneas the pictures of her suitors from many
lands and criticizes each in turn. As we listen to her
sharp comments and to her hints of where her heart is
given we seem to have quitted Carthage for Portia's
Belmont.

The reappearance of Juno at this crisis in III. ii. is
ingeniously associated with a design to take her revenge
for the insults to her deity by murdering in his sleep

> Aeneas' cursed brat,
> The boy wherein false Destiny delights,
> The heir of Fame, the favourite of the Fates.

But Venus, warned by her doves, saves Ascanius.

Thereafter, as in *Aeneid*, iv. 90–128, the two goddesses make a truce and Juno sets forth her plan for bringing Dido and Aeneas together in a cave while they are hunting. How the Shakespeare of *A Midsummer Night's Dream* would have delighted in III. iii in loading with Warwickshire detail the Virgilian 'odora canum vis' and the 'sonipes' champing his bit! But animals appealed little to Marlowe. He prefers to make further play with the rivalry between Iarbas and Aeneas, with the counterfeit bragging of Cupid-Ascanius, and with the idea, suggested by the stage-setting, that the hunt is in the wood where Aeneas and his followers had first set foot.

So, too, with the fateful meeting in the cave. It is over the personal aspects that the dramatist lingers. Dido is still the woman who half reveals and half conceals her passion (III. iv. 26–34):

> And yet I'll speak—and yet I'll hold my peace.
> Do shame her worst, I will disclose my grief:
> Aeneas, thou art he—what did I say?
> Something it was that now I have forgot.
> *Aen.* What means fair Dido by this doubtful speech?
> *Dido.* Nay, nothing; but Aeneas loves me not.
> *Aen.* Aeneas' thoughts dare not ascend so high
> As Dido's heart which monarchs might not scale.

When the queen retorts, 'It was because I saw no king like thee', Aeneas offers his heart and vows, with oath on oath,

> Never to leave these new-upreared walls,
> Whiles Dido lives and rules in Juno's town—
> Never to like or love any but her.

In ecstasy she cries (III. iv. 51–3):

> What more than Delian music do I hear,
> That calls my soul from forth his living seat
> To move unto the measures of delight.

She hails him as King of Carthage and bestows on him the ring with which her first husband had wooed her.

They retire to the back of the cave,[1] where their union takes place. And it is noteworthy that here, for once, Marlowe omitted a cosmic background to the scene, though Virgil had given him the lead in *Aeneid*, iv. 166–8:

> Prima et Tellus et pronuba Iuno
> Dant signum; fulsere ignes et conscius aether
> Conubiis, summoque ulularunt vertice Nymphae.

'The ritual of a Roman marriage is here undertaken', as J. W. Mackail has said,[2] 'by the elemental Powers.' But the dramatist ignores the significance of this and the omen of woe to come in the words that follow:

> Ille dies primus leti primusque malorum
> Causa fuit.

Events move swiftly to their tragic close. Iarbas, stung to fury by the sight of the lovers coming from the cave, first, with a Marlovian gesture, curses 'unrevenging Jove' (IV. i. 17), and then in the next scene, in a more Virgilian temper, seeks to appease him with sacrifice on his altars, and prays for his help against his rival (IV. ii. 19–22):

> Now if thou be'st a pitying god of power,
> On whom ruth and compassion ever waits,
> Redress these wrongs, and warn him to his ships
> That now afflicts me with his flattering eyes.

But even with celestial intervention Aeneas' announcement of his departure is unplausibly abrupt after his unconditional vows of fidelity to Dido (IV. iii. 1–7):

> Carthage, my friendly host, adieu!
> Since destiny doth call me from the shore:
> Hermes this night, descending in a dream,
> Hath summon'd me to fruitful Italy;

---

[1] This seems the interpretation of the S.D. *Exeunt to the cave*, taken in connexion with the S.D. at the beginning of the scene, *Enter* Aeneas *and* Dido *in the cave, at several times.* In IV. i. 16 Anna cries, 'Behold where both of them come forth the cave'.

[2] *The Aeneid*, ed. by J. W. Mackail, p. 138. Mackail illustrates the statement quoted above in detail.

> Jove wills it so; my mother wills it so;
> Let my Phoenissa grant and then I go.
> Grant she or no, Aeneas must away.

The remainder of Act IV, representing a first attempt
of Aeneas to sail away, of which Virgil gives no hint, is
a tamer anticipation of his final leave-taking in Act V.
It gives Marlowe the opportunity of lingering over the
relations between the lovers and of again embroidering
them with luxuriant fancies. When Anna at Dido's command stays the Trojan from sailing, he pleads that he was
merely bidding farewell to Achates and that he would not
have left his only son. In an ecstasy of relief the queen
invests him with her crown and sceptre, and cries (IV. iv.
45 ff.):

> Now looks Aeneas like immortal Jove:
> O where is Ganymede, to hold his cup,
> And Mercury, to fly for what he calls?
> Ten thousand Cupids hover in the air,
> And fan it in Aeneas' lovely face!
>
> .   .   .   .
>
> Heaven, envious of our joys, is waxen pale,
> And when we whisper, then the stars fall down,
> To be partakers of our honey talk.

It is an elemental love that here annihilates space, as
in ll. 121–3 it annihilates time:

> If he forsake me not, I never die;
> For in his looks I see eternity,
> And he'll make me immortal with a kiss.

It is a steep descent from such transcendental flights to
Dido's manœuvres in sending for Aeneas' oars, tackling,
and sails, round which she lets her fancies run riot in
IV. iv. 126–65, and in bidding the nurse take Ascanius to
her country home. The idyllic picture of this in IV. v.
4–11, and the aged crone's amorous musings, prompted
by Cupid-Ascanius, form a lighter interlude before the
final tragedy in Act V, where the play returns to its

Virgilian source. At Jupiter's command Hermes, now appearing not in a dream but in person, warns Aeneas, as he is drawing the 'platform' of a statelier Troy, that he

> must straight to Italy,
> Or else abide the wrath of frowning Jove.

It is, of course, an excrescence on the original tale that Aeneas, robbed by Dido of his ships' furniture, should have his needs supplied by Iarbas who, in his eagerness to get rid of his rival, shows himself in a gracious guise, inconsistent with his previous utterances.

Then comes the dramatist's hardest task—to reproduce the agony of a woman scorned, crystallized in the words (*Aen.* iv. 300–1):

> Saevit inops animi totamque incensa per urbem
> Bacchatur.

It is here that Marlowe does not stand the test. There is little of Bacchic frenzy in the queen's words, making play with her lover's 'farewell' (v. i. 105):

> Farewell! is this the mends for Dido's love?
> Do Trojans use to quit their lovers thus?
> Fare well may Dido, so Aeneas stay;
> I die, if my Aeneas say farewell.
> *Aen.* Then let me go, and never say farewell.
> *Dido.* 'Let me go; farewell; I must from hence.'
> These words are poison to poor Dido's soul.

Was Marlowe himself half-conscious of his limitations when, as the queen becomes more impassioned, he puts into her mouth three of Virgil's own lines (*Aen.* iv. 317–19):

> *Si bene quid de te merui, fuit aut tibi quicquam*
> *Dulce meum, miserere domus labentis et istam,*
> *Oro, si quis adhuc precibus locus, exue mentem.*

answered similarly by the Trojan (*Aen.* iv. 360–1):

> *Desine meque tuis incendere teque querelis;*
> *Italiam non sponte sequor.*

Then follow lines not unworthy to be the sequel of even Virgilian music (v. i. 141–8):

> Hast thou forgot how many neighbour kings
> Were up in arms, for making thee my love?
> How Carthage did rebel, Iarbas storm,
> And all the world calls me a second Helen,
> For being entangled in a stranger's looks?
> So thou wouldst prove as true as Paris did,
> Would, as fair Troy was, Carthage might be sack'd,
> And I be called a second Helena.

The name of Helen had always a talismanic effect on Marlowe. But when Aeneas at last forsakes her, Dido again gives rein to her exuberant fancy. She will follow her lover in the air like Icarus, or ride to him on a dolphin's back. She cheats herself into the belief that she sees him coming back to her arms. Then with a swift revulsion of feeling she resolves to (v. i. 269–71)

> die in fury of this oversight.
> Ay, I must be the murderer of myself;
> No, but I am not; yet I will be straight.

In the epic the harrowing picture of the deserted woman dooming herself to death on the sacrificial pyre fills some two hundred lines, which are compressed by Marlowe into fifty. The queen's last agony finds voice in only a single speech (v. i. 289–313), consigning her faithless lover's relics to the flames, foretelling the Punic conqueror who would take revenge for her on Rome, and with her last breath again using Virgil's own words (*Aen.* iv. 628–9 and 660):

> *Litora litoribus contraria, fluctibus undas*
> *Imprecor, arma armis; pugnent ipsique nepotes!*
> Live false Aeneas! truest Dido dies;
> *Sic, sic juvat ire sub umbras.*

With the cry, 'Dido, I come to thee', Iarbas too kills himself, and with the echoing cry:

> Now, sweet Iarbas stay! I come to thee

Anna falls lifeless over his body.

With the prominence given in the play to Iarbas and Anna it was natural that Marlowe should associate them in death with the Carthaginian queen. But here he showed himself unequal to his august source. Dido in the *Aeneid* stands out alone in tragic grandeur. 'While she is there', in Mackail's words,[1] 'she fills the whole canvas. . . . Into her Virgil pours all his insight into the human heart and his sense of purely human tragedy.' Nor was her tragedy purely human—

> Tantae molis erat Romanam condere gentem.

It was Dido's fate to be sacrificed in the course of the divinely ordained sequence of events that linked the fall of Troy with the rise of Rome. It was that mighty conception that lay at the heart of the *Aeneid*. What were Iarbas and Anna to Virgil that he should weep for them? It was otherwise with Marlowe. His translation from Lucan shows an interest in Roman history. But it was not through history that antiquity laid upon him its chief spell. The Virgilian conception of the world-destiny of Rome was outside his ken. He was absorbed, as has been seen, in the emotional aspects of the story of Dido, and he decked them out with a lavish wealth of fantasies.

It was not only Virgil's theme, but his art, that offered a challenge to the English dramatist. The secret of that art was incommunicable. Its poignant expression in haunting cadences of the pathos of mortal things is far removed from all that is most distinctive in Marlowe's genius. Such key-lines as

> Sunt lacrimae rerum et mentem mortalia tangunt

or

> Non ignara mali miseris succurrere disco

have no counterpart in the English play.

It is just because Marlowe had already found his own voice that so many lines and phrases in his later writings

---

[1] *The Aeneid*, ed. by J. W. Mackail, lxvii.

are anticipated in *Dido*. Yet any one who had speculated
on his future as a dramatist from *Dido* would probably
have gone astray. In the relations of Aeneas and Dido,
Iarbas and Anna, sexual love has a relatively far larger
place than it was to fill in his other plays. Never again
was a woman to be the protagonist in his theatre.[1] The
representation of Jupiter and the other Olympians on the
traditional classical lines gave no hint of the speculative
flights of the 'atheist' Marlowe into the supersensual
sphere, as in *Tamburlaine* and *Doctor Faustus*. Nor does
there throb through *Dido* the passionate aspiration after
the fullness of power and beauty and knowledge which,
in one aspect or another, links Marlowe's other plays. He
may have instinctively felt that the Children of the Chapel
could not 'boy' the 'greatness' of such themes. He was
to find interpreters of them on the public stage.

There were three principal adult companies acting
in London when Marlowe arrived there in 1587. The
Queen's men had been formed in 1583 and had absorbed
a number of the chief players from the companies of the
Earls of Leicester and Oxford and others. The period of
their special vogue was ended by the death of Richard
Tarlton in 1588. The company of Ferdinando Stanley,
Lord Strange, were both players and tumblers, and it is
of their feats of activity that there is the fuller record.
Perhaps by 1588–9, and certainly by 1590–1, they amal-
gamated till 1594 with the Lord Admiral's company.
This company, serving Lord Howard of Effingham, bore
the title of the Admiral's men after his appointment to
this high office in July 1585. It may have been either then
or some years later that Edward Alleyn joined the company and became its star actor. We know for certain from
the 1590 title-page of *Tamburlaine* that it was by the
Admiral's men that both Parts were produced, but it is
doubtful, though probable, that Alleyn was already with

---

[1] Unless his hand is to be seen in *Arden of Feversham*. See below,
pp. 198–200.

them to create the hero's role of which he became the great exponent. And the vague reference on the title-page of the earliest editions to the two Parts having been 'shewed vpon Stages in the Citie of London' suggests that Marlowe may have first won dramatic fame not in one of the few theatres built by 1587 but in one or other of the inn-yards still used for playhouse purposes.

Tamburlaine

the Great.

Who, from a Scythian Shephearde,
by his rare and woonderfull Conquests,
became a most puissant and migh-
tye Monarque.

And (for his tyranny, and terrour in
Warre)was tearmed,

The Scourge of God.

Deuided into two Tragicall Dis-
courses, as they were sundrie times
shewed vpon Stages in the Citie
of London.

By the right honorable the Lord
Admyrall, his seruantes.

Now first, and newlie published.

LONDON.
Printed by Richard Ihones: at the signe
of the Rose and Crowne neere Hol-
borne Bridge. 1590.

V

THE FIRST PART OF
'TAMBURLAINE THE GREAT'

IT is a paradox that when they presented to the reading public the two most epoch-making of pre-Shakespearian plays, *The Spanish Tragedy* and *Tamburlaine the Great*, the publishers decked them out with flowery title-pages but did not give the names of their authors. In the former case the omission was rectified by Thomas Heywood in his *Apology for Actors* (1612), where, in quoting three lines from *The Spanish Tragedy*, Act IV. i, he names Kyd as the writer. In tantalizing fashion, twenty-one years later, he just avoided doing the same service for *Tamburlaine* when in his Cockpit prologue to *The Jew of Malta* he said:

> We know not how our Play may pass this stage,
> But by the best *of Poets in that age   *Marlo.
> The *Malta Jew* had being, and was made;
> And He, then by the best of *Actors play'd: *Allin.
> In *Hero and Leander*, one did gain
> A lasting memory; in *Tamberlaine*,
> This *Jew*, with others many: th'other wan
> The attribute of peerless.

Here Marlowe is saluted as the author of *The Jew of Malta* and of *Hero and Leander*; Alleyn as the creator on the stage of the parts of Tamburlaine and Barabas, 'with others many'. There is no allusion to the authorship of *Tamburlaine*, though the introduction of it alone by name, out of the many plays in which Alleyn had figured, between *The Jew of Malta* and *Hero and Leander* seems to imply that Heywood attributed it to Marlowe.

More unquestionable had been the implication almost half a century before in Greene's epistle 'to the gentlemen

readers' prefixed to his *Perimedes the Blacksmith* (1588),
where he complains that he is derided

'for that I could not make my verses jet upon the stage in tragicall
buskins, everie word filling the mouth like the Faburden of Bo-Bell,
daring God out of heaven with that Atheist *Tamburlan*, or
blaspheming with the mad preest of the sonne: but let me rather
openly pocket up the Asse at *Diogenes* hand: then wantonlie set
out such impious instances of intollerable poetrie, such mad and
scoffing poets, that have propheticall spirits as bred of *Merlins* race.'

The last words in conjunction with the gibe at the
Atheist Tamburlaine and with the Cambridge documentary evidence that the dramatist's name was often known
as Marlin can leave no reasonable doubt that Marlowe is
here attacked as the writer of *Tamburlaine*. Nor is there
anything in favour of another authorship. Even if, which
is doubtful, Sir John Suckling in *The Goblins*, Act IV. i
(published 1646),[1] intended to imply that Nicholas
Breton wrote *Tamburlaine*, his view can be discounted,
though it misled, of all people, Edmund Malone. Equally
unfounded is the attribution to Thomas Newton by
Edward Phillips in *Theatrum Poetarum* (1675). Rogers and
Ley and Edward Archer in their play-lists of 1656, and
Francis Kirkman in his of 1661, had entered the two
Parts of *Tamburlaine* without an author's name. But
Kirkman in his second list of 1671 had assigned it to
'Chr. Marloe'. Phillips, therefore, as Gerard Langbaine
and Anthony Wood were quick to point out in 1691, had
no excuse for his error, and except Malone no one of
weight has since questioned Marlowe's authorship.

It is therefore unnecessary to labour the internal
evidence. The arresting music of the blank verse, unique
in its combination of sonorous ring and liquid flow, the
cosmic imagery, the pervading impress of an endlessly
aspiring mind stamp both Parts of *Tamburlaine* with the
unmistakably authentic Marlovian signature. As any
annotated edition will show, there are a multitude of
passages linking the two *Parts* with the plays bearing

[1] See *Tamburlaine the Great*, ed. Una Ellis-Fermor, p. 14.

Marlowe's name on the title-page. It is scarcely too much
to say that the lines, Part II, Act II. iv. 87–8,

> Helen, whose beauty summoned Greece to arms,
> And drew a thousand ships to Tenedos,

compared with *Doctor Faustus*, v. i. 107–8, and with *Dido*,
v. i. 146–8, would be sufficient to show that they all came
from the same pen.

The publication of the octavo of 1590 (entered in the
Stationers' Register on 14 August) gives an upward limit
of date. Greene's reference in the prefatory epistle to
Perimedes brings this down to 1588, and as Miss Ellis-
Fermor has pointed out, his gibing phrases seem to be
more fully applicable to Part II than to Part I.[1] The date
appears to be still more narrowly fixed by the following
letter from Philip Gawdy to his father on 16 November
1587:

'My L. Admirall his men and players having a devyse in ther playe
to tye one of their fellowes to a poste and to shoote him to deathe,
having borrowed their callyvers one of the players handes swerved
his peece being charged with bullett, missed the fellowe he aymed
at and killed a chyld and a woman great with chyld forthwith and
hurt an other man in the head very sore.'[2]

As the two 'tragical discourses' of *Tamburlaine* were
acted, according to the title-page, by the Lord Admiral's
company, it can scarcely be questioned that the fatality
which he recounts took place during the performance of
Act v. i. 148 ff. of Part II, where the Governor of Babylon
is hung in chains upon the walls of the town and is shot at
by the besiegers. Marlowe's last period of residence in
Corpus Christi College was for five weeks and a half
between Christmas 1586 and Lady Day 1587. He may,
as already suggested,[3] have begun *Tamburlaine* towards the
end of his Cambridge period. Otherwise both Parts must
have been written in the summer and autumn of 1587.

[1] Op. cit., pp. 6–8.
[2] Quoted by Sir E. K. Chambers, *T.L.S.*, 28 Aug. 1930, and in *Eliz.
Stage*, ii. 135, from *Letters of Philip Gawdy*, ed. I. H. Jeayes, p. 23.
[3] See above, p. 27.

Two objections, however, to that date have to be met. Tamburlaine's speech to his sons about fortifications in Part II, Act III. ii. 62–82, is taken almost verbally from a passage in Paul Ive's *Practise of Fortification*, published in 1589. F. C. Danchin, who first noted this, has therefore concluded that Part II cannot be earlier than 1589, and that Greene's allusions were to Part I which Danchin would assign to 1588.[1] Miss Ellis-Fermor would get over the difficulty by assuming that Marlowe had seen Ive's work in manuscript, especially as he was a Kentish man and dedicated it to Sir Francis Walsingham.[2]

There has also to be noted another similar but more extensive problem concerning both Parts of *Tamburlaine*. In each of them there are considerable borrowings from the early Books, especially the first, of *The Faerie Queene*.[3] The two most notable are in Part II, Act IV. iii. 119–24:

Like to an almond tree ymounted high, &c.,

compared with *F.Q.* I. vii. 32, ll. 5–9; and Act IV. i. 188–92:

As when an herd of lusty Cimbrian bulls, &c.,

compared with *F.Q.* I. viii. 11, ll. 5–8.

But Part I also borrows from *The Faerie Queene*, e.g. Act v. ii. 227–30:

O highest lamp of ever-living Jove, &c.,

compared with *F.Q.* I. vii. 23, ll. 1–5; and Act v. ii. 239–40:

Then let the stony dart of senseless cold, &c.,

compared with *F.Q.* I. vii. 22, ll. 7–8.

In the light of these and other parallels Mincoff, like Miss Ellis-Fermor in the case of *The Practise of Fortification*, assumes that Marlowe must have seen part of *The*

---

[1] *Revue Germanique*, Jan.–Feb. 1912.

[2] Op. cit., pp. 9–10.

[3] See Marco K. Mincoff, *Christopher Marlowe: A Study of his Development*, pp. 14–16 (1937, Sofia), following, in part, Schoeneich, *Der literarische Einfluss Spensers auf Marlowe* (1907, Halle).

Faerie Queene in manuscript. We know from Spenser's correspondence with Gabriel Harvey that he had begun his epic in 1580, but from that year till towards the close of 1589 he was in Ireland. Is it likely that the young Cambridge student would have had access to his unpublished work or felt at liberty to draw so freely upon it? *The Faerie Queene* (Books I–III) was entered in the Stationers' Register on 1 December 1589; the entry of *Tamburlaine* followed eight and a half months later. We are learning more and more that Marlowe was an adept at turning his reading quickly to dramatic use. I think it probable that before Richard Jones published the first edition of *Tamburlaine* in the latter half of 1590, Marlowe revised the two 'tragical discourses' and inserted the passages lifted with slight change from Spenser and Ive. If they are looked at in their context, it will be found that they can be detached from these and are little more than embroidery. They need not, therefore, weigh against the evidence of date supplied by Gawdy's 1587 letter and Greene's 1588 allusions.

Moreover, the *Tamburlaine* plays are linked to *Dido* by metrical similarities and parallelisms of phrase which favour a date as close as possible to Marlowe's Cambridge period. And as I shall try to show, there are other insufficiently recognized traces of the influence of Marlowe's academic studies upon the first of the 'tragical discourses' which when 'shewed upon Stages in the Citie of London' took the public by storm.

The name of *Tamburlaine* has been so long associated with that of Marlowe as the first heir of his invention produced on a public stage that we scarcely pause to consider how it was that the young dramatist chose so exotic a subject, so different from the themes of classical, Italian, or British origin which had hitherto supplied the chief material for tragedy or tragi-comedy in England. Yet a close examination suggests that Marlowe's Cambridge studies and translations of Latin poetry may well have led him to the choice of the career of the Scythian

conqueror for his first play. Though the First Book of Lucan
has as its central theme the march of Caesar in 49 B.C.
from Gaul towards Rome, it takes in its sweep part of the
territories which fourteen centuries later were to be the
scene of Tamburlaine's exploits. It was the defeat of
Crassus by the Parthians and his 'wretched death' at
Carrhae that broke up the triumvirate and that set in
motion, as Lucan laments, the train of events that
culminated in the Civil War. Romans turned on one
another the arms by which (19–20)

> Scythia and wild Armenia had been yok'd,
> And they of Nilus' mouth.

So the chief centurion appeals to Caesar (368–9):

> Well, lead us then to Syrtes' desert shore,
> Or Scythia or hot Libya's thirsty sands.

And in Lucan's later Books the civil war shifts to Greece
and Egypt and Asia Minor. From the moment that
Caesar crosses the Rubicon and cries (228–9):

> Fortune, thee I follow.
> War and the Destinies shall try my cause

till he attains supreme power after his triumphs at
Pharsalia, Thapsus, and Munda, his career is that of a
world-wide conqueror. And that Marlowe thought of
Caesar and Tamburlaine as warriors of similar breed is
shown by *1 Tamburlaine*, III. iii. 153–6:

> My camp is like to Julius Caesar's host
> That never fought but had the victory,
> Nor in Pharsalia was there such hot war
> As these my followers willingly would have.

Tamburlaine speaks of himself in terms of Roman
dignities when he cries to Theridamas (I. ii. 196–7):

> Both we will reign as consuls of the earth,
> And mighty kings shall be our senators.

And the lines that immediately follow show that behind Marlowe's reminiscences of Lucan and Roman

history there floated images from Ovid and classical mythology (198–200):

> Jove sometimes masked in a shepherd's weed,
> And by those steps that he hath scal'd the heavens,
> May we become immortal like the gods.

The shepherd revealing himself as a god prefigures the shepherd who in the play rises to earthly omnipotence.

The mythologists tell also of the overthrow of one celestial dynasty by another, thus giving countenance to similar revolutions on earth (II. vii. 12–17):

> The thirst of reign and sweetness of a crown,
> That caused the eldest son of heavenly Ops
> To thrust his doting father from his chair,
> And place himself in the imperial heaven,
> Mov'd me to manage arms against thy state.
> What better precedent than mighty Jove?

Thus Tamburlaine addresses the defeated puppet king of Persia, Cosroe, who had boasted that he would overthrow him as Jove had crushed the Titans (II. vi. 1–8):

> What means this devilish shepherd to aspire
> With such a giantly presumption,
> To cast up hills against the face of heaven,
> And dare the force of angry Jupiter?
> But as he thrust them underneath the hills
> And pressed out fire from their burning jaws,
> So will I send this monstrous slave to hell,
> Where flames shall ever feed upon his soul.

Thus Marlowe's imagination was richly stored with classical analogies when accounts of Tamburlaine's meteoric career fell into his hands. His chief source appears to have been the Latin *Magni Tamerlanis Scythiarum Imperatoris Vita* (1553) by Petrus Perondinus. The description of Tamburlaine's appearance in II. i. 7–30, beginning,

> Of stature tall, and straightly fashioned
> Like his desire, lift upwards and divine,

is evidently based upon chapter xxi of the *Vita* by Perondinus, *De statura Tamerlanis et moribus eius*, with the
omission of his lameness, and the addition of transfiguring
Marlovian touches. Perondinus's whole conception of
Tamburlaine as a figure 'insatiable, irresistible, ruthless,
destructive, but instinct with power'[1] gives the cue
upon which Marlowe worked. It was not the aim of the
daring young dramatist to follow in the Senecan tradition
and to stress with appropriate moralizing the mutations
of Fortune. There is only one passage in which this theme
is dominant, v. ii. 285–309, where Zenocrate drives home
the lesson of the miserable fate of the captive Turkish
emperor and his wife. Here Marlowe is following another
source, Thomas Fortescue's *The Foreste or Collection of
Histories* (1571),[2] an English version, through the French,
of Pedro Mexia's Spanish *Silva de Varia Lection* (1542),
which contained in Part II, chapter xxviii, the story of
Tamburlaine. The tragic fate of Bajazeth, which in
Fortescue's words 'might suffice to withdrawe men from
this transitorie pompe, and honour', provokes the warning
from Zenocrate:

> Those that are proud of fickle empery,
> And place their chiefest good in earthly pomp,
> Behold the Turk and his great emperess!

But such moralizing was incidental and was in contradiction with the essential spirit of the play. In it Marlowe
achieved the revolution of bringing on the English public
stage a figure, who was not the sport of Fortune but her
lord; who held the Fates fast bound in iron chains, and
who throbbed with a stupendous vitality that made him
the fitting mouthpiece of the dramatist's own tumultuous
energies and aspirations.

The Prologue heralds his appearance by assuring the
audience that they

> shall hear the Scythian Tamburlaine
> Threatening the world with high astounding terms
> And scourging kingdms with his conquering sword.

[1] Introduction to *Tamburlaine*, by U. Ellis-Fermor, p. 31. [2] But see p. 87.

But the stage is first occupied by a strangely different figure, the Persian King Mycetes, a nerveless ruler, with aesthetic susceptibilities, who holds "'tis a pretty toy to be a poet', and who is a feebler forerunner of Marlowe's Edward II and Shakespeare's Richard II. Though he deplores his lack of 'a great and thundering speech' with which to voice his wrongs, he can make play with fanciful images and conceits as he sends forth his 'chiefest captain', Theridamas, to do battle with Tamburlaine (I. i. 65 ff.):

Rich. II

> Go frowning forth, but come thou smiling home,
> As did Sir Paris with the Grecian dame
>
> .   .   .   .   .   .
>
> Go, stout Theridamas, thy words are swords,
> And with thy looks thou conquerest all thy foes:
> I long to see thee back return from thence,
> That I may view these milk-white steeds of mine
> All loaden with the heads of killed men,
> And from their knees even to their hoofs below
> Besmeared with blood that makes a dainty show.

But Theridamas yields to the Scythian's 'strong enchantments' and deserts to him, as does also Cosroe, the more virile brother of Mycetes, planning himself to be King of Persia, with Tamburlaine as his regent. But when Mycetes has been defeated,[1] Tamburlaine turns upon Cosroe, whom he has made king only in sport, and takes from him both his crown and his life. The fortunes of the Persian royalties which fill the greater part of Acts I and II do not in themselves move us much. But our ears are enchanted with the billowy music of the verse, and with the sonorous roll of eastern place-names to whose magic Marlowe, like Milton after him, had the key.

Though in several of the scenes in these earlier Acts Tamburlaine does not himself appear, yet through the descriptions of him alike by friends and enemies, through

---

[1] His opening speech in Act II. iv, beginning, 'Accursed be he that first invented war', expresses well the pacifist point of view. But his attempt to hide the crown and his dialogue with Tamburlaine have an incongruous air.

the magnetism that he exerts, and through 'the high
astounding terms' of his proclamations, his figure swells
to more and more stupendous proportions. The panegyric
on his physical attributes, with comparisons to Atlas and
Hercules, a glorified version of the account by Perondinus, has been noted above. It is put into the lips of the
Persian lord, Menaphon, and it is echoed by his royal
countryman, Cosroe (II. i. 31–6):

> Well hast thou pourtrayed in thy terms of life
> The face and personage of a wondrous man:
> Nature doth strive with Fortune and his stars
> To make him famous in accomplished worth:
> And well his merits shew him to be made
> His fortune's master and the king of men.

And yet another Persian, Theridamas, cries at first
sight of him (I. ii. 154–6):

> Tamburlaine! A Scythian shepherd so embellished
> With nature's pride and richest furniture!
> His looks do menace heaven and dare the gods.

One of his Scythian followers, Techelles, exclaims when
he views him in full warlike array (I. ii. 52–4):

> As princely lions when they rouse themselves,
> Stretching their paws, and threatening herds of beasts,
> So in his armour looketh Tamburlaine.

His own utterances are pitched in a corresponding key.
In almost his first words he speaks of himself as one who
(I. ii. 38–40)

> means to be a terror to the world,
> Measuring the limits of his empery,
> By east and west, as Phoebus doth his course.

He and his men (I. ii. 64–5)

> in conceit bear empires on our spears
> Affecting thoughts coequal with the clouds.

And in yet another of Marlowe's favourite cosmological
parallels (I. ii. 173–6):

> I hold the fates fast bound in iron chains,
> And with my hand turn Fortune's wheel about,

> And sooner shall the sun fall from his sphere
> Than Tamburlaine be slain or overcome.

The magnetic effect of this magniloquence is proved in
the scene which brings Act II to an effective close when
Tamburlaine, after Cosroe's defeat and death, crowns
himself King of Persia and is acclaimed by 'all':

> Long live Tamburlaine, and reign in Asia!

And with a superb flourish he greets this popular
recognition (II. vii. 65-7):

> So; now it is more surer on my head
> Than if the gods had held a parliament,
> And all pronounc'd me king of Persia.

It was doubtless as a warrior victor of superhuman
mould that Tamburlaine took Elizabethan theatre-goers
by storm. But had he been no more than this he would
not have been truly representative of Marlowe's genius.
Tamburlaine can not only, as has been seen, find Olympian precedent for his limitless ambition, but in lines
where he is the mouthpiece of his creator he traces the
passion for sovereignty to the same ultimate source as
the insatiable scientific impulse (II. vii. 18-29):

> Nature that fram'd us of four elements
> Warring within our breasts for regiment,
> Doth teach us all to have aspiring minds;
> Our souls, whose faculties can comprehend
> The wondrous architecture of the world,
> And measure every wandering planet's course,
> Still climbing after knowledge infinite,
> And always moving as the restless spheres,
> Will us to wear ourselves and never rest,
> Until we reach the ripest fruit of all,
> That perfect bliss and sole felicity,
> The sweet fruition of an earthly crown.

Allied in Marlowe's vision with the quest for power
and the quest for knowledge is the quest for beauty,
personalized for Tamburlaine in Zenocrate, the captive

daughter of the Soldan of Egypt. Thus from the beginning there blends with the Scythian's martial grandiloquence a softer strain. Neither Perondinus nor Fortescue
speaks of Tamburlaine in his relation to women, but the
Byzantine historian Chalcondylas, whose account of the
Scythian was available to Marlowe in the Latin version
by Conradus Clauserus (1556),[1] mentions his first wife.
Here was a hint of 'feminine interest', and the translator
of the *Amores* could not but remember that with a soldier
Cupid was only less potent than Mars.

The question, however, has to be asked—why does Marlowe present Tamburlaine, when he first appears in Act I.
ii, as already enamoured of Zenocrate? I would suggest,
in answer, that Marlowe was here influenced by Virgil,
who in the later part of his epic makes Aeneas, when he
comes to Italy, win the hand of Lavinia, the daughter of
King Latinus, who was already betrothed to Turnus,
King of Rutilia. Similarly, Zenocrate has been betrothed
to the King of Arabia, who in the last scene of Part I
does battle with Tamburlaine for his country and his
love. In the warning words of a messenger (v. ii. 316–20):

> th' Arabian king,
> The first affecter of your excellence,
> Comes now as Turnus 'gainst Aeneas did,
> Armed with lance into the Egyptian fields,
> Ready for battle 'gainst my lord the king.

And Zenocrate herself prays for a similar issue to the
conflict as when

> the gods to end the Trojans' toil,
> Prevented Turnus of Lavinia.

It is evident that Marlowe's debt to the *Aeneid* is not
confined to his *Dido*.

Tamburlaine is at first no very devout lover. Zenocrate
seems to stir his imagination rather than his heart. She
is 'lovelier than the love of Jove', 'fairer than whitest
snow'; she shall be drawn 'with milk-white harts upon an

---

[1] Ethel Seaton in 'Fresh Sources for Marlowe' (*R.E.S.*, Oct. 1929) has
shown that Marlowe knew this work.

ivory sled'. Agydas, one of the Median lords escorting
Zenocrate, must have forgotten these flowers of speech
when in a later scene he warns her (III. ii. 40–6):

> How can you fancy one that looks so fierce,
> Only disposed to martial stratagems?
> Who, when he shall embrace you in his arms,
> Will tell how many thousand men he slew;
> And when you look for amorous discourse,
> Will rattle forth his facts of war and blood,
> Too harsh a subject for your dainty ears.

Zenocrate's reply proves that Tamburlaine can exercise
as potent an enchantment over women as over men.
Again Marlowe has recourse for the expression of passion
to the images of Ovidian mythology:

> As looks the sun through Nilus' flowing stream,
> Or when the Morning holds him in her arms,
> So looks my lordly love, fair Tamburlaine;
> His talk much sweeter than the Muses' song
> They sung for honour 'gainst Pierides,
> Or when Minerva did with Neptune strive;
> And higher would I rear my estimate
> Than Juno, sister to the highest god,
> If I were matched with mighty Tamburlaine.

These high-flown classical parallels are wasted on
Agydas, who still pleads the cause of the young Arabian
king. Tamburlaine, who has meanwhile entered and over-
heard this dialogue, now takes Zenocrate (as the stage-
direction runs) 'away lovingly by the hand looking wrath-
fully on Agydas, and says nothing'. The terror inspired
by Tamburlaine's mere look is realized when Agydas
moans (III. ii. 72–3):

> Upon his brows was pourtrayed ugly death,
> And in his eyes the fury of his heart.

Thereupon Techelles enters 'with a naked dagger' and
the grim exhortation:

> See you, Agydas, how the King salutes you,
> He bids you prophesy what it imports.

Characteristically argumentative to the end, with an echo perhaps of some disputation in the Cambridge schools on the value of words, Agydas retorts:

> I prophesied before and now I prove
> The killing frowns of jealousy and love.
> He needed not with words confirm my fear,
> For words are vain where working tools present
> The naked action of my threatened end.

Therewith he takes his own life. But neither his Stoic *apologia* for his suicide, nor the tributes of the Persian lords, should divert attention from what is the only dramatic justification of this curious episode, of Marlowe's own devising, that it is the first example (apart from the fate of Cosroe in battle) of Tamburlaine's terrible short way with those who stand in his path. It is the first glimpse of the sadistic element in his complex nature and it prepares the audience for worse atrocities to come.

The decadent royal house of Persia has been an easy prey to Tamburlaine, but in Act III he faces a more formidable enemy. Bajazeth, the Emperor of the Turks, who has been on the point of crowning his victorious career by the conquest of Constantinople, raises the siege to stay the onset of Tamburlaine in Asia. In dispatching beforehand a Basso with a threatening message to the Scythian, Bajazeth speaks of himself in magniloquent style as (III. i. 23–6):

> Dread Lord of Afric, Europe and Asia,
> Great king and conqueror of Graecia,
> The Ocean, Terrene and the coal-black sea,
> The high and highest monarch of the world.

Yet in some subtle way the Turk's braggadocio lacks the dominant note that rings through Tamburlaine's utterances as in his proclamation of himself (for which his biographers give warrant) to the Basso (III. iii. 44–5):

> I that am term'd the Scourge and Wrath of God,
> The only fear and terror of the world.

When Bajazeth appears with his contributory kings and his wife, Zabina, the dialogue for about one hundred lines (III. iii. 60–163) is cast in virtually strophic form, the leaders on either side with their followers taking equally balanced parts in an elaborate 'flyting'. And when the battle begins off-stage, the acrimonious strife of tongues is continued for nearly another fifty lines by Zenocrate and Zabina and their waiting-women. At last Bajazeth has to acknowledge defeat, and Zenocrate places his imperial crown on Tamburlaine's head. He then in the most sweepingly grandiose of all his visions beholds himself as master not only of the lands but of the seas, with his Persian fleet and men-of-war sailing about the Indian continent,

> Even from Persepolis to Mexico,
> And thence unto the Straits of Jubalter,
> Where they shall meet and join their force in one,
> Keeping in awe the Bay of Portingale,
> And all the ocean by the British shore;
> And by this means I'll win the world at last.

The last lines seem to be almost an ironic anticipation of the proud aims with which Philip of Spain was so soon after the production of the play to send the Invincible Armada to its doom. They would seem to be a fitting climax to this Act, but for the groundlings a more spectacular close was provided by the order to bind and lead in the Turk and his empress. In their agony the pair turn with execrations upon the Prophet who has betrayed their trust in him:

> *Baj.* Ah villains, dare ye touch my sacred arms?
>   O Mahomet! O sleepy Mahomet!
> *Zab.* O cursed Mahomet, that makest us thus
>   The slaves to Scythians rude and barbarous!

The barbarous humiliation of Bajazeth by carrying him about like a wild beast in a cage is related by all the authorities available to Marlowe, but the additional outrage of his being made Tamburlaine's footstool (IV. ii. 1) seems to be taken from Perondinus. It is not mentioned by Fortescue, who at this point abridges Mexia's Spanish original.[1] In fantastic contrast with the primitive savagery of his treatment of his victim, Tamburlaine as 'he gets up upon him to his chair' again emblazons himself in celestial imagery (IV. ii. 33–40):

> Smile, stars that reign'd at my nativity,
> And dim the brightness of their neighbour lamps:
> Disdain to borrow light of Cynthia,
> For I, the chiefest lamp of all the earth,
> First rising in the east with mild aspect,
> But fixed now in the meridian line,
> Will send up fire to your turning spheres,
> And cause the sun to borrow light of you.

It is a steep descent from this glowing vision to the curt command, 'Put him in again', and the order to Zabina to feed him with scraps from the conqueror's board. The banquet scene (IV. iv) in which Bajazeth's humiliation is elaborated is partly written in crude prose (ll. 32 ff.) and may be a remnant of those 'fond and frivolous gestures' of which the publisher complained. But if this be so the interpolation testifies to the delight of 'vain, conceited fondlings' in these monstrosities. Their cup was doubtless filled to the brim when in Act V. ii. 241 Bajazeth brains himself against his cage, and Zabina seeks the same fate after a frenzied outburst in which there are singular anticipations at once of Lady Macbeth and of Ophelia:

'Let the soldiers be buried. Hell, death, Tamburlaine, hell. Make ready my coach, my chair, my jewels. I come, I come, I come!'

[1] Miss Ellis-Fermor in her edition of *Tamburlaine*, p. 140, note, states that Raleigh in his *History of the World*, The Preface, ed. 1820, ii, p. xiii, recalls this scene from the play, when he writes, 'God, who is the Author of all our tragedies, hath written out for us, and appointed us all the parts we are to play: and hath not in their distribution, beene partiall to the most mighty Princes of the world . . . that appointed *Bajazet* to play the *Gran Signior* of the *Turkes* in the morning and in the same day the *Footstoole* of *Tamerlane*.' This seems to be an echo of IV. ii. 1 'Bring out my footstool'. Yet it must be noted that the camp has now moved from Bithynia to Damascus, that it is not 'the same day', and that Raleigh uses the form *Tamerlane* as in Perondinus.

With the Persians and the Turks overthrown, the
Soldan of Egypt remains to confront Tamburlaine, who
keeps his daughter captive and who has laid siege to his
city of Damascus. Even when warned of his power and
ruthlessness the Soldan pours contempt on him (IV. i.
65–8):

> Merciless villain, peasant, ignorant
> Of lawful arms or martial discipline;
> Pillage and murder are his usual trades,
> The slave usurps the glorious name of war!

And with Ovidian parallels on his lips the Soldan goes
forth 'with streaming colours' to relieve his beleaguered
city from 'this presumptuous beast' (IV. iii. 1–6):

> Methinks we march as Meleager did,
> Environed with brave Argolian knights,
> To chase the savage Calydonian boar;
> Or Cephalus, with lusty Theban youths,
> Against the wolf that angry Themis sent
> To waste and spoil the sweet Aonian fields.

Joined with the Soldan is the King of Arabia to whom
Zenocrate has once been pledged. Her fears are, however,
not for him but for her father and her country. In vain
she pleads with Tamburlaine to raise the siege of Damascus and make a truce with the Soldan (IV. iv. 67 ff.).
Tamburlaine, after the fashion reported by his biographers, has already changed the colour of his tents from
the merciful white of the first day to the red of the second,
with himself 'all in scarlet',[1] portending death to all combatants. And at the opening of Act V, on the third day, as
the Governor of Damascus laments, the tents have taken
on 'the last and cruel'st hue'.

> His coal-black colours, everywhere advanced,
> Threaten our city with a general spoil.

In vain four virgins with branches of laurels in their
hands come forth to plead with Tamburlaine 'all in black
and very melancholy'. He greets them with the derisive

---

[1] 'Tamberlane's breeches of crymson velvett' are included in an inventory
made on 13 March 1598. *Henslowe Papers*, ed. Greg, p. 120.

cry, 'What, are the turtles frayed out of their nests?' and orders his horsemen to show them

> my servant Death
> Sitting in scarlet on their armed spears.

This massacre of the innocents which Fortescue associates with the siege of an unnamed 'strong and riche citie' is legitimately transferred by Marlowe to the assault on Damascus. But it is a glaringly unsuitable prelude to the immediately following lyric invocation of 'fair Zenocrate, divine Zenocrate', mounting line by line to the superb rhapsody, in which the romantic impulse, ever yearning after an unrealizable ideal of perfection, finds its expression once and for ever (v. ii. 98–110):

> If all the pens that ever poets held
> Had fed the feeling of their masters' thoughts,
> And every sweetness that inspir'd their hearts,
> Their minds and muses on admired themes;
> If all the heavenly quintessence they still
> From their immortal flowers of poesy,
> Wherein as in a mirror we perceive
> The highest reaches of a human wit—
> If these had made one poem's period,
> And all combin'd in beauty's worthiness,
> Yet should there hover in their restless heads
> One thought, one grace, one wonder, at the least,
> Which into words no virtue can digest.

Did Marlowe himself recognize how incongruous such words were on the Scythian's lips when he made him break into an apology for harbouring 'thoughts effeminate and faint', and utter the plea that every warrior 'must needs have beauty beat on his conceits'?

Little wonder that Zenocrate is distracted between the barbarous deeds and the honeyed speeches of her captor or that her 'martyred soul' is torn by divided loyalties, when the Soldan and the King of Arabia arrive to do battle with Tamburlaine (v. ii. 326–7):

> My father and my first betrothed love
> Must fight against my life and present love.

The issue, as has been seen above, is modelled on that at the close of the *Aeneid*. The Arabian king dies on the field like Turnus, and Tamburlaine comes to terms with the father of Zenocrate as Aeneas with the father of Lavinia. But there is no Virgilian echo in the Scythian's defiant boast (v. ii. 388–94):

> The god of war resigns his room to me,
> Meaning to make me general of the world;
> Jove, viewing me in arms, looks pale and wan,
> Fearing my power should pull him from his throne.
> Where'er I come the fatal Sisters sweat,
> And grisly Death, by running to and fro,
> To do their ceaseless homage to my sword.

If Marlowe had already thought of a sequel to this play, in this insensate challenge to the deities he may have foreshadowed the end when Tamburlaine himself has to yield to Death. But for the present his victims carry his glory to the depths and heights of the universe (v. ii. 403–5):

> Hell and Elysium swarm with ghosts of men
> That I have sent from sundry foughten fields
> To spread my fame through hell and up to heaven.

The crowning of Zenocrate as Queen of Persia and the preparations for the solemnization of the marriage rites between her and Tamburlaine bring the play to a triumphant close.

Note 2 to p. 76.

In *Modern Language Notes*, June 1943, T. C. Izard makes a strong claim for G. Whetstone's *The English Myrror* as the chief immediate source of *Tamburlaine*, Part I, instead of T. Fortescue's *The Foreste*.

VI

THE SECOND PART OF
TAMBURLAINE THE GREAT

THE resounding success of Marlowe's play on Tamburlaine evidently led to an instant popular demand for
a sequel. But how was it to be provided? The young
dramatist had already used up practically the whole of the
material which Fortescue and Perondinus and others supplied for the Scythian's career. The invention of entirely
original episodes was never to be one of his major qualifications as a playwright. But he could turn to his purposes the fruits of his extensive Cambridge reading. The
classical poets were at his hand to supply further parallels
and decorations. The geographical details of Tamburlaine's more or less historical campaigns could not well be
duplicated in a second Part, but with Abraham Ortelius's
atlas, *Theatrum Orbis Terrarum*, before him, the dramatist
could associate striking place-names with imaginary military exploits.[1] History could be similarly manipulated.
Who among the London theatre-goers knew or cared anything about the details of Oriental annals? Marlowe felt
himself free to exercise some chronological legerdemain
and to dovetail incidents of Turkish history into the later
fortunes of Tamburlaine. Miss Seaton has proved beyond
doubt that Marlowe was well acquainted with the
Chronicorum Turcicorum tomi duo by Philippus Lonicerus,
of which the second edition had appeared at Frankfurt in
1578.[2] In this edition he would also find reprinted
Antonii Bonfinii Rerum Ungaricarum decades tres (1543),

---

[1] See 'Marlowe's Map', by Ethel Seaton, in The English Association
Essays and Studies, vol. x (1924). The *Theatrum Orbis Terrarum* was first
published at Antwerp in 1574.
[2] In *T.L.S.*, 16 June 1921, and 'Fresh Sources for Marlowe', *R.E.S.*,
Oct. 1929.

together with *Callimachi Experientis de clade Varnensi
Epistola*. These relate that King Vladislaus of Poland and
Hungary swore a truce with the Sultan Amurath II, and
afterwards violating his oath marched into Turkish territory while the Sultan was attacking the King of Carmania. Vladislaus paid the penalty of his treachery by his
defeat in the battle of Varna, 1444. Marlowe substitutes
Sigismund of Hungary for Vladislaus; Orcanes, King of
Natolia, for Amurath II; and Tamburlaine for the King
of Carmania. In the most solemn fashion on the banks
of the Danube, in I. ii. 56 ff., Sigismund swears by 'sweet
Jesus Christ' and Orcanes by 'sacred Mahomet' to 'keep
this truce inviolable'. But in II. i Frederick of Buda and
Baldwin of Bohemia persuade Sigismund to break his
oath. And here Marlowe puts into the lips of the two
lords the arguments with which Cardinal Julian, as reported by Bonfinius,[1] had justified the breach of faith
with the Turks (ll. 33 ff.):

Bald.   with such infidels
          In whom no faith nor true religion rests,
          We are not bound to those accomplishments
          The holy laws of Christendom enjoin.

                .   .   .   .   .   .

Fred.   And should we lose the opportunity
          That God hath given to venge our Christians' death,
          And scourge their foul blasphemous paganism,
          As fell to Saul, to Balaam, and the rest,
          That would not kill and curse at God's command,
          So surely will the vengeance of the highest,
          And jealous anger of his fearful arm,
          Be pour'd with rigour on our sinful heads,
          If we neglect this offered victory.

Similarly, when Orcanes hears that the Christians are
advancing against him, he displays, like Amurath II at
Varna, the broken treaty, and in words borrowed mainly
from Bonfinius[2] adjures the God of the Christians to

---

[1] *De Rer. Ung.* Dec. III, Lib. VI, pp. 457–9, quoted by Una Ellis-
Fermor, op. cit., pp. 206–7 n.   [2] Op. cit., p. 465.

avenge the outrage which His followers have offered to
His name (II. ii. 39):

> Then, if there be a Christ, as Christians say,
> But in their deeds deny him for their Christ,
> If he be son to everliving Jove,
> And hath the power of his outstretched arm,
> If he be jealous of his name and honour,
> As is our holy prophet Mahomet,
> Take here these papers as our sacrifice,
> And witness of thy servant's perjury.

This is dramatically appropriate on the lips of the Turk.
But in his revolt against the orthodoxy of his age Marlowe may well have taken an ironical pleasure in an
episode which showed the followers of Mahomet in favourable contrast with those who bore the name of Christ.
Yet this is not all. Breaking loose suddenly from Bonfinius, Marlowe, with one of his characteristic upward
flights, makes Orcanes invoke the God (II. ii. 49–52)

> that sits on high and never sleeps,
> Nor in one place is circumscriptible,
> But everywhere fills every continent
> With strange infusion of his sacred vigour

and is 'of endless power and purity'. It is a conception of
the Deity, as Miss Bradbrook has pointed out,[1] akin to
Sir Walter Raleigh's as of 'an understanding, which only
itself can comprehend, an essence eternal and spiritual'.
Till after the defeat of Sigismund in II. iii Tamburlaine,
as in the earlier scenes of Part I, plays a relatively passive
part, though his temper is unchanged, for to Zenocrate's
question, 'When wilt thou leave these arms?' he answers
(I. iv. 12–14):

> When heaven shall cease to move on both the poles,
> And when the ground, whereon my soldiers march,
> Shall rise aloft and touch the horned moon.

Yet if Marlowe took any account of chronology many
years must have passed since Tamburlaine's exploits in

---

[1] *The School of Night* (1936), pp. 106–7.

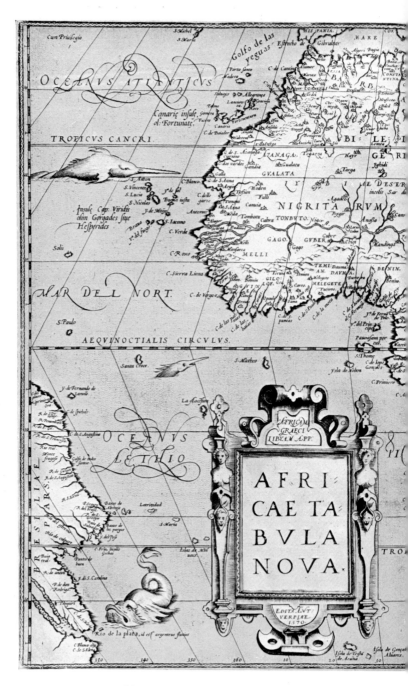

Map of Africa in *Theatrum Orbis Terrarum* of Ortelius, th

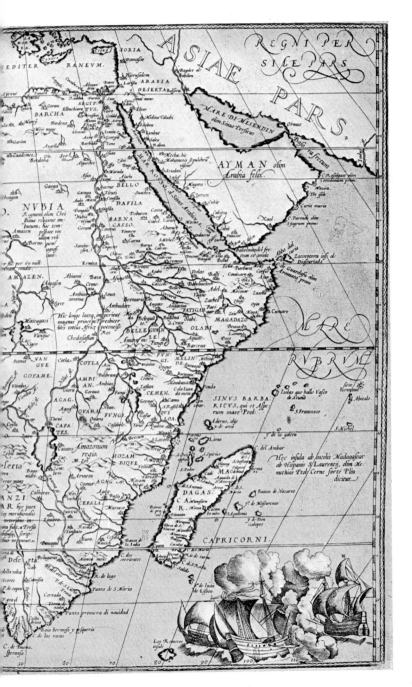

of Marlowe's geography in *The Second Part of Tamburlaine*

Part I. For his three sons by Zenocrate are now nearing military age and he is preoccupied with their future (ll. 21 ff.):

> methinks their looks are amorous,
> Not martial as the sons of Tamburlaine;
>
> . . . . . .
>
> Their fingers made to quaver on a lute,
> Their arms to hang about a lady's neck,
> Their legs to dance and caper in the air.

The two younger boys satisfy him by their protestations that they will become like him the scourge and terror of the world. But the eldest, Calyphas, infuriates him by his pacifist plea with which Marlowe adroitly sounds a softer note amidst the clang of trumpets and drums. From his parental cares Tamburlaine turns in scenes v and vi to welcome his generals and tributary kings, Theridamas, Techelles, and Usumcasane, now gathering to his standard for the conflict with Orcanes. Here Marlowe had recourse to the map of Ortelius for supplying details of imaginary campaigns by the three generals. Techelles, in particular, by the recital of his march (i. vi. 59–78), including Zanzibar, 'the western part of Afric', confounded all commentators, who thought Marlowe as revolutionary in geography as in theology, till Miss Seaton discovered that Ortelius had given the name of Zanzibar to a western province of Africa.[1]

The clash of arms is hushed for a time in ii. iv, where Tamburlaine reappears as the poet-lover, bending over the bed of state where Zenocrate lies dying. Again, as in passages of Part I,[2] the blank verse falls into almost strophic form in the lines 15–33 wherein Tamburlaine pictures her advent in heaven, with the refrain, 'To entertain divine Zenocrate'. Then with a new note of complete self-surrender he pleads (ll. 55–6):

> Live still, my love, and so conserve my life,
> Or, dying, be the author of my death;

---

[1] *Marlowe's Map*, pp. 16–18.   [2] See above, p. 83.

whereto she makes the antiphonal response:

> Live still, my lord; O let my sovereign live!

. . . . . .

> But let me die, my love; yet, let me die:
> With love and patience let your true love die.

Never does Marlowe come so near to striking a note of pure tenderness as in this scene where Zenocrate dies to the sound of music, kissing her lord and blessing her 'sweet sons'. The episode is of the dramatist's own imagining, but echoes from the classical poets were floating through his brain and inspired the dithyrambic outburst (ii. iv. 85–91):

> Her sacred beauty hath enchanted heaven,
> And had she liv'd before the siege of Troy,
> Helen, whose beauty summoned Greece to arms,
> And drew a thousand ships to Tenedos,
> Had not been nam'd in Homer's Iliads,
> Her name had been in every line he wrote.

As Helen was to Marlowe the incarnation of absolute beauty this was his supreme tribute. But the translator of Ovid was impelled to add, even though in anticlimax:

> Or had those wanton poets, for whose birth
> Old Rome was proud, but gazed a while on her,
> Nor Lesbia nor Corinna had been nam'd;
> Zenocrate had been the argument
> Of every epigram or elegy.

So it is with classical imagery that Tamburlaine bids his generals bring Zenocrate back to him by haling the fatal Sisters from the infernal vaults, or by shivering the starry firmament where Jove means to make her the queen of heaven. Then for the first time the Scythian hears from the lips of Theridamas that there are limits to his power (ii. iv. 119–20):

> Ah, good my lord, be patient! she is dead,
> And all this raging cannot make her live.

He must content himself with carrying her body wherever he goes in a golden coffin, and with burning down the town where she has breathed her last.

From this flaming spectacle, which must have taxed the scenic equipment of the company, Tamburlaine turns abruptly (III. ii. 53 ff.) to give his sons a lecture on 'the rudiments of war', in particular the methods of carrying a besieged city by assault, borrowed from Paul Ive's *Practise of Fortification*.[1] When Calyphas again shows the white feather, Tamburlaine gives him a further lesson in soldiering by cutting his own arm:

> A wound is nothing, be it ne'er so deep;
> Blood is the god of war's rich livery.

To Calyphas it is a pitiful sight, but his younger brothers are eager to offer their arms to the knife.

Marlowe may have wished to point an ironic contrast between the recreant heir of Tamburlaine and Callapine, the son of Bajazeth, who, having bribed his keeper to help him to freedom, joins Orcanes after his victory over Sigismund and in III. i is crowned emperor by the tributary kings, who, with the aid of Ortelius's map, have gathered forces from many parts to oppose the Scythian's advance. The two armies come face to face in III. v, and as in Part I, Act III. iii, the battle is preluded by a contest in 'flyting' between the rival leaders. This opens superbly with Marlowe again turning to his own purpose a romanticized version of Greek epic story,[2] when Tamburlaine cries (III. v. 64–74):

> Ye petty kings of Turkey, I am come,
> As Hector did into the Grecian camp,
> To overdare the pride of Graecia,
> And set his warlike person to the view
> Of fierce Achilles, rival of his fame.
> I do you honour in the simile;
> For if I should, as Hector did Achilles,
> (The worthiest knight that ever brandished sword)
> Challenge in combat any of you all,
> I see how fearfully ye would refuse,
> And fly my glove as from a scorpion.

[1] See above, p. 72.

[2] The episode was a post-Homeric addition. Miss Ellis-Fermor points out that Marlowe may have found it in Lydgate's *Troy Book*, III. ii. 3755 ff.

A dozen magical lines transforming the two supreme figures of the *Iliad* into the likeness of jousting knights of medieval chivalry! Thence it is a steep descent to the abusive railing between the commanders on either side, including some apparent gags in prose.

When at last the battle is joined off-stage in Act IV. i, Calyphas, despite the taunts of his younger brothers, lingers in his tent, declaring (ll. 27–9):

> I know, sir, what it is to kill a man;
> It works remorse of conscience in men,
> I take no pleasure to be murderous.

The lines gain added significance from our knowledge that Marlowe himself was in September 1589[1] to be put on trial for his part in a fatal affray. And in what follows there seems to be an anticipation of Falstaff's *apologia* on the field of Shrewsbury (IV. i. 45 ff.):

> Take you the honour, I will take my ease.
>
> .   .   .   .   .   .
>
> The bullets fly at random where they list;
> And should I go and kill a thousand men,
> I were as soon rewarded with a shot,
> And sooner far than he that never fights;
> And should I go and do nor harm nor good,
> I might have harm, which all the good I have
> Join'd with my father's crown, would never cure.

But inaction cannot save Calyphas from harm. Tamburlaine returning victorious stabs him to death for cowardice, justifying his unnatural deed in terms more suited to an academic lecture-room than a Scythian camp (IV. i. 111–15):

> Here, Jove, receive this fainting soul again,
> A form not meet to give that subject essence,
> Whose matter is the flesh of Tamburlaine,
> Wherein an incorporeal spirit moves,
> Made of the mould whereof thyself consists.

He denounces Jupiter for sending

> to my issue such a soul
> Created of the massy dregs of earth,

---

[1] See below, pp. 101 ff.

whereby he has made of Tamburlaine a greater enemy than the mountain-hurling Titans. Yet a moment afterwards he proclaims himself (IV. i. 151-2)

> arch-monarch of the world,
> Crown'd and invested by the hand of Jove,

and announces that (199-201)

> till by vision or by speech I hear
> Immortal Jove say 'Cease my Tamburlaine',
> I will persist a terror to the world.

Somewhat irrelevantly intermingled with the above episodes are three scenes (III. iii and iv, and IV. ii) concerned with the Captain of Balsera, his wife, and his son. Marlowe was here apparently indebted to Belleforest's story in his *Cosmographie Universelle*, ii. 750, of the Governor of Rhodes and his mistress,[1] and less directly to Ariosto's account in *Orlando Furioso*, cantos xxviii and xxix, of Isabella and Rodomont.[2] But in III. iii, where Theridamas and Techelles summon the Captain to yield up the fort, Marlowe takes another opportunity of displaying his knowledge of military technicalities, especially regarding siege methods. When in the next scene, after the Captain's death, his wife Olympia kills their son to save him from the Scythian's cruelty, she may be intended as a foil to the gentle Zenocrate.

> 'Twas bravely done and like a soldier's wife,

exclaims Techelles, who saves her from suicide and carries her to Tamburlaine's camp. Here in Act IV. ii by a stratagem akin to that by which Isabella foils the advances of Rodomont she lures Theridamas, who has become deeply enamoured of her, to give her a fatal wound. And as a pendant to Tamburlaine's vision of the heavenly powers entertaining Zenocrate is Theridamas's vision of Hell glorified by the advent of Olympia (IV. ii. 87-96):

> Now hell is fairer than Elysium.
> A greater lamp than that bright eye of heaven
> From whence the stars do borrow all their light

---

[1] Quoted by Ethel Seaton, 'Fresh Sources for Marlowe', *R.E.S.*, Oct. 1929, pp. 395-6.   [2] See Una Ellis-Fermor, op. cit., pp. 44-5.

> Wanders about the black circumference;
> And now the damned souls are free from pain,
> For every Fury gazeth on her looks;
> Imperial Dis is courting of my love,
> Inventing masks and stately shows for her,
> Opening the doors of his rich treasury
> To entertain this queen of chastity.

Lines of such sombre splendour would redeem the most irrelevant of excrescences.

It is a crudely grotesque transition to the next scene where Tamburlaine appears drawn in his chariot by two of the conquered kings, 'with bits in their mouths, reins in his left hand, and in his right hand a whip with which he scourgeth them'. This barbaric episode repeated in intensified form the resounding theatrical hit in Part I of Bajazeth being carried about in a cage and used as his victor's footstool. And this second appeal by Marlowe to the sadistic instincts of his audience, not based, as before, on his sources but of his own invention, proved even more successful than the first. Not the most notorious ejaculations of Hieronimo in *The Spanish Tragedy* gained wider *réclame*, as we know from the lips of Ancient Pistol and others, than Tamburlaine's rebuke to his sluggish human steeds (iv. iii. 1–2):

> Holla, ye pampered jades of Asia!
> What, can ye draw but twenty miles a day?

With this monstrous mode of transport his objective now is Babylon, but beyond it he sees himself riding in triumph through his native city of Samarcand. Once again he can find no lesser parallel than Jove on his passage through the firmament (iv. iii. 125–32):

> Then in my coach, like Saturn's royal son
> Mounted his shining chariot gilt with fire,
> And drawn with princely eagles through the path
> Pav'd with bright crystal and enchas'd with stars,
> When all the gods stand gazing at his pomp,
> So will I ride through Samarcanda streets,
> Until my soul, dissevered from this flesh,
> Shall mount the milk-white way, and meet him there.

With this characteristic flourish, closing Act IV, Tamburlaine for the first time recognizes that even for him there must at last be an end of his career on earth. Yet in his final exploit, the capture of Babylon, he fills the measure of his savageries to the brim. The Governor tarnishes the glory of his brave defence of the city by seeking to save his life by revealing the secret of the gold hidden in the neighbouring lake. Deaf to his plea Tamburlaine has him hung in chains upon the walls, and bids his followers shoot him to death.[1] He hangs up, too, the broken-winded jades, the kings of Trebizond and Zoria, and bridles in their stead the two 'spare kings' of Natolia and Jerusalem. He orders the 'burghers' to be bound hand and foot and thrown into the lake, and their wives and children to suffer the like fate. Then he gives to the flames (v. i. 172–5)

> the Turkish Alcaron
> And all the heaps of superstitious books
> Found in the temples of that Mahomet
> Whom I have thought a god.

It is significant that Marlowe should here fly in the face of the historians who depict Tamburlaine as showing favour to the temples of the Prophet. All orthodox forms of religion come in turn under the dramatist's lash. As Christianity had been put to scorn in Act II by the perfidy of its adherents, so Mohammedanism is now made a mock through the helplessness of its Prophet to avenge the millions of his followers slain by Tamburlaine, or to save his sacred writ from the flames (v. i. 191–8):

> Why send'st thou not a furious whirlwind down,
> To blow thy Alcaron up to thy throne,
> Where men report thou sitt'st by God himself,
> Or vengeance on the head of Tamburlaine
> That shakes his sword against thy majesty,
> And spurns the abstracts of thy foolish laws?
> Well, soldiers, Mahomet remains in hell:
> He cannot hear the voice of Tamburlaine.

---

[1] On P. Gawdy's letter referring to this episode see above, p. 71.

It is the voice not of Tamburlaine but of Marlowe, in realistic derision of direct divine intervention in human affairs, and repeating from II. ii. 49, 'he that sits on high and never sleeps', the conception of a transcendent deity:

> Seek out another Godhead to adore;
> The God that sits in heaven, if any god,
> For he is God alone, and none but he.

Then once again, in v. iii, we hear the voice of Tamburlaine himself, who, stricken with sudden sickness, threatens war against heaven (ll. 42 ff.):

> What daring god torments my body thus,
> And seeks to conquer mighty Tamburlaine?
> .   .   .   .
> Come, let us march against the powers of heaven,
> And set black streamers in the firmament,
> To signify the slaughter of the gods.

Yet when Techelles seeks to comfort him with the assurance that his malady is too violent to last, he confesses that he is mortal:

> Not last, Techelles! no, for I shall die.

His slave, Death, is tremblingly creeping nearer him, but will be scared away if Tamburlaine keeps him busy on the field of battle. Then in contrast with these imaginative flights Marlowe characteristically introduces a detailed report, in the medical terminology of the day, on Tamburlaine's condition. It is not, however, the physician, but a messenger announcing the advance of the Turkish forces who provides the Scythian with a medicine to 'recure' his pain. For the last time he fights and is victor but has not strength to pursue the foe. He calls for a map—it must have been the *Theatrum Orbis Terrarum* which had done yeoman service to Marlowe—wherein he traces his past conquests and contemplates enterprises still unfulfilled, including what seem to be prophetic anticipations of the cutting of the Suez Canal and the discovery of Australia. These he leaves as legacies for the future to his two sons. The terms in which the trio emphasize their essential unity

(v. iii. 164–74) again savour of the philosophic lecture-room rather than of the camp.

The reluctance of Amyras to assume his father's state strikes a more natural note, and the bringing in of Zeno-crate's hearse at Tamburlaine's bidding to 'serve as parcel' of his funeral reminds us that he had been a lover as well as a warrior. But he is the Scythian savage when, after crowning his heir, he bids him (v. iii. 229–30)

> scourge and control those slaves,
> Guiding thy chariot with thy father's hand.

The only classical parallels for which it is hard to forgive Marlowe are those in which Tamburlaine warns Amyras to beware lest 'these proud rebelling jades' should drag him to a fate like that of Phaeton or Hippolytus.

It is merely the extravagant *pietas* of Amyras that in the closing couplet can pronounce the elegy:

> Let earth and heaven his timeless[1] death deplore,
> For both their worths will equal him no more.

For in Part II of *Tamburlaine* the protagonist is a coarser and more incredible figure than in Part I. There even the brutalities to Bajazeth and the massacre at Damascus could do no more than blur the resplendent picture of a world-conqueror whose ambition was in essence the divine intoxication of the spirit and the senses which is the creative fount of all the arts. And in Part II something of this radiant image survives. By the deathbed of Zenocrate Tamburlaine appears as the poet-lover, and even when his hands are red with blood, phrases of pure gold flow ever and again from his lips. But through the later acts of Part II he becomes more and more the primitive barbarian, heaping outrage upon outrage and challenging the very deities whose instrument he had claimed to be. A Macbeth driven from crime to crime by a brooding sense of guilt and haunted by imaginative terrors; a Lear goaded to madness by encountering obstacles upon

[1] untimely.

which his imperious will is broken—these were destined
after the turn of the century to become figures of tragic
grandeur. But in their fate there is nothing akin to Tamburlaine's cumulative enormities or his frenzied defiance
of mortal limitations. His career closes at last merely
because all that live must die, and he looks forward to its
continuation by his sons.

It is in other ways than in the presentation of Tamburlaine himself that Part II shows a ripening of Marlowe's
powers as a dramatist. There is less concentration of
interest upon the central figure. Many of the subordinate
characters are little more than puppets, but the contrast between Tamburlaine's eldest son and his brothers
and between Zenocrate and Olympia, though not fully
developed, indicates the use of a wider canvas than before.

What is more notable is the technical advance in the
manipulation of source-materials. Instead of following
more or less closely in the track of Fortescue and Perondinus, Marlowe now borrows in turn from Lonicerus and
Bonfinius, from Belleforest and Ariosto, and welds them
together for his purposes, though in the borrowings from
Paul Ive and in some other technical passages there is
more than a suspicion of 'padding'. So dexterous was his
use of the map of Ortelius that the secret has been discovered only after three centuries and a half. Behind his
exposure of the weaknesses of Christianity and Islam we
seem to come closer than before to his own creed. And
what is more fundamental in Marlowe than any religious,
or irreligious, belief, his passion for beauty embodied in
classical legend and myth irradiates, as has been seen, with
flashes of dazzling splendour even the most murky and
ensanguined episodes of Part II of *Tamburlaine the Great*.
The play may thus fitly claim to be the counterpart in the
western world of the Scythian conqueror's mausoleum in
Samarkand, with its brilliant interior adornment of marble,
precious stones, arabesques in turquoise, and inscriptions
in gold.[1]

[1] *The Times*, 20 Jan. 1939.

LIFE IN LONDON

I

THE BRADLEY AFFRAY AND NEWGATE

THERE is a remarkable contrast between the large amount of evidence extant concerning Marlowe's career at Cambridge and the almost complete dearth of it for his first two years in the capital after his triumph on the stage with the *Tamburlaine* plays. And when the earliest record of him for this period leaps to light it is startlingly at variance with the certificate of the Privy Council in 1587 that in all his actions he had behaved himself orderly and discreetly.

It has taken exactly half a century for the full significance of this record to be gradually pieced out. In 1886 J. C. Jeaffreson in his *Middlesex County Records*, i. 189, translated and summarized an entry in the Middlesex Sessions Roll 284, 1 October, 31 Elizabeth (1589), according to which 'Richard Kytchine' and 'Humfrey Rowland' became sureties that Christopher Marley of London, gentleman, should appear at the next sessions of Newgate to answer charges against him. On 18 August 1894 in *The Athenaeum* Sidney Lee identified the Christopher Marley of this entry as the dramatist. In 1926 Leslie Hotson threw new light upon the two sureties,[1] but it was not till 1934 that Mark Eccles discovered that it was no less serious a charge than homicide upon which Marlowe had been arrested and held to bail.[2]

The documents in which the whole story is unfolded are in the Public Record Office among the Chancery Miscellanies, Bundle 68, file 12, no. 362, consisting of a writ and a return into Chancery of a Gaol Delivery at

---

[1] In 'Marlowe among the Churchwardens', *Atlantic Monthly*, July 1926.   [2] *Marlowe in London*, pp. 9 ff.

Newgate, reciting the Coroner's inquest, together with a Pardon contained in the Patent Rolls for Elizabeth, part 4, C 66/1340, and the Sessions Roll 284 in the Middlesex Guildhall mentioned above. The opening part of the finding at the inquest held by Ion Chalkhill, with a jury of twelve 'probi et legales homines', on 19 September 1589 runs as follows:

'Vbi ... willelmus Bradley et quidam Cristoferus Morley nuper de London generosus vicesimo octavo die Septembris Anno vicesimo primo [Regine Elizabethe] fuerunt insimul pugnantes in quadam venella vocata hoglane in parochia Sancti Egidij extra Creplegate ... inter horas secundam et terciam post meridiem eiusdem diei. Ibi intervenit eisdem die et anno et infra horas predictas quidam Thomas Watson nuper de London generosus super clamorem populi ibidem a[d]stantis ad separandum prefatos willelmum Bradley et Christoferum Morley sic pugnantes et ad pacem dicte domine Regine conservandam. Et gladium suum eam ob causam tunc et ibidem extraxit. Super quo prefatus [Christoferus][1] Morley seipsum retraxit & a pugnando desistit. Et super hoc predictus willelmus Bradley videns eundem Thomam Watson sic intervenientem ibidem cum gladio suo extracto dixit ei in his Anglicanis verbis sequentibus videlicet (arte thowe nowe come then I will haue a boute wth thee).'

Bradley then, according to the sworn statement of the jury, so beset and maltreated Watson with a sword in one hand and a dagger in the other that to save his life Watson had to retreat to a ditch and turning at bay gave Bradley a wound with his sword in the right breast of which he instantly died. And the jury found that he had killed him in self-defence.

Who were the persons involved in this fatal affray, and what was the sequel? Eccles has supplied the answers. William Bradley was the son of the landlord of the Bishop Inn at the corner of Gray's Inn Lane and Holborn. In the summer of 1589 he had asked for sureties of the peace against Hugo Swift, John Allen, and Thomas Watson of whom, according to the formula, he went in fear of his

---

[1] The document has by mistake 'will[elmus]'.

life.[1] Bradley had thus some cause of quarrel with Thomas Watson, who must have been the poet of that name, the author of ʽΕκατομπαθία, for Hugo Swift was his brother-in-law. Watson was a friend of Thomas Walsingham of Scadbury, Kent, to whom he dedicated his *Meliboeus* in 1590, and who three years later is known to have been a host to Marlowe. I do not put as much weight as Eccles on the Walsingham link between the two men, and Kyd does not mention Watson among Marlowe's friends.[2] But as poets, dramatists, and translators the two had much in common and, as will be seen, there are further circumstances that justify the belief that the Christoferus Morley of the inquest is Christopher Marlowe, the playwright.

Thus another record discovered by Eccles[3] not only calls him by the more familiar name but reveals his place of residence as what was in 1589 the main theatrical neighbourhood. The Middlesex Sessions Roll 284 which begins with Marlowe's recognizance ends with 'a sort of matriculation register' of the prisoners who arrived in Newgate between 9 September and 2 October 1589. It includes the following entry:

Thomas Watson nuper de Norton ffowlgate in Comitatu Middlesex generosus & Christoferus Marlowe nuper de Eadem yoman qui ducti fuerunt Gaole xviij° die Septembris per Stephanum wyld Constabularium ibidem pro Suspicione Murdri viz pro Morte [*blank*] et Commissi fuerunt per Owinum Hopton Militem.

This shows that Watson and Marlowe were neighbours in the suburban district of Norton Folgate, close to the Shoreditch playhouses *The Theater* and *The Curtain*, where it was convenient for dramatists and actors, including Shakespeare in his earlier London years, to live. It is curious that while Watson is called 'generosus' Marlowe, though a university graduate, is here described

[1] The record in the Queen's Bench Controlment Rolls found by J. L. Hotson is quoted by Eccles, op. cit., p. 57.
[2] See below, p. 112.   [3] Op. cit., p. 34.

as 'yoman'. Was it because he was a shoemaker's son?[1] In any case after Bradley's death they were for a time treated alike. They were arrested by the constable who dealt with affrays in Hog Lane, Stephen Wyld, who brought them before Sir Owen Hopton, Lieutenant of the Tower, then living in Norton Folgate. Hopton committed them both to Newgate. On the following day the Coroner's jury found that Watson had killed Bradley in self-defence. But this did not at once set him or Marlowe free. Watson was confined in Newgate till the Gaol Delivery at the Old Bailey on 3 December, when the Coroner's inquisition was laid before the Middlesex justices who remanded him again to prison to await the Queen's pardon which was granted on 12 February 1589/90, after he had endured the rigours of Newgate for nearly five months.

Marlowe, who had no part in the actual homicide, was in prison for less than a fortnight, as he was admitted to bail on 1 October. But short as his confinement was there is a curious echo of it outside the Newgate calendar. Among the charges brought against him in 1593 by Richard Baines was the intention to coin money about which he had learnt from 'one Poole a prisoner in newgate who hath great Skill in mixture of mettals'.[2] It was tempting to see in 'one Poole' the Robert Poole or Poley who was to be with Marlowe on the day of his death. But Eccles has shown[3] that he was a John Poole who had been confined in Newgate on or before July 1587 on suspicion of coining, and who remained there for several years. The inference, in my opinion, must further be drawn that the allegations of Baines, however exaggerated, cannot be dismissed as mere inventions.

---

[1] Similarly Ben Jonson is called 'yoman' in the indictment against him for the manslaughter of Gabriel Spencer on 22 Sept. 1598. In relation to the episode Henslowe writing to Allen calls him 'bengeman Jonson bricklayer' (*Ben Jonson*, ed. Herford and Simpson, i. 18 n. and 219).

[2] See below, pp. 251-2.

[3] 'Marlowe in Newgate', in *T.L.S.*, 6 Sept. 1934.

The recognizance may be summarized in English as follows:[1]

'Richard Kytchine of Clifford's Inne, gentleman, & Humfrey Rowland of East Smithfeilde in the county aforesaid, horner, came before me, William Fletewoode, Serjeant at Law and Recorder of the City of London, one of the Justices of our Lady the Queen appointed in the county aforesaid, & became sureties for Christopher Marley of London, gentleman: to wit, each of the sureties aforesaid under the penalty of twenty pounds, and he, the said Christopher Marley, undertook for himself, under penalty of forty pounds . . . on condition that he the said Christopher shall personally appear at the next Sessions of Newgate to answer everything that may be alleged against him on the part of the Queen, and shall not depart without the permission of the Court.'

The bail was heavy and was not forfeited. A marginal memorandum on the recognizance, added by the clerk, 'reu & del' per proclam' was first noted by Eccles and interpreted as *reuertitur et deliberatur per proclamacionem*, implying that Marlowe had presented himself at the Old Bailey on 3 December and had been discharged by the Court 'by proclamation' after hearing the Coroner's inquisition. It was a formidable Bench before which to appear, consisting of four Judges, including the Master of the Rolls and Sir Roger Manwood, Chief Baron of the Exchequer; the Lord Mayor, William Fleetwood the Recorder of London, and two Aldermen; Robert Wroth of Enfield and other Middlesex justices. As he stood in court Marlowe could not foresee that by the end of December 1592 he would be writing an epitaph on Manwood,[2] whose country seat was near Canterbury, and that Fleetwood before his death in 1594 was to buy one of the early editions of *Tamburlaine*.[3]

Who were Marlowe's two sureties? The investigations of Tucker Brooke[4] and Hotson,[5] supplemented by those

---

[1] A facsimile of the Latin original is given by J. H. Ingram, op. cit., p. 149. The text in expanded form is reproduced by Tucker Brooke, op. cit., pp. 96–7.   [2] See below, p. 237–8.
[3] John Bakeless, op. cit., pp. 160–1, 341.   [4] Op. cit., pp. 41–2.
[5] 'Marlowe among the Churchwardens.'

of Eccles,[1] have identified them. Richard Kitchen came
from Skipton in Yorkshire where his family had long been
in the service of the Cliffords. He entered Clifford's Inn
before his marriage to Agnes Redman in January 1579/80,
for in the licence he is described as Richard Kitchen, Gent.
of Clifford's Inn. In Hilary term 1586 he appears as
attorney for Thomas Meeres of Kent and thenceforward
in a number of cases of very varied interest. In one of
these, in a deposition on 15 April 1591, he describes himself as of Great St. Bartholomew's near Smithfield. This
tallies with an assessment of five shillings on his land in
that parish in 1588, the year before he became a surety
for Marlowe. Five years later he was himself the principal
in a similar episode to that of the Hog Lane affray, though
it had not a fatal termination. On 11 April 1594 he was
indicted at the Guildhall for an assault on John Finch,
and after the case had been removed to the Queen's
Bench it was discharged in 1595/6.

Richard Kitchen's many-sided activities may have
brought him later into relation with Philip Henslowe.
Though there were other legal Kitchens he is probably
meant when on 9 August 1598 Henslowe lent Richard
Alleyn eight shillings and sixpence 'to geue the atorney
ceachen for the bande wch he hade in his hande', and also
'layd owt for hime the same time to m^r ceatchen' fifty
shillings.[2] In any case it was Marlowe's surety who gave
evidence in a Star Chamber case, on 1 June 1600, on
behalf of William Williamson, landlord of the Mermaid
Tavern in Bread Street, who had declined to provide music
on a previous March evening for a company of revellers.
Eccles stretches a point when he asserts that, 'since Kitchen
knew the host of the Mermaid, he must have known
Shakespeare and Jonson as well as Marlowe', but it is a
plausible speculation. In November 1604 Kitchen died,
leaving his house in Skipton to his wife for her life and
his other goods and chattels to her absolutely.

[1] Op. cit., chap. iv, 'Marlowe's Sureties'.
[2] Eccles, op. cit., p. 86, quoting from *Henslowe's Diary*, ed. Greg, i. 205.

Humphrey Rowland was of inferior station and less substance. In the recognizance he is called a 'horner', and in the parish register of St. Botolph's church, Aldgate, 'hornbreaker'. In a letter of the Lord Mayor, 30 June 1583, in answer to one from Lord Burghley asking permission for Rowland, 'a very honest poore man', to be admitted to the Cutlers' Company, he is more specifically described as 'a maker of Lanterne hornes'. He also made shoeing horns, for the Barber-Surgeons granted him in September 1586 a lease of a house in East Smithfield at an annual rent of six pounds on condition that he delivered eighteen of them to the Company every year frank and free.

He had been a householder in St. Botolph's parish as early as 7 November 1571, when his son Edmund was christened. From that date till 1593 the church registers record christenings and burials of his many children by his first wife, Mary, who was herself buried on 27 February 1585/6, and his second wife, Eve Ashe, whom he married on the following 4 May. There are also entries of the burials of several of his servants.

Though he was one of the constables for East Smithfield for several years including 1585, he was in that year, as is shown by an entry in the King's Bench Controlment Rolls, summoned to answer for 'quibusdam transgressis & extorcionibus' and he was outlawed in the following Hilary term. Notwithstanding, he was elected a churchwarden of St. Botolph's on 11 December 1586 for two years. This appointment together with the size of his family and household would seem to argue a fair degree of prosperity, but in 1598 his goods were assessed at only three pounds, upon which he paid a tax of eight shillings, and when he died in January 1600/1 his estate came to only thirty-five shillings and his widow renounced the administration. It is one of the minor mysteries of Marlowe's career how this East Smithfield maker of lanterns and churchwarden should have been one of his sureties and been accepted for the considerable sum of twenty pounds.

II

FIRST CHARGES OF ATHEISM

WHEN Christopher Marlowe walked out of the Old Bailey
after his discharge on 3 December 1589, he had suffered
the unpleasant experiences of an arrest on suspicion of
murder and of nearly a fortnight's confinement in Newgate. Yet otherwise up to this date, so far as our evidence
goes, Marlowe at each successive turn of his career had
been singularly fortunate. He had obtained a scholarship
at the King's School just before he would have become
ineligible. After an unusually brief attendance there he
had been chosen by John Parker to hold one of his father's
scholarships at Corpus Christi College. He had taken
his Cambridge B.A. within the shortest legal limit. He
had held his scholarship at Corpus Christi for the maximum period of six years, though before the end of this
period he must have decided against a clerical career.
He had been given some temporary government employment in which he had acquitted himself so well that the
Privy Council had taken the very unusual step of directing
the University authorities not to delay the conferment
on him of the M.A. degree. While yet in his twenty-
third year he had won such an instant triumph with his
first play performed on a public stage that he had been
obliged to follow it at once with a second Part, though
he had really used up his original materials for Tamburlaine's career. And in the latter part of 1589 he was
probably busy upon *The Jew of Malta*, with which he
was to have another immediate theatrical success. Even
when he was involved in one of the affrays which were
so common a feature of Elizabethan life, his luck did not
desert him. Though he was Bradley's first antagonist, it
was Watson, the intervener, who killed the innkeeper's
son, and had to endure five months of Newgate before
he was pardoned, while Marlowe came off comparatively lightly. There was apparently in December 1589
nothing to indicate that he was doomed to meet within

a few years as tragic a fate as any of the protagonists in his dramas.[1]

Yet a cloud perhaps at the time no bigger than a man's hand had already appeared in the sky. The times were critical, with the Queen's government constantly faced by perils at home and abroad. It was dangerous for any man to step outside the bounds of the Elizabethan *via media* in Church and State. Marlowe had already incurred in certain quarters the suspicion of intending to join the Roman Catholic recusants abroad. Now a deadlier charge was beginning to make itself heard against him. The term 'Atheism' had in the sixteenth century much of the sweeping sinister associations that 'Bolshevism' has in the twentieth. It was a useful slogan with which to denounce doctrines or actions that challenged constitutional ecclesiastical or secular authority. Thus among 'certain objections' laid before the Privy Council against the admission of George Gascoigne, the poet and satirist, to be a burgess of Parliament it is alleged that 'he is a notorious Ruffianne and especialli noted to be bothe a spie, an atheist and godlesse personne'.[2]

That Marlowe, while he was in residence at Cambridge, had come under the suspicion of being 'an atheist and godlesse personne' seems to me to be most improbable. The extension of his scholarship to the full limit and the

---

[1] The documentary evidence of Marlowe's residence in London between September and December 1589 is alone sufficient to dispose of a suggestion made by E. St. John Brooks in 'Marlowe in 1589–92?' (*T.L.S.*, 27 Feb. 1937). Lady Shrewsbury, writing to Burghley on 21 Sept. 1592, stated that 'one Morley', who had attended at Hardwick on her granddaughter, Lady Arabella Stuart, 'and read to her for the space of three years and a half', had been dismissed because he was discontented and because Lady Shrewsbury had of late 'some cause to be doubtful of his forwardness in religion'. Brooks suggested that 'one Morley' was Christopher Marlowe, and that he had been recommended by the Privy Council as tutor to Lady Arabella, who stood in close succession to the Crown. But a doubt about 'forwardness in religion' is something very different from the charges of 'atheism' against Marlowe which now begin to claim attention.

[2] *State Papers (Domestic)*, vol. lxxxvi. no. 159. I owe this reference to C. T. Prouty.

signing of his 'supplicat' for the M.A. by the Master of Corpus Christi are in my opinion conclusive evidence to the contrary. It has indeed been recently proved from the College Buttery books that Francis Kett, who had been a Fellow of the College from 1573 to July 1580, remained in residence during the earlier part of 1581 after Marlowe had entered.[1] But a young freshman was not likely to come into contact with a senior man no longer in an official position. It is very improbable, therefore, that Kett had any influence on Marlowe, though the heresies with which he was charged in later years and for which he suffered death at Norwich on 14 January 1588/9 are of the Arian type to which the dramatist was afterwards inclined.[2]

Just before Marlowe took his M.A. in July 1587 there came to Corpus Christi College Thomas Fineaux or Phineaux. It is apparently to him that Henry Oxinden refers in his note:[3] 'Marloe had a friend named Phineaux at Dover, whom he made an Atheist, but who was made to recant.' But of his later career at Cambridge or elsewhere there seems to be no record.

The other later Kentish admirer of Marlowe, Simon Aldrich, who entered Trinity College, Cambridge, about 1593,[4] told Oxinden 'that Marlowe was an Atheist and wrote a book against the Scriptures, how that it was all one man's making; and would have printed it, but it could not be suffered to be printed'.

These memoranda are important as traditional links, though scanty, between the dramatist and men of his own county and university, but they do not imply that Marlowe's 'atheism' dated back to his Cambridge days. Yet the violation by the Archbishop's scholar of the understood obligation to take holy orders and his sensational début immediately afterwards as a London playwright must have caused no little scandal. And it was

---

[1] Bakeless, op. cit., p. 50.   [2] See below, pp. 111–12.
[3] On Oxinden's memoranda see above, p 19.
[4] See above, p. 19.

At my last being wth yor Lp. to entreate some speaches from you in my favor
to my Lorde, whoe (though I thinke he rest not doubtfull of myne inocence) hath yet
in his discreeter iudgmt feared to offende in his reteyning me, wthout yor honors
former pryvitie. So is it nowe R. ho: that the denyall of that favor (to my
thought resonable) hath mov'de me to coniecture some suspicion, that yor Lp holds me
in, concerning Atheisme, a deadlie thing wch I was undeservedlie chargd wthall, &
therfore have I thought it requisite, aswell in duetie to yor Lp, & the lawes, as
also in the feare of god, & freedom of my conscience, therein to satisfie the
world and you:

218

The first and most (thoughe insufficient surmize) that euer as therein
might be raisde of me, grewe thus. When I was first suspected for that
libell that concern'd the state, amongst those waste and idle papers (which I carde
not for) & which unaskt I did deliuer up, were founde some fragmentes of a
disputation toching that opinion, affirmed by Marlowe to be his, and shufled
wth some of myne (unknowne to me) by some occasion of our wrytinge in one
chamber twoe yeares synce.

My first acquaintance wth this Marlowe, rose upon his bearing name to
serve my Lo: although his Lp never knewe his service, but in writing for

Part of a letter from Thomas Kyd to Sir John Puckering, the Lord Keeper, accusing Marlowe of atheism

natural that some of the most challenging tirades of his first tragic hero should be interpreted by unfriendly hearers as the utterances of the dramatist himself. Among these, as has been seen in discussing the date of the *Tamburlaine* plays, was Robert Greene,[1] who at St. John's College had been Marlowe's senior at Cambridge by two years, and who was envious of the younger man's triumph in the theatre while his own only venture as yet was 'to palter up some thing in Prose'. The first known use of the term 'Atheist' in any connexion with Marlowe is the phrase from the preface to *Perimedes the Blacksmith* in 1588,[1] 'daring God out of heaven with that Atheist *Tamburlan*', followed by the sneer at 'mad and scoffing poets, that have propheticall spirits as bred of *Merlins* race'. Here Greene evidently insinuates that the atheism of Tamburlaine was characteristic of the 'scoffing' poet, his creator, versed in the black art of his namesake, the wizard Merlin.

A much more serious and illuminating allegation of atheism was to be made against Marlowe by his chief rival as a tragic dramatist, Thomas Kyd. And its importance lies in the fact that it arose out of the personal contact of the two men. In circumstances to be discussed later Kyd was arrested on 12 May 1593.[2] Among his papers were found fragments of a disputation which the authorities endorsed as 'vile hereticall conceiptes denyinge the deity of Jhesus Christe o[r] Savio[r]'. This is in itself a sufficiently accurate description, but the discovery brought upon Kyd the charge of atheism against which he protested in an undated letter, written after Marlowe's death, to the Lord Keeper, Sir John Puckering. He there asserts that the fragments belonged to Marlowe and that they were 'shuffled wth some of myne (vnknown to me) by some occasion of o[r] wrytinge in one chamber twoe yeares synce'. This dates the association of the two dramatists at least as far back as the early summer of 1591.

The object of the treatise was to deny the divinity of

---

[1] See above, pp. 69–70.   [2] See below, p. 242.

Jesus Christ. It quotes texts from the New Testament Epistles calling God 'Euerlasting, Inuisible, Incõmutable, Incomprehensible, Iõmortall', and maintains that if 'Jhesus Christ euen he which was borne of Marie was God so shall he be a visible God comprehensible & mortall', which is a contradiction. It has been shown[1] that the fragments found in Kyd's possession are part of an anonymous treatise quoted in full for purposes of confutation by John Proctor in 1549 in a book called *The Fal of the Late Arrian*. And good reason has been given[2] for concluding that the 'late Arrian' was John Assheton who had denied the doctrine of the Trinity, had been examined by Archbishop Cranmer in 1549, and had afterwards recanted.

It is surprising evidence of the range of Marlowe's reading that he had once in his possession these portions of a heretical treatise more than thirty years old by an obscure parish priest. And it shows how wide an interpretation could be given to atheism if charges of it could be brought against Kyd and Marlowe based on this Socinian disputation. How far it may have at all approximated to Marlowe's views will be discussed later.

It is fortunate that in support of his assertions Kyd asks Puckering to inquire of those with whom Marlowe 'conversed', Harriot, Warner, Roydon, and some stationers in Paul's Churchyard. Whether the Lord Keeper approached them or not, we must be grateful for getting this short list of the dramatist's intimates. The St. Paul's stationers must include Edward Blount, whose shop was in the Churchyard, and who was in 1598 to publish *Hero and Leander* with an effusive tribute to the author's memory.[3] The identity of Warner is doubtful. The association of his name in the letter with that of Harriot suggests that he was Walter Warner, the mathematician.

---

[1] By W. Dinsmore Briggs in 'A Document concerning Christopher Marlowe', *Studies in Philology*, April 1923.

[2] By George T. Buckley in 'Who was the Late Arrian?', *Mod. Lang. Notes*, Dec. 1934.   [3] See below, p. 282.

But he may have been William Warner, the poet, in whose *Albion's England* there is a definition of the nature of the deity[1] not unlike that in the treatise of 'the late Arrian' and in *Tamburlaine*, Part II, II. ii. 49-53.

Thomas Harriot, an Oxford graduate, was four years senior to Marlowe. He had been taken by Sir Walter Raleigh into his household as a mathematical tutor, and in 1585 accompanied his expedition to Virginia. In 1588 he published *A Brief and True Report* of this 'newfound land', displaying his powers of scientific observation and lucid statement. This was his only publication during his lifetime; his important work on algebra was edited by Walter Warner in 1631, ten years after his death. Modern investigation has somewhat tardily done increasing justice to his achievements in mathematics, astronomy, and optics where he may be mentioned in association with some of the greatest names. These were the studies, disturbing to traditional conceptions of the universe, that excited suspicions among the orthodox of the period. Harriot and his employer were widely credited with keeping a 'School of Atheism' in the latter's house. It is to Harriot that the Jesuit pamphleteer, Robert Parsons, refers in his *Responsio ad Elizabethae edictum* (1592) as 'Astronomo quodam necromantico', the preceptor of the 'schola frequens de Atheismo'. The English summary of the *Responsio* has the entry:

'Of Sir Walter Rawleys school of Atheisme by the waye, & of the Conjurer that is M[aster] thereof, and of the diligence vsed to get yong gentlemen of this schoole, where in both Moyses, & our Sauio^r, the olde, and the new Testamente are iested at, and the schollers taughte, amonge other thinges, to spell God backwarde.'

The 'Conjurer' here is, of course, Harriot, and a year later Richard Baines was to accuse Marlowe of affirming 'that Moyses was but a Iugler and that one Heriots being Sir

---

[1] See M. C. Bradbrook, *The School of Night*, pp. 65-6.

W. Raleighs man Can do more then he'.[1] It was of Harriot too that Thomas Nashe was thinking when he declared in *Pierce Pennilesse* (1592): 'I heare say there be Mathematicians abroad, that will prove men before Adam.' This finds support in Harriot's manuscript papers which include calculations about the chronology of Genesis. And according to Baines, Marlowe similarly was of opinion that 'the Indians and many Authors of antiquity haue assuredly writen of aboue 16 thowsande yeeres agone, whereas Adam is proued to have lived within 6 thowsand yeares'.

But so far as has been discovered, in spite of some tantalizing coincidences of names, there is no mention of Christopher Marlowe in Harriot's voluminous papers.[2] The 'Morly' who drew Harriot's attention to a point to be considered in working with the planisphere of Gemma Frisius seems to have been Captain Edmund Marlowe, author of *Ars Naupegica*, from which Harriot took notes, and whom he mentions in the entry 'I invented this Feb. 28th 1607–1608 and gave it to E. Marlow for Mr. Baker the shipwrite'. Captain Edmund is also probably the 'Mr Marlo' in a short list of names, including 'Mr Alisbury', i.e. Thomas Ailesbury, who was secretary to two Lord High Admirals, and whose association with Harriot was later than Marlowe's death. And a more intimate reference among 'remembrances' to 'a horse for Kit' seems to be concerned not with Kit Marlowe, but with one of Harriot's servants, either Christopher Tooke or Christopher Kellett.

Of Matthew Roydon, the other friend of Marlowe named by Kyd, it is preferable to speak later.[3] But whatever may have been Marlow's degree of intimacy with persons popularly suspected of heresy, and whatever rumours may have begun to circulate about his own atheism, his career, except for his arrest and fortnight's

---

[1] See below, p. 251.
[2] On the points that follow see John Bakeless in *T.L.S.*, 2 Jan. 1937, and the comments by Ethel Seaton, ibid., 5 June 1937.   [3] pp. 243-4.

imprisonment in September 1589, seems to have run prosperously from his success with the *Tamburlaine* plays till the spring of 1592. Nor was there then any check to the flow of his genius, but during the last year of his life clouds increasingly blackened his firmament, presaging the final tragedy of 30 May 1593.

VIII

ROBERT POLEY

PLOT AND COUNTERPLOT: 1585–8

AT this point it is advisable to bring into the narrative
of Marlowe's fortunes the enigmatic figure of Robert
Poley, who was to be one of the actors in the tragedy of
Deptford, who in his tortuous career was brought into
relation with members of the dramatist's circle, and who
probably knew something of him personally before their
last fatal meeting, though of this there is no documentary
proof. In any case Poley's equivocal activities as a Government agent and his double-faced attitude to recusants
and plotters throw vivid light on the feverish and turbulent
atmosphere in which suspicions of treasonable intentions
by Marlowe, whether in his Cambridge or London days,
might easily be roused and entertained.

In tracing the career of Robert Poley we are again faced,
though in a less degree than with Christopher Marlowe,
with the difficulties arising from variant Elizabethan
spellings of proper names. Poley appears as 'Pooley',
'Pollye', 'Poole', and 'Pole', and allusions to him in the
State Papers have thus been indexed as if they referred
to different persons. But there were also other Poleys or
Pooles, among them John Poole the Newgate prisoner
and coiner; another John Pooley who was in the service
of the Earl of Essex; and Edmund Poley, nephew to Lord
Wentworth.[1] References therefore merely by surname
can only be identified with Robert Poley if the circumstances appear to be relevant.

He may have been the Robert Pollye who matriculated
as a sizar from Clare College, Cambridge, in Michaelmas
1568, and who had perhaps been a chorister at King's in

[1] See Ethel Seaton in *R.E S* (Jan. 1931), p. 88, with references to
Cal. S. P.

1564.[1] He was a man of education, but, so far as I know, neither in his own statements nor in contemporary allusions to him is there any reference to a connexion with Cambridge. In any case he does not seem to have taken a degree. There is a plausible, though not conclusive, reason for identifying him as the 'Master Pooley' who was in the service of Lord North in 1578.[2] But our first certain knowledge of him is in the earlier part of 1583. It is derived from a deposition by Richard Ede, apparently lodge-keeper at the Marshalsea, in a case against Poley for alienating the affections of Joan, the wife of William Yeomans, a London cutler. The case came in January 1588/9 before William Fleetwood, the London Recorder who in the December of the same year was to be on the Bench when Marlowe was set free after the killing of Bradley. Ede deposed that on a date not specified in 1583 Poley was committed by Sir Francis Walsingham to the Marshalsea and remained there till the 10th of May following. One half of the time he was a close prisoner; and the other half he had 'the liberty of the house'. He made use of this 'enlargement' to entertain Mistress Yeomans at 'fine bankets' in his chamber, while refusing to have anything to do with his own wife, who often tried to see him. This ill-used lady (as we learn from Yeomans) was 'one Watson's daughter', and was married to Poley by a seminary priest in the house of one Wood, a tailor dwelling in Bow Lane, who circulated prohibited books like *The Execution of Justice* and *The Treatise of Schism*.

Whatever the reason for Poley's committal to the Marshalsea, he cannot have been in want of money at this time, for he entrusted Mistress Yeomans with £110 of 'good gould'. After a time he sent Mistress Ede to borrow £3 from Yeomans, who was not at home. Mistress Yeomans, however, sent him back by the messenger £3 of his own money. Yeomans afterwards sent by his brother another £3, and when Mistress Ede declared that

[1] Ethel Seaton in *R.E.S.* (Apr. 1931), p. 147, quoting from John and J. A. Venn's *Alumni Cantabrigienses*.   [2] See below, p. 123 n.

the money had already been received by Poley, Yeomans thought his wife had robbed him and was angry with her. But when Poley came out of prison the matter was explained, and Ede brought about a reconciliation, confirmed by a gift from Poley to Yeomans of a silver bowl double gilt, and to Ede of two angels for his pains in the matter. But the intrigue between Poley and Joan Yeomans continued, and to facilitate it she arranged for him to have a chamber at the house of her mother, a widowed .Mistress Browne.

Apparently, however, Mistress Browne did not suspect the guilty relations between her daughter and Poley, which had a remarkable sequel. One of the deponents who gave evidence before the Recorder on 7 January 1588/9 was Agnes Hollford, wife of Ralph Hollford, hosier. She deposed that on a Friday about Shrovetide, 1585, she met Mistress Browne, mother of Mistress Yeomans. Mistress Browne told her that 'one Mr. Polley laye in her howse, and her daughter comminge to her howse to drye clothes' she 'fownde her daughter sitting vpon the said Polleys knees, the syght thereof did soe stryke to her hart that she shoulde never recover yt. She prayed God to cutt her of verie quickly or ells she feared she shoulde be a bawde vnto her owne daughter.' Her prayer was quickly answered, for when Mistress Hollford called on Mistress Browne on the Monday following she found her 'departed and readie to be caried to the Church to be buried, she dyinge vppon the Saterdaie before'. Even this divine visitation, however, did not, as will be seen, put a stop to the relations between Poley and Mistress Yeomans.

By 1585, however, Poley had become associated with a very different circle from that of the London cutler and his wife. Charles and Christopher Blunt (or Blount) were younger brothers of William, seventh Lord Mountjoy. Charles, who was a favourite of Elizabeth, succeeded to the title in 1594, and afterwards became Earl of Devonshire and Lord Deputy of Ireland. Christopher was Master of the Horse to Lord Leicester, whose widow he married about 1589. He was knighted for his military services in Flanders in 1587–8. He afterwards took part in the ill-fated campaign of the Earl of Essex in Ireland, and in the abortive conspiracy against Elizabeth, for which he was executed on 18 March 1601. This was the culmination of a long series of treasonable practices. By 1585 Christopher Blunt, who became a convert to Roman Catholicism, had thrown himself ardently into the plots on behalf of the unfortunate Queen of Scots. For this purpose he chose as his agent Robert Poley, as appears to · be first mentioned in a letter from Thomas Morgan to Mary, dated 10 July 1585. Morgan, one of Mary's agents abroad, was at this time a prisoner in the Bastille, but he was able to communicate in cipher with the Queen of Scots, then at Tutbury in the custody of Sir Amias Poulet.

'Aboute fiftene dayes past or thereaboutes, there arrived here a speciall messenger from London, sent hither expresselye by Mr. Blunt vnto me with letters, declaring by the same that he was bound to serve & honor the only Sainct that he knowes living vppon the grownd—so he termed your majestie . . . which bringer of Blunt his letters is a gentleman & named Robert Poley. I am, as I was, still prisonner & he cold not be permitted to have accesse vnto me.'

Poley, however, refused to deal with Morgan through any intermediary, 'declaring that he wold not deliver his charge to none living till he spake with my selfe or hard me speak'. Some of Morgan's friends became apprehensive, beginning 'to dout the sayd Poley was sent by England to practise my death in prison by one meanes or other'. Morgan, however, was not influenced by their fears:

'I fownd the meanes to have him conducted as nere as might be to the window of the chamber where I am a prisoner, and through the window I spoke so moch to him as satisfied him, who at the last delivered the letters where I appoynted, & so they came to my handes with ample Instrucions of the state of England . . .

'And so vppon conference and conclusion with the sayd Poley I fownd nothing but that he ment well, and a Catholike he showeth himselfe to be, and moch disposed to see some happye & speedye reformation in that state . . . I have retorned Poley in fine well contented and confirmed, I hope, to serve your majestie in all he may, but I wrote not one line with him, but signified that Blunt shold heare from me by some other meanes.'

The last words suggest that Morgan did not trust Poley fully, but in any case he got him recompensed for 'his viage and charges hither'. He persuaded the Archbishop of Glasgow to send Poley 30 pistolets through Charles Paget.

'He hath receaved the same, & is gone to England wher he promised Paget to do some good offices, & prayed him to assure me thereof, for I cold not be permitted to speak with him but once, as I tolde you alredye.'

Morgan's caution in not communicating with Blount through Poley proved fruitless. For as Charles Paget, another fervent adherent in Paris of the Queen of Scots, wrote to Mary on 15 July, Poley himself on his first arrival there 'committed an error in writing hence to Mr. Christopher Blunt' and 'sent it by an ordinary messenger, so that it was taken'. This is confirmed on 18 July by Morgan: 'I hear that the said Poleys letters were intercepted at the port in England and sent to the Council.' In all probability Poley did not 'commit an error' but deliberately arranged that the correspondence should fall into the hands of the English Government.

Exactly six months afterwards, on 18 January 1586, Morgan gives further news of Poley:

'Hert [i.e. Charles Paget] and I recommend the French Embassador some English in London to doe him some pleasure & service there and amongst others one Robert Poley who hath geven me assurance to serve and honor your majestie to his power being but a poore gentleman. He is moch at Chr[istopher] Blunt his devotion and both of them do travell to make an intelligence for your majestie. The sayd Embassador & his Secretarye Courdaillot have sithence theyr arrivall in London reported well to Hert and to my selfe of the sayd Poley who hath bene heretofore in Scotland & knoweth the best wayes to passe into Scotlande. If you know not how to be better served for conveyance to Scotland you may cause the Embassador to addresse the sayd Poley with your letters into Scotland. But order must be taken to make his charges in such viages. And if your majestie will have him to remayne in some place nerer for your purpose & service he will accommodate himself accordinglye to your pleasure. He is a Catholike and Blunt has placed him to be Sir Phillipp Sydneys man that he may more quietlye live a Christian life vnder the sayd Sydney.'

What an exquisite compliment to the *preux chevalier* of the Elizabethan age (though the *Calendar of the Scottish State Papers* cynically omits it)! But it was of course not with Poley's progress in the religious life that Mary's supporters were concerned. They secured him a place in Sidney's service because on 20 September 1583 Sir Philip had married Frances, daughter of Sir Francis Walsingham, and had taken up his abode in his father-in-law's house. Poley would thus be in a favourable position for learning 'Mr. Secretary's' movements and plans.

In a later letter to the Queen of Scots, dated 21 March 1586, Morgan states this without any disguise:

'Having written thus farre I receaved letters out of England from London from Poley, in my former letters mentioned, who writeth vnto me that he hath bene in the partes where your majesty remayneth, and there addressed the meanes to convey such letters as I commended to his care to serve to make an intelligence with your majesty. We have applyed him this twelve monthe or thereabouts & have fownd him to deale well & verye willing to serve your majesty. Hert can tell yow he was first recommended vnto me by Christopher Blunt who never abused [i.e. deceived] me, but continueth well affected to serve & honor your majesty. And I am of opinion that you entertayne the sayd Poley who by Bluntes labours & my advise is placed with the Ladye Sydney, the dowghter of Secretarye Walsingham, & by that means ordinarilye in his Howse and therebye able to picke owt many things to the information of your majesty. . . . As I have sayd, [Poley] is in a place to discover many thinges which he beginneth to doe to the disadvantage of the common enemies.'

Morgan goes on to tell Mary that 'eyther Rawley, the mignon of her of England is wearye of her or els she is wearye of him, for I heare she hath now entertayned one [Charles] Blunt, brother of the Lord Mountjoye, a yong gentilman, whose grandmother she may be for her age and his'. It is therefore expedient that Mary should make Poley understand that she thinks well of this gentleman's brother, Christopher, 'who is at present in Holland with Leicester, & has sent for Poley to come to him'.

There is no evidence as to whether or not Poley obeyed this summons. But on 10 April, Charles Paget wrote, as Morgan had done ten days before, emphasizing the advantage to Mary's cause of Poley's position in Sidney's service.

'There be two other which be in practyse to gayne others to serve your majesty for intelligence, whereof one is called Poley, a great friend to Christopher Blunt, of whome I suppose your majesty hath harde here tofore. Morgan and I have had conference with the sayd Poley and hope he is in soch place, being servant to Sir Phillipp Sydney, and thereby remayneth with his Ladye and in house with Secretarye Walsingham, so as he shalbe able to give your majesty advertisement from time to time.'

As Sir Philip had left England on 16 November 1585, to take up his post as Governor of Flushing, and as he remained in the Netherlands till his death on 17 October 1586, Poley can have had little personal intercourse with him. But as both Morgan and Paget state, he remained with Lady Sidney, who followed her husband about the end of March. Poley, as his own words will show, while acting as an agent for Sir Francis, was brought into direct association with Thomas Walsingham, son of a cousin of Sir Francis, who thus appears as a link between Marlowe and Poley as well as between Marlowe and Thomas Watson. It may well have been at his Chislehurst home, or at one of the two residences of 'Mr. Secretary', in London or at Barn Elms, that Marlowe and Poley first met.

An episode in Mr. Secretary's presence, which if William Yeomans's memory on 7 January 1589 is to be trusted, took place early in 1586, throws a remarkable light on Poley's mentality. 'About three years past', according to Yeomans, Poley was examined before Sir Francis Walsingham 'by the space of two hours touching a book which was made against the Earl of Leicester'. This was evidently the notorious *Leicester's Commonwealth*, published in 1584, and prohibited by the Privy Council on 28 June 1585.

'Although Mr. Secretary did vse him very cruelly yet woulde he never confes ytt. And he saied that he putt Mr. Secretary into that heate that he looked out of his wyndowe and grynned like a dogge.' Yeomans asked Poley how he 'durst to denye the having of the said booke because he verie well knewe that he had the same'.[1] 'Marye', answered Poley, 'it is noe matter for I will sweare and forsweare my selffe rather then I will accuse my selffe to doe me any harm.' What an avowal from one of the trio on whose evidence the Coroner's jury were to be dependent later for their verdict on how Marlowe met his death!

During the summer of 1586 Poley was becoming more and more deeply involved in plots and counterplots. He wrote an unsigned letter of thanks to Mary, Queen of Scots, which evidently caused her some perplexity. She refers on July 27 to 'a letter of Poleyes as I judge by reason of some reward he thanketh me for therein receaved beyond sea. Otherwise the letter being an unknowne hand without subscription or name therein I am not assured from whence it came. Neyther can I tell by whome to send back my answer agayne.'

Mary had far deeper reason for being distrustful of

---

[1] One reason for Poley having a copy of *Leicester's Commonwealth* is that he is probably the 'Master Pooley' mentioned on p. 86 (edition of 1641). Lord North was one of those present at the marriage of Leicester to Lettice, Countess of Essex, on 21 Sept. 1578, and received in consequence a letter of sharp rebuke from the Queen. According to the writer of *Leicester's Commonwealth* he told 'his trusty Pooly', who repeated the words to Sir Robert Jermine, that 'he was resolved to sinke or swimme with my Lord of Leicester'. If Poley was in the service of Lord North as early as 1578, this would be a sidelight on his career about five years previous to any documentary information.

Poley than she knew. For by July 1586 he had already wormed his way into the secrets of the hot-headed youth, rich and well born, who staked everything for her sake and in losing brought doom upon her as well as himself. Into the well-known story of the conspiracy of Anthony Babington it is not necessary to go here. It is sufficient to say that about April 1586 Babington, largely inspired by John Ballard, a priest from Rheims, formed a plot that included the murder of Elizabeth; that in July he communicated the scheme to Mary; that Ballard was seized early in August; that Babington afterwards fled but was discovered; and that he and Ballard were executed on 20 September. The plot, though completely mismanaged, is of first-rate historical importance because it led directly to Mary's own trial and execution.

Poley's relation to the conspiracy is curiously equivocal. He appears to have been an agent of Walsingham, but he won Babington's complete confidence, and after the arrest of the conspirators he was committed to the Tower, where he was examined on various charges and made a lengthy confession. From this we learn that he was introduced to Babington in the middle of June, that he might procure him a licence from Walsingham for some years of continental travel:

'I labored . . . that I might accompanye him betwene the condicyon of a servaunte & companion beinge vtterly vnhable to maintaine myselfe in all this jorneye, thinkinge with myselfe that I should bothe better my selfe thereby bothe in language and experience and allso do the State much better servyze in that coursse abroade then in that wherein I remained att hoame . . . Babington agreed to supplie all my charges of travell, and to give me some yeerly stipende att my retorne . . . and I tellinge him that I remained bownd with 2 sureties with me to appear every 20 dayes att the Court, he offered me £40 or £50 to make means for my discharge, which money I receyved of him afterwards to that ende the daye before my Lady Sidnies going hence towards Flushinge.'[1]

[1] The dates are difficult to reconcile, for Lady Sidney had gone to Flushing before the middle of June, when, according to Poley, he first met Babington.

Here incidentally we get an important sidelight on Poley's dubious activities. How was it that he, while in the service of the Sidneys, and in touch with Walsingham, 'remained bownd with two sureties to appear every 20 dayes at the Court', and had to buy his discharge through a gift from Babington? Was it a sequel to his examination concerning *Leicester's Commonwealth*?

Poley procured Babington a couple of interviews with Walsingham, who evidently encouraged further confidences by speaking favourably of the go-between. On Babington's asking by what means Poley's credit grew with Mr. Secretary,

'I towlde him by dealinge with his honor in some busines of my master, Sir Philipp Sidney, but he seeminge to discredite that & urge me further, I towld him further I was in a like coursse of doinge servize to the state as him self had nowe vndertaken. He answered mee that was impossible, because he knew thatt all the menn of note in England being Catholikes had me in vehemente suspicyon.'

For some time longer Poley continued to play his double part, while Walsingham made excuses for postponing a further interview with Babington or the grant of his passport. Then, when all was ready, the Government struck. They just missed the chance of rounding up on 2 August 'a whole knot' of the conspirators at supper in Poley's garden, including 'Skyrres', who is probably Nicholas Skeres, afterwards to be present with Poley at Marlowe's death. But on 4 August Ballard was arrested at Poley's lodging, immediately after a visit by Thomas Walsingham 'to whom I had delivered such speeches as Mr. Secretary had commanded me the day before'. Babington's flight followed, and before his arrest he wrote Poley a last letter in which affection and doubt are pathetically mingled:

'I am the same I allwayes pretended. I pray god yow be, and ever so remayne towards me. Take hede to your owne parte least of these my mysfortunes yow beare the blame ... ffarewell sweet Robyn, if as I take the, true to me. If not adieu *omnium bipedum nequissimus*. Retorne me thyne answere for my satisfaction,

& my dyamond, & what els thow wilt. The fornace is prepared wherin our faith muste be tried. ffarewell till we mete, which god knowes when.'

When the conspirators were arrested, Poley was committed to the Tower, where his confession was written. On 2 July 1588 it is officially recorded that he had been a 'prisoner one year xi monthes'. It is difficult to reconcile this with the evidence of the bills of the Lieutenant of the Tower which include one for the expenses connected with the imprisonment of Robert Poley from 18 August 1586 to 'the laste of September the next folowinge beinge syx wicks' amounting in all to vi*li* xiij*s*.[1] There is no further similar bill relating to Poley till one from Christmas Day 1587 till 25 March 1588. There is no bill extant for the following quarter, but from 24 June till 29 September the Lieutenant of the Tower records the expenses in connexion with his imprisonment as xv*li* xij*s*. viij*d*. All the bills may not have been preserved or he may have been at liberty during intervals. But he was regarded with suspicion by the Government, as is plain from his protests in a petitioning letter apparently addressed to the Earl of Leicester in which he begs the Earl to employ him in some service at home or abroad. The letter is not dated, but it gives some clues to the time of its composition. It includes the phrases, 'then went your honour immediately to Kylingworth' (Kenilworth) and 'your honour's great business of Parliament'. It must therefore have been written after 29 November 1586, when Leicester returned from the unsuccessful campaign in Flanders, and probably between 15 February and 23 March 1587, when a Parlia-

---

[1] The details of this and the two other bills mentioned here are printed by Miss de Kalb in *The Nineteenth Century and After*, Nov. 1927. They are preserved among the bills of the Lieutenant of the Tower in the Public Record Office, and are numbered E 407/56, Nos. 44, 47, 50. A minor conspirator in the Babington plot, James Tipping, is also mentioned in the Tower bills, and like Poley had on 2 July 1588 been a prisoner for a year and eleven months. See further Ethel Seaton, *R.E.S.*, July 1929, pp. 277–9.

ment was sitting, which the Earl regularly attended. It is remarkable that Poley speaks of having recently introduced to Christopher Blunt a Thomas Audley who had 'married a near kinswoman of your honour's first wife', and who wanted to 'move some suit' to the Earl. What can Leicester have thought of such a reminder of Amy Robsart, if the reference be really to her? Audley had accompanied Poley among other places to Seething Lane, 'where I attended Mr. Thomas Walsingham for my secret recourse to Mr. Secretary, but all to lost labour then and my distress now'. Here again we have direct evidence of Poley's association with Marlowe's patron.

His confinement in the Tower cannot have been close, for, as before in the Marshalsea, Joan Yeomans was able to visit him, with 'one W. Golder', and to bring him letters from overseas from Christopher Blunt, who was serving in Flanders in 1587–8. Yeomans gives a vivid account in his evidence of how he found his wife reading one of these letters and of her throwing it into the fire.

Ede and Yeomans both confirm the information from the Tower bills that Poley was released about Michaelmas 1588. This was apparently due to the intervention of Sir Francis Walsingham. 'Had not I good lucke to gett owt of the Tower?' Poley asked Yeomans, declaring that 'Mr. Secretarie did deliver him owt'. 'You are greatlie beholding vnto Mr. Secretarie', answered Yeomans. 'Naye', said Poley, 'he is more beholding vnto me then I am vnto him for there are further matters betwene hym & me then all the world shall knowe of.' He further declared that Walsingham had contracted a disreputable disease in France.

On his release Poley quartered himself on the unfortunate Yeomans, who took Ede 'into his nether room and made very great mone that Poley was come to lodge and did lodge in his house again'. Ede sensibly advised Yeomans to get rid of him, as otherwise he would 'beguile him either of his wife or of his life'. And so it proved. On 10 November Poley got Yeomans committed to the

Marshalsea for disregard of a warrant of the Vice-Chamberlain, Sir Thomas Heneage. Richard Ede again intervened as a peacemaker, but his efforts, though they got Yeomans out of prison, ended in failure, for Mistress Yeomans, on pretence that she was going to market, finally eloped with Poley. Yet neither his private misconduct nor his dubious political record prevented him from being re-engaged before the end of the year in the service of the Government. And, as will be seen, he was actively employed therein on the day when Marlowe met his doom in May 1593. But till then the dramatist was to continue the triumphant theatrical career which had begun with the *Tamburlaine* plays.

IX

THE TRAGEDY OF THE JEW OF MALTA

THOUGH the only extant edition of *The Famous Tragedy of the Rich Jew of Malta* is the quarto of 1633, the date of the play can be fixed within fairly close limits. The words in the original prologue, l. 3, 'And now the Guise is dead', refer to the assassination of the third Duke of Guise on 23 December 1588, and would have particular point if the event was comparatively recent. Henslowe in his *Diary* records a performance of *The Jew of Malta* by Lord Strange's men on 26 February 1591/2, when fifty shillings was taken, and he does not mark it as a new play. 1589 may be taken as the approximate date.

Henslowe's *Diary* gives evidence of the popularity of the play, thirty-six performances being recorded up to 21 June 1596. There was a revival of it in 1601, when Henslowe notes: 'Lent vnto Robert shawe & mr. Jube the 19 of Maye 1601 to bye divers thinges for the Jewe of malta the some of . . . v^{li}. lent mor to the littell tayller the same daye for more thinges for the Jewe of malta some of . . . x^{s}.'[1] Some of the properties and costumes evidently had to be renovated.

It is improbable that so popular a piece did not find its way into print till forty years after Marlowe's death. It was entered in the Stationers' Register on 17 May 1594 to Nicholas Linge and Thomas Millington. If they published an edition, not a single copy has survived. Thomas Heywood in dedicating the 1633 quarto to his worthy friend Mr. Thomas Hammon speaks of the play as 'being newly brought to the Presse'. This is ambiguous, as 'newly' may either mean 'for the first time' or 'anew'.

In his epistle to Hammon Heywood proclaims himself the threefold sponsor of the play:

'As I vsher'd it unto the Court, and presented it to the Cock-pit,

[1] *Henslowe's Diary*, ed. Greg, i. 137.

K

with these Prologues and Epilogues here inserted, so now being newly brought to the Presse, I was loath it should be published without the ornament of an Epistle.'

The further question arises: did Heywood confine himself to writing prologues and epilogues when *The Jew of Malta* was revived first at the Court and afterwards at the Cockpit in Whitefriars with Richard Perkins in the title-role, and providing 'the ornament of an Epistle' for the quarto published by Nicholas Vavasour? Or did he edit and revise the play? His own words seem to negative this: 'Sir, you have been pleased to grace some of mine own works with your courteous patronage; I hope this will not be the worse accepted because commended by me.' Here Heywood draws a definite contrast between his own works and one only commended by him. In the prologue spoken at Court he craves pardon for boldly daring to present among plays 'that now in fashion are . . . this writ many years ago'. And in the prologue at the Cockpit he declares that by Marlowe

the best of Poets in that age
The *Malta Jew* had being, and was made.

But with seventeenth-century standards such statements are not entirely conclusive. The similarity, within limits, of the episode of the two Friars in *The Jew of Malta*, Act IV. ii and iii, to the underplot of Heywood's *The Captives* has naturally suggested the presence of his hand in the 1633 version of Marlowe's play. The scenes of which Bellamira, the courtesan, is the centre have been similarly suspected. The points involved are somewhat more complicated than may appear at first sight and they are discussed in an appendix to this chapter. In the light of the whole evidence I agree with the latest editor of *The Jew of Malta* that 'we must . . . give a verdict of *Not proven* at the very least when asked to believe these scenes are by Heywood'.[1] They are not marked by his peculiarities of diction and they are not so extraneous to

<hr/>

[1] *The Jew of Malta*, ed. H. S. Bennett, p. 9 (1931).

the structure of the play as might be supposed. On the other hand, it is very unlikely that after more than forty years the play, especially if it survived only in the play-house in manuscript, has reached us exactly as it came from Marlowe's pen.

In his search for materials for Part II of *Tamburlaine* Marlowe, as has been seen, made use in the earlier Acts of *Chronicorum Turcicorum tomi duo* of P. Lonicerus narrating the events which led up to the battle of Varna. In this Chronicle he also came across an account of a Portuguese Jew, Juan Miques or Michesius, who in the later half of the sixteenth century became a favourite of the Sultan Selim II, and was raised by him to a position of great authority as Duke of Naxos.[1] In this he proved himself a consistent opponent of the Christian powers, and particularly urged the Sultan in 1569 to break faith with the Republic of Venice and to seize the isle of Cyprus. A similar account is given in another source available to Marlowe, Belleforest's *Cosmographie Universelle*, ii. 580, where 'Micqué' is called 'un paillard Iuif . . . homme subtil, rusé et malicieux'. This is amplified in a later section of the same work (ii. 785), which also tells of his widely dispersed financial interests, 'car il auoit demeuré un long temps à Lyon negotiant en France, puis à Marseille, de là passa à Rome, visita la Sicile, et puis prit son adresse à Venise'. Recent research has made it increasingly evident that Marlowe found the chief materials for his plays in books that he had read. J. Kellner was therefore probably right when he suggested half a century ago[2] that Miques was the prototype of Barabas, though he was unaware that Marlowe had the opportunity of making his acquaintance in the pages of Lonicerus and Belleforest.

---

[1] See 'Fresh Sources for Marlowe', by Ethel Seaton. Miss Seaton quotes the account of Miques in Lonicerus, op. cit., 2nd edit., 1584, ii. 3. She also gives in full the passages concerning 'Micqué' in Belleforest's *Cosmographie Universelle*.

[2] In *Englische Studien*, x. 80 ff. (1887).

But in Part II of *Tamburlaine* the dramatist had already shown that he could unify materials drawn from different sources, and he probably did not draw his Jew from a single model. He may well, as Tucker Brooke has suggested,[1] have borrowed features from the personality of another Jew of Constantinople, David Passi, 'whose career reached its culmination after half-a-dozen years of European notoriety in March 1591'. Passi was involved in the Turkish designs against Malta, but he 'pursued a boggling policy, playing off Turk against Christian after the fashion of Marlowe's Barabas. He was closely connected with English diplomacy in the Mediterranean'. An opponent of Passi at the Turkish court was another Jew, Alvaro Mendez, who was a kinsman of Miques, and brother-in-law of Dr. Roderigo Lopez. In the eighteen months preceding Marlowe's death he twice sent Jews of his household to England on pro-Turkish missions.[2] It was open to the dramatist to supplement his book-knowledge of Ottoman affairs by conversations at first hand.

Whatever were the exact sources of his information it was an easy transition for a playwright to pass from the feuds and treacheries of Scythians, Turks, and Christians in the Orient to those of Jews, Turks, and Christians in the Mediterranean. The third of the great religious systems known to Marlowe was now to suffer at his hands the same mockery as its rivals. The choice of the name Barabas, with its sinister associations, for the Jew of Malta was in itself significant. Yet Barabas, as first conceived by Marlowe, was more than a representative of the Hebrew race and religion. Within the narrower sphere of finance he is cast in the same mould as Tamburlaine. We see him on his chosen field of battle, with his munitions of war, when in the opening scene of the play he 'is discovered in his counting-house with heaps of gold before him'. He turns contemptuously from the 'paltry silver-

[1] In *T.L.S.*, 8 June 1922.
[2] 'Fresh Sources for Marlowe', p. 392.

lings' pursed from his humbler clients, and finds his com-
peers in those who traffic in the virgin treasures of the
Orient (1. i. 19-24):

> Give me the merchants of the Indian mines
> That trade in metal of the purest mould;
> The wealthy Moor, that in the eastern rocks
> Without control can pick his riches up,
> And in his house heap pearl like pibble-stones,
> Receive them free and sell them by the weight.

Of like quality is his own treasure in precious stones,

> Bags of fiery opals, sapphires, amethysts,
> Jacinths, hard topaz, grass-green emeralds,
> Beauteous rubies, sparkling diamonds.

He gloats over the names of each of the costly 'seld-seen'
heaps as Tamburlaine over the titles of each conquered
province; and as the Scythian seeks a world-wide empery
so Barabas covets

> Infinite riches in a little room.

Like a general reviewing his forces he keeps track of
the movements of his merchant fleet (1. i. 41-7):

> I hope my ships
> I sent for Egypt and the bordering isles
> Are gotten up by Nilus' winding banks:
> Mine argosy from Alexandria,
> Loaden with spice and silks now under sail,
> Are smoothly gliding down by Candy-shore
> To Malta, through our Mediterranean sea.

When a shipmaster in his employment enters with the
news that his ships are safely riding 'in Malta road' and
asks him to come there to pay the 'custom' duties, Barabas
answers him in the imperious tone of a master of men,
whose word is law in his own sphere (1. i. 55-8):

> go bid them come ashore
> And bring with them their bills of entry:
> I hope our credit in the custom-house
> Will serve as well as I were present there.

When the shipmaster demurs because the duties come to so immense a sum, the Jew cuts him short,

> Go tell 'em the Jew of Malta sent thee, man:
> Tush, who amongst 'em knows not Barabas?

and there comes the instant response, 'I go'. In the same tone of authority, when a second shipmaster announces the arrival of his richly laden argosy from Alexandria, Barabas cries:

> Well, go
> And bid the merchants and my men despatch
> And come ashore, and see the fraught discharg'd,

and again the answer comes at once, 'I go'. Even the elements are yoked to do him service and to fulfil Old Testament prophecy (1. i. 101–9):

> Thus trowls our fortune in by land and sea,
> And thus are we on every side enrich'd:
> These are the blessings promis'd to the Jews,
> And herein was old Abram's happiness:
> What more may heaven do for earthly man
> Than thus to pour out plenty in their laps,
> Ripping the bowels of the earth for them,
> Making the seas their servants, and the winds
> To drive their substance with successful blasts?

Barabas, like Tamburlaine, is greedy of sovereignty, but for him it lies not in kingship but in riches—

> who is honour'd now but for his wealth?

He rolls off the names of Jewish millionaires in many lands (1. i. 125–31):

> wealthy every one,
> Ay, wealthier far than any Christian.
> I must confess we come not to be kings:
> That's not our fault: alas, our number's few,
> And crowns come either by succession
> Or urg'd by force: and nothing violent,
> Oft have I heard tell, can be permanent.

Again Marlowe shows his skill in dovetailing materials drawn from very diverse sources. Barabas, who had been quoting Scripture at the beginning of his monologue, is echoing in the three last lines a typical passage in Chapter II of Machiavelli's *The Prince*.[1] And in the first words of another Jew, who now enters with two compatriots,

> Tush, tell not me; 'twas done of policy,

we hear the keynote of the Machiavellian doctrine as popularly interpreted in England, especially by readers of Gentillet's French counterblast to it in his *Discours sur les moyens de bien gouverner. . . . Contre N. Machiavel*, published in 1576.

The central problem of Marlowe's work and career lies in his exceptional union of two almost conflicting Renaissance elements. There was in him the soaring aspiration after power and knowledge and beauty in their ideal and absolute forms. Side by side with this there was the critical, analytic impulse which led to the questioning of orthodox creeds and standards of conduct. As the myths of classical antiquity had fed his 'aspiring mind', so his critical faculty, sharpened by his governmental service, was fortified further by the study of the maxims of sixteenth-century Italian statecraft, considered without relation to the special conditions in which they originated. Thus the Machiavelli who speaks the Prologue to the *Jew of Malta* is to Marlowe one and the same, whether alive in his native land, or embodied in France in the Guise, or after his death come to frolic with his friends in England (ll. 9–15):

> Admir'd I am of those that hate me most:
> Though some speak openly against my books,
> Yet will they read me, and thereby attain
> To Peter's chair; and when they cast me off,
> Are poison'd by my climbing followers.
> I count religion but a childish toy,
> And hold there is no sin but ignorance.

The two last lines misrepresent Machiavelli, but they

---

[1] See the note on p. 44 of H. S. Bennett's edition of the play.

could be made use of by the enemies of the 'atheist' Marlowe. There is a closer approach to the Florentine's
doctrine in what follows:

> Many will talk of title to a crown:
> What right had Caesar to the empery?
> Might first made kings and laws were then most sure
> When, like the Draco's, they were writ in blood.
> Hence comes it that a strong-built citadel
> Commands much more than letters can import.

It is in this spirit of what is now known as *Realpolitik*
that the action of the play develops. Barabas's compatriots have hastened to consult him in an emergency,
'for he can counsel best in these affairs'. They bring the
startling news that a Turkish fleet has arrived, that the
Maltese authorities are entertaining the newcomers in
the Senate house, and that all the Jews in Malta have been
summoned there. After discussing the situation they take
their leave, and Barabas dismisses them contemptuously
(I. i. 177-83):

> These silly men mistake the matter clean.
> Long to the Turk did Malta contribute;
> Which tribute all in policy, I fear,
> The Turks have let increase to such a sum
> As all the wealth of Malta cannot pay;
> And now by that advantage thinks, belike,
> To seize upon the town; ay, that he seeks.

But Barabas can counter State 'policy' with the older
doctrine of individual self-preservation, and Terence can
be quoted (not quite correctly) against Machiavelli:

> Ego mihimet sum semper proximus.[1]

Things, however, do not go according to his plan. The
Turks in I. ii grant the knights of Malta a month's respite
for the collection of the arrears of tribute, and the

---

[1] *Andria*, IV. i. 12, 'Proximus sum egomet mihi.' Marlowe seems to
have adapted the words to fill a five-foot line. This is his only quotation
from a classical comic dramatist.

Governor passes on the levy to the Jews with the unctuous justification (1. ii. 63-5):

> through our sufferance of your hateful lives,
> Who stand accursed in the sight of heaven,
> These taxes and afflictions are befall'n.

Each Jew is to pay one-half of his estate, or else to become at once a Christian; if he refuses he is to lose all he has. The other Jews immediately promise to give half, but Barabas shows his masterful spirit when he declares 'I will be no convertite', and to the demand, 'then pay thy half', proudly retorts (1. ii. 86-8):

> Half of my substance is a city's wealth.
> Governor, it was not got so easily;
> Nor will I part so slightly therewithal.

But at the threat to seize all his wealth he abruptly recants:[1]

> *Corpo di Dio!* Stay: you shall have half;
> Let me be us'd but as my brethren are.

When this is denied him he asks in bitter irony,

> Will you then steal my goods?
> Is theft the ground of your religion?

To which the Governor replies with the plea of Caiaphas:

> No, Jew; we take particularly thine,
> To save the ruin of a multitude:
> And better one want for a common good,
> Than many perish for a private man.

This he follows with the self-righteous excuse (1. ii. 108-10):

> If your first curse fall heavy on thy head,
> And make thee poor and scorn'd of all the world,
> 'Tis not our fault, but thy inherent sin.

The indignant retort leaps from the Jew's lips:

> What, bring you Scripture to confirm your wrongs?
> Preach me not out of my possessions.

[1] I see no reason for A. M. Clark's assumption (*Thomas Heywood*, p. 290) that there has been a cut here, and that 'a rebellious speech by Barabas at the very least must have been omitted'.

He claims that the individual must be judged according
to his actions, that 'the man that dealeth righteously
shall live', but he speaks to deaf ears. The Governor
plumes himself upon sparing the Jew's life:

> to stain our hands with blood
> Is far from us and our profession—

provoking the damning reply,

> Why, I esteem the injury far less,
> To take the lives of miserable men
> Than be the causers of their misery.

After the swift thrust and parry of this dialogue, with
its Scriptural basis, it is an unexpected transition to Marlowe's metaphysical terminology when, after the exit of
the Maltese, Barabas appeals to the 'great *Primus Motor*'
to deliver their souls to everlasting pains. When one of
his countrymen exhorts him to patience and bids him
remember Job, he bursts out angrily, 'What tell you me
of Job?'—whose wealth could not compare with his. And
he appropriates to himself the words in which the
patriarch pours forth his lamentations (i. ii. 197–9):

> For only I have toil'd to inherit here
> The months of vanity, and loss of time,
> And painful nights, have bin appointed me.[1]

But it is in the loftier spirit of a defeated commander
that he takes leave of his compatriots:

> give him liberty at least to mourn,
> That in a field, amidst his enemies,
> Doth see his soldiers slain, himself disarm'd,
> And knows no means of his recovery.

When their backs are turned, however, he again pours
contempt on them as 'slaves' and witless 'villains' who
mistake him for 'a senseless lump of clay'. He knows
himself to be 'fram'd of finer mould than common men',
with the future open to him to retrieve his fortunes.

[1] H. S. Bennett in his edition of the play, p. 58, note, quotes Job vii. 3:
'So am I made to possess months of vanity, and wearisome nights are
appointed to me.'

Herein he finds a helpmeet in his daughter Abigail. She appears to be an invention of the dramatist. As classical allusions are relatively fewer in *The Jew of Malta* than in Marlowe's other plays it is notable that when Barabas first mentions Abigail he speaks of her (I. i. 135–6) as

> one sole daughter whom I hold as dear
> As Agamemnon did his Iphigen.

Agamemnon's readiness to sacrifice his daughter for the welfare of the Greek host may have suggested to Marlowe the idea of a daughter whom Barabas would be willing to sacrifice on his own behalf. Agamemnon might well have used to Iphigeneia at Aulis the words of Barabas to Abigail (I. ii. 272–3):

> Be rul'd by me, for in extremity
> We ought to make bar of no policy.

Against the evil day that has befallen he had hidden under a plank in the upper chamber of his house

> Ten thousand portagues,[1] besides great pearls,
> Rich costly jewels and stones infinite.

As the Governor has now turned the house into a convent he instructs Abigail to gain admission to it by applying to become a novice under the pretence that she wishes to make atonement for sin and want of faith. He has told her that he will be at the door at dawn, but, sleepless with excitement, he arrives with a light before midnight at the moment when Abigail has risen to search for, and find, the hidden treasure. As it is before the appointed time each is uncertain of the other's presence (II. i. 41–4):

Bar. But stay: what star shines yonder in the east?
The loadstar of my life, if Abigail.
Who 's there?
Abig.   Who 's that?
Bar.   Peace, Abigail! 'tis I.
Abig. Then, father, here receive thy happiness.

---

[1] Portuguese gold coins of high value.

As the bags containing the treasure come tumbling
from above into his arms, Barabas breaks into tumultuous
ecstasy:

> O my girl,
> My gold, my fortune, my felicity;
>
> .   .   .   .   .
> O girl! O gold! O beauty! O my bliss!

And as, in the original stage-direction, he 'hugs his
bags' he chants over them a paean of loverlike rapture
(II. ii. 60–3):

> Now Phoebus, ope the eyelids of the day,
> And for the raven, wake the morning lark,
> That I may hover with her in the air;
> Singing o'er these, as she does o'er her young.

Up to this point the action of the play has been in the
main closely knit and convincing. But even with the
recovery of his hidden store it strains our belief to find
Barabas in II. iii become again as wealthy as before, with
a new house 'as great and fair as is the Governor's'.
Abigail, released from the convent, is again with him, and
is now to play a different part in his schemes. It has
already been noted as a feature of Marlowe's dramatic
technique that he provides every prominent woman in
his plays with rival lovers.[1] In *The Jew of Malta* Abigail
is first beloved of Don Mathias, who describes her to
Lodowick, the Governor's son, as (I. ii. 378–9)

> A fair young maid, scarce fourteen years of age,
> The sweetest flower in Cytherea's field.

Lodowick determines to see her beauty for himself, and
is hypocritically greeted by Barabas, who is yearning for
revenge on the Governor. Though restored to wealth,
the iron has entered into his soul, and there is a new note
of coarse-grained venom in his outburst against the
'swine-eating Christians' (II. iii. 23–9):

> I learned in Florence how to kiss my hand,
> Heave up my shoulders when they call me dog,
> And duck as low as any bare-foot friar;

[1] See above, pp. 54–5.

> Hoping to see them starve upon a stall,
> Or else be gather'd for in our synagogue,
> That, when the offering-basin comes to me,
> Even for charity I may spit into 't.

With equivocal phrases of welcome, and muttered threatening 'asides', Barabas guides Lodowick to his house, where he bids Abigail feign love for him and plight him her troth, though at the same time he assures Don Mathias that the girl shall be his and stirs him to angry jealousy. When Abigail protests that Mathias and not Lodowick is her lover Barabas applies, *mutatis mutandis*, the argument that Baldwin of Bohemia had used in Part II of *Tamburlaine*, ii. i, for breaking faith with the Turks[1] (ii. iii. 310–13):

> It 's no sin to deceive a Christian;
> For they themselves hold it a principle,
> Faith is not to be held with heretics:
> But all are heretics that are not Jews.

When the rival lovers, though friends from youth, have thus been manœuvred into enmity, Barabas brings his plot to a head by forging a challenge from Lodowick and sending it to Mathias. In the duel that follows (iii. ii) they are both slain, to the horrified amazement of their relatives, who, with incredible *naïveté*, do not scent the Jew's hand in the fatality. It is Abigail only who denounces his ruthless and tortuous 'policy' (iii. iii. 43–51):

> Admit thou lov'dst not Lodowick for his sire,
> Yet Don Mathias ne'er offended thee:
> But thou wert set upon extreme revenge,
> Because the Governor dispossess'd thee once,
> And couldst not venge it, but upon his son;
> Nor on his son, but by Mathias' means;
> Nor on Mathias, but by murdering me.
> But I perceive there is no love on earth,
> Pity in Jews, nor piety in Turks.

The feigned challenge had been carried to Mathias by Ithamore, a Turk captured in a sea-fight by Spaniards,

---

[1] See above, p. 89.

and bought by Barabas in the Maltese slave-market. With
the entry of Ithamore there is a subtle change in the atmosphere of the play. Hitherto the Jew, with his imaginative
idolatry of riches, his racial and religious fanaticism, his
passion for revenge, and his 'policy', has been a figure
of wellnigh tragic stature. Even his earliest instructions to Ithamore are in a typically Machiavellian strain
(II. iii. 170–3):

> First, be thou void of these affections,
> Compassion, love, vain hope, and heartless fear,
> Be mov'd at nothing, see thou pity none,
> But to thyself smile when the Christians moan.

In the Turk's retort, 'O brave, master! I worship your
nose for this', there is the first allusion in the dialogue to
the Jew's grotesque facial make-up. As if in response to
the consequent lowering of tone Barabas proceeds to give
a detailed, hair-raising recital of the villainies that he has
practised as murder, poisoner, and usurer, to which
Ithamore replies in similar vein. So crudely naïve is the
Jew's self-exposure that a modern critic, himself a
dramatist, takes the view that Barabas as here presented
is meant to be a 'prodigious caricature'.[1] I agree with
the latest editor of the play in rejecting such an interpretation, which 'seems to postulate considerable powers of
detachment from contemporary taste and practice on the
part of Marlowe'.[2] But henceforward the figure of the
Jew degenerates and he again is drawn in his derisory
aspect when Ithamore exclaims to Abigail (III. iii. 9–11):
'O mistress! I have the bravest, gravest, secret, subtle,
bottle-nosed knave to my master that ever gentleman had.'

After the revelation of her father's villainous plot
Abigail again enters the convent not now to serve him
but to escape from him. And the earlier iniquities of
Barabas are eclipsed when through a poisoned pot of
porridge, in the guise of a present on Saint Jacques' Even,
he does not only his daughter but all the nuns to death.

---

[1] T. S. Eliot in *The Sacred Wood*, p. 84.
[2] *The Jew of Malta*, ed. H. S. Bennett, p. 17.

Abigail, however, has had time, in III. vi, to disclose her father's practice against her lovers to Friar Bernardine, who without directly violating the seal of confession warns Barabas that he knows of his guilt (IV. i. 44–8). In terror he offers to be baptized and to bestow his wealth on some religious house. For a moment in describing his treasure his accents catch again something of the rich glow of the opening scene (IV. i. 66–70):

> Cellars of wine, and sollars full of wheat,
> Warehouses stuff'd with spices and with drugs,
> Whole chests of gold, in bullion, and in coin,
> Besides I know not how much weight in pearl,
> Orient and round have I within my house.

It is characteristic of Marlowe to make Friar Bernardine contend as to who shall convert Barabas with Jacomo, a friar of another order, who had admitted Abigail to the sisterhood. The Jew plays off one against the other, as he had done with the two lovers, and seeks to make himself safe by getting rid of both (IV. i. 120–4):

> Now I have such a plot for both their lives,
> As never Jew nor Christian knew the like:
> One turn'd my daughter, therefore he shall die;
> The other knows enough to have my life.

Barabas, however, makes a false boast when he claims that his plot is entirely novel. Its most remarkable features had been anticipated at least as early as 1476 in a story by Masuccio di Salerno.[1] Having strangled Bernardine, with Ithamore's aid, at midnight under his roof, he lets him be propped up outside, leaning on his staff, as if alive. Jacomo then arrives eager to convert the Jew and secure his gold for his order. Finding Bernardine blocking his way, he strikes him down with the staff, and confesses to Barabas and Ithamore who rush out that he

---

[1] On the relation of Masuccio's *novella* and the English jest-book story of 'Dane Hew, Munk of Leicester' to *The Jew of Malta* and Heywood's *The Captives* respectively, see Appendix to this chapter.

has killed him. When the friar begs to be let go, the Jew
primly refuses (IV. iii. 24 ff.):

> No, pardon me; the law must have his course
>
> .   .   .   .   .   .
>
> To-morrow is the Sessions, you shall to it.

And is there a reminiscence of Marlowe's own appearance at the Newgate Sessions in December 1589 in
Barabas' order?—

> Take in the staff too, for that must be shown:
> Law wills that each particular be known.

Less fortunate, however, than Marlowe in 1589 Jacomo
pays the penalty for his imagined crime, with Ithamore
accompanying him at the gallows-foot and ironically
describing his last moments (IV. iv. 25–9):

> 'I never knew a man take his death so patiently as this friar; he
> was ready to leap off ere the halter was about his neck; and when
> the hangman had put on his hempen tippet, he made such haste
> to his prayers, as if he had had another cure to serve.'

So the Turk soliloquizes on his way to the house of the
courtesan, Bellamira, whose attendant 'bully', Pilia-
Borza, has brought him a letter of invitation from her.
The bully must have had an extravagantly hirsute make-
up, for Ithamore speaks of him as 'a fellow . . . with a
muschatoes like a raven's wing', and Barabas amplifies this
(IV. v. 7–9):

> a shaggy, totter'd, staring slave,
> That when he speaks, draws out his grisly beard,
> And winds it twice or thrice about his ear.

Whether Marlowe or another wrote the scenes, mainly
in prose, in which Bellamira and Pilia-Borza appear, they
are inferior in quality to what has gone before. Yet they
cannot be dismissed as merely irrelevant. They serve to
reveal the crimes of Barabas who had fancied himself
safe when Abigail and Bernardine were put out of the
way. Ithamore, to obtain the favours of the courtesan,
blackmails his master into sending him three hundred,
and then five hundred, crowns. After a drinking-bout

with Bellamira and her bully he discloses the full tale of
his own and the Jew's villainies (iv. vi. 17–21). Barabas
counters his servant's treachery by visiting the two in the
disguise of a French musician, with a posy of poisoned
flowers in his hat whose smell will kill them all. But before
it completes its deadly work, Bellamira and Pilia-Borza
have time (v. i. 11 ff.) to tell the Governor of the Jew's
misdeeds, in which Ithamore confesses his share. When
soon afterwards the death of the poisoned trio is an-
nounced, the body of Barabas, who has simulated his own
death by drinking poppy and mandrake juice, is borne in
and thrown over the city walls to be a prey to birds and
beasts.

Thenceforward the play, though it does not recapture
the glow and colour of the early scenes, becomes once
more an arresting exposition of Machiavellian plot and
counterplot. When Selim Calymath returns, after the
month's respite stipulated in i. ii, to collect the Maltese
tribute to the Turks, the Governor, persuaded by the
Spanish Vice-Admiral, has closed the gates and broken
his pledge. Barabas is opportunely at hand, outside the
walls, to guide a company of Turks through a secret
passage into the town, and then to admit their main body.
For his services Calymath appoints him Governor, and
thus he has Fernese as much in his power as Tamburlaine had Bajazeth. But even in his dizzying elevation
Barabas does not forget the maxims of *The Prince*. He
knows that the Maltese hate him and that he must find
means to make his place secure (v. ii. 34–7):

> No, Barabas, this must be look'd into;
> And, since by wrong thou gott'st authority,
> Maintain it bravely by firm policy;
> At least, unprofitably lose it not.

Therefore instead of taking Fernese's life he promises
on receipt of great sums of money to deliver Malta from
the Turks, and by a stratagem to destroy Calymath and
his men. To the new Governor's invitation to a banquet

before he sets sail the Turkish prince answers with royal magnanimity (v. iii. 21-5):

> I fear me, messenger, to feast my train
> Within a town of war so lately pillag'd
> Will be too costly and too troublesome:
> Yet would I gladly visit Barabas,
> For well has Barabas deserv'd of us.

There is a flash of the Jew's old grandiloquence in the retort through his messenger's lips:

> thus saith the Governor
> That he hath in his store a pearl so big,
> So precious, and withal so orient,
> As, be it valu'd but indifferently,
> The price thereof will serve to entertain
> Selim and all his soldiers for a month.

The Turkish prince, with his bassoes, is to be feasted in the citadel, and his soldiers in the more spacious quarters of a monastery, which stands as an outhouse to the town. When Fernese returns with a hundred thousand pounds collected from the citizens Barabas discloses his policy (v. v. 24 ff.). The monastery has been mined underneath, with explosives ready to be discharged, and in the citadel Barabas himself has been very busy with a hammer helping to make

> a dainty gallery
> The floor whereof, this cable being cut,
> Doth fall asunder, so that it doth sink
> Into a deep pit past recovery.

At the sound of a warning-piece the monastery is to be fired and Fernese is to cut the cord that will send Calymath to his doom. But Fernese double-crosses Barabas. He has the charge sounded and cuts the cable at the moment when the Jew is on the gallery floor waiting to welcome the guests. Thereupon, as the original stage-direction has it, there is 'a cauldron discovered', the 'j cauderon for the Jewe' which is listed among the properties of the Lord Admiral's company in

March 1598.[1] After fruitless cries for help to the Christian onlookers Barabas, resuming at the last something of his first dignity, determines to die with 'resolution', and boasts of his misdeeds (v. v. 81–6):

> Know, Governor, 'twas I that slew thy son,
> I fram'd the challenge that did make them meet;
> Know, Calymath, I aim'd thy overthrow:
> And, had I but escap'd this stratagem,
> I would have brought confusion on you all,
> Damn'd Christians, dogs, and Turkish infidels!

But his intolerable pangs from the heated cauldron cut short his speech and force him to a last, long-drawn, agonized cry:

> Die, life! fly, soul! tongue, curse thy fill and die!

Yet the work of Barabas in an unforeseen sense lives after him. Though the Turkish prince has been saved his soldiers in the monastery have been massacred by the explosion, and Calymath is thus in effect a prisoner in the hands of the Maltese. It is, as Fernese caustically terms it,

> a Jew's courtesy,
> For he that did by treason work our fall,
> By treason hath deliver'd thee to us.

And his final warning to the Turkish prince anticipates in its ring the words of Faulconbridge at the close of Shakespeare's *King John*:

> for come all the world
> To rescue thee, so will we guard us now,
> As sooner shall they drink the ocean dry,
> Than conquer Malta, or endanger us.

Though spoken by a Maltese Governor they sound like England's defiant challenge from her sea-girt shores to all enemies in the immediate post-Armada years.

---

[1] *Henslowe Papers*, ed. W. W. Greg, p. 118. I think that Bakeless is mistaken in saying (op. cit., pp. 38–9) that Barabas 'was boiled to death in a cauldron exactly like the unfortunate Friar Stone of Canterbury'. His extracts from the city accounts, 1539–95, seem to show that the friar was hanged and that the kettle in which he was 'parboiled' was used for one of the grim sequels to a Tudor execution for treason.

APPENDIX TO CHAPTER IX

Thomas Heywood and 'The Jew of Malta'

THE view held by F. G. Fleay[1] that Heywood interpolated scenes into the 1633 text of *The Jew of Malta* has been set forth more precisely and exhaustively by Arthur Melville Clark in Appendix III to his volume *Thomas Heywood: Playwright and Miscellanist* (1931). One preliminary assumption of Fleay and Clark may be dismissed at the outset. The last line of the Epilogue spoken at Court,

> We only act and speak what others write

they interpret as implying that there was more than one author of the play. But the words are merely a general allusion to the relations between actors and dramatists.

But there is an undeniable similarity up to a point between Act IV, scenes ii and iii, and the underplot of Heywood's *Captives* (1624). It is clear that Heywood took this underplot from a *novella* by Masuccio di Salerno, printed in 1476. A friar, Maestro Diego, falls in love with a beautiful lady, wife of Messer Roderico, who entraps and strangles him, with the aid of his servant. The servant conveys the corpse on his back to the convent and there props it up. It is found by another friar, an enemy of Diego, who thinking him to be alive throws a stone at him, and when he falls, believes that he has murdered him. He then carries the body to the door of Roderico, who again helped by his servant sets the murdered Diego upon a stallion, and places a lance in his hands. Meanwhile the second friar, to escape the consequences of his supposed guilt, rides forth on a mare which is chased by the stallion till the friar in terror announces that he has killed Diego and is handed over to justice. Thereupon to save him Roderico confesses that he is the murderer and is pardoned by the king.

With changes of names and of other details not of the first importance Heywood skilfully introduces the whole of this complicated story into *The Captives*.[2]

In *The Jew of Malta* Barabas lures the friar Bernardine to his

---

[1] *Biographical Chronicle of the English Drama*, i. 298 and ii. 61–2 (1891). A. H. Bullen in his edition of *Marlowe's Works*, i. xl (1885), thought that 'another hand' filled in the details of Acts III–V. Tucker Brooke, op. cit. (p. 232), thinks it 'not improbable' that Heywood altered the play, but suspends judgement.

[2] See *The Captives*, ed. by A. C. Judson, pp. 17–24 (1921).

house and strangles him, with Ithamore's help, because through Abigail's confession he knows that her father had forged the challenge which caused the fatal duel between Lodowick and Mathias. At Ithamore's suggestion the body is propped upon a staff, and is encountered by Jacomo, a friar of a rival order, who strikes him down, and believing that he has killed him confesses his guilt to Barabas and Ithamore when they come forth. The points of contact with *The Captives* are obvious. But it is necessary to emphasize that there are also striking divergences. In *The Jew of Malta* there is no mention of the triangle of husband, wife, and amorous friar. The whole episode of the stallion and the mare is omitted. Instead of being saved through a confession by the real murderers, Jacomo pays the death penalty, and the opening part of Act iv. iii, where Ithamore is encountered by Pilia-Borza and describes the execution, contains what seem to me to be touches of Marlowe's 'highbrow' humour (e.g. ll. 14–15 'driven to a nonplus'; l. 21 *Hodie tibi, cras mihi*; l. 22 'the exercise' used for 'the execution'). On the other hand, as Margarete Thimme has shown in an exhaustive analysis,[1] neither here nor elsewhere in the play is there any evidence of Heywood's characteristic vocabulary and syntax.

An entry in Sir Henry Herbert's office-book shows that *The Captives* was licensed as a new play on 3 September 1624. In the same year Heywood included in his encyclopaedic Γυναικεῖον or *Nine Books of Various History Concerning Women*, under the title *The Faire Ladie of Norwich*, a version of the underplot of *The Captives* much compressed yet containing the chief episodes. Is it likely that Heywood, having thus twice made use of the whole story, would nine years afterwards drag its central incident into *The Jew of Malta*?

On the other hand Marlowe, if he had not read Masuccio's *novella* nor its French translation by Antoine de Saint-Denis in *Les Comptes du Monde Adventureux* (1555), could have drawn upon *A Mery Iest of Dane Hew, Munk of Leicester* (printed before 1584),[2] though there the two friars are replaced by a monk and an abbot. The central episode fitted into the scheme of Barabas for getting rid of both the friars, though for this it was necessary that Jacomo, unlike the abbot, should pay the death penalty. It is far more characteristic of Marlowe than of Heywood to show the two men

---

[1] *Marlowes 'Jew of Malta': Stil- und Echtheitsfragen* (1921).
[2] A summary of the story in *Dane Hew* is given by Judson, op. cit., pp. 18–19.

of religion meeting their fate while trying to steal a march on each other for the acquisition of the Jew's wealth.

Clark would also attribute to Heywood the scenes, beginning with Act III. i, introducing the courtesan Bellamira and her 'bully' Pilia-Borza, in whom he finds duplicates of Mistress Mary and Brabo in *How a Man may Choose a Good Wife from a Bad*. It is true that the scenes, IV. iv–vi, in which Bellamira makes love to Ithamore and through him and Pilia-Borzia blackmails Barabas till the Jew in the disguise of a musician kills the trio with the scent of poisoned flowers, are spun out and somewhat loosely connected with the main plot. The rhymed lines, IV. iv. 95–105, in which Ithamore declares to Bellamira that they 'will sail from hence to Greece, to lovely Greece', sound like a skit upon Marlowe's classical references and upon the refrain of his poem *The Passionate Shepherd*.[1] Yet in the earlier part of the scene there are, as I think, traces of Marlowe, as quoted above. Moreover, Barabas's use of poisoned flowers (IV. vi. 35–43) is akin to the use of scented gloves in *The Massacre at Paris* for poisoning the Queen Mother of Navarre. And in *Edward II* Lightborn boasts:

> I learned in Naples how to poison flowers.

The Jew has a motive for this crime that links it with the main action of the play. He is afraid that Ithamore will reveal his misdeeds to his new confederates (IV. v. 63–5):

> Well, I must seek a means to rid 'em all,
> And presently[2]; for in his villainy
> He will tell all he knows, and I shall die for 't.

His fears are well founded, for in his cups Ithamore does tell all (IV. vi. 14–24), and as soon as they feel the poison working on them Bellamira and Pilia-Borza disclose the whole black record to the Governor (V. i. 10–15):

> *Bell.* I bring thee news by whom thy son was slain:
>   Mathias did it not; it was the Jew—
> *Pilia.* Who, besides the slaughter of these gentlemen,
>   Poison'd his own daughter and the nuns,
>   Strangled a friar, and I know not what
>   Mischief beside.

Some way of bringing the crimes of the Jew to light was necessary to the plot of the play. It seems therefore probable that the Bellamira scenes are originally Marlowe's work, though it may have been touched up for revivals of *The Jew of Malta* by Heywood or another.

---

[1] See below, pp. 220–2.   [2] immediately.

X

THE MASSACRE AT PARIS

THE only edition of *The Massacre at Paris*, an octavo printed by Edward Allde for Edward White, has the name of Christopher Marlowe on the title-page. The octavo is undated and is not entered in the Stationers' Register, probably because, as the corrupt text indicates, it was a stolen and surreptitious copy. If the so-called 'Collier leaf' is accepted as authentic, and as reproducing the original text of scene xvi, ll. 1–16, in the octavo, light is thrown on the relation of the octavo version, of some 1,250 lines, to Marlowe's manuscript.[1]

The Massacre at Paris must have been written after the death of Henry III of France on 2 August 1589, and probably after that of Pope Sixtus V on 17 August 1590, as his 'bones' are spoken of in scene xxi, l. 100. On the other hand, it has to be dated before 26 January 1592/3, when Henslowe entered in his *Diary*:

R[eceived] at the tragedey of the gvyes 30[2] . . . iij^{li} xiiij^s.

The Guise, as with characteristic variants of spelling he frequently calls the play, was marked by him on this occasion as a new piece, and had probably been written not long before, in the latter part of 1592. It was one of a group of plays acted by Lord Strange's men at the 'Rose' during January–February 1592/3, and the sum of £3 14s. taken at the performance was the highest of the season. On 28 January the Privy Council forbade acting of plays in London on account of the plague, and there is no record of *The Massacre* being performed again till 19 June 1594, when it was staged by the Admiral's men at the 'Rose', and was given ten times between that

---

[1] See Appendix to this chapter.

[2] A mistake for 26 Jan. See Greg's edition of the *Diary*, i. 15, ii. 157, and the Malone Society reprint of *The Massacre at Paris*, p. vi.

date and 25 September.[1] As the title-page of the octavo
states that it was 'plaide by the right honourable the Lord
high *Admirall* his Seruants', the edition seems to have been
published after the 1594 performances and before 1596,
when his company became known as the Earl of Notting-
ham's men.[2]

But there is one, at first sight, very strong argument for
dating the octavo not earlier than 1600 or 1601. In scene
xviii, l. 66, Guise declares, 'Yet Caesar shall go forth', in
words identical with Shakespeare's *Julius Caesar*, ii. ii. 28.
It has been generally assumed that the octavo line is an
echo from Shakespeare's play, acted probably about 1600.
But this conclusion is not necessary when we take into
account the pervasive classical influence on Marlowe's work.
Recalling his Lucan the dramatist may well have seen in
the attempt of the Guise to overthrow the constitutional
government in France and in his death by assassination a
close counterpart to Caesar's ambitions and kindred fate.
From the illustrations given below it may be legitimately
contended that Guise's words were in Marlowe's original
text and not foisted in later from Shakespeare's play.

After arriving at this conclusion I found that it has
been reached independently and from a different angle by
John Bakeless, who writes:

'A more careful study of the pamphlet literature of the French
wars of religion . . . shows that the Catholic party habitually
referred to their champion, the Duke of Guise, as "Caesar", and
one of their partisans even drew up a laborious comparison
between the two heroes which occupies four printed pages.
Plainly then Marlowe wrote the line first.'[3]

Two other close parallels between *The Massacre*, scene
xv, ll. 1–2, and scene xx, 4–5, and passages in *The True
Tragedy* and *3 Henry VI* raise the question of priority,
but do not bear directly on the date of the octavo, and

---

[1] *Henslowe's Diary*, ed. Greg, i. 17–19.
[2] For later performances in Elizabeth's reign, see below, pp. 167–8.
[3] Op. cit., p. 299.

may be considered together with the similar and more extensive series of parallels between *Edward II* and the Shakespearian plays.[1]

Whatever views may be taken on these disputable points, my own belief, as will be seen, is that the octavo of *The Massacre*, in spite of its textual corruption, preserves more of the play as it came from Marlowe's hand, and has a more important place in the canon of his works, than his editors have been willing to allow. Any fruitful discussion of these questions must start, in my opinion, from the relation of the play in its present form to its source. That source for the first ten scenes is unquestionably Book X of *Commentaries of the Civill Warres in Fraunce* (1576), by Jean de Serres, translated by T. Timme. Marlowe's obligation to de Serres was first pointed out by A. H. Bullen,[2] who quoted some striking parallels between the *Commentaries* and the text of *The Massacre*. To these one very remarkable instance has been added by H. S. Bennett,[3] though his general conclusion is that 'nowhere do we get the feeling that' Marlowe 'was working with his source before him'. My own view is that the evidence proves that he *was* working in this way; that nothing of importance in his source that was material to his purpose seems to be omitted in the octavo version; and that this version is shown, by comparison with Book X of *The Commentaries*, to preserve with general, if not purely textual, accuracy the details of successive episodes in the action. Full confirmation of these points could be given only in a complete editorial apparatus, but the illustrations brought forward below indicate that Marlowe was as faithful in the first half of *The Massacre* to de Serres, in Timme's translation, as he was in the *Tamburlaine* plays

---

[1] See Appendix to Chapter XI.

[2] *Works of Marlowe* (1885) ii, 243, 253. Book X, however, does not belong, as Bullen seems to have thought, to *Three Partes of Commentaries*, published in Timme's translation in 1574, but to *The Fourth Parte* of which Timme's version followed in 1576.

[3] See below, p. 158 n.

to Fortescue and Ortelius, in *Edward II* to Holinshed, and in *Doctor Faustus* to 'P. F.'[1] I can see nothing to support the view that 'Marlowe's friends probably helped to provide material for the play . . . he probably gained still more from the Huguenot refugees who had streamed to England'.[2]

For the scenes subsequent to the accession of Henry III to the French throne no similar single source has been traced, though Marlowe was probably acquainted with the pamphlet controversy concerning the papal responsibility for the murder of King Henry. In any case there does not seem sufficient material for the view tentatively advanced by Tucker Brooke that certain passages in the play 'suggest first-hand acquaintance with political and religious conditions in France'.[3]

Though he was dealing with French historical events and personages, and using French sources, it is important to stress the fact that Marlowe in this play drew his inspiration mainly from Italy, both in its classical and its Renaissance periods. The central figure, the Duke of Guise, adopts more than once the very role of Julius Caesar. In the significant monologue in which he reveals his ambition to win the crown of France he quotes (ii. 98–9) one of the Roman dictator's maxims:

> As Caesar to his soldiers, so say I,—
> Those that hate me will I learn to loathe.

King Henry, in a later scene, proves that he realizes what is in the Duke's mind when he cries (xvi. 55–7):

> Guise, wear our crown, and be thou King of France,
> And, as dictator, make or war or peace,
> Whilst I cry *placet*, like a senator!

In a similarly classical vein the Guise proclaims (xviii. 51–3):

---

[1] See below, pp. 203–4, 207 ff.   [2] Bakeless, op. cit., pp. 252–3.
[3] *Life of Marlowe*, p. 34 n.

As ancient Romans o'er their captive lords,
So will I triumph o'er this wanton King;
And he shall follow my proud chariot's wheels.

Most significant of all is his imperious dismissal of the
warning that if he enters the next room he will be murdered; 'therefore, good my lord, go not forth' (65–6):

Yet Caesar shall go forth.[1]

And with his last breath he flourishes the proud parallel
between himself and the great *imperator*:

Thus Caesar did go forth, and thus he died.

In these classical analogies the Guise recalls some of
Tamburlaine's speeches, and his ambition has the same
boundless scope as the Scythian's (ii. 43–7):

Set me to scale the high Pyramides,
And thereon set the diadem of France;
I'll either rend it with my nails to naught,
Or mount the top with my aspiring wings,
Although my downfall be the deepest hell.

There is the very ring of Tamburlaine's voice in the
words (ii. 100–2):

Give me a look that, when I bend the brows,
Pale death may walk in furrows of my face;
A hand that with a grasp may grip the world.

If the Guise is thus linked with Caesar-Tamburlaine,
he is also akin to Barabas. The opening lines of the
Prologue to *The Jew of Malta* testify that the Duke was to
Marlowe a reincarnation on this side of the Alps of Machiavelli as conceived by most Englishmen. The combination
of 'resolution' and craft distinctive of the Florentine's
'policy', which had been practised by Barabas, reappears
in the Guise. He can play alternately both active and
passive parts to attain his end—the crown (ii. 48–9):

For this I wake, when others think I sleep,
For this I wait, that scorns attendance else.

---

[1] On the relation between this line and the same words in Shakespeare's
Julius Caesar, ii. ii. 28, see above, p. 152.

He has the same contempt as the Jew for his intellectual and social inferiors, 'peasants', as he repeatedly calls them. He alone is competent to deal with

> Matters of import aimèd at by many,
> Yet understood by none.

Machiavelli's slogan in the Prologue to *The Jew* 'I count Religion but a childish toy' is re-echoed by the Guise (ii. 66–9):

> Religion! *O Diabole!*
> Fie, I am asham'd, however that I seem,
> To think a word of such a simple sound,
> Of so great matter should be made the ground!

Thus the Duke, as presented by Marlowe, though the character-drawing is not entirely consistent in this respect, looks on religion merely as an instrument of policy. The Pope has bestowed on him a largesse and a pension, the Spanish Catholics send him Indian gold, Paris maintains five hundred colleges on behalf of the faith. But all these are to be turned to serve his personal ambitions (ii. 88–91):

> Then, Guise,
> Since thou hast all the cards within thy hands,
> To shuffle or cut, take this as surest thing,
> That, right or wrong, thou deal thyself a king.

To this end the Catholics are to be hounded on to murder the Huguenots and, in their turn, the royalist leaders are to be sacrificed. As Turks and Christians are counters in the game to Barabas, so are the contending factions in France to the Duke.

Thus the marriage of King Charles IX's sister Margaret to Henry of Navarre, with which the play opens, is an offence to him not only because Henry is a prominent Huguenot but because the houses of Valois and Bourbon are thereby politically united. De Serres tells how, as a compromise between the opposed religious views of the two houses, the marriage was celebrated 'in the porch of the great church of Paris', and that after the ceremony the bride was led into the church to hear mass, while the bridegroom, with the Prince of Condé and the Admiral, 'walked without the churche dore, wayting for the Brides return'. This account is faithfully followed by Marlowe, and is skilfully used to give the Huguenot leaders when left alone the opportunity of inveighing against the designs of 'th' aspiring Guise'.

De Serres is similarly followed, though with less skill (at any rate in the octavo text), in the opening part of scene ii. The Guise orders an apothecary to present perfumed gloves, whose smell is death, to the Queen Mother of Navarre,

> For she is that huge blemish in our eye,
> That makes these upstart heresies in France.

The Duke's action becomes dramatically more plausible when we know that Marlowe learned from de Serres that the Queen of Navarre had played a leading part in bringing about the marriage of her son and Margaret. And the details of the outrage are taken from the French chronicler. The Queen 'died in the Court at Paris of a sodane sicknesse . . . she was poysoned with a venomed smell of a payre of perfumed gloues dressed by the Kings Apothecarie'. This was not found out at first, but afterwards they opened her head and found traces of the poison in her brain. This is echoed in her dying cry (iii. 19–20):

> the fatal poison
> Works within my head: my brain-pan breaks.

The other outrage that abruptly follows in the same scene, the shooting of the Admiral through the arm by a soldier from an upper window, also follows closely the account by de Serres.

These crimes are the prelude to the general massacre of the Huguenots in which the Guise has as his chief confederates the Queen Mother, Catherine de Medici, and the heir to the throne, the Duke of Anjou. Halfhearted opposition comes from King Charles, another of the weak sovereigns who are foils to Marlowe's men of

destiny. He pleads against the proposed massacre to
Catherine (iv. 5–12):

> Madam, it will be noted through the world
> An action bloody and tyrannical;
> Chiefly, since under safety of our word
> They justly challenge their protection:
> Besides, my heart relents that noble men,
> Only corrupted in religion,
> Ladies of honour, knights and gentlemen,
> Should, for their conscience taste such ruthless ends.

But he weakly lets himself be overruled, and he pays
a visit to the Admiral, 'discovered in bed', to give him
a hypocritical assurance that he will be guarded from
further harm. It has only recently been proved how
closely Marlowe follows de Serres at this point. The King
gives orders (iv. 64–6):

> Cossin,[1] take twenty of our strongest guard,
> And, under your direction, see they keep
> All treacherous violence from our noble friend.

This is based on the chronicler's statement: 'Therewith the Duke of *Aniou* the Kings brother commanded
Cossin Captaine of the Kings guarde to place a certaine
band of souldiers to warde the Admiralles gate.' And the
details of the Admiral's murder in scene v are also taken
from de Serres, and skilfully adapted to stage conditions.
The Admiral is again 'discovered in bed', but this time
on the upper stage, for when he is killed, the Duke cries,
'Then throw him down'. When this is done, Anjou bids
Guise

> view him well,
> It may be it is some other, and he escap'd.

And the Duke replies, 'Cousin, 'tis he; I know him by his
look.' All this is based directly upon the chronicle, where

---

[1] This was printed 'Cosin' in the octavo, in roman type, not in the
italic used for names. The printer, like a long series of editors, took it to
mean 'Cousin'. It was H. S. Bennett who first pointed out, in his edition
of the play, p. 196 n., that it stands for 'Cossin', the captain of the guard,
here and in v. 20.

the Admiral's body is thrown out of the window and 'owing to the blood on the face, they could not well discerne him. The Duke kneeling wiped away the blood, and sayd "now I know him, it is he".'[1]

Thereupon an ordinance is shot off and a bell tolled as the signal for the beginning of the general massacre. Marlowe gets over the difficulty of representing this on the stage by giving some vivid 'snapshots', displaying incidentally the acid humour which has been an insufficiently recognized element in his genius. When the Protestant Loreine proclaims himself 'a preacher of the word of God', the Guise with a mockery of Puritan phraseology retorts, as he stabs him (v. 69), 'Dearly beloved brother—thus 'tis written', and Anjou adds, 'Stay, my lord, let me begin the psalm'. When another Huguenot, Seroune, faced with death, cries, 'O Christ, my Saviour', his murderer throws the prayer back in his teeth (v. 80):

> Christ, villain !
> Why, darest thou presume to call on Christ,
> Without the intercession of some saint?
> *Sanctus Jacobus*, he's my saint; pray to him.

The cries of hunted victims shatter the silence of what should be a sanctuary of learning, the study of the King's Professor of Logic, Petrus Ramus, 'sitting at his book'. Here again de Serres furnished Marlowe with a starting-point when he related that among those murdered were 'many singularly learned professors and teachers of good artes and among the rest *Petrus Ramus*, that renowned man throughout the worlde'. This was enough to recall to the dramatist echoes of the academic controversies of his Cambridge days. Ramus in his lectures in the Uni-

---

[1] There are two points in Marlowe's representation of the Admiral's death which suggest that he may also have used *The lyfe of . . . Jasper Colignie* by de Serres, translated by A. Golding (1576). The mention there of 'certein Swissers of the Duke of Anjous guard' may account for Anjou's order (v. 17), 'Switzers, keep you the streets'; and the Admiral's last words, 'I commende my sowle to Gods mercy', seem to be echoed in (v. 30), 'O God, forgive my sins!'

versity of Paris had created a sensation by attacks upon
the Aristotelian system of logic. Translations of his
Dialectica had appeared in England in 1574 and 1581,
and two editions of the original Latin in 1576 and 1584,
the latter of which was published at Cambridge, where
the University was for long divided between the partisans
of the rival systems.[1] The controversy is now transferred
by Marlowe from the classroom to the death-chamber,
and no discourse by Tamburlaine on the battle-field upon
poetry or cosmology is more incongruous than Guise's
apologia for Aristotelian logic before bidding Anjou stab
Ramus to death (vi. 26–7):

> Was it not thou that scoff'dst the *Organon*,
> And said it was a heap of vanities?

Scoffingly quoting a 'quiddity' of Ramus about the
argumentum inartificiale he gives it a practical refutation
(vi. 35–7):

> To contradict which, I say, Ramus shall die:
> How answer you that? your *nego argumentum*
> Cannot serve, sirrah.—Kill him.

Ramus pleads for a pause in which to purge himself:

> I knew the *Organon* to be confus'd,
> And I reduc'd it into better form;
> And this for Aristotle will I say,
> That he that despiseth him can ne'er
> Be good in logic or philosophy.

But the recantation is of no avail. The 'collier's son'
is sent to his doom. And he is speedily followed by two
other men of learning, the 'schoolmasters' of Navarre and
Condé who here, as in de Serres, are killed while their
patrons' lives are saved. Then the Guise silences the bell
that rings 'to the devil's mattins', and the fury is stayed
in Paris itself, though the heretics who hold their 'syna-
gogue' in the neighbouring woods are to be hunted out and
killed, and those in the provinces are to be put to the sword.
From this point the play develops on lines that are

[1] For the influence of Ramus on Cambridge studies see J. B. Mullinger's
The University of Cambridge, ii. 404–13.

independent, so far as has been traced, of any particular source. Catherine, the Queen Mother, determines to get rid of her faint-hearted son Charles, who has begun to lament the Guise's 'late night's work' in Paris, and whom she suspects of plotting with his brother-in-law Navarre (viii. 40–5):

> As I do live, so surely shall he die,
> And Henry then shall wear the diadem;
> And if he grudge or cross his mother's will,
> I'll disinherit him and all the rest;
> For I'll rule France, but they shall wear the crown,
> And if they storm, I then may pull them down.

In scene x Charles is stricken with 'a sudden pang, the messenger of death', which, in spite of Catherine's hypocritical lamentations, he suspects may be the work of his 'dearest friends'. Henry III succeeds, recalled to France from the elective throne of Poland. It is to be noted that Marlowe discriminates the characters of the two brothers. Charles had been weak but high-principled : Henry is dissolute and pleasure-loving. In almost his first words after his accession he asks (xi. 16–17):

> What says our minions? think they Henry's heart
> Will not both harbour love and majesty?[1]

His thoughts run at once to revelry (39–42):

> Our solemn rites of coronation done,
> What now remains but for a while to feast,
> And spend some days in barriers, tourney, tilt,
> And like disports, such as do fit the court?[2]

In the frivolous preoccupations of the new king his mother sees the opportunity of establishing her own authority with the aid of an army raised by the Guise, nominally against the Huguenots but really to overawe

---

[1] Bennett points out in his edition of the play, p. 217 n., that this is a reminiscence of Ovid, *Met.* ii. 846.

[2] Marlowe here transfers to Henry a love of 'disports' which de Serres had attributed to Charles: 'So great was the preparation of playes, so greate was the magnificence of banquets and shewes, and the King so earnestly bent to those matters.'

the throne. Again she proclaims her ruthless ambition
(xi. 63–6):

> if he do deny what I do say,
> I'll despatch him with his brother presently,
> And then shall Monsieur wear the diadem.
> Tush, all shall die unless I have my will.

In the next scene a personal factor in the Guise's
hostility to Henry and his retinue is abruptly introduced.
The Duchess is discovered by her husband writing a letter
of assignation to one of the King's minions, Mugeroun,
who in scene xvi pays with his life for his amorous intrigue.
As has been shown, it is an almost constant factor of
Marlowe's technique to attach rival lovers to the women
in his plays.[1] But even if the episode is imperfectly rendered in the octavo text,[2] the Duke's enmity to the King
falls to a lower plane when motived by revenge for a minion's
wrongdoing rather than by ambition for a throne.

By Navarre the Guise is seen in another aspect, as one
of a trio with the Pope and the King of Spain (xiii. 5 ff.):

> Who set themselves to tread us underfoot,
> And rend our true religion from this land
>
> .   .   .   .
>
> Spain is the council-chamber of the Pope,
> Spain is the place where he makes peace and war;
> And Guise for Spain hath now incens'd the king
> To send his power to meet us in the field.

To audiences in the post-Armada years such lines must
have had more than a merely dramatic significance, as
also the dialogue between Navarre and Bartus after the
Huguenot victory over the royalist army led by Joyeux,
closing with Navarre's clarion-call (xv. 12–17):

> But God we know will always put them down
> That lift themselves against the perfect truth:
> Which I'll maintain so long as life doth last.
> And with the Queen of England join my force
> To beat the papal monarch from our lands,
> And keep those relics from our countries' coasts.

[1] See above, pp. 54–5 and 140.   [2] See Appendix to this chapter.

Meanwhile the rift between the French court and the faction of the Guise widens. The Duke proclaims that he must stand on his guard against his enemies, and therefore 'being able, I'll keep an host in pay'. Epernoun, another of Henry's minions, retorts tauntingly (xvi. 37–40):

> Thou able to maintain an host in pay,
> Thou livest by foreign exhibition! [1]
> The Pope and King of Spain are thy good friends;
> Else all France knows how poor a duke thou art.

When the King echoes the taunt, the Duke tries to disarm suspicion by asserting that he is moved by religious zeal and a desire for Henry's safety, but that he will speedily break up his camp. Warned again by Epernoun Henry determines to forestall him, 'as I live, so sure the Guise shall die'. He double-crosses him much as Ferneze does Barabas in *The Jew of Malta*. The words with which the King has him admitted to the audience-chamber from which he is not to depart alive recall the fate of the Jew (xviii. 31–2):

> Come, Guise, and see thy traitorous guile outreach'd,
> And perish in the pit thou mad'st for me.

To the last he acts in character. He disdains the warning of the doom that awaits him (68–70):

> Let mean consaits and baser men fear death:
> Tut, they are peasants; I am Duke of Guise;
> And princes with their looks engender fear.

When wounded to death he haughtily disdains the murderer's admonition 'to pray to God, and ask forgiveness of the King'. It is not pardon, divine or human, that he craves:

> Trouble me not; I ne'er offended Him,
> Nor will I ask forgiveness of the King.

---

[1] maintenance.

Like Barabas in his extremity he dies defiant and execrating his enemies (82–7):

> Ah, Sixtus, be reveng'd upon the King!
> Philip and Parma, I am slain for you!
> Pope, excommunicate, Philip, depose
> The wicked branch of curs'd Valois his line!
> *Vive la messe!* perish, Huguenots!
> Thus Caesar did go forth, and thus he died.

Over the body of Guise the King speaks words addressed more to the Londoners in the audience than to the French courtiers on the stage (100–6):

> This is the traitor that hath spent my gold
> In making foreign wars and civil broils.
> Did he not draw a sort of English priests
> From Douay to the Seminary at Rheims,
> To hatch forth treason 'gainst their natural queen?[1]
> Did he not cause the King of Spain's huge fleet
> To threaten England and to menace me?

But there was a sadistic as well as a patriotic strain in the Elizabethan groundlings that was now gratified by seeing the Duke's high-spirited boy brought in to gaze on his murdered father, and hurried to prison after a childish effort at revenge. There is more justification, dramatic and historical, for Henry's order to kill the Guise's brothers, the Cardinal and Dumaine. In his shrewdly caustic phrase (132–3):

> These two will make one entire Duke of Guise,
> Especially with our old mother's help.

But for his old mother, entering as he speaks, the Guise's death means the end of all things. To Henry's plea that he killed the Duke because 'I would be king' she turns a deaf ear, denouncing him as a changeling, not her son. And when the King leaves her to 'grieve

---

[1] Is this an echo of the accusation against Marlowe himself in 1587 from which he was defended by the Privy Council?

her heart out', she shows more unmistakably than before
that it is for her faith that she has sought power
(155–60):

> To whom shall I bewray my secrets now
> Or who will help to build religion?
> The Protestants will glory and insult;
> Wicked Navarre will get the crown of France;
> The Popedom cannot stand; all goes to wrack
> And all for thee, my Guise!

Then follows an unforeseen turn of the wheel. Dumaine has escaped his brothers' fate and becomes the
confidant of a Jacobin friar bent on the 'meritorious' deed
of killing a king who had been lukewarm in the Papal
cause. Henry with his ally Navarre is besieging Paris, still
faithful to the house of Guise. Entering his camp the
Friar hands him a letter, and as he reads it stabs him with
a knife, 'and then the king gets the knife and kills him'.
Again Henry addresses the audience rather than those
on the stage (xxi. 47–52):

> all rebels under heaven
> Shall take example by his punishment,
> How they bear arms against their sovereign.
> Go call the English agent hither straight:
> I'll send my sister England news of this,
> And give her warning of her treacherous foes.

To the agent he pours forth, without historical warrant,
a violent diatribe against 'accursed Rome', and vows
eternal love to Navarre,

> And to the Queen of England specially,
> Whom God hath bless'd for hating papistry.

His declamation is cut short by the surgeon's announcement that his wound is fatal from a poisoned knife—a re-
finement added by Marlowe, recalling the poisoned porridge
and flowers in *The Jew of Malta*. Henry has only time
to announce to his courtiers that Navarre is 'your lawful

king, and my next heir', and to urge them to avenge his death. Navarre accepts the legacy, vowing that

> Rome, and all those popish prelates there,
> Shall curse the time that e'er Navarre was king,
> And rul'd in France by Henry's fatal death.

Whenever these words were written they were to be given a surprisingly ironic significance in July 1593, two months after Marlowe's death, by Navarre's conversion to Roman Catholicism.

In the above interpretation of *The Massacre at Paris* I have attempted to suggest that the play is of greater merit, and has more significance in the Marlovian canon, than has hitherto been recognized. For what seems to me to be its undervaluation there are three chief reasons. The first and most important is the corrupt octavo text. But when all its imperfections have been taken into account, much of the action is closely knit and the dialogue often has a keen edge. There are none of the dazzling purple passages of *Tamburlaine* and *Doctor Faustus*, but there is scarcely a scene which has not in some of its lines or phrases the distinctive Marlovian note.

Secondly, even the editors who have known that Marlowe drew chiefly from de Serres have not, as I think, sufficiently considered the play in that special relation, and in the light of what we now realize to have been Marlowe's fidelity to his sources. A play called *The Massacre at Paris* may be excused for containing an unduly rapid succession of blood-curdling incidents, and it has been shown above that in these the dramatist is closely following his original, and often skilfully adapting his material to the resources of the contemporary stage.

Thirdly, in the scene of the murder of the Guise it has been generally assumed that the Duke's identification of himself with Caesar was inserted at a revival of *The Massacre* subsequent to the performance of Shakespeare's *Julius Caesar*, and that the words were borrowed from that play. But in view of Marlowe's delight in classical allusions and parallels, and the frequency of his references to Caesar in particular, it is probable that the debt to Shakespeare is imaginary and that the octavo here represents Marlowe's own text.

Consistent character-drawing is never to be expected from Marlowe, and it is not found in any of the too slightly sketched figures in *The Massacre*. Yet, as has been seen, the two French kings are differentiated in their failings. The dominant and aspiring personalities of the Guise and the Queen Mother are also discriminated and, though the drawing wavers, the Duke's ambition is pictured as primarily for himself alone and Catherine's as in the interests of her faith. Both are set off by the selflessly righteous aims of Navarre. His outspoken Protestant sentiments combined with Henry III's sympathetic references to Elizabeth and England doubtless found a ready response in the theatre and account for the play's continued popularity throughout the Queen's reign.

After its first production by Henslowe at the 'Rose' in January 1593 it was revived at the same theatre on 19 June 1594, and had ten performances between that date and 25 September.[1] A later revival took place in or soon after November 1598 when Henslowe on the 19th lent William Borne or Birde, who acted the Guise, twelve shillings that he might 'Jmbrader his hatte',[2] and on the 27th a further sum of twenty shillings that he might 'bye a payer of sylke stockens' in which to perform the part.[3] It was evidently an expensive play to dress. When it was again revived in November 1601, three pounds were paid for 'stamell cllath'[4] for a cloak, and other sums to the 'littell taylor Radford' for further materials and for work upon suits for the play. After final payment of his bill on 26 November, £7. 14*s*. 6*d*. had been laid out on costumes.[5]

---

[1] See above, pp. 151–2.   [2] *Henslowe's Diary*, ed. Greg i. 78.

[3] Ibid. i. 72. Below this entry, without a date, appears another loan to Borne for the same amount 'to bye his stockens for the gwisse'. Is this in addition or a duplicate?

[4] a red woollen fabric.   [5] For full details see ibid. i. 149–51.

About seven weeks afterwards, on 18 January 1602, the Admiral's men bought the play, with two others, from Edward Alleyn for six pounds.[1] But so far as *The Massacre at Paris* was concerned, this was probably not a profitable investment. In the following July the British Ambassador in Paris, Sir Ralph Winwood, objected to the performance of a play introducing Queen Elizabeth. The retort was made 'that the Death of the Duke of Guise hath been plaied at London', and 'that the Massacre of St. Bartholomew hath been publickly acted, and this King[2] represented upon the Stage'.[3] The English Government's anxiety not to ruffle French susceptibilities may well account for the apparent disappearance of *The Massacre at Paris* henceforward from the stage.

APPENDIX TO CHAPTER X

The Collier Leaf of 'The Massacre at Paris'

J. P. COLLIER in his Introduction to *The Jew of Malta* in volume viii of his edition of Dodsley's *Old Plays* (1825) stated that 'a curious manuscript fragment of one quarto leaf' of *The Massacre at Paris* was in the hands of Rodd, a London bookseller. He printed a transcript of it, showing that it was an expanded form of the very short scene in which a soldier, hired by Guise, kills Mugeroun. When Collier published his *History of English Dramatic Poetry* (1831) he printed a corrected transcript of the leaf, with a note showing that it was now in his possession. From his hands it passed successively into those of J. O. Halliwell-Phillipps, M. J. Perry, and H. C. Folger, and is now preserved in the Folger Shakespeare Library in Washington.

While it was in Folger's hands in New York it was inaccessible and could not be seen by Tucker Brooke for his edition of Marlowe's Works (1910), by W. W. Greg for the Malone reprint of *The Massacre* (1928), or by H. S. Bennett for his edition of the

---

[1] Ibid. i. 153.
[2] The reigning king of France, Henry IV, the Navarre of *The Massacre*.
[3] Quoted, in more detail, by J. Bakeless, op. cit., p. 251, from E. Sawyer, *Memorials of Affairs of State* (1725), i. 425.

play (1931). Their views upon its authenticity had therefore to be tentative. But it has now been examined by J. Quincy Adams, its custodian in the Folger Shakespeare Library, who reproduced it in facsimile with a transcript in modernized spelling and punctuation in *The Library*, March 1934.[1] I print his transcript here for comparison with the octavo version which follows, also with modernized spelling and punctuation, in Bennett's edition of the play, but in both cases with the omission of such stage-directions as they have added.

[MS. VERSION]

Enter a Soldier with a musket.

Soldier. Now, sir, to you that dares make a Duke a cuckold, and use a counterfeit key to his privy-chamber: though you take out none but your own treasure, yet you put in that displeases him, and fill up his room that he should occupy. Herein, sir, you forestall the market, and set up your standing where you should not. But you will say you leave him room enough besides. That's no answer; he's to have the choice of his own free land. If it be not too free—there's the question! Now, sir, where he is your landlord, you take upon you to be his, and will needs enter by default. What though you were once in possession, yet coming upon you once unawares he frayed you out again! Therefore your entry is mere intrusion. This is against the law, sir; and though I come not to keep possession (as I would I might!) yet I come to keep you out, sir. You are welcome, sir; have at you.

Enter minion. He kills him.

Minion. Traiterous Guise! Ah, thou hast murdered me.

Enter Guise.

Guise.   Hold thee, tall soldier. Take thee this and fly.
Thus fall, imperfect exhalation,
(Which our great sun of France could not effect),
A fiery meteor in the firmament!
Lie there the King's delight, and Guise's scorn!
Revenge it, Henry, if thou list, or dar'st.
I did it only in despite of thee.
Fondly hast thou incens'd the Guise's soul,
That of itself was hot enough to work
Thy just digestion with extremest shame!

[1] At the end of Adams's article Greg adds an 'unedited transcript' in the original spelling and punctuation.

The army I have gathered now shall aim
More at thy end than exterpation;
And when thou think'st I have forgotten this,
And that thou most reposest on my faith,
Then will I wake thee from thy foolish dream
And let thee see thyself my prisoner.

Exeunt.

[OCTAVO VERSION]

Enter a Soldier.

Soldier. Sir, to you, sir, that dares make the duke a cuckold, and use a counterfeit key to his privy-chamber-door; and although you take out nothing but your own, yet you put in that which displeaseth him, and so forestall his market, and set up your standing where you should not; and whereas he is your landlord, you will take upon you to be his, and till the ground that he himself should occupy, which is his own free land; if it be not too free—there's the question; and though I come not to take possession (as I would I might!) yet I mean to keep you out: which I will, if this gear hold.

Enter Mugeroun.

What, are ye come so soon? have at ye, sir!

He shoots at him and kills him

Enter the Guise

Hold thee, tall soldier, take thee this, and fly.   *Exit Soldier*
Lie there, the king's delight, and Guise's scorn!
Revenge it, Henry, as thou list or dare;
I did it only in despite of thee.

Take him away

Adams shows that Collier was wrong in speaking of 'a quarto leaf'; it is the lower portion of a folio leaf. The recto has been filled by the scribe and nine lines added on the verso which has otherwise been left blank. Adams suggests that 'the manuscript is a preliminary or tentative draft of a single episode, written on a bit of blank paper that happened to be at hand'; the bit was one of the 'foul sheets' often used by Elizabethan dramatists before making their fair copy. If so, it would naturally be in Marlow's own script, though we have no undoubted specimen by which to test it. It might even, if fancy is given rein, have been shuffled among the 'waste and idle papers' when Marlowe and

Kyd were writing in one chamber in 1591 and which were seized by the Government agents on 12 May 1593.[1]

This, in whole or part, is an attractive speculation, and Adams, in my opinion, rebuts successfully Samuel A. Tannenbaum's attacks upon the authenticity of the manuscript[2] on the grounds of its ink, its penmanship, and other considerations. Yet in the light of Collier's record as a forger a doubt remains, and one would like to know the *provenance* of the leaf before it came into the hands of the bookseller Rodd.

But I agree with Adams that the strongest internal evidence of the genuineness of the leaf lies in two passages which at first sight are questionable. The word 'digestion' in l. 10 of Guise's speech here means dissolution by heat, and carries on the metaphor of 'incens'd' and 'hot' in the two previous lines. This is a verbal use natural to Marlowe, but which is very unlikely to have occurred to a forger. And when Guise declares, ll. 11–12, that his aim now will be more at effecting King Henry's end than at 'exterpation' of the Huguenots he is continuing the contrast of the two motives that drive him in different ways.

If the leaf is genuine I look upon it as a support to my view formed on other grounds that in the octavo text of *The Massacre at Paris* we have, though in a cut version, the essential features of Marlowe's play. The differences in the two versions of the soldier's prose speech do not amount to much. It is true that only four out of the sixteen lines of Guise's speech were printed, but except in two small points they are identical in the manuscript and the octavo, and they contain the pith of the matter which is expanded and decorated in the other lines.

[1] Adams, however, is not accurate in saying that Kyd states in his letter to Puckering that Marlowe occasionally left fragments of his work lying about. The fragments belonging to Marlowe which got shuffled with Kyd's papers were parts of a theological treatise by 'the late Arrian'.

[2] In *Shakesperian Scraps*, pp. 177–86 (1933).

XI

THE TROUBLESOME REIGN OF EDWARD
THE SECOND, KING OF ENGLAND

*E*DWARD *II* was entered in the Stationers' Register
to William Jones on 6 July 1593, little more than a
month after Marlowe's death. An edition may have appeared in that year. An imperfect copy of the 1598 quarto
of the play in the South Kensington Museum has the
first two leaves, containing the title-page and seventy lines
of the text, supplied in manuscript.[1] The date on the title-
page is 1593 and the imprint is 'at London for William
Jones'. There are textual variants between the manuscript and all the printed editions, but it is much closer
to that of 1594 than of 1598.[2] Some of its readings are
preferable but others are evident mistakes. It looks
probable, as H. B. Charlton and A. D. Waller have suggested,[3] that there was an edition of *Edward II* in 1593
hastily printed from manuscript to catch a public still
excited by Marlowe's death. In such circumstances the
copies would be quickly exhausted, and there would soon
be a call for a new edition.

However this may have been, there appeared in 1594
an octavo published by Jones, with a title-page which
ran: The troublesome | raigne and lamentable death of |
Edward *the second, King of* | England: with the tragicall |
fall of proud Mortimer: | As it was sundrie times publiquely
acted | *in the honourable Citie of London, by the* | right
honourable the Earle of Pem- | *brooke his seruants.* | *Written
by* Chri. Marlow *Gent.* Of this edition only two copies are

---

[1] These are reproduced in facsimile in the Malone Society reprint of
Edward II, edited by W. W. Greg. The neat Italian script probably
belongs to the earlier seventeenth century.
[2] The title-page is identical in wording with that of the 1594 octavo,
but 'Marlow' is abbreviated to 'Mar:'.
[3] See their edition of *Edward II*, p. 4 (1933).

known, both in continental libraries, one in Cassel and the other in Zürich. Another quarto edition, also published by Jones, and giving the name of the printer, Richard Bradocke, followed in 1598. It added on the title-page after 'Mortimer': 'And also the life and death of *Peirs Gaueston*, | the *Great Earle of* Cornewall and mighty favourite of King Edward the Second'. It omitted the particular reference to performances in London.

Hitherto Marlowe's plays had been acted by the Lord Admiral's company which was in combination with Lord Strange's men from about 1590 to 1594. If, as Tucker Brooke has suggested,[1] it was Lord Strange who was the employer of Kyd and Marlowe when they were writing together in 1591, and who was outraged by the latter's atheism, Marlowe may have looked out for another theatrical patron in the Earl of Pembroke. But nothing is known of his company till near the close of 1592 when it was at Leicester.[2] On 26 December 1592 and 6 January 1593 it performed at court. A provincial tour followed, and when the company returned to London in the middle of August it was bankrupt. Henslowe wrote to Alleyn on 28 September: 'As for my Lord of Pembroke's . . . they are all at home and have been these five or six weeks, for they cannot save their charges with travel, as I hear, and were fain to pawn their apparel.'

Unless therefore Pembroke's company was in being earlier than we have any record it seems that *Edward II* cannot have been acted in London before December 1592, and it probably was written in that year. But the question of its date is involved with the problem of a perplexing series of parallel passages between *Edward II* and several other Elizabethan plays which needs separate consideration.[3]

The reference by Machiavelli in the prologue to *The Jew of Malta* to the death of the Guise in whom he was

[1] *Life of Marlowe*, p. 48.
[2] J. T. Murray, *English Dramatic Companies*, i. 72 and II. 305.
[3] See Appendix to this chapter.

reincarnate has focused attention on the relation between that play and *The Massacre at Paris*. It has thus
helped to prevent recognition of the parallelism between
The Massacre, in its later scenes, and *Edward II, King
of England*.

In the French historical play, after the death of
Charles IX the throne is occupied by a king, Henry III,
who neglects affairs of state for shows and festivities, and
who lavishes affection on the 'minions' who minister to
his pleasures. His sovereignty is overshadowed in his own
capital by an aspiring noble and his associates. He alien-
ates the woman who stands nearest to the throne, and he
brings upon himself the hostility of the Papacy and its
adherents.

When Marlowe laid aside his de Serres and opened his
Holinshed he found in the English chronicler's account of
'the pitifull tragedie' of Edward II's reign all these elements reproduced. The perspective is largely altered, but
it is scarcely too much to say that scenes xi–xxi of *The
Massacre* are something in the nature of a preliminary
sketch for *Edward II*. It will be seen that there are even
some striking verbal correspondences. Hence I cannot
share the view of Charlton and Waller[1] that 'the dramatist's imagination was no doubt first drawn to the subject
by the pathos and horror of Edward's end, which had
already produced the most moving parts of Holinshed's
account'. Marlowe, I believe, plunged into his plots
without much forethought of what the ending was to be.
Why, then, out of all the rich material provided by
Holinshed did he choose the comparatively unattractive
reign of Edward II? The reason is, I believe, to be mainly
found in the relation between the king and Gaveston
which he brings into the forefront of the play. Homosexual affection, without emphasis on its more depraved
aspects, had (as has been seen) a special attraction for
Marlowe. Jove and Ganymede in *Dido*, Henry III and
his 'minions' in *The Massacre*, Neptune and Leander in

[1] Op. cit., p. 36.

Hero and Leander,[1] are all akin, though drawn to a slighter scale, to Edward and Gaveston. The parallel to Jupiter and his cup-bearer is a fact brought home to the audience by the deserted queen (I. iv. 178–81):

> Like frantic Juno will I fill the earth
> With ghastly murmur of my sighs and cries;
> For never doted Jove on Ganymede
> As much as he on cursed Gaveston.

Even more significant is the roll-call of illustrious precedents in I. iv. 390–6:

> The mightiest kings have had their minions:
> Great Alexander lov'd Hephaestion;
> The conquering Hercules for Hylas wept;
> And for Patroclus stern Achilles droop'd.
> And not kings only, but the wisest men:
> The Roman Tully loved Octavius;
> Grave Socrates, wild Alcibiades.

Among the classical influences to which Marlowe as poet and dramatist was so readily responsive the particular feature of which these lines are a partly distorted record had no unimportant place. Hence, while Holinshed in his detailed account of Edward's reign gives only limited space to Gaveston, Marlowe makes him the centre of the first half of the play. This deals with the five years of his career as the king's favourite (1307–12), while the second half covers the much longer period till the execution of Mortimer in 1330.[2] The selection and rearrangement of material thus involved presented a series of problems to Marlowe which he met, if not with perfect accomplishment, yet with a technical skill and artistry that raised the chronicle-history for the first time to the true level of tragedy.

The opening paragraphs of Holinshed's account of the reign gave the dramatist just the cue that he wanted.

---

[1] See below, p. 227.

[2] A valuable time-analysis, in which Holinshed's dates are affixed to each of Marlowe's scenes, is provided by Charlton and Waller, op. cit., pp. 33–5.

Gaveston, recalled from exile and loaded with honours, humoured the king, who was 'passing his time in voluptuous pleasure, and riotous excesse'. He 'furnished his court with companies of iesters, ruffians, flattering parasites, musicians, and other vile and naughtie ribalds, that the king might spend both daies and nights in iesting, plaieing, blanketing, and in such other filthie and dishonorable exercises'. These words are echoed by Gaveston as he sets foot again in London, and prepares to run into Edward's arms (i. i. 51–6):

> I must have wanton poets, pleasant wits,
> Musicians that with touching of a string
> May draw the pliant king which way I please.
> Music and poetry is his delight;
> Therefore I'll have Italian masks by night,
> Sweet speeches, comedies, and pleasing shows.

And then follow classical embellishments, added by Marlowe, of nymphs and satyrs, Diana and Actaeon—

> Such things as these best please his majesty.

Holinshed further states that the King using Gaveston as 'a procurer of his disordred dooings . . . began to have his nobles in no regard, to set nothing by their instructions, and to take small heed vnto the good gouernement of the commonwealth'. It is on this and similar statements that Marlowe bases the display of hostility to Gaveston by the barons even before he meets the king on his return. Of the peers named by Holinshed as the favourite's chief enemies only the Earl of Warwick is here introduced. For the Earl of Lincoln the dramatist substitutes his son-in-law, the Earl of Lancaster, who was finally possessed of five earldoms. 'He was', says the chronicler, 'the greatest Pere in the Realm, and one of the mightiest Erles in Christendom.' He was thus the nearest counterpart in fourteenth-century England to the Duke of Guise in sixteenth-century France, and it might have been expected that Marlowe would make him play the corresponding role of protagonist in the opposition of the nobility to the king, who even denounces him as 'aspiring Lancaster'. But he died five years before Edward, and it would have been too violent a distortion of history to represent him as responsible for the king's final tragedy. Marlowe preferred the minor liberty of pre-dating the rebellious activities of Roger Mortimer of Chirk and his nephew Roger Mortimer of Wigmore. In Holinshed's account they do not come to the fore till after Gaveston's fall, but in the play they take from the first the lead in the opposition to him. When the Earl of Kent, the king's half-brother, rebukes their insolence, Mortimer (as the nephew will here be called) retorts in fury (1. i. 125–6):

> Come, uncle, let us leave this brain-sick king,
> And henceforth parley with our naked swords.

This is in the Guise-Tamburlaine vein, and Lancaster uses plainer and coarser threats:

> Adieu, my lord; and either change your mind,
> Or look to see the throne, where you should sit,
> To float in blood; and at thy wanton head,
> The glozing head of thy base minion thrown.

The nobles gone, Edward speaks after the manner of Henry III in *The Massacre*:

> I cannot brook these haughty menaces;
> Am I a king and must be overrul'd?

When Gaveston comes forward and presents himself he embraces him rapturously, and, in spite of warning words from Kent, showers titles and offices upon him. The favourite in his adroit reply uses a classical simile which had come more aptly from the lips of the Guise:[1]

> It shall suffice me to enjoy your love,
> Which whiles I have, I think myself as great,
> As Caesar riding in the Roman street,
> With captive kings at his triumphant car.

The episode that follows, the arrest of the Bishop of Coventry, who had procured Gaveston's banishment,

---

[1] See above, pp. 155–6, and Appendix.

comes from Holinshed, but is skilfully elaborated by Marlowe to reveal the spiteful cruelty of the king and the favourite. The latter lays hands on the Bishop, with the mocking words, 'Saving your reverence, you must pardon me', and the dialogue continues (i. i. 187 ff.):

K. Edw. Throw off his golden mitre, rend his stole,
           And in the channel christen him anew.
Kent. Ah, brother, lay not violent hands on him!
           For he'll complain unto the see of Rome.
Gav. Let him complain unto the see of hell;
           I'll be reveng'd on him for my exile.
K. Edw. No, spare his life, but seize upon his goods.

         .   .   .   .   .   .

Gav. He shall to prison and there die in bolts.

         .   .   .   .   .   .

K. Edw. But in the meantime, Gaveston, away,
           And take possession of his house and goods.

This outrage further incenses the peers, who resent the favourite's insolent familiarity with his sovereign (i. ii. 23–4):

Thus leaning on the shoulder of the king,
He nods and scorns, and smiles at those that pass.

While they are conferring, the most hapless victim of the king's infatuation, his young queen, enters hurriedly and is significantly first addressed by Mortimer, to whom she confides that she is fleeing to the forest 'to live in grief' (i. ii. 49–52):

For now my lord the king regards me not,
But dotes upon the love of Gaveston,
He claps his cheeks, and hangs about his neck,
Smiles in his face, and whispers in his ears.

Yet when the lords threaten to take up arms on her behalf she protests:

for rather than my lord
Shall be oppress'd by civil mutinies,
I will endure a melancholy life
And let him frolic with his minion.

As yet, in spite of his neglect, Edward still holds sway over Isabella's heart. The Archbishop of Canterbury is also against violence, and on his advice the Lords of the Council meet at the New Temple to re-enact Gaveston's banishment. While they are in session the king enters with the favourite, whom he places in the highest seat next himself. The elder Mortimer voices his indignation in an Ovidian phrase, *Quam male conveniunt*, which had been more explicitly anglicized in *The Massacre*.[1] After a brisk interchange of abuse Gaveston is forcibly removed, and again Edward speaks in the very tones of Henry III[2] (I. iv. 36–8):

> Here, Mortimer, sit thou in Edward's throne;
> Warwick and Lancaster, wear you my crown;
> Was ever king thus overrul'd as I?

He refuses his assent to his minion's banishment till the Archbishop, as Papal Legate, threatens to release the lords from their duty and allegiance to him. Even then he attempts further parrying, but at last signs the edict, though with characteristic sentimental flourishes:

> Instead of ink, I'll write it with my tears.
>
> . . . . . .
>
> 'Tis done, and now, accursed hand, fall off.

When the lords hurry forth to see that the decree is enforced, Edward cries in rage (I. iv. 96–103):

> Why should a king be subject to a priest?
> Proud Rome, that hatchest such imperial grooms,
> For these thy superstitious taper-lights,
> Wherewith thy antichristian churches blaze,
> I'll fire thy crazed buildings and enforce
> The papal towers to kiss the lowly ground.
> With slaughter'd priests make Tiber's channel swell,
> And banks rais'd higher with their sepulchres.

This violent anti-Papal outburst is of a piece with Henry III's tirade in *The Massacre*,[3] and in lines 100–1

---

[1] *The Massacre*, xi. 16–17.
[2] Ibid. xvi. 55–7.   [3] Ibid. xxi. 60–71.

is verbally almost identical. It comes more appropriately from a king who has been fatally wounded by a friar than from one who has been merely cautioned to banish a minion. But in either case it makes capital out of the passionate Protestant feeling in the theatre audience.

Edward's sentimental mood recurs when Gaveston re-enters to take his leave, and hears from the king's lips, 'Thou from this land, I from myself am banished'. He is appointed governor of Ireland and 'pictures' are exchanged as mementoes. But the queen's entrance stirs Edward to a further outburst, 'Fawn not on me, French strumpet; get thee gone', and both he and Gaveston accuse her of being too familiar with Mortimer. She repudiates the charge, for which no word or action of hers in the play has hitherto given ground. Indeed Marlowe skilfully makes the love that she still bears to her husband the pivot on which Gaveston's recall from exile is to turn. The king angrily declares:

> There weep, for till my Gaveston be repeal'd,
> Assure thyself thou com'st not in my sight.

When, therefore, he departs with the favourite and the barons enter, Isabel cries (1. iv. 200–3):

> I am enjoin'd
> To sue unto you all for his repeal;
> This wills my lord, and this must I perform,
> Or else be banish'd from his highness' presence.

Lancaster and Warwick would have Gaveston return only as 'a ship-wreck'd body'. When Mortimer asks in surprise, 'But madam, would you have us call him home?' the queen answers:

> Ay, Mortimer, for till he be restor'd,
> The angry king hath banish'd me the court;
> And therefore, as thou lovest and tendrest me,
> Be thou my advocate, unto these peers—

and she takes him aside to give him weighty 'reasons' why he should agree to Gaveston's recall. This whispered colloquy marks the beginning of the queen's amorous

entanglement with Mortimer. It has been seen that every
woman playing a leading part in Marlowe's plays has two
rivals for her love. Here there is a variant on this theme.
A woman through her husband's wanton neglect is step
by step urged into the arms of a paramour.

Mortimer's argument, as the queen's mouthpiece, to
the still protesting lords is that Gaveston in Ireland will
purchase friends with his store of gold, and will be difficult
to overthrow, while at home he is so detested that it will
be easy to make away with him. Moreover, his banishment and recall will have taught him respect for the
nobility, and should he offend again an armed rising will
be justified (I. iv. 280–1):

> For howsoever we have borne it out,
> 'Tis treason to be up against the king.

Here Marlowe may well have had in mind not only the
lords, who reluctantly yield to Mortimer's persuasion, but
also Elizabeth's government, which did not welcome the
presentation of rebellion on the stage.

In his joy at the news of Gaveston's recall the king
welcomes Isabel in 'a second marriage', scatters titles and
offices among the lords, and proclaims a tilt and tournament in honour of the favourite's return and his coming
marriage to his niece. Mortimer is thus stirred to an outburst in singular contrast with his plea of justification for
the favourite's 'repeal'. He rails at his fantastically rich
array, on which the national treasure is wasted, and denounces his insolence (I. iv. 415 ff.):

> Whiles others walk below, the king and he
> From out a window laugh at such as we,
> And flout our train, and jest at our attire.
>
> .   .   .   .   .   .
>
> But whiles I have a sword, a hand, a heart,[1]
> I will not yield to any such upstart.

In Act II the lords are far from politic when they
flaunt in the king's face ironic 'devices' to be borne in

[1] Cf. *The Massacre*, ii. 52.

the tournament that he has proclaimed, and when they sarcastically salute Gaveston with the titles of his great offices. He retorts with a Gascon thrust (II. ii. 74–5):

> Base, leaden earls, that glory in your birth,
> Go sit at home and eat your tenants' beef.

Mortimer replies with his sword and is banished from Court, but before he goes finds fresh cause of offence in the king's refusal to ransom his uncle, who has been taken prisoner by the Scots. He and Lancaster are thus galled into a stern arraignment (of which the details are not all historical) of Edward's misgovernment. It ends with a mocking reference to his behaviour at Bannockburn (II. ii. 180–5):

> When wert thou in the field with banner spread?
> But once, and then thy soldiers march'd like players,
> With garish robes, not armour, and thyself
> Bedaub'd with gold rode laughing at the rest,
> Nodding and shaking of thy spangled crest,
> Where women's favours hung like labels down.

This is based on Holinshed's picture of Edward's invading army 'bravely furnished, and gorgeously apparelled, more seemely for a triumph than meet to encounter with the cruel enimie in the field'. But the 'jig' with which 'the fleering Scots' celebrated their victory, 'Maids of England, sore may you mourn', seems to have been taken by Marlowe from Fabyan's Chronicle.

The king takes comfort from these accusations in grandiose images (II. ii. 201–3):

> Yet shall the crowing of these cockerels
> Affright a lion? Edward, unfold thy paws,
> And let their lives' blood slake thy fury's hunger.

When Kent, hitherto his unflinching supporter, urges him to get rid of Gaveston, the king turns on him angrily: 'Traitor, begone! whine thou with Mortimer.' Kent thereupon joins the revolted barons who have laid siege to Tynemouth Castle where Gaveston, now married to the king's niece, 'frolics' with him. As the besiegers

force their way in the favourite and his bride take ship
to Scarborough, whither the rebels follow by direction of
the queen, who for the first time openly confesses to herself her growing love for Mortimer (II. iv. 59–62):

> So well hast thou deserv'd, sweet Mortimer,
> As Isabel could live with thee for ever.
> In vain I look for love at Edward's hand,
> Whose eyes are fix'd on none but Gaveston.

Holinshed records in detail what follows: the arrest of
Gaveston by his pursuers, the plea sent by the king to
see him again, the offer of the Earl of Pembroke to conduct him safely to and fro, the Earl's visit by the way to
his own house, and Warwick's seizure and execution of
the favourite. All this is not easily digestible into dramatic
form, and Marlowe is somewhat overloaded by his material, but he introduces vivid touches. When Warwick
after ordering Gaveston to be hanged countermands this
for the 'honour' of beheading, the Gascon has at once his
cynical jest ready (II. v. 29–31):

> I thank you all, my lords: then, I perceive,
> That heading is one and hanging is the other,
> And death is all.

In grimmer vein is Warwick's last retort before Gaveston
goes to his doom (III. i. 15–16):

> *Gav.* Treacherous earl, shall I not see the king?
> *War.* The king of heaven perhaps, no other king.

It was unfortunate for Marlowe that the death of
Gaveston was immediately followed in the Chronicle by
prominent mention of the king's new favourites, the
Spensers, father and son, 'which were notable instruments
to bring him vnto the liking of all kind of naughtie and
euill rule'. The feud between the king and his foreign
minion and the English barons gave obvious dramatic
opportunities of which Marlowe had made the most,
though they were just beginning to drag in the middle
of the play. But it was impossible to turn to similarly

effective account the hostility to the Spensers, who were
of like stock with their enemies.

Marlowe, however, shows skill in dealing with this
awkward dramatic problem. He connects the fortunes of
the earlier and later favourites by making the younger
Spenser a member of the Earl of Gloucester's household,
where he had won the good graces of Gaveston's bride,
and had thus been promoted to the royal service. As he
tells his fellow retainer, the Oxonian Baldock, in a scene
which brings a lull into the clash of factions, the way to
rise is to (II. i. 31 ff.)

> cast the scholar off,
> And learn to court it like a gentleman
> .   .   .   .   .   .
> You must be proud, bold, pleasant, resolute,
> And now and then stab, as occasion serves.

Baldock assures him that he is merely

> curate-like in mine attire,
> Though inwardly licentious enough,
> And apt for any kind of villainy.

Such a pair are well fitted to make their way rapidly
in the hectic atmosphere of Edward's court, and Marlowe foreshortens history in order to accelerate Spenser's
rise to favour. On the news of Gaveston's execution the
king at once creates him Earl of Gloucester and appoints
him to the vacant office of Lord Chamberlain. But this
does not allow of sufficient display of his evil influence
to make plausible the immediate demand of the barons
to the king (III. ii. 161–3):

> That from your royal person you remove
> This Spenser, as a putrefying branch,
> That deads the royal vine.

Edward's answer is to embrace the new Lord Chamberlain in front of the barons' herald, with the threat:

> hie thee, get thee gone.
> Edward with fire and sword follows at thy heels.

After the royal victory at Boroughbridge, which is advanced in the time-scheme of the play, the king takes vengeance for Gaveston's death by beheading Warwick and Lancaster and sending Mortimer to the Tower, though captivity cannot quench his spirit (III. iii. 71–4):

> What, Mortimer! can ragged stony walls
> Immure thy virtue that aspires to heaven?
> No, Edward, England's scourge, it may not be:
> Mortimer's hope surmounts his fortunes far.

Spenser now shows himself to be not merely a minion. He seeks to ensure the quiet of the land through the dispatch of an agent loaded with gold to frustrate the designs of the queen, who has fled with her young son to her brother, Philip of Valois. But the aid against her husband, denied in France, she finds in Flanders, and joined by Kent and Mortimer, escaped from the Tower, she prepares to invade England. Edward characteristically bids them welcome in terms that Juliet uses as she awaits the coming of her lover (IV. iv. 45–8):

> Gallop apace, bright Phoebus, through the sky,
> And dusky night, in rusty iron car,
> Between you both shorten the time, I pray,
> That I may see that most desired day.

Marlowe again seems to have remembered that successful rebellion was a delicate subject on a Tudor stage, for as Isabel lands near Harwich she laments (IV. ii. 4–9)

> a heavy case
> When force to force is knit, and sword and glaive
> In civil broils makes kin and countrymen
> Slaughter themselves in others, and their sides
> With their own weapons gor'd. But, what's the help?
> Misgoverned kings are cause of all this wrack.

Mortimer, always practical, cuts short her rhetoric:

> Nay, madam, if you be a warrior,
> You must not grow so passionate in speeches.

In the name of the lords he swears fealty to prince Edward, whom, after the king is defeated near Bristol, the queen proclaims Lord Warden of the realm. This complete reversal of fortune dumbfounders the Earl of Kent, who shrinks from physical outrage to the king, and who realizes that there is guilty love between Isabel and Mortimer. His question to the queen 'How will you deal with Edward in his fall?' is followed by a piece of significant dialogue (IV. v. 41–6):

P. Edw. Tell me, good uncle, what Edward do you mean?
Kent. Nephew, your father! I dare not call him king.
Mort. My lord of Kent, what needs these questions?
'Tis not in her controlment, nor in ours.
But as the realm and parliament shall please,
So shall your brother be disposed of.

Mortimer's own ruthless mood is shown when he orders the elder Spenser, taken prisoner in the battle, to be beheaded, and sends forth a Welshman, Rice ap Howell, in pursuit of the 'rebellious runagates', as he calls the King, Spenser, and Baldock, who have escaped from the stricken field to the Abbey of Neath.

During the greater part of Acts III and IV Marlowe's conscientious endeavour to compress a somewhat unmanageable amount of historical material within restricted dramatic limits had produced an episodic and overcrowded effect. But from the point where the King takes refuge in the Abbey the interest becomes concentrated on him as the principal figure, and Marlowe's art moves steadily onwards to a superb climax. In his downfall Edward clings to his passion for making a 'situation' out of everything that happens to him. He offers himself to the Abbot's compassion as an exemplar of the tragic fortunes of princes (IV. vi. 12–15):

Stately and proud, in riches and in train,
Whilom I was, powerful, and full of pomp:
But what is he whom rule and empery
Have not in life or death made miserable?

He begs from his companions in woe moralizing consolations which have no reality for him:

> Make trial now of that philosophy
> That in our famous nurseries of arts
> Thou suckedst from Plato and from Aristotle.

He tries to cheat himself into the belief that he would find contentment within monastic walls:

> Father, this life contemplative is heaven,
> O that I might this life in quiet lead!
> But we, alas, are chas'd; and you, my friends,
> Your lives and my dishonour they pursue.

His fears are at once realized, for his pursuers are guided to the Abbey and their leader, the Earl of Leicester, as he catches sight of the king sitting disguised, takes his turn at moralizing with a Senecan adage (IV. vi. 43–4):

> Too true it is, *Quem dies vidit veniens superbum,*
> *Hunc dies vidit fugiens iacentem.*

After arresting Spenser and Baldock in the queen's name, he tells Edward that he must go to Killingworth. Again he generalizes and fantasticates the situation (IV. vi. 81 ff.):

> *K. Edw.* Must! 'tis somewhat hard when kings must go.
> *Leic.*   Here is a litter ready for your grace.
>
> .   .   .   .   .   .
>
> *K. Edw.* A litter hast thou?   Lay me in a hearse,
>   And to the gates of hell convey me hence;
>   Let Pluto's bells ring out my fatal knell,
>   And hags howl for my death at Charon's shore.

When, at Killingworth, Leicester seeks to comfort him he retorts with another grandiose image (V. i. 8–12):

> The griefs of private men are soon allay'd,
> But not of kings.   The forest deer, being struck,
> Runs to an herb that closeth up the wounds;
> But, when the imperial lion's flesh is gor'd,
> He rends and tears it with his wrathful paw.

But there is a note of real anguish in another, more exquisite image (v. i. 26–7):

> But what are kings when regiment is gone
> But perfect shadows in a sunshine day?

And with Edward's recital that follows of his own griefs and humiliations the dramatist begins to excite the revulsion of feeling on behalf of the king who had hitherto by his words and deeds alienated every sympathy. The Bishop of Winchester presses him to resign the crown to his son, but he declares that it is 'for Mortimer, not Edward's head' and refuses the demand. At last he forces himself to submit (v. i. 56–7):

> Here, take my crown; the life of Edward too.
> Two kings in England cannot reign at once—

only forthwith to retract:

> But stay awhile, let me be king till night,
> That I may gaze upon this glittering crown.

But he is pressed for an instant answer:

> My lord, the parliament must have present news,
> And therefore say, will you resign or no?

Thereupon, in the original stage-direction, 'the king rageth', and cries 'I'll not resign'. Even in the 'reluctant pangs of abdicating royalty' there is an element of pose, as Edward alternately gives and takes back the crown, and when he finally parts with it, sends also to the queen his handkerchief wet with tears and dried again with sighs.

Yet he has only begun to tread his *via dolorosa*. He is now to be surrendered to the Earl of Berkeley, who in his turn proves too gentle a custodian, and gives place to Matrevis and Gurney, with orders to move him hither and thither by night, and by the way (v. ii. 63–5)

> Speak curstly to him; and in any case
> Let no man comfort him if he chance to weep,
> But amplify his grief with bitter words.

When the king is seen in their custody, Mortimer's

commands are being ruthlessly obeyed. Edward moans
(v. iii. 18–20):

> all my senses are annoy'd with stench.
> Within a dungeon England's king is kept,
> Where I am starv'd for want of sustenance.

Holinshed mentions the stench, but to emphasize the
king's humiliation Marlowe here introduces an episode
for which Stow is the authority. Edward pleads for water
to cool his thirst:

> *Mat.* Here's channel water, as our charge is given;
> Sit down, for we'll be barbers to your grace.
> *K. Edw.* Traitors, away! What, will you murther me
> Or choke your sovereign with puddle water?
> *Gur.* No, but wash your face and shave away your beard,
> Lest you be known, and so be rescued.

In effect an abortive attempt at rescue is made by the
Earl of Kent, who is seized and sent to be judged. But
Mortimer realizes that there are other sympathizers with
Edward (v. iv. 1–2):

> The king must die, or Mortimer goes down:
> The commons now begin to pity him.

He sends a message in equivocal Latin phrasing that
will procure Edward's death, without making him responsible for it, and he uses as agent Lightborn, a character
of the dramatist's invention, who has graduated in the
Italian criminal school. As Lightborn speeds on his fateful
mission Mortimer speaks again in the very tones of the
Guise (v. iv. 48–52):

> The prince I rule, the queen I do command,
> And with a lowly congé to the ground,
> The proudest lords salute me as I pass :
> I seal, I cancel, I do what I will,
> Fear'd am I more than lov'd; let me be fear'd.

He even challenges Fate in the Ovidian line:

> *Major sum quam cui possit fortuna nocere.*[1]

---

[1] *Metamorphoses*, vi. 195.

Immediately after the coronation of prince Edward
as the new king, Mortimer shows that he is master by
ordering Kent, who is brought in a prisoner, to be beheaded. Neither the young king's counter-order, 'he is
my uncle, and shall live', nor his petition to the Protector
can save Kent from the block. His execution (antedated
in the play by three years) is the prelude to Edward's last
agony in Berkeley Castle. Lightborn delivers to Matrevis
and Gurney the letter from Mortimer which includes an
order in Latin for his own death after Edward's murder.
The trio make their preparations for the deed (v. v. 29–
35):

> *Light.* See that in the next room I have a fire,
> And get me a spit, and let it be red-hot.
> *Mat.* Very well.
> *Gur.*   Need you anything besides?
> *Light.* What else? A table and a feather-bed.
> *Gur.* That's all?
> *Light.* Ay, ay; so when I call you, bring it in.
> *Mat.* Fear you not that.

This homely dialogue, fraught with tragic significance,
is a masterpiece of art in its contrast with the imaginative
realism of Edward's description of his prison, when Lightborn enters it (v. v. 55 ff.):

> This dungeon where they keep me is the sink
> Wherein the filth of all the castle falls.
>
> .   .   .   .   .
>
> And there in mire and puddle have I stood
> This ten days' space; and lest that I should sleep,
> One plays continually upon a drum.
> They give me bread and water being a king.

His tortures have now robbed Edward's speech of its
flourishes, save for one last hectic flash:

> Tell Isabel, the queen, I look'd not thus,
> When for her sake I ran at tilt in France,
> And there unhors'd the Duke of Claremont.

It is a final irony that sleep which the king has for ten
days sought in vain should now deliver him to his doom.

But there is no detailed lingering over the murder itself, and Lightborn swiftly follows his victim. Mortimer thus feels secure (v. vi. 13–14):

> All tremble at my name, and I fear none;
> Let's see who dare impeach me for his death.

There is, however, one who dares, the young king:

> Think not that I am frightened with thy words.
> My father's murdered through thy treachery,
> And thou shalt die.

Gurney has betrayed Mortimer, who, like Barabas and Guise, finds himself double-crossed and is sentenced to the terrible death of a traitor. Even in face of this he takes his leave in words that embody the spirit of all Marlowe's supermen (v. vi. 59–66):

> Base Fortune, now I see, that in thy wheel
> There is a point, to which when men aspire,
> They tumble headlong down; that point I touch'd,
> And seeing there was no place to mount up higher,
> Why should I grieve at my declining fall?
> Farewell, fair queen; weep not for Mortimer,
> That scorns the world, and, as a traveller,
> Goes to discover countries yet unknown.

A last plea for him from the queen is in vain, and she herself, as a suspected accomplice in the murder of Edward, is committed (unhistorically) to the Tower. But like the Queen Mother in *The Massacre* after the death of Guise, she has no longer the will to live:

> Then come, sweet death, and rid me of this grief.

The exhibition of Mortimer's head, as an offering by the young king to his father's murdered ghost, appealed to the same spirit in the theatrical audience that in the next decade was to welcome the entrance of Macduff with the head of Macbeth. To-day it is the indubitable proof of Marlowe's transfiguration of his historical material into tragic art that such an episode in its crude physical horror strikes us as incongruous at the close of *Edward II* as of Shakespeare's play.

APPENDIX TO CHAPTER XI

I

'Edward II', 'The First Part of the Contention (2 Henry VI)' and 'The True Tragedy of Richard Duke of York (3 Henry VI)'

THE presence in *Edward II* of a number of parallels with lines in *The First Part of the Contention* and *The True Tragedy of Richard Duke of York* and of *2 and 3 Henry VI* is an outstanding feature of the baffling problem of the interrelation of these plays and their authorship. For the detailed discussion, from very varied standpoints, of the problem reference should be made to (1) Miss J. Lee, 'Parts II and III of *Henry VI* and their Originals', in *Transactions of the New Shakespeare Society* (1875); (2) Tucker Brooke, 'The Authorship of *2 and 3 Henry VI*', in *Transactions of the Connecticut Academy of Arts and Sciences* (1912); (3) Peter Alexander, *Shakespeare's 'Henry VI' and 'Richard III'* (1929), with an Introduction by A. W. Pollard; (4) Sir E. K. Chambers, *William Shakespeare: A Study of Facts and Problems*, i (1930); (5) *Edward II*, ed. by H. B. Charlton and R. D. Waller, pp. 10 ff. (1933). In this Appendix only the main aspects of the subject can be summarized.

On 12 March 1593/4 Thomas Millington entered in the Stationers' Register a play which was published in 1594 in quarto as *The First Part of the Contention between the two famous houses of York and Lancaster*. Without further entry Millington published in 1595 another quarto, *The True Tragedy of Richard, Duke of York, and the death of good King Henry the Sixth . . . as it was sundry times acted by the Right Honourable the Earl of Pembroke his servants.* In 1600 Millington republished both plays in the same form. He afterwards parted with his rights to Thomas Pavier, who on 19 April 1602 entered both plays as *The Whole Contention* which he published in 1619, with continuous signatures with *Pericles*. In this edition there were a number of verbal changes and a few additions, and 'W. Shakespeare Gent.' appeared on the title-page as author. In 1623 the two plays, much enlarged and altered, especially *The Contention*, were included in the First Folio entitled *The Second and Third Parts of Henry VI*, as sequels to the hitherto unpublished *First Part of Henry VI*.

A false start, as is now generally recognized, was given to the problem aroused by these successive publications, by Malone, through the misinterpretation of a passage in the address to his fellow playwrights in Greene's *Groatsworth of Wit*, warning them against actors:[1]

'Yes trust them not: for there is an upstart Crow, beautified with our feathers, that with his *Tygers hart wrapt in a Players hyde*, supposes he is as well able to bombast out a blanke verse as the best of you: and being an absolute *Iohannes fac totum*, is in his owne conceit the onely Shake-scene in a countrey.'

Malone took the phrase 'beautified with our feathers' to mean that Greene was accusing the 'upstart' Shakespeare of plagiarizing from the plays of himself and his friends. From his parody of the line,

O tygers hart wrapt in a womans hyde

found both in *The True Tragedy* and *3 Henry VI*, i. iv. 137, Malone inferred that this was one of Shakespeare's borrowings and that Greene and one or other of his associates, preferably Marlowe, were the originators of the plays which Shakespeare revised into *2 and 3 Henry VI*. This view, with modifications, found much support, and was most fully expounded by Miss J. Lee in the article mentioned above.[2]

But Greene's phrase, 'an upstart Crow, beautified with our feathers', has to be interpreted in the light of an earlier passage in his *Never too Late* (1590), where he rebukes an actor for presumption, though he owes everything to the playwright who has provided him with words to speak:

'Why, *Roscius*, art thou proud with *Esops* Crow, being pranct with the glorie of others feathers? of thy selfe thou canst say nothing.'

Greene, therefore, in his *Groatsworth of Wit* was attacking the actor, Shakespeare, for daring to compete with his superiors, the dramatists, in their own field. But he was not making a charge of plagiarism. This was recognized by Tucker Brooke and has been pressed home conclusively by Alexander. But with the elimination of Greene's supposed claim, Tucker Brooke has championed Marlowe as the author of *The Contention* and *The True Tragedy* on grounds which may be summarized broadly as follows.

Thomas Millington, who entered *The Contention* on the

[1] *Dissertation on the Three Parts of Henry VI* (1787), pp. 19 ff.
[2] A summary of it is given in my *Shakspere and his Predecessors*, pp. 540–2.

4427   o

Stationers' Register on 12 March 1593/4, on the following 17 May entered, with Nicholas Ling, *The Jew of Malta*. In neither case was the author's name given, nor did it appear on the title-page of *The Contention* (1594) or *The True Tragedy* (1595). But the latter play and presumably the former was acted by Pembroke's company, for which Marlowe wrote *Edward II*, and with which Shakespeare is not known to have been associated. Millington's 1600 quartos were also anonymous, and Shakespeare's name first appears on the 1619 edition of Pavier, who had previously not hesitated to place it on the title-pages of *Sir John Oldcastle* (1600) and *The Yorkshire Tragedy* (1608).

The literary quality of *The Contention* and *The True Tragedy*, in Brooke's view, points to Marlowe as being their author. They exhibit 'a brilliant synthesis of plot and emotion', and 'the whole tangled story is resolutely pitched in a single key'. Moreover, the respective relations of Henry VI, Queen Margaret, Suffolk, and Prince Edward in these two plays are closely akin to those of Edward II, Queen Isabel, Mortimer, and Prince Edward in *Edward II*. The versification, with its predominant number of end-stopped lines, and its absence of double endings, is characteristic of Marlowe. But the most concrete support for Marlowe's claim is found by Brooke in the remarkable number of passages in *The Contention* and *The True Tragedy* which have parallels in Marlowe's accepted plays or which are repeated in the quartos themselves. Such parallelism and repetition are both characteristic of Marlowe's technique. Brooke gives a list of twenty-eight parallels with plays in the recognized Marlovian canon, fourteen of which are with *Edward II* and nine with *The Massacre at Paris*. He gives also fifteen examples of repetitions within *The Contention* and *The True Tragedy*. He notes further that there are absent from these plays six additional parallels between *Edward II* and *2 and 3 Henry VI*. Hence he infers that the 1594 and 1595 quartos did not reproduce the full text of the plays as written by Marlowe, and later revised by Shakespeare. The revision, he holds, took place before Greene's death in September 1592, as otherwise his parody of a line in *The True Tragedy* loses its pertinence.

The view of *The Contention* and *The True Tragedy* as incomplete versions of the texts on which they are based, which is incidental in Brooke's theory, is fundamental in Alexander's and is developed to an entirely different conclusion. Alexander holds that the two plays are 'bad quartos' of *2 and 3 Henry VI*, and that Shakespeare alone is the author. He believes that these quartos are not based, according to an earlier view of some critics, on an imperfect short-hand transcript taken in the theatre but on a report by the actors in Pembroke's company who took the parts of Warwick in *The Contention* and *The True Tragedy* and of his chief interlocutors, Suffolk in the earlier play and Clifford in the latter, which are noticeably far closer to the corresponding parts in *2 and 3 Henry VI* than any others, except in some of the prose episodes, including detailed stage-directions, which, in Alexander's view, are derived from a transcript. On the general relation of the quarto and the folio texts Alexander makes a strong case. But Sir E. K. Chambers, while adopting his view of this, would substitute the book-keeper for actors as the reporter and is doubtful about the supplementary transcript. And A. W. Pollard, another supporter, puts in the qualification that the inclusion of the plays in the First Folio does not imply a guarantee by Heminge and Condell that they are the unaided work of Shakespeare.

The evidence of the Folio is therefore not in itself conclusive on the question of authorship. Pavier's ascription of *The Contention* and *The True Tragedy* to Shakespeare in 1619 counts, for reasons already given, for very little. The strongest external evidence in his favour, in my opinion, is Greene's in 1592. His parody of a line in *The True Tragedy*, bitterly applied to the upstart actor-dramatist, would lose, if not all, at any rate most of, its significance if it were not an example of the blank verse that the upstart had ventured to bombast out. And there was probably little else of Shakespeare's blank verse before September 1592 to gibe at except in these historical plays.

The strongest internal evidence for Shakespeare's authorship lies, as I think, in the Jack Cade scenes. The view that Marlowe had no humour and could not write prose is no longer tenable. But, in opposition to Tucker Brooke, I cannot see his hand in these scenes which are unlike anything in the Marlovian canon and which are written in exactly the same spirit as Shakespeare always treats demagogues and their dupes. And though Marlowe has drawn weak kings in Mycetes, Henry III of France, and Edward II, they have a kinship that differentiates them all from the ineffec-tively saintly Henry VI. Richard, Duke of Gloucester, in *The True Tragedy*, is consistent in character (though the attempt has been made to question this) with Richard III. And the pastoral images and allusions are foreign to Marlowe's interest while they fall naturally from the pen of the young actor-playwright lately come from Stratford-on-Avon.

On the other hand, on Alexander's own showing that *The Contention* and *The True Tragedy* are bad quartos of the existing *2 and 3 Henry VI*, there are, as I think, points that tell in favour of Marlowe. Chambers has noted that the quartos omit the classical quotations found in the folio text of the plays. It has been one of my endeavours in the present study to illustrate the wide-reaching classical influence on Marlowe. He has, of course, no monopoly of Latin quotations. But when we find them from Ennius (*2 Henry VI*, I. iv. 65), Virgil (*2 Henry VI*, II. i. 24, and IV. i. 117), Ovid, *Heroides* (*3 Henry VI*, I. iii. 48) it is in accord with the usual practice of Marlowe and not of Shakespeare. And while a good many classical allusions are common to the quarto and the folio texts, many of the most striking are found only in the latter. Among these are the references to Althea and her son Meleager, prince of Calydon (*2 Henry VI*, I. ii. 35-6); Ascanius and 'madding Dido' (*2 Henry VI*, III. ii. 116-18); 'Ajax Telamonius' in his madness killing sheep and oxen (*2 Henry VI*, v. i. 26-7); and in *3 Henry VI* two that are specially noticeable (II. ii. 146-9):

> Helen of Greece was fairer far than thou,
> Although thy husband may be Menelaus,
> And ne'er was Agamemnon's brother wrong'd
> By that false woman, as this king by thee.

and (IV. ii. 19-22):

> That as Ulysses and stout Diomede
> With sleight and manhood stole to Rhesus' tents
> And brought from thence the Thracian fatal steeds.

The mention of Helen together with Menelaus has its counter-part in one of the greatest passages in *Doctor Faustus* (v. i. 115 ff.), and Marlowe's reiteration of the theme of Helen's peerless beauty is elsewhere absent, except in passing reference, from Shakespeare's pages. Nor is there in these any other allusion to the exploit concerned with the horses of Rhesus, which is here unconvincingly dragged in by way of simile, and which was known to Marlowe from the *Amores* I. ix. 23-4, and had been introduced also as a simile, in *Dido* I. i. 70-4. With *The Massacre at Paris*, too, *2 and 3 Henry VI* are closely related not only through parallel passages but through the strikingly similar portraiture of the Dukes of Guise and of York, and their relations to the sovereigns whom they plot to overthrow.

These, briefly set forth are the chief conflicting factors of a problem which is rendered the more difficult because we do not know the chronological order of the plays. The comparative relevance to their context of some of the parallel passages suggests that it is as follows: *The Massacre at Paris, 2 and 3 Henry VI, Edward II.* On the assumption of the priority of the two *Henry VI* plays to *Edward II* Charlton and Waller have suggested that Marlowe was influenced by Shakespeare to turn to English history: 'he forsook his high astounding terms to adopt a new technique.' But if Shakespeare had written in 1591 or 1592 the two *Henry VI* plays more or less as they appear in the First Folio he had himself played the sedulous ape to Marlowe. And the latter who has been seen to be at all times a ready borrower would then seem in his turn to have 'conveyed' a number of lines and phrases from the upstart's English history plays to his own. On this theory it is not Shakespeare but Marlowe who turns out to be the plagiarist. *Mutato nomine de te fabula narratur!*

On the other hand, *Edward II* may be the earliest of the three plays. If so, Shakespeare must after all have lifted lines from this play and from *The Massacre*, and the charge of plagiarism, scarcely recognized as an offence in the Elizabethan code, would have to be revived, not on behalf of Greene or on his testimony, but in relation to Marlowe on internal evidence alone. Yet again we do not know what may be due to the book-keeper of the Pembroke company, or to the respective editors, 'pirate' or otherwise.

Every suggested solution seems to me to have its own difficulties. The only certainty is that *2 and 3 Henry VI*, with their 'bad quartos', stand in a peculiarly intimate relation to *Edward II* and to *The Massacre at Paris*, and that had Marlowe never written, they would not be what they are. And whether with Tucker Brooke we claim *The Contention* and *The True Tragedy* for Marlowe, or with Alexander see in them bad quartos of Shakespeare's folio *2 and 3 Henry VI*, both of these critics, in my opinion, from their opposing standpoints, exaggerate the literary and dramatic merits of the texts that they champion as compared with *Edward II*.

II
Edward II, Arden of Feversham, and Solyman and Perseda

Edward II has also a number of parallels with two plays, *Arden of Feversham* and *Solyman and Perseda*, which for different reasons have become associated with Thomas Kyd. One line in *Edward II*, I. i. 151, 'I have my wish in that I joy thy sight' is repeated exactly in *Arden*, v. i. 342 (Temple edition); and *Edward II*, II. ii. 30–1,

> Is this the love you bear your sovereign?
> Is this the fruit your reconcilement bears?

is closely echoed in *Arden*, I. i. 186–7,

> Is this the end of all thy solemn oaths?
> Is this the fruit thy reconcilement buds?

There are other parallels quoted by Charlton and Waller in the Introduction to their edition of *Edward II*, pp. 17–18.

Arden of Feversham was entered on the Stationers' Register on 3 April 1592 to Edward White who published an edition, with a flamboyant title, in the same year. Another edition by White followed in 1599, and a third by Elizabeth Allde in 1633. All were anonymous. The attempt first made in 1770 to claim the play for Shakespeare by a Faversham antiquary, which found its most eloquent advocate in Swinburne, needs, in my opinion, no refutation. Neither in subject-matter nor style does it recall Shakespeare at any period. A much more plausible claim has been advanced for Kyd by Fleay, Crawford, Dugdale Sykes, and Tucker Brooke. His prose tract, *The Murder of John Brewen*, published in 1592, shows his interest in a notorious contemporary case closely analogous to that of Thomas Ardern, as the name was really spelt, and his guilty wife and her lover. But I remain of the opinion stated in my edition of Kyd's Works (1901), p. xc, that the palpable imitation, with a far less harrowing background, of a famous episode in *The Spanish Tragedy* (II. v. 1–4) in *Arden*, III. i. 88–80:

> *Franklin.* What dismal outcry calls me from my rest?
> *Arden.* What hath occasioned such a fearful cry?
> Speak, Michael: hath any injured thee?

is very unlikely to be from the pen of Kyd who, so far as we can judge, was not given to repetition. Marlowe, on the other hand, was a frequent borrower, and he might readily have adapted Kyd's lines to his own use, especially at a time when they were in close contact. And apart from the parallels with *Edward II*, there are other passages in *Arden* that have a distinctively Marlovian stamp. The invocation, in the *Amores*, I. xiii. 39, to the horses of the night not to hasten, repeated in his tragic hour by Dr. Faustus, falls with exquisite tenderness from Arden's lips, I. i. 60–4:

> Sweet love, thou knowest that we two, Ovid-like,
> Have chid the morning when it 'gan to peep.
> And often wished that dark night's purblind steeds
> Would pull her by the purple mantle back,
> And cast her in the Ocean to her love.

And another line in the same elegy of the *Amores*, translated freely by Marlowe,

> The Moon sleeps with Endymion every day

prompts Alice Arden's passionate outburst about Mosbie, v. i. 155–7:

> Had chaste Diana kissed him, she like me
> Would grow love-sick, and from her watery bower
> Fling down Endymion and snatch him up.

The lines in *Arden*, I. i. 252–5:

> For as sharp-witted poets, whose sweet verse
> Makes heavenly gods break off their nectar draughts
> And lay their ears down to the lowly earth,
> Use humble promise to their sacred Muse—

might be a pendant to the passage in *1 Tamburlaine*, v. ii. 98–110, beginning, 'If all the pens that ever poets held'. In very different vein the description of a villain in *Arden*, II. i. 49–54, ending,

> His chin was bare, but on his upper lip
> A mutchado, which he wound about his ear—

is reminiscent of the description of Pilia-Borza in *The Jew of Malta*, IV. i. 7–8:

> That, when he speaks, draws out his grisly beard,
> And winds it twice or thrice about his ear.

And in the speeches of Mosbie and Alice in Act II. v, there is that mingling of romantic feeling and classic lucidity of phrase of which Marlowe is master, and which differs from Kyd's cloudier and more sombre interpretation of passion. Marlowe, as we know from *The Jew* and *The Massacre*, was keenly interested in the devices for poisoning employed by Clarke, the painter, as described by Mosbie in Act I. i. 228 ff. and 610 ff. And what has been seen to be a constant feature from *Dido* onwards in Marlowe's dramatic technique, the emphasis upon the rivalry of two men for a woman's love, is illustrated by the contest between Clarke and Michael for Susan's hand, of which there is no hint in Holinshed, as a pendant to the conflict of passion, of which Alice is the centre, between Arden and Mosbie.

It is, of course, true that this tragedy of *bourgeois* domestic life is on a very different plane from the subjects of Marlowe's recognized plays. But it has become increasingly clear from recent investigation that he made as profitable use as was possible of his reading. When turning over his Holinshed for material for *Edward II* he may have been struck with the chronicler's detailed account of a *cause célèbre* connected with a Kentish town through which he had probably passed on his way from Canterbury, where Alice Ardern had in 1551 been burnt at the stake. If he felt drawn to dramatize it, *Arden of Feversham* is the masterpiece that would result, and I agree with E. H. C. Oliphant[1] that there is no other known playwright of the time whose hand can be traced in its finest flights, not even Kyd, though the villains might owe something to the creator of Pedringano and Serberine in *The Spanish Tragedy*. If *Arden* is anonymous in all its editions so is *Tamburlaine*. But with the domestic tragedy there is no support from contemporary references for the authorship of Marlowe or any other known playwright, and there may have been some unidentified genius who could bring the touch of Marlowe's magic into a dramatic field unvisited by him in any of his accepted works.

Another anonymous play, *Solyman and Perseda*, entered in the Stationers' Register, 20 November 1592, and published by Edward White in an undated quarto and in another dated 1599 has a number of parallels with *Edward II*. Two of the most notable are *Edward II*, II. iv. 296–7:

> And when this favour Isabel forgets,
> Then let her live abandoned and forlorn.

---

[1] *Shakespeare and his Fellow Dramatists*, pp. 281–2.

Solyman and Perseda, iv. i. 198–9:

> My gracious Lord, when Erastus doth forget this favour
> Then let him live abandoned and forlorn.

and *Edward II*, v. ii. 104–5:

> I tell thee, 't is not meet that one so false
> Should come about the person of a prince.

Solyman and Perseda, i. v. 71–2:

> It is not meet that one so base as thou
> Shouldst come about the person of a king.

Other parallels are given by Charlton and Waller in their edition of *Edward II*, pp. 18–19.

In my edition of Kyd's Works, pp. lvi ff., I have summarized the evidence in favour of his authorship of *Solyman and Perseda*, though this cannot be proved beyond a doubt. In any case the date of the entry in the Register makes it probable that it was later than *Edward II*, in which case the author of *Solyman and Perseda* would be the borrower.

There are also some notable parallels quoted by Charlton and Waller (op. cit., pp. 9–10) with Peele's *Edward I* entered in the Stationers' Register, 8 October 1593 and published in the same year. The dates suggest that Peele, or whoever was responsible for the corrupt 1593 text, was the borrower. But as Charlton and Waller point out, one or two of the passages are more approximate to their context in *Edward I* than in Marlowe's play.

The Tragicall History
of the Life and Death
of Doctor Faustus.

With new additions.

Written by *Ch. Marlot,*

Printed at London for *Iohn Wright*, and are to be sold at his
shop without Newgate. 1628.

? ⌒ 2

THE TRAGICAL HISTORY OF DOCTOR FAUSTUS

TILL comparatively recently it was usual to assign *The Tragical History of Doctor Faustus*, of which the earliest-known quarto is dated 1604, to the earlier period of Marlowe's dramatic career. The academic atmosphere and echoes, especially in the opening scenes, suggested a date of composition not long after Marlowe had left Cambridge. In a number of passages there is kinship in thought and style with the *Tamburlaine* plays, and there are links with *Dido* and the *Amores*. A date within 1588–9 was therefore widely accepted and was thought to be supported by the entry in the Stationers' Register on 28 February 1588/9 of *A Ballad of the life and death of Doctor Faustus*, and by the performance, not as a new play, of Greene's *Friar Bacon and Friar Bungay*, recorded by Henslowe on 19 February 1591/2. But nothing is known of the origin or contents of the ballad, and Sir A. W. Ward's view that Greene's play was written to rival the success of *Doctor Faustus*[1] is merely a speculation.

It now seems highly probable on bibliographical grounds that *Doctor Faustus* cannot be dated earlier than 1592. The ultimate source of the play is the German *Historia von D. Johann Fausten*, published at Frankfurt-on-the-Main in 1587, and reissued with additional chapters in the same year, in 1589, 1590, 1592, and 1599. But Marlowe probably did not know German, and his practice of close adherence to the text of his sources proves beyond doubt that he based his play not on any edition of the original *Historia* but on an English translation by an unidentified 'P. F.', of which the earliest extant edition has the following title-page:

The | HISTORIE | of the damnable | life and deserued death

---

[1] See pp. xxi–xxii of his edition of *Doctor Faustus* and *Friar Bacon and Friar Bungay* (1901).

of | *Doctor Iohn Faustus,* | Newly imprinted, and in conueni- | *ent places imperfect matter amended*: | according to the true Copie printed | at Franckfort, *and translated into* | *English* by P.F. Gent. | Seene and allowed. | [Device] | *Imprinted at London by Thomas Orwin, and are to be* | solde by Edward White, dwelling at the little North | doore of Paules, at the signe of the Gun. 1592.

As this edition was newly imprinted and amended it was not the first and it was possible to assume that there was an earlier one which Marlowe could have used from about 1588 onwards. But an entry on 18 December 1592 in Register B of the Stationers' Company, first made public in 1930,[1] shows that after Orwin's publication of P. F.'s translation, Abel Jéffes asserted that he had a prior right based on a claim made in or about the preceding May. This claim he appears to have made good. As it did not rest on an entry in the Register, it apparently depended on a publication of the translation in or about May. This would seem to have been the first printing of P. F.'s version, for Orwin, who had procured his manuscript from Richard Olive, did not make a counter-claim on a previous publication. Unless, therefore, we make the purely arbitrary assumption that Marlowe had access to a manuscript of the translation, it seems that his play must be later than May 1592.[2]

In any case, no entry of it was made during the sixteenth century in the Register, and paradoxically about fourteen lines of it, together with some thirty from *Tamburlaine*, Parts I and II, were printed for the first time, so far as we know, with modifications, in 1594 in the anonymous Pembroke company's piece, *The Taming of a Shrew*. It was not till 7 January 1600/1 that Thomas Bushell entered *A booke called the plaie of Doctor Faustus*. Even then he brought out no edition (unless one has

---

[1] *Records of the Court of the Stationers' Company, 1576 to 1602, from Register B*, ed. by W. W. Greg and E. Boswell, p. 44.

[2] See W. W. Greg's note on pp. 7–8 of the introduction to *Doctor Faustus*, ed. F. S. Boas (1932).

totally disappeared) till the quarto of 1604, represented by one surviving copy in the Bodleian, with a title-page as follows:

THE | TRAGICALL | History of D. Faustus, | *As it hath bene Acted by the Right* | *Honorable the Earle of Nottingham his seruants.* | Written by Ch. Marl. | [Device] LONDON | Printed by V[alentine] S[immes] for Thomas Bushell, 1604.

This edition was reprinted with minor variants in 1609 and 1611 after the copyright had passed to John Wright. Then in 1616, without a prefatory word or even an announcement on the title-page, Wright brought out a radically altered edition of which only one copy is extant in the British Museum. To the approximately 1,500 lines of the 1604 quarto about 550 were now added, including some entirely new or considerably expanded scenes. And even in those that run parallel there are so many textual variants that it is evident that Wright was not basing this 1616 edition on any of the earlier quartos but on an independent manuscript. The long additions to the scenes at the Papal Court (Act III. i. 55 ff. and ii. 1–93), the new scenes (Act IV. i, iii, iv, and the additional matter in ii) at or near the Emperor's Court, and the inserted dialogues in Act V. ii between the fiends and between the good and bad angels are all clearly not from Marlowe's pen. Light on their *provenance* is thrown by an entry in Henslowe's *Diary*, 22 November 1602, of a payment of £4 to William Birde and Samuel Rowley 'for their adicyones in doctor Fostes'. This has been supported by the investigations of H. Dugdale Sykes[1] and others, especially in respect of Rowley. The episodes at the Papal and Imperial Courts in the 1616 version are strikingly akin in treatment and in versification to scenes in Rowley's *When You See Me You Know Me*.[2] The additions evidently hit the taste of the time for *Doctor Faustus* in its revised form

[1] *The Authorship of 'The Taming of A Shrew', 'The Famous Victories of Henry V', and the Additions to Marlowe's 'Faustus'* (1920).

[2] *Doctor Faustus*, ed. Boas, pp. 29–30.

was reissued by Wright in 1619, 1620, 1624, 1628,[1] and 1633.

By the majority of modern editors of the play, including Sir A. W. Ward, A. H. Bullen, and Tucker Brooke, the 1616 text has been treated as throughout inferior to that of 1604 because of its later date and its inclusion of scenes not from Marlowe's hands. They did not take account of the fact that the quotations from *Doctor Faustus* in the 1594 *The Taming of a Shrew* are considerably closer to the 1616 than the 1604 version. Recent examination of the 1616 quarto in relation to P. F.'s translation of the German *Historia* has vindicated its claim to give on the balance a better text than the 1604 quarto, so far as they run parallel, especially in Acts I–IV.

In Act III the opening chorus contains thirteen lines, beginning:

He views the clouds, the planets and the stars

which the *English Faust Book* (as P. F.'s translation may be called) shows to be a necessary part of this prologue and which are omitted in 1604. Some other omitted lines and a large number of preferable readings are preserved in the 1616 quarto.[2] In the comic scenes common to both versions this quarto presents a demonstrably superior text without a number of the 1604 corruptions.[3] On the other hand, the 1604 quarto retains some lines which were omitted in 1616 apparently for fear of the Censor's ban, and it has the superior rendering of Faustus's great final monologue.

Thus to reconstruct, as far as may be, the original play recourse must be had to both the 1604 and 1616 texts, with the omission, of course, of the additions by Birde

---

[1] Two copies of this hitherto unknown edition recently came to light in Lincoln College, Oxford, and the Royal Library, Stockholm.

[2] For details, see *Doctor Faustus*, ed. Boas, pp. 22–6.

[3] On these corruptions, see P. Simpson's 'The 1604 Text of Marlowe's "Doctor Faustus"' in *Eng. Assoc. Essays and Studies*, vol. vii (1921).

and Samuel Rowley. This abnormally short version without any indications of act or scene division, must present *Doctor Faustus* in mutilated form. Yet the loss that we have thus suffered may well have been exaggerated. Speeches have doubtless been cut and some episodes may have disappeared entirely. But as in the case of *The Massacre at Paris* a close comparison of *Doctor Faustus* with its source suggests that when corruptions and additions are removed, the main lines of Marlowe's presentation of his theme are preserved. There seems to me to be nothing vital to this presentation which is found in the *English Faust Book* and which is missing from the play. Its structural deficiencies have been unduly emphasized by the practice of most modern editors of dividing it merely into scenes though, in spite of its comparative brevity, it falls naturally enough into the usual five Acts.

In any case the play, as it has come down to us, whatever its imperfections, shows that in the *English Faust Book* Marlowe found a subject fitted above all others to his distinctive genius. And, paradoxically enough, it was fortunate that he made the acquaintance of the legend in this translation and not in the original *Historia von D. Johann Fausten*. For the German *Historia* was written avowedly as an awful example of the terrible fate that befell any one who to gratify his unlawful desires sold himself to the devil. Yet writing under Renaissance influences the anonymous author could not help endowing his Doctor Faustus with something of humanist intellectual ardour.

This feature became much more prominent in P. F.'s English version, together with a more subdued presentation of the Doctor's sins and vices. It is in this version, and there only, that Marlowe could find the statement that Faustus at Padua 'entred his name into the Vniuersitie of the Germane nation, and wrote himself Doctor *Faustus*, the vnsatiable Speculator'. Could any two words have more aptly fitted not only the wandering scholar,

but the playwright, who had cried through the lips of
Tamburlaine:

> Our souls whose faculties can comprehend
> The wondrous architecture of the world,
> And measure every wandering planet's course,
> Still climbing after knowledge infinite,
> And always moving as the restless spheres,
> Will us to wear ourselves and never rest.

And in more specific ways Marlowe must have recognized in Faustus his own counterpart. The Canterbury
boy through the bounty of Archbishop Parker had
reached Cambridge to qualify himself there for the clerical
career. His studies had earned him the Bachelor's and
Master's degrees, but he had turned his back on the
Church, and on arrival in London had gained a reputation
for atheism. Similarly, Faustus through the bounty of a
rich uncle had been sent to Wittenberg to study divinity,
and had obtained with credit his doctorate in the subject.
But his interests lay elsewhere, and he had turned secretly
to the study of necromancy and conjuration.

The opening scene in which Faustus takes one by one
the chief subjects of the academic curriculum, philosophy,
medicine, law, and divinity, and rejects them as insufficient is, however, not directly suggested by the *English
Faust Book* but, as the use of Cambridge technical terms
helps to show, by Marlowe's own studies at Corpus Christi
in connexion wherewith some lines from the scene have
been quoted and discussed.[1] In comparison with the
orthodox curriculum

> These metaphysics of magicians
> And necromantic books are heavenly.

By them as Marlowe's own speculative faculty and
Harriot's precepts may have led him to believe, more
could be effected than by Tamburlaine's conquering arms,
or the gold of Barabas, or the statecraft of the Guise.

---

[1] See above, pp. 16-17.

The power that they conferred was universal and illimitable:

> Emperors and Kings
> Are but obey'd in their several provinces
> Nor can they raise the wind, or rend the clouds;
> But his dominion that exceeds in this,
> Stretcheth as far as doth the mind of man:
> A sound magician is a demi-god.

Thus when by the exercise of incantations at night Faustus has raised Mephistophilis, who asks what he would have him do, the Doctor assumes totalitarian authority (1. iii. 38–41):

> I charge thee wait upon me whilst I live,
> To do whatever Faustus shall command,
> Be it to make the moon drop from her sphere,
> Or the ocean to overwhelm the world.

But Mephistophilis is himself merely the servant of the arch-fiend, Lucifer, concerning whom Faustus now questions him. In the *English Faust Book* the passage runs:

Here *Faustus* said: but how came thy Lord and Master *Lucifer* to haue so great a fal from heauen?

Mephistophiles answered: My Lord *Lucifer* was a faire Angell created of God as immortal, and being placed in the Seraphins, which are aboue the Cherubins, he would haue presumed vnto the Throne of God with intent to haue thrust God out of his seate. Vpon this presumption the Lord cast him downe headlong, and where before he was an Angel of light, now dwels hee in darkenes.

Marlowe's genius for transfiguring his material, while keeping faithful to it, made superb use of the opportunity presented to it here (1. iii. 65–82):

> *Faust.* Tell me what is that Lucifer thy lord?
> *Meph.* Arch-regent and commander of all spirits.
> *Faust.* Was not that Lucifer an angel once?
> *Meph.* Yes, Faustus, and most dearly lov'd of God.
> *Faust.* How comes it then that he is prince of devils?
> *Meph.* O, by aspiring pride and insolence:
> For which God threw him from the face of heaven.
> *Faust.* And what are you that live with Lucifer?

> *Meph.* Unhappy spirits that fell with Lucifer,
> Conspir'd against our God with Lucifer,
> And are for ever damn'd with Lucifer.
> *Faust.* Where are you damn'd?
> *Meph.*   In hell.
> *Faust.* How comes it then that thou art out of hell?
> *Meph.* Why this is hell, nor am I out of it.
> Think'st thou that I, that saw the face of God,
> And tasted the eternal joys of heaven,
> Am not tormented with ten thousand hells.
> In being depriv'd of everlasting bliss?

Here the 'atheist' Marlowe's presentation of hell is far more spiritual than that of the Puritan Milton in the next century. But the agonized accents of the fallen angel have no power to move Faustus:

> What, is great Mephistophilis so passionate
> For being deprived of the joys of heaven?
> Learn thou of Faustus manly fortitude,
> And scorn those joys thou never shalt possess.

The Doctor is ready to sell his soul to Lucifer so he may live twenty-four years in all voluptuousness, with Mephistophilis at his commandment. The effective dramatic episodes in Act II. i, when Faustus signs the bond in due legal form at night with his own blood, which congeals and has to be melted with a chafer of fire, and when he disregards the warning inscription that suddenly appears on his arm, *Homo fuge*—these are closely based on the *English Faust Book*. In this source, too, Faustus thereafter returns to the quest of what hell is, and is told that 'wee Diuels know not what substance it is of, but a confused thing ... but to bee short with thee, Faustus, we know that hell hath neither bottome nor end'. Here again Marlowe spiritualizes what he borrows (II. i. 122–7):

> *Meph.* Hell hath no limits, nor is circumscrib'd
> In one self place, but where we are is hell,
> And where hell is, there must we ever be:
> And to be short, when all the world dissolves,
> And every creature shall be purified,
> All places shall be hell that is not heaven.

It is because Faustus, so far as appears in the play, spends his time with Mephistophilis chiefly in such discussions and in the disputation in academical fashion on 'divine astrology' in Act II. ii. 33–67, rather than in all voluptuousness, that there is a sense of unreality in the Doctor's periodical outbursts of repentance and in the rival admonitions of the good and bad angels, a legacy from medieval drama that fits awkwardly into the Marlovian technique. And there is another echo of medievalism when Faustus violates his bond by calling upon his saviour, Christ, and when Lucifer, with his attendant devils, appears to rebuke him and, after his promise not to think henceforth on God, to divert him with the pageant of the seven deadly sins.

Intermingled with the main action of these first two acts are scenes forming more or less a parallel comic underplot. In Act I. ii and iv the chief figure is the Doctor's servant, Wagner, who has been taken over from the *English Faust Book.* In his talk with the two scholars and afterwards with the clown he uses Latin tags which would drop naturally from Marlowe's pen. And the agreement in I. iv, by which the clown is to become his man and serve him for seven years parodies the contract by which Mephistophilis is to wait upon Faustus for twenty-four years.

There is no other comic scene till II. iii, where Wagner and the Clown have dropped out and their places have been taken by two characters unknown to the *English Faust Book*, Robin and Dick.[1] This change seems to indicate another hand than Marlowe's, and the frequent use of phrases which are found also in the Additions presumably from Samuel Rowley's pen suggests that he may have possibly contributed to the play in its original form.[2] In any case in this scene and in III. iii the idea of a burlesque underplot is continued. Robin has got hold of one of the Doctor's conjuring books, from which he reads

---

[1] He is so called in the 1616 quarto. In the 1604 quarto the name is Ralph.　　　[2] See further *Doctor Faustus*, ed. Boas, pp. 27–8.

a mock incantation. At the second reading of it in III. iii, to escape the hands of a vintner whose cup they have stolen, Mephistophilis unexpectedly appears and turns Robin into an ape and Dick into a dog.

Mephistophilis announces angrily that he has been summoned from Constantinople by these villains' charms, and that he must fly back forthwith 'unto my Faustus at the Great Turk's Court'. But in neither version of the play is there any other reference to such a visit. The Court at which Faustus, after a tour in a dragon-drawn chariot of the stellar universe, and a more circumscribed terrestrial ride on a dragon's back, first gives a display of his magic art is that of the Pope in Act III. i and ii. The episode, without the lengthy, pseudo-historical additions of 1616, closely follows the account in the *English Faust Book*. The childish tricks played upon the Pope at a banquet by the invisible conjurer and his ministering spirit seem to us equally unworthy of Faustus and the august victim of his practical jokes. And the solemn cursing by Friars, with the bell, book, and candle used in the office of excommunication, of the supposed offending 'ghost' seems an ironic comment on the view attributed to Marlowe by Baines that if there is 'anie good Religion then it is the Papistes, because the service of God is performed with more ceremonies, as elevation of the masse, organs, singing men, shaven crowns, &c.' But the episode is probably one where Marlowe has been content merely to follow his source and from which no implication as to his opinions is to be drawn.

The *English Faust Book* served him better in its account of the Doctor's visit to the imperial court of Carolus the Fifth. The mention of one of the great figures of Greece or Rome always struck a responsive chord in Marlowe's breast. In *Tamburlaine*, Part II, v. i. 69–70, he had spoken of 'great Alexander' as one of the potentates who had ridden in triumph through Babylon. Now he fastened eagerly on the passage in P. F.'s narrative which tells how the Emperor Carolus desired that Faustus should show him that 'great and mighty monarch of the worlde', who 'was such a lanterne & spectacle to all his successors', together with his paramour. In lines closely based on P. F.'s prose, yet fraught with Marlovian music, the Emperor thus makes his request in Act IV. ii. 19 ff.:

> Then, Doctor Faustus, mark what I shall say.
> As I was sometimes solitary set
> Within my closet, sundry thoughts arose
> About the honour of mine ancestors.
>
> . . . .
>
> Amongst which kings is Alexander the Great,
> Chief spectacle of the world's pre-eminence,
> The bright shining of whose glorious acts
> Lightens the world with his reflecting beams;
> As when I hear but mention made of him
> It grieves my soul I never saw the man.
> If, therefore, thou by cunning of thine art,
> Canst raise this man from hollow vaults below,
> Where lies entomb'd this famous conqueror,
> And bring with him his beauteous paramour
>
> . . . .
>
> Thou shalt both satisfy my just desire,
> And give me cause to praise thee while I live.

The Emperor's wish is gratified and it is a disconcertingly sudden change from this majestic vision to the jocular episode, also taken from the *English Faust Book*, wherein the Doctor revenges himself upon a knight of the Court, who had doubted his magical art, by making horns sprout upon his head. Coming from the same source and belonging to a similar order of conjuring feats are the tricks that Faustus plays upon the horse-courser (IV. v) and the exhibition of his art at the Court of the Duke of Anholt (IV. vii). But for a credulous Elizabethan audience that took seriously the exercise of sorcery such scenes must have had a far greater significance than for us to-day. And now and again, though incongruously with their immediate setting, come confessions from Faustus that he is not unmindful of the doom to which he is ever drawing nearer. Thus he leaves the Emperor's Court with the cry:

> Now, Mephistophilis, the restless course
> That time doth run with calm and silent foot
> Shortening my days and thread of vital life
> Calls for the payment of my latest years.

And in the middle of his fooling with the horse-courser he is arrested by agonizing thoughts from which he seeks relief in slumber:

> What art thou, Faustus, but a man condemn'd to die?
> Thy fatal time doth draw to final end;
> Despair doth drive distrust unto my thoughts:
> Confound these passions with a quiet sleep:
> Tush, Christ did call the thief upon the Cross;
> Then rest thee, Faustus, quiet in conceit.

In Act V the awful end is at hand. The Doctor has made his will and again is seeking to distract his thoughts, not in sleep but in festive 'belly-cheer' with his friends among the scholars of Wittenberg. And here once more the *English Faust Book* offered Marlowe a golden opportunity. Of all the figures of the ancient world that had captured his imagination Helen of Troy stood foremost. She was the paragon of loveliness and charm by whom all other women—a Dido or a Zenocrate, were to be measured. What a joy, therefore, it must have been to the dramatist to find one of the Wittenberg scholars declaring that he 'neuer was so desirous of any thing in this world as to haue a sight (if it were possible) of fayre *Helena* of Greece, for whom the worthy towne of Troie was destroyed', and Faustus replying that he would bring her into their presence personally, 'and in the same forme of attyre as she vsed to go when she was in her cheefest flowre and pleasauntest prime of youth'. P. F.'s phrases have a charm of their own, but again Marlowe's pen adds a new magic (v. i. 21-4):

> You shall behold that peerless dame of Greece,
> No otherwise for pomp or majesty,
> Than when Sir Paris cross'd the seas with her,
> And brought the spoils to rich Dardania.

And when Helen passes over the stage before their eyes the scholars vie with one another in outbursts of lyrical ecstasy:

    2. Schol. Was this fair Helen, whose admired work
             Made Greece with ten years' wars afflict poor Troy?
             Too simple is my wit to tell her praise,
             Whom all the world admires for majesty.
    3. Schol. No marvel though the angry Greeks pursued
             With ten years' war the rape of such a queen,
             Whose heavenly beauty passeth all compare.
    1. Schol. Now we have seen the pride of Nature's work,
             And only paragon of excellence,
             We'll take our leaves; and for this glorious deed
             Happy and blest be Faustus evermore!

But Faustus does not think himself 'happy and blest' by a momentary vision of Helen. The *English Faust Book* tells how he bade Mephistophilis bring her to him and how he 'made her his common concubine and bedfellow'. So in the play (v. i. 100–4) he craves

        That I may have unto my paramour
        That heavenly Helen which I saw of late
        Whose sweet embraces may extinguish clean
        Those thoughts that do dissuade me from my vow,
        And keep my oath I made to Lucifer.

And when she again appears companioned by two Cupids his rapturous greeting echoes some of the loveliest lines in *Dido* and *Tamburlaine*:

        Was this the face that launch'd a thousand ships,
        And burnt the topless towers of Ilium?
        Sweet Helen make me immortal with a kiss—
        Her lips suck forth my soul: see where it flies.

But nowhere in his plays, not even here, does Marlowe dwell on the merely sensual side of sex relationships. He apostrophizes Helen in the diction of medieval chivalry:

        I will be Paris, and for love of thee,
        Instead of Troy, shall Wittenberg be sack'd;
        And I will combat with weak Menelaus,
        And wear thy colours on my plumed crest,
        Yea, I will wound Achilles in the heel,
        And then return to Helen for a kiss.

And he etherializes her in cosmic and mythological similitudes till one is tempted to cry,

> Was ever woman in this humour wooed?

Had Marlowe vouchsafed us a sight of Faustus in his sinful pleasures it would have been a fitter prelude to his fast approaching doom. Goethe two centuries later was wiser in his generation when he exhibited his Faust as the seducer of the simple maiden, Gretchen.[1]

Another attitude of Marlowe's Faustus that makes his iniquity more difficult to realize is the affectionate relation till the end between him and his scholar-friends. For this the *English Faust Book* gave the cue, but the dramatist must have been thinking of those who shared the same room with him at Corpus Christi College, when Faustus addresses one of the scholars as 'my sweet chamber-fellow'. It is the scholars who are his companions on his last night, and who seek to comfort him when Faustus agonizes over his sin and its inevitable penalty in accents where Marlowe's prose for once rivals in effect his finest verse (v. ii. 39–52):

2. Schol. Yet Faustus, look up to heaven; remember God's mercies are infinite.

Faust. But Faustus' offence can ne'er be pardoned; the serpent that tempted Eve may be saved, but not Faustus. . . . O would I had never seen Wittenberg, never read book! and what wonders I have done, all Germany can witness, yea, all the world; for which Faustus hath lost both Germany and the world; yea, heaven itself, heaven, the seat of God, the throne of the blessed, the Kingdom of joy; and must remain in hell for ever—hell, oh, hell for ever.

Even in his anguished expectation of the coming of the fiends, he thinks of his friends' safety. 'Gentlemen, away, lest you perish with me.' They may pray for him in the next room, but 'what noise soever you hear, come not unto me, for nothing can rescue me'. So one hour before midnight, Faustus is left to face his awful destiny alone.

[1] On the relation between Marlowe's and Goethe's treatment of the Faustus story see *Doctor Faustus*, ed. Boas, pp. 45–6.

In all Marlowe's plays the death-scenes are specially memorable. Dido, with Virgil's words on her lips, flinging herself into the flames; Tamburlaine gazing before his eyes close for ever on Zenocrate's hearse and on the son whom he has crowned as his heir; Barabas with his last breath hurling curses from the burning cauldron upon his enemies; the murdered Guise crying *'Vive la messe*; perish the Huguenots'; Edward II pleading in vain for his life to the assassins in the vaults of Berkeley Castle—all these are haunting figures. But here Marlowe had to deal with the yet more tremendous situation of a man conscious that by his own will he is on the very brink of eternal damnation. His lamentations, in P. F.'s prose, though on conventional lines, have a poignant ring:

'Ah, *Faustus*, thou sorrowful and wofull man, now must thou go to the damned company in vnquenchable fire, whereas thou mightest haue had the joyfull immortalitie of the soule, the which thou hast now lost. . . . Ah grievous paynes that pearce my parting heart, whom is there now that can deliuer me? Would God that I knew where to hide me, or into what place to creepe or flie. Ah, woe, woe is me, be where I will, yet am I taken. Now thou *Faustus*, damned wretch, howe happy wert thou if as an vnreasonable beast thou mightest die without soule, so shouldest thou not feele any more doubts? But now the diuell will take thee away both body and soule, and set thee in an vnspeakable place of darknesse.'

Never did Marlowe's genius for both keeping true to his source and gloriously transfiguring it display itself more irresistibly than in the last-hour soliloquy that he built on the foundation provided in the *English Faust Book*. Never did he employ to such moving effect his passionate cosmic interest as when he makes Faustus cry (v. ii. 140–5):

> Stand still you ever-moving spheres of heaven,
> That time may cease, and midnight never come
> Fair Nature's eye, rise, rise again, and make
> Perpetual day; or let this hour be but
> A year, a month, a week, a natural day,
> That Faustus may repent and save his soul.

And never did his classical ardour leap into such startlingly miraculous flame as when he puts into the lips of the doomed Faustus the invocation of the poet of the *Amores* as he lay with Corinna by his side,

O lente, lente currite, noctis equi!

Then with the swift transition, in which to the Renaissance dramatist there was nothing incongruous, comes the cry of the sinner whom the Crucified had died to save:

O, I'll leap up to my God!—Who pulls me down?—
See, see, where Christ's blood streams in the firmament!
One drop would save my soul, half a drop; ah, my Christ!
Ah rend not my heart for naming of my Christ!
Yet will I call on him: O spare me, Lucifer!

Then he turns again to Nature, prays to the hills to fall and cover him, to the earth to gape and harbour him, to the stars of his nativity to draw him up into the clouds. As the clock strikes the half-hour, the thought of the eternity of his damnation forces from him the agonized outburst:

Let Faustus live in hell a thousand years,
A hundred thousand, and at last be sav'd,
O, no end is limited to damned souls.

And the contrast between himself, with the fatal dower of immortality, and the beasts that perish finds voice in a last wistful recall of classical lore:

Ah, Pythagoras' *metempsychosis* were that true,
This soul should fly from me, and I be changed
Into some brutish beast!

But the midnight hour strikes that ends the twenty-four allotted years. The devils come to claim their victim, and he vanishes with the despairing cry, 'I'll burn my books'. So, some twenty years later, another magician, Prospero, abjures the practice of his art with the declaration, 'I'll drown my book'. Look on this picture and on that!

Yet, with all the horror of the closing scene, of the two tragic purgative emotions, pity and fear, it is the former that has the chief mastery over us at the end. It is the

note of pity that is heard in the three first lines of the
Epilogue:

> Cut is the branch that might have grown full straight,
> And burnèd is Apollo's laurel-bough,
> That sometimes grew within this learned man.

If these lines were written by Marlowe they have the
ring of unconscious prophecy. Among the playwrights of
his day he was noted for his learning which was reverenced
even beyond the circle of his friends.[1] Apollo's laurel-
bough that grew within him seemed destined to put forth
many a new and brave shoot. But within about a year
(if the play has been rightly dated above) Marlowe lay
dead in Deptford, and for him, as for his Faustus, the
branch was cut for ever.

[1] Chettle, while disclaiming any desire for his acquaintance, says that he
reverences his learning (see below, p. 240).

XIII

MARLOWE'S POEMS

I

THE SHORTER PIECES

WITH the lyrical and descriptive elements in Marlowe's genius it would not have been surprising if even in his short career he had left behind him a body of original poetic achievement outside of the dramatic sphere. But his one notable legacy of this kind is the unfinished *Hero and Leander*. Unlike Lyly before him and Shakespeare and Jonson after him, he did not write songs to fit aptly into the action of his plays. The one lyric that we can identify from his pen is more notable for its associations than its content, though it has its own silvery charm. It is the set of four-lined stanzas entitled *The Passionate Shepherd to his Love*, beginning:

> Come, live with me and be my love,
> And we will all the pleasures prove,
> That valleys, groves, hills, and fields
> Woods, or steepy mountains yields.
>
> And we will sit upon the rocks,
> Seeing the shepherds feed their flocks,
> By shallow rivers to whose falls
> Melodious birds sing madrigals.
>
> And I will make thee beds of roses
> And a thousand fragrant posies,
> A cap of flowers and a kirtle,
> Embroidered all with leaves of myrtle.

With three other stanzas these are printed in the anthology, *England's Helicon* (1600), with the signature, Chr. Marlow. The first three stanzas (with some variants) and one of the others had already appeared, without title or signature, in *The Passionate Pilgrim* (1599). This volume bore Shakespeare's name on the title-page, but it was a miscellaneous collection, and Marlowe's stanzas were included in the second part, which had a separate title, *Sonnets to Sundry Notes of Music*. But though not written by Shakespeare, they were certainly known to him, for he makes Sir Hugh Evans in *The Merry Wives of Windsor*, III. i, sing some of the lines in a maudlin mood, when he has 'a great dispositions to cry'—scarcely a compliment to the 'dead shepherd'. Did the Welsh parson use the musical setting included in William Corkine's *Second Book of Ayres* (1612)?

More of a compliment, though a left-handed one, was paid by Raleigh when he wrote a *Reply* to the shepherd's invitation in the same metre and in answering phrases. Its cynical burden is the swift passing of all pleasure and beauty, wherefore the loved one will not lend an ear:

> But could youth last, and love still breed;
> Had joys no date, nor age no need;
> Then those delights my mind might move
> To live with thee and be thy love.

The *Reply* was printed, together with Marlowe's poem, in *England's Helicon*. They were both published together in a broadside, preserved in *The Roxburghe Ballads* (i. 205), printed by the assigns of Thomas Symcock, between 1618 and 1629. In a commonplace book kept by John Thornborough (1551–1641), successively Dean of York and Bishop of Worcester, there is an additional antepenultimate stanza which in modernized spelling runs:

> Thy dishes shall be filled with meat
> Such as the gods do use to eat:
> Shall one and every table be
> Prepared each day for thee and me.

This might have been looked on as an interpolation had not Izaak Walton, who introduces the poem into *The Compleat Angler* (1653 and 1655), added a similar stanza in the second edition:

> Thy silver dishes for thy meat
> As precious as the gods do eat,
> Shall on an ivory table be
> Prepar'd each day for thee and me.

Walton puts it into the lips of a milkmaid, as 'that smooth song which was made by Kit Marlowe, now at least fifty years ago'. It certainly comes much more suitably from a milkmaid than from Ithamore in *The Jew of Malta* who in IV. iv. 104–5 ends a highly coloured invocation to Bellamira with the couplet:

> Thou in those groves by Dis above,
> Shalt live with me and be my love.

The nearest parallels to the song in Marlowe's plays are to be found in *Dido*, especially in the Nurse's invitation to Cupid (IV. v. 4–12). But pastoralism does not sit easy on Marlowe. Coral clasps and amber studs, silver dishes and an ivory table mingle strangely with the simple joys of the country-side.

There is something of the same blending of diverse features in the tantalizing fragment, subscribed 'Ch. Marlowe', included in another 1600 anthology, *England's Parnassus*. The fragment has no separate title, but is included in the section headed 'Description of Seas, Waters, Rivers, &c.' It consists of two full stanzas in *ottava rima*, preceded by the four last lines of a stanza and followed by the first four lines of another. Short as it is, this specimen serves to show that Marlowe could handle the elaborate rhyme scheme of the poem with easy mastery. And it is marked by his characteristic boldness of imagery and wealth of colour. The poet is walking beside 'a stream for pureness rare' and feasts his eyes upon

> the glorious prey
> That in the pebble-paved channel lay.

There ran

> Nature's richest alchemy,
> Diamonds resolv'd, and substance more divine
> Through whose bright gliding current might appear
> A thousand naked nymphs, whose ivory shine,
> Enamelling the banks, made them more dear
> Than ever was that glorious palace gate
> Where the day-shining sun in triumph sate.

The comparison with the sun's palace gate is in the true
Marlovian vein as, in different wise, is the similitude in the
next stanza of the trees overarching the stream to 'a
costly valance o'er a bed'. And the striking expression of
the poet's sense of form and colour in the last lines of the
fragment,

> Their leaves that differed both in shape and show,
> (Though all were green), yet difference such in green,
> Like to the checker'd bent of Iris' bow,
> Prided the running main as it had been—

deepens our sense of loss in the disappearance of the rest
of the poem.

The recent fresh evidence in support of Marlowe's
authorship of the Latin elegy on Sir Roger Manwood[1]
and the prose dedication of Thomas Watson's *Amintae
Gaudia*[2] may warn us against rejecting too summarily
other pieces that have been attributed to him. An
anonymous contributor to *Notes and Queries*, 18 May
1850, claimed to have a later sixteenth-century manuscript which had among its contents an eclogue, *Amor
Constans*, beginning 'For shame, man, wilt thou never
leave this sorrow', and signed 'Infortunatus Ch. M.'
This was followed by sixteen sonnets, including two
addressed to a painter, Seager, otherwise apparently unknown. The sonnets were also signed 'Ch. M.' While
Marlowe's authorship is highly improbable, it is to be
regretted that the communication in *Notes and Queries*
raised no further inquiry and that the manuscript has
disappeared.

Another attribution is, on the face of it, much more
plausible. Thomas Warton asserted, on the authority of
Thomas Coxeter's manuscript papers, that Marlowe had
'translated Coluthus's *Rape of Helen* into English rhyme
in the year 1587'. Coxeter, an antiquarian collector in the
earlier eighteenth century, has a doubtful reputation, and
no one else had seen a copy of the translation. But in the

---

[1] See below, pp. 237-8.
[2] Eccles, *Marlowe in London*, pp. 162-71.

light of Marlowe's association with Thomas Watson, it is
notable that the latter had in 1586 published a Latin
version, *Helenae Raptus*, of the Greek epic in 400 hexameters by Coluthus, a sixth-century poet of Lycopolis
in the Egyptian Thebaid. With Marlowe's passionate
adoration of Helen it would have been natural for him
to turn Watson's Latin verse into English. And how apt
a counterpart it would be to Marlowe's *Hero and Leander*,
inspired by a kindred source (also probably through a
Latin translation), the Greek poem of the fifth-century
Alexandrian, 'divine Musaeus'.

II

HERO AND LEANDER

On 28 September 1593 'a booke intituled *HERO and
LEANDER* beinge an amorous poem devised by CHRIS-
TOFER MARLOW' was entered on the Stationers'
Register to John Wolf. If he published an edition, no
copy has survived. By 1598 he had made over his right
to Edward Blount who in that year brought out a quarto,
printed by Adam Islip, and dedicated to Sir Thomas
Walsingham,[1] containing Marlowe's unfinished portion of
the poem. Of this edition only one copy survives, now
in the Folger Shakespeare Library in Washington. On
2 March 1597/8 Blount in his turn transferred his interest
(though not wholly) to Paul Linley, who later in the year
published a quarto, printed by Felix Kingston, containing
'HERO AND LEANDER: Begun by *Christopher Marloe*;
and *finished by* George Chapman'. Two copies of this
previously unknown edition were discovered in 1857 at
Lamport Hall. One is in the British Museum and the
other in the Huntington Library. Linley's edition contains Marlowe's two 'Sestiads', followed by four by Chapman, who in a separate dedication to Lady Walsingham
profusely apologizes for concerning himself with so trifling
a subject.

[1] See further, pp. 281-2.

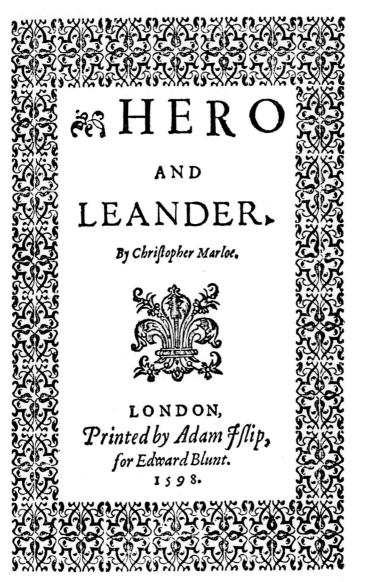

HERO

AND

LEANDER.

By Chriſtopher Marloe.

LONDON,
Printed by Adam Iſlip,
for Edward Blunt.
1598.

Title-page of the only edition of *Hero and Leander* in its unfinished
state, without Chapman's continuation

Mention has already been made of the passing of the copyright in *Hero and Leander*, as well as of the translation of *Lucan*, from Linley to John Flasket,[1] who published editions of the poem, with Chapman's continuation, in 1600 and 1606.

As *Hero and Leander* was left unfinished, it has been natural to assign it to the end of Marlowe's career. Blount's dedication of it to Sir Thomas Walsingham may even suggest that the poet was engaged on it while he was visiting Scadbury. And internal evidence in the main favours a late date. This is supported by the large proportion of run-on lines and double endings in *Hero and Leander* as contrasted with the end-stopped couplets of the *Elegies*, though allowance has to be made for a difference of technique in a translation of Ovid's elegiacs and in an original poem. Another less noticed point is the absence in *Hero and Leander* of the colloquial phrases which, as has been seen, often produced in the *Elegies* a jarring effect. Marlowe's verbal artistry is more mature.

On the other hand the poem has links with what are usually accounted Marlowe's earlier works. Apart from minor points of contact one line in *Hero and Leander*, i. 382,

Threat'ning a thousand deaths at every glance

is identical with *Dido*, ii. i. 231. And, as will be seen, Marlowe when writing the poem was steeped in Ovidian memories of the *Amores* and the *Heroides*. It is possible that in the *Lucan* translation and in *Hero and Leander* Marlowe may have made use, even at an early period, of run-on lines which had little place in his dramatic dialogue.

At whatever period *Hero and Leander* was written echoes from Ovid's *Elegies* were ringing in Marlowe's ears. When the youth enamoured of the maiden at first sight cries (i. 207–8):

My words shall be as spotless as my youth,
Full of simplicity and naked truth—

---

[1] See above, pp. 42–3.

he is repeating the plea of Ovid to his mistress (*El.* i. iii. 5–6, and 13–14):

> Accept him that will serve thee all his youth,
> Accept him that will love with spotless truth
>
> .   .   .   .
>
> My spotless life, which but to gods gives place,
> Naked simplicity, and modest grace.

And when Leander urges (i. 231–42):

> Vessels of brass oft handled, brightly shine,
>
> .   .   .   .
>
> Rich robes themselves and others do adorn;
> Neither themselves nor others, if not worn.
> Who builds a palace and rams up the gate,
> Shall see it ruinous and desolate;
> Ah simple Hero, learn thyself to cherish,
> Lone women like to empty houses perish—

he is expanding and turning to his use the argument of the *lena*, Dipsas (*El.* i. viii. 51–2):

> Brass shines with use: good garments would be worn;
> Houses not dwelt in are with filth forlorn.

And there are other parallels, though not so close and indisputable.

In the *Elegies* there is only one incidental reference to Hero and Leander (ii. xvi. 31–2)

> The youth oft swimming to his Hero kind,
> Had then swum over, but the way was blind.

But in the *Heroides*, xviii and xix, the two lovers exchange lengthy epistles, which Marlowe doubtless had in mind when Leander (ii. 14–15)

> after her a letter sent,
> Which joyful Hero answer'd.

It was the confession of Leander in *Heroides* (xviii. 13–14)

> Non poteram celare meos, velut ante, parentes,
>   quemque tegi volumus, non latuisset amor

that prompted Marlowe's (ii. 136–7):

> Leander's father knew where he had been,
> And for the same mildly rebuk'd his son.

So, too, Hero's fears and suspicions in her epistle seem to have suggested the line (ii. 43):

> Now wax'd she jealous, lest his love abated.

Leander's father and Hero's jealousy are equally absent from the main source of Marlowe's poem, the *Hero and Leander* of Musaeus, whether in the original Greek or in a translation. Printed in Greek, apparently for the first time in 1484, it had been translated into Italian by Tasso in 1537, into French by Marot in 1541, and into Latin by F. Paulinus in 1587. Minor links have been suggested between Marlowe's poem and the Italian and French versions, but he probably drew the story of the lovers chiefly from the Latin of Paulinus. Not only in its main incidents, but in some special details, as will be seen, Marlowe reproduced the neo-classic romance.

But as handled by the English poet it becomes, even though uncompleted, far more than the tale of the two star-crossed lovers. I have already stressed the fact that the *Amores*, in addition to its other aspects, is a storehouse of mythological lore.[1] And in the *Heroides* Leander and Hero sprinkle their epistles fully with allusions to Greek deities and legendary figures. Influenced in part by Ovid, Marlowe crowds his canvas with such elaborate extraneous detail from the classical Pantheon that his hero and heroine become often obscured. This is flagrantly so in the last hundred lines of Sestiad I where quite irrelevantly Marlowe turns aside to tell a tale of Mercury, Jove, Cupid, and the Destinies, ending with a lament over the poverty which is in consequence the heritage of Mercury's devotees. No less redundant is the long episode (ii. 155–226) narrating the passion of Neptune for Leander. And the same homosexual element enters into the lines, i. 77–86, beginning

> Had wild Hippolytus Leander seen,
> Enamoured of his beauty had he been,

---

[1] See above, pp. 31–2.

and, in part, into those that describe (i. 143–56)

> the gods in sundry shapes
> Committing heady riots, incest, rapes,

pictured on the 'radiant floor' of Venus' temple in Sestos.

Marlowe even introduces Hero with a mythological flourish, seemingly of his own invention (i. 5–7):

> Hero the fair,
> Whom young Apollo courted for her hair,
> And offer'd as a dower his burning throne.

The sleeves of her garment were (i. 11–14)

> bordered with a grove,
> Where Venus in her naked glory strove
> To please the careless and disdainful eyes
> Of proud Adonis that before her lies.

Leander, too, makes his entry amid a shower of mythological allusions (i. 55–62):

> His dangling tresses that were never shorn,
> Had they been cut, and unto Colchos borne,
> Would have allur'd the vent'rous youth of Greece
> To hazard more than for the golden Fleece.
> Fair Cynthia wish'd his arms might be her sphere:
> Grief makes her pale, because she moves not there.
> His body was as straight as Circe's wand,
> Jove might have sipt out nectar from his hand.

Besides these set pieces there is a running fire throughout the two Sestiads of classical similes and references. It is scarcely too much to say that Marlowe had, at any rate subconsciously, a double object in *Hero and Leander*, to tell the story of the lovers and to load every rift with mythological ore. It is, therefore, in a sense, beside the point to criticize the poem for its lack of unity. Marlowe is joyously travelling in 'the realms of gold', and glories in exploring their by-ways rather than in steering a direct course.

None the less he shows a mastery in the conduct of his central theme and stamps his own genius upon it. He

borrows from Musaeus the introductory episode of the
festival in the Sestian temple of Venus where Hero and
Leander first meet. But he fills in the picture with fresh
and vivid detail, as in the dazzling description of the
temple itself (i. 135–42):

> So fair a church as this, had Venus none:
> The walls were of discoloured jasper stone,
> Wherein was Proteus carved, and o'erhead
> A lively vine of green sea-agate spread;
> Where by one hand, light-headed Bacchus hung,
> And with the other, wine from grapes outwrung.
> Of crystal shining fair the pavement was;
> The town of Sestos call'd it Venus' glass.

Musaeus describes the youths from the islands near and
from Phrygia hasting on the day to pay their vows to the
fair ones of Sestos. Marlowe heightens the picture with
characteristic celestial imagery (i. 94–103):

> Thither resorted many a wand'ring guest
> To meet their loves: such as had none at all,
> Came lovers home, from this great festival:
> For every street like to a firmament
> Glistered with breathing stars, who where they went,
> Frighted the melancholy earth, which deem'd
> Eternal heaven to burn, for so it seem'd,
> As if another Phaëton had got
> The guidance of the sun's rich chariot.
> But far above the loveliest Hero shined.

Then follows an elaborate comparison of Hero to the
moon 'crown'd with blazing light and majesty', succeeded
by an unexpected image that brings us abruptly into the
atmosphere of *Tamburlaine*:

> And as in fury of a dreadful fight,
> Their fellows being slain or put to flight,
> Poor soldiers stand with fear of death dead-strooken,
> So at her presence all surpris'd and tooken
> Await the sentence of her scornful eyes;
> He whom she favours lives; the other dies.

Yet it is difficult, on the face of it, to associate with the author of *Tamburlaine*, at any period of his career, the couplet (i. 167–8):

> It lies not in our power to love, or hate,
> For will in us is over-rul'd by fate.

If the second line is taken in its naked simplicity, and in its natural interpretation to-day, it is the negation of the dominant spirit of Marlovian drama where the human will soars above all limitations and boasts that it holds 'the fates fast bound in iron chains'. But in the light of the first line, 'will' is here to be interpreted in its narrower Elizabethan sense of amorous desire, or its opposite. This does not spring from conscious reasoning; but from a primal impulse that, in modern phrase, is stronger than ourselves and carries us headlong.

> Where both deliberate, the love is slight;
> Who ever lov'd that lov'd not at first sight?

So is it with Leander and Hero, with Tamburlaine and Zenocrate, with Faustus and Helen. Is it really a compliment to Marlowe that Shakespeare in *As You Like It* should put the last line into the mouth of Phebe to vindicate her sudden infatuation for Rosalind disguised as a youth?

But though love is not the offspring of reasoning it can make use of it for its own purposes. Though Hero was enamoured, she displayed a maidenly coyness towards Leander.

> At last, like to a bold sharp sophister,
> With cheerful hope thus he accosted her.

The use of the term 'sophister' borrowed from the academic schools prepares us for a 'disputation' from Leander's lips on the superiority of wedlock to spinster-hood, very different from the conventional lover's pleas in Musaeus. He first plies Hero with the arguments, already noted, borrowed from Ovid, and then advances to

a more subtle dialectic, for which Aristotle gives the cue
(i. 255):

> One is no number; maids are nothing then,
> Without the sweet society of men.
> Wilt thou live single still? one shalt thou be,
> Though never-singling Hymen couple thee.
>
> .   .   .   .
>
> Base bullion for the stamp's sake we allow;
> Even so for men's impression do we you;
> By which alone, our reverend fathers say,
> Women receive perfection every way.
> This idol which you term Virginity,
> Is neither essence subject to the eye,
> No, nor to any one exterior sense,
> Nor hath it any place of residence,
> Nor is 't of earth or mould celestial,
> Or capable of any form at all.
> Of that which hath no being do not boast,
> Things that are not at all are never lost.

Is Marlowe here remembering discussions in his class
at Cambridge, or later metaphysical arguments with
Harriot and Raleigh? In any case we may well again cry:

> Was ever woman in this humour wooed?
> Was ever woman in this humour won?

For Hero is won, though she still makes a pretence of
fight (i. 329–32):

> These arguments he us'd, and many more,
> Wherewith she yielded, that was won before;
> Hero's looks yielded, but her words made war;
> Women are won when they begin to jar.

Though she forbids Leander—and here Marlowe follows Musaeus—to embrace her or to touch her 'sacred
garments', she surrenders the key of the fort (i. 345 ff.):

> 'Upon a rock, and underneath a hill,
> Far from the town (where all is whist and still
> Save that the sea, playing on yellow sand,
> Sends forth a rattling murmur to the land)
>
> .   .   .   .

My turret stands . . .
Come thither.' As she spake this, her tongue tripp'd,
For unawares 'Come thither' from her slipp'd.

It is an exquisite vignette, rare in Marlowe, of nature
in a peaceful, gentle mood, fit background to the maiden
who is herself so 'whist and still' that she can only whisper
the two inviting words. And then in more characteristic
vein the poet whirls us upwards to the empyrean (i.
361–4):

And like a planet moving several ways
At one self instant, she poor soul assays,
Loving, not to love at all, and every part
Strove to resist the motions of her heart.

It is at this point that Marlowe breaks off to tell the
tale of Mercury, Cupid, Jove, and the Destinies. But
when he returns at the beginning of the second Sestiad
to his main theme, Leander, who in Musaeus after his
first meeting with Hero recrosses the Hellespont to
Abydos, is already entering her tower (ii. 19–21):

Wide open stood the door, he need not climb, .
And she herself before the pointed time
Had spread the board, with roses strowed the room.

The remainder of the Sestiad, except for the Neptune
interlude, is a minute study of the stages by which the
lover progresses to the full possession of his mistress. It is
a frankly sensuous revelation, in which Marlowe proves
himself a disciple of Ovid rather than of Musaeus. He
shows how Leander, as yet a novice, becomes a master
of the art of love. At their first encounter in the tower he
has to be content with kisses and embraces. Hero though
'seeming lavish, sav'd her maidenhead'.

Jewels being lost are found again, this never,
'Tis lost but once and once lost, lost for ever.

It is after the first night in the tower that Marlowe
represents Leander as returning to Abydos. And once

again he goes to astronomy for an image of his distracted
state (ii. 123–8):

> Like as the sun in a diameter
> Fires and inflames objects removed far,
> And heateth kindly, shining laterally:
> So beauty sweetly quickens when 'tis nigh,
> But being separate and removed,
> Burns where it cherish'd, murders where it loved.
>
> . . . .
>
> His secret flame apparently was seen
> Leander's father knew where he had been.

But parental rebuke could not stay him from plunging
into the Hellespont, nor Neptune's amorous enticements
from crossing the strait to Sestos. He ran breathless to
Hero's tower:

> And knock'd and called; at which celestial noise
>
> . . . .
>
> She stayed not for her robes, but straight arose
> And drunk with gladness, to the door she goes.

The purest rapture of expectant love thrills through
these lines and glorifies what follows. Marlowe had
evidently here in mind, and repeats some of the phrases
from, one of the most sensuous of the *Elegies* (i. v). But
the grossness of the verses in which Ovid tells of his
intercourse with Corinna is purged by the brisk ani-
mation and delicate humour of Marlowe's narrative.
Leander 'through numbing cold all feeble, faint and wan',
begs if not for love, yet for pity, to be taken into Hero's
bed. When Hero 'affrighted' shrinks away, and makes
room for him (ii. 259–66):

> His hands he cast upon her like a snare;
> She overcome with shame and sallow fear,
> Like chaste Diana when Acteon spied her,
> Being suddenly betrayed, div'd down to hide her,
> And as her silver body downward went,
> With both her hands she made the bed a tent,
> And in her own mind thought herself secure,
> O'ercast with dim and darksome coverture.

But it is a false security, and soon 'the poor silly maiden at his mercy was'.

Then with one of his characteristic abrupt transitions Marlowe confronts Love as an elemental force, reckless of all but its own ends (ii. 287–93):

> Love is not full of pity, as men say,
> But deaf and cruel where he means to prey.
> Even as a bird, which in our hands we wring,
> Forth plungeth, and oft flutters with her wing,
> She trembling strove, this strife of hers (like that
> Which made the world) another world begat
> Of unknown joy.

Marlowe seems to be a forerunner of the 'metaphysical' school when he here, with another reminiscence of the Cambridge classroom, prays in aid as a parallel the Empedoclean doctrine that strife begot the universe. And when 'the pleasure of the blessed night' is over, and Hero stands blushing beside the bed, the loveliest of all Marlowe's cosmic images irradiates the scene (ii. 318–22):

> And from her countenance behold ye might
> A kind of twilight break, which through the hair,
> As from an orient cloud, glimps'd here and there;
> And round about the chamber this false morn
> Brought forth the day before the day was born.

It is such images, strewn through the poem, that even in its most sensuous episodes make its raptures, in Drayton's words, 'all air and fire'. They are 'magic casements opening' from Hero's tower upon sky and sea, and purifying its heated atmosphere.

And throughout *Hero and Leander* Marlowe shows a linguistic and metrical mastery. His vocabulary is akin to that of his translation of the *Amores* in its admixture of words, either rare or used in an unusual sense, e.g. 'thirling' (flying through the air), 'parled' (spoke), 'idiot' (ignorant person), 'put' (repelled), 'affied' (betrothed), 'pais'd' (weighed), 'ringled' (? marked with rings), 'dang'd' (threw). There is also a copious use, as in the *Elegies*, of compound epithets, 'night-wandering', 'deep-drench'd', 'never-singling', 'flint-breasted,' 'sapphire-visaged', 'dead-strooken'. On the other hand, there is almost a complete absence of the colloquialisms, and of the occasional obscurities that are found in the translation. The language of *Hero and Leander* is almost uniformly lucid and, in the best sense of the word, elegant.

Metrically the frequent double rhymes and epigrammatic couplets connect the poem with the *Elegies*. And as has been seen, there are passages in the translation which reach a high rhythmical level. But the general metrical quality of the *Elegies* and of *Hero and Leander* is strikingly different. Where the one makes its best effects by the cumulative massing of a series of sonorous couplets the latter relies mainly on the 'run-on' line. Its music is thus far more subtle, and the flow of the verse far more rapid. It is these that, in spite of the delaying interludes, give *Hero and Leander* as a whole so exhilarating a movement and make us deplore that it was left incomplete. Had Marlowe intended to keep, however broadly, to the proportions of Musaeus' poem, he is more likely to have added one Sestiad than the four of Chapman's continuation.

But if we are to speculate about what might have been, we may perhaps regret that Marlowe did not make a play out of the tragic story, and provide what might have been a companion piece to *Romeo and Juliet*, as *Edward II* is to *Richard II*. But, as has been seen, in his only accepted play where love is the dominant theme, *Dido, Queen of Carthage*, it is not passion between a youth and a maiden wrecked by raging seas or family feuds. It is the mature love between two figures of heroic mould which has to be sacrificed to a divine decree, and to an imperial destiny.

XIV

MARLOWE'S ACCUSERS

I

GREENE AND KYD

ABOUT the same time that P. F.'s *English Faust Book* was being published and furnishing Marlowe with material so attractive to his genius, he seems to have been again getting into trouble with the Shoreditch legal authorities. Mark Eccles discovered from an entry in Middlesex Sessions Roll 309, no. 13, that 'Christopherus Marle de London generosus' entered on 9 May 1592 into a recognizance under a penalty of £20 to appear at the next General Session of the Peace, and meanwhile to keep the peace towards Allen Nicholls, Constable of Holywell Street and Nicholas Helliott, sub-constable.[1] It is true that there were five other Christopher Morleys living in London in 1592, but as Eccles has shown, none of them resided near Holywell Street.[2] In this theatrical neighbourhood the dramatist seems to have continued living since appearing at the Gaol delivery in December 1589. There is no entry to show that on this later occasion he made the requisite appearance in the first week after Michaelmas.

In any case the charge was a less serious one than the suspicion of murdering Bradley. The memory of the Hog lane affray and its consequences must have come home to Marlowe in September 1592 when Thomas Watson died. On 10 November his *Amintae Gaudia* was entered in the Stationers' Register, and was published with a Latin dedication to the Countess of Pembroke signed 'C. M.'[3] In the light of what is now known of the association of Marlowe and Watson there is good reason

---

[1] The document is quoted in the original Latin in *Christopher Marlowe in London*, p. 105. [2] Op. cit., pp. 109–13.

[3] Printed in full by Eccles, op. cit., p. 164.

for identifying 'C. M.' as the dramatist. The profusion of classical allusions in the dedication is characteristic of him. Thus the high-flown invocation begins:

Illustrissimæ Heroinæ omnibus et animi et corporis dotibus ornatissimæ, Mariæ Pembrokiæ Comitissæ.

Laurigera stirpe prognata Delia, Sydnæi vatis Apollinei genuina soror; Alma literarum parens, ad cuius immaculatos amplexus, confugit virtus, barbariei & ignorantiae impetu violata, vt olim a Threicio Tyranno Philomela.

Then follow allusions to Ariadne, Phoebus, Jupiter, to the 'littorea myrtus Veneris' and 'Nymphæ Peneiæ [Daphne] semper virens coma'. It seems to me also in Marlowe's dialectical vein, after he has declared that the renown of the Countess cannot be increased by the praise of mortals, to add 'quomodo enim quicquam possit esse infinito plus?' On the other hand, even allowing for the conventions of Elizabethan dedications, it is surprising to find the author of *Tamburlaine* and *Doctor Faustus* belittling his own powers to the degree implied in these words:

'Dia proles, quæ iam rudi calamo, spiritus infundis elati furoris, quibus ipse misellus, plus mihi videor præstare posse, quam cruda nostra indoles proferre solet.'

There was certainly no mark of 'cruda indoles' in *Edward II* which the players of the Countess of Pembroke's husband were performing in this same year.

Thomas Watson was almost immediately followed to the grave by one of the leading figures on the Bench at the Gaol-Delivery of 3 December 1589. Sir Roger Manwood, Chief Baron of the Exchequer, died on 14 December 1592, and was buried in the church of his manor of Hawe, near Canterbury. Manwood had been guilty of malpractices in his high office, and had been arraigned before the Privy Council. Yet in the Oxinden Commonplace books and the Heber copy of *Hero and Leander*[1] there is found an epitaph on him in twelve Latin hexameter lines, 'made by Christopher Marlo'. The ascription of the epi-

[1] See above, p. 19 n.

taph to Marlowe thus goes back to 1640, within half a
century of his death, and apparently rests on a well-
authenticated tradition, though it is difficult to see why
the dramatist, who had apparently neglected to keep up
any ties with his native city, should have taken occasion
to celebrate the somewhat doubtful virtues of this deceased neighbouring 'worthy'. The lines, if they are by
Marlowe, would have an interest as being the only extant
Latin verses from his pen, but they are in the conventional vein of an epitaph, bidding criminals rejoice, and
the innocent mourn for the death of 'fori lumen, vene-
randæ gloria legis'. Perhaps the prayer to 'livor' or
'malice' to spare his ashes may be a veiled hint that all
was not well with his name.

The deaths of Watson and Manwood had been preceded by some months by that of a more familiar figure
who had also come within Marlowe's orbit. Robert
Greene died on 3 September 1592. In his last hours he
penned the pamphlet *Greenes Groats-worth of Wit bought
with a Million of Repentance*, including towards its close
an exhortation 'To those Gentlemen his Quondam acquaintance that spend their wits in making Plaies'. There
are five of these Gentlemen whom he bids learn by his
woeful experience to look back with sorrow on their time
past, and endeavour with repentance to spend that which
is to come.

He then first singles out Marlowe (for no other can be
meant), and now in sorrow, instead of anger as in 1588,[1]
reproves him for atheism:

'Wonder not (for with thee wil I first begin) thou famous gracer
of Tragedians, that *Greene* who hath said with thee like the foole
in his heart, there is no God, should now giue glorie vnto his
greatnesse: for penetrating is his power, his hand lies heauie
vpon me, he hath spoken vnto me with a voice of thunder, and
I haue felt he is a God that can punish enemies. Why should thy
excellent wit, his gift, be so blinded, that thou should giue no
glory to the giuer?'

---

[1] See above, pp. 70 and 111.

The words that follow show that Greene is thinking of atheism in terms not only of doctrine but of morals, for though '*The Prince* reveals a consistent theory of life which quietly and temperately sets aside the laws of Christianity'[1] its author was not directly concerned with religious belief or unbelief.

'Is it pestilent Machiuilian pollicie that thou hast studied? O peeuish follie! What are his rules but meere confused mockeries, able to extirpate in small time the generation of mankinde. For if *Sic Volo, sic iubeo,* hold in those that are able to commande, and if it be lawfull *Fas & nefas* to doe any thing that is beneficiall, onely Tyrants shuld possesse the earth, and they striuing to exceede in tyranny, shuld each to other bee a slaughter man; till the mightiest outliuing all, one stroke were left for Death, that in one age man's life shuld ende.'

Here Greene, addressing Marlowe, catches for the moment the secret of his soaring and sombre rhetoric in this vision of the final catastrophe of mankind. He continues with a somewhat enigmatic reference:

The brocher of this Diabolicall Atheisme is dead, and in his life had neuer the felicitie he aimed at. . . . Wilt thou my friend be his Disciple? Looke vnto me, by him perswaded to this libertie, and thou shalt finde it an infernall bondage. I knowe the least of my demerits merit this miserable death, but wilfull striuing against knowne truth exceedeth al the terrors of my soule. Defer not (with me) till this last point of extremitie; for little knowest thou how in the end thou shalt be visited.'

In the light of the tragedy at Deptford on 30 May 1593 the last words were to be more luridly prophetic than the dying Greene could have foreseen. Then after milder admonitions to two other dramatists, almost certainly Nashe and Peele, he warns the trio against putting any trust in actors, though he acknowledges that they have consorted more with him than with them:

'Base minded men al three of you, if by my miserie ye be not warned: for vnto none of you (like me) sought those burres to cleaue:

---

[1] Una Ellis-Fermor, *Christopher Marlowe*, p. 91.

those Puppits (I meane) that speake from our mouths, those
Anticts garnisht in our colours.'

Then follows the outburst against Shakespeare the 'vp-
start' actor, who has had the temerity also to pose as a
playwright.[1] From this Greene turns to entreat Marlowe
and the other dramatists to adopt 'more profitable courses
. . . for it is a pittie men of such rare wits should be
subiect to the pleasures of such rude groomes'. It is a
paradox to hear the arch-Bohemian Robert Greene at the
end of his days denouncing professional players as vio-
lently as the most stiff-necked of the contemporary
academic enemies of the public stage.

Soon after Greene's death his *Groatsworth of Wit* was
edited by Henry Chettle, and the letters to divers play-
makers was 'offensively by one or two of them taken'.
This is acknowledged by Chettle in an introduction to his
Kind-Harts Dreame, registered on 8 December 1592, in
which he disclaimed any part in *The Groatsworth of Wit*,
except for rewriting the 'copy', as 'sometime *Greenes* hand
was none of the best'. Chettle asserts that 'with neither
of them that take offence was I acquainted'. But with
one of them, who would seem to be Shakespeare, he implies that he has since then been in contact, 'because my
selfe haue seene his demeanor no less ciuill than be exelent
in the qualitie he professes'. He has also heard from
'diuers of worship' of 'his uprightnes of dealing' and of
his 'facetious grace in writing'. Thus Chettle makes
handsome amends to Shakespeare for Greene's attack by
a comprehensive tribute to his personal character, his
talent as an actor, and his achievement as a writer. In
sharp contrast is his attitude towards the other offended
playwright, who can be no other than Marlowe. With
him he cares not if he never became acquainted, though
he reverences his learning, 'and at the perusing of *Greenes*
Booke stroke out what then in conscience I thought he
in some displeasure writ; or had it been true, yet to
publish it was intollerable'. With all respect for Chettle's

[1] See above, p. 193.

creditable scruples one cannot help regretting that he omitted details from Greene's exhortation to Marlowe which might have thrown light on the 'intollerable' accusations which were in a few months to be brought against him from other quarters.

It has been seen, on the word of Thomas Kyd, that he and Christopher Marlowe had been associated at least as early as the first summer months of 1591, when they were writing in one chamber together.[1] But their acquaintance probably dated back farther, for after the reference to 'twoe yeares synce', Kyd immediately proceeds to tell the Lord Keeper, 'My first acquaintance with this Marlowe, rose vpon his bearing name to serve my Lord although his Lordship never knewe his service, but in writing for his plaiers.' It is one of the most tantalizing problems in Marlovian biography that Kyd omits to give a clue to the identification of this lord of whose household he had been a member in some unspecified capacity for nearly six years,[2] and for whose company Marlowe wrote. On the evidence of title-pages and of Henslowe's diary the companies known to have acted Marlowe's plays during his lifetime were those of the Lord Admiral (*Tamburlaine*), Lord Strange (*The Jew of Malta* and *The Massacre at Paris*), and Lord Pembroke (*Edward II*). On the assumption that Henry Herbert, Earl of Pembroke, had no company before 1592 he is ruled out. Charles Howard, 2nd Lord Howard of Effingham, who had been Lord Chamberlain, and afterwards Lord High Admiral from 8 July 1585 and had held the chief command against the Armada was, it may be assumed, too august a personage for Kyd to assure the Lord Keeper that he 'wold no waie move the Leste suspicion of his Loves and cares both towardes hir sacred Majestie your Lordships and the lawes'. Ferdinando Stanley, Lord Strange, though soon to succeed as 5th Earl of Derby, was of less exalted station,

---

[1] See above, p. 111.
[2] In my edition of *Kyd's Works*, p. cix, for 'theis iij yeres nowe' read 'theis vj yeres nowe'.

and had a connexion with Kyd as his men acted *The Spanish Tragedy* in 1591/2–1592/3. He may have been the patron-lord,[1] but the matter must remain in doubt. In any case it is important to keep clear the circumstances in which Kyd's letter to the Lord Keeper was written. He was arrested on 12 May 1593 on suspicion of being guilty of what he calls in his letter 'that libell that concern'd the state', and 'that mutinous sedition towr'd the state'. On the previous day the Privy Council had directed a body of commissioners appointed by the Lord Mayor to arrest and examine any persons suspected of lately setting up 'diuers lewd and mutinous libells' within the city of London, to search their chambers for writings or papers, and, in default of confession to 'put them to the Torture in Bridewell'.[2] There can be little doubt that it was under this general warrant that Kyd was arrested, and as he speaks of 'my paines and vndeserued tortures' he appears to have been put on the rack. But in his letter he is careful to distinguished between the offence against the state of which (as he protests) he was unjustly suspected and the further charge of atheism which only arose after the discovery among his papers of the heretical disputation which had belonged to Marlowe. In his feverish anxiety to clear himself of this deadlier charge Kyd does not hesitate to minimize the extent of his association with Marlowe and to defame his character.

Never cold my Lord endure his name or sight, when he had heard of his conditions, nor wold indeed the forme of devyne praiers vsed duelie in his Lordships house haue quadred wth such reprobates.

That I shold loue or be familer frend wth one so irreligious were verie rare . . . besides he was intemperate & of a cruel hart, the verie contraries to w[ch], my greatest enemies will saie by me.

Kyd then refers Puckering to Marlowe's more intimate associates for more detailed information, but apparently

---

[1] His claims are set forth by Tucker Brooke (op. cit., p. 47), who states objections to my suggestion, in op. cit., p. lxiv, of Robert Radcliffe, 5th Earl of Sussex.   [2] See *Kyd's Works*, p. lxvii.

the Lord Keeper pressed him to amplify his statement. For there is another letter, unsigned but in his hand,[1] as follows:

Pleaseth it your honorable lordship toching marlowes monstruous opinions as I cannot but with an agreved conscience think on him or them so can I but particulariz fewe in the respect of them that kept him greater company. Howbeit in discharg of dutie both towardes god your lordships & the world thus much haue I thought good breiflie to discover in all humblenes.

ffirst it was his custom when I knewe him first & as I heare saie he contynewd it in table talk or otherwise to iest at the devine scriptures gybe at praiers, & stryve in argument to frustrate & confute what hath byn spoke or wrytt by prophets & such holie menn.

1. He wold report St John to be our savior Christes *Alexis*. I cover it with reverence and trembling that is that Christ did loue him with an extraordinary loue.

2. That for me to wryte a poem of St *paules* conversion as I was determined he said wold be as if I shold go wryte a book of fast & loose, esteeming *Paul* a Jugler.

3. That the prodigall Childes portion was but fower nobles, he held his purse so neere the bottom in all pictures, and that it either was a iest or els fowr nobles then was thought a great patrimony not thinking it a parable.

4. That things esteemed to be donn by devine power might haue aswell been don by observation of men all which he wold so sodenlie take slight occasion to slyp out as I & many others in regard of his other rashnes in attempting soden pryvie iniuries to men did ouerslypp thogh often reprehend him for it & for which god is my witnes aswell by my lordes comaundment as in hatred of his life & thoughts I left & did refraine his companie.

Then in a final sentence Kyd turns from the discussion of Marlowe's heretical utterances and his personal qualities to bring against him a political charge of a treasonable nature.

He wold perswade with men of quallitie to goe vnto the k[ing] of *Scotts* whether I heare *Royden* is gon and where if he had liud he told me when I sawe him last he meant to be.

[1] Identified by Ford K. Brown and first printed, not quite accurately, in *T.L.S.*, 2 June 1911.

Matthew Roydon is the only friend of Marlowe mentioned by Kyd in both his letters. He is best known by his elegy on Sidney and by the very complimentary references to him by Nashe and Chapman. There is further probable evidence of his association with the group of whom Raleigh was patron. But nothing has come to light of any such political activities as are suggested by Kyd.

Kyd's letters to Puckering were written after Marlowe's death, but they doubtless echo statements made by him when examined by the Lord Mayor's commissioners after the discovery of the disputation among his papers on 12 May. And in consequence thereof, a few days later, on 18 May, the Privy Council issued a warrant for Marlowe's arrest. They directed Henry Maunder, one of the messengers of Her Majesty's Chamber,

'to repair to the house of Mr Tho. Walsingham in Kent, or to anie other place where he shall vnderstand Christofer Marlow to be remayning, and by vertue thereof to apprehend, and bring him to the Court in his Companie. And in case of need to require aid.'

Maunder had no difficulty in carrying out the Council's order, for on 20 May there follows an entry:

'This day Christofer Marley of London, gentleman, being sent for by warrant from their Lordships, hath entered his appearance accordinglie for his *Indemnity* therein; and is commaunded to giue his daily attendaunce on their Lordships vntill he shalbe lycensed to the contrary.'

The good luck that Marlowe had so often enjoyed at critical periods still followed him. Instead of being imprisoned and tortured like Kyd he was ordered after the customary formula to give his daily attendance on their lordships till he was licensed to the contrary.

The Privy Council evidently did not think it necessary to deal severely with Marlowe. But I cannot accept the view of Tucker Brooke that he was summoned as a witness rather than as a malefactor. In such cases the Council merely sent an order to the person in question to attend. It was a very different procedure to dispatch a messenger to 'apprehend' Marlowe, with the significant proviso, 'and in case of need to require aid'.

But the exercise of force was not needed, and it was doubtless in the dramatist's favour that he had been staying with Thomas Walsingham at Scadbury. Thomas was related in a younger generation to the late Secretary of State, Sir Francis Walsingham, who had thought well of him and employed him as a political agent. He was in favour, too, with the Queen, who was later to visit him at Scadbury and there knight him. He was a patron of men of letters, and it may have been Thomas Watson who brought Marlowe to his notice.

Scadbury, in the Chislehurst neighbourhood, was a pleasant haven at a time when the plague was raging in London and the theatres had been closed. But it may not have been ready to open its gates to him again after Henry Maunder's visit. At any rate on 30 May, ten days after his appearance before the Privy Council, Marlowe is found to be at Deptford. Meanwhile, however, further charges were being formulated against him not by fellow-playwrights, but by an informer, one Richard Baines.

II

RICHARD BAINES'S NOTE

WHO was this Richard Baines who so suddenly steps into the foreground with 'A Note Containing the opinion of one Christopher Marly, concerning his damnable iudgment of religion and scorn of Gods word'? It helps to the identification that Richard Baines (with its surname variants, Baynes and Banes) does not seem to have been a common name at the period. There was a Richard Baynes of Christ's College, Cambridge, who matriculated in November 1568, took his B.A. in 1572–3, and his M.A. (at Caius) in 1576. There is nothing, however, to connect him with Marlowe's circle in London, with which the writer of the 'Note' must have been familiar. This also applies to Richard Baynes, a son of Thomas Baynes, of Whaddon, Cambridgeshire, who mentions him in his will of 11 May 1593, apparently as a minor. A Richard Banes, a witness to the will of William Arnall of Southwell, on 6 March 1541, is out of the question, owing to the date. Of another Richard Banes merchant-tailor, buried in St. Mary Abchurch on 6 February 1596/7 nothing seems otherwise to be known.[1] It would therefore seem that Tucker Brooke was warranted in seeking to identify the author of the 'Note' with Richard Baines of the Middle Temple, son of an elder Richard Baines, merchant of the Staple in London, a dealer in wool, and a landowner in Shropshire and Montgomeryshire,[2] who was wealthy, unscrupulous and litigious, cast in the same mould as the William Gardiner in Hotson's *Shakespeare versus Shallow*.

The younger Richard was born in 1566 towards the end of October, for the registers of St. Peter's, Cornhill (Harl. Soc. Regs., i. 12), contain the following entry:

1566   Nouem 1 Monday Christning of Richard Baynes sonne of . . .

The name of the father is unfortunately omitted here and in a later entry:

1568   Februa 2 Thursday Christning of Mary Banes daughter of . . .

But there is ample proof in documents quoted later that they were the children of Richard Baines, merchant of the Staple, who is mentioned in two further entries:

1577   June 23 Sonday Christning of Fraunces Baines daughter of Richard Baines, merchant of ye Staple, born the 19th daye of June.

1580   Nouem 6 Sonday Christning of Vrsula Baynes daughter of Richard Banes Merchant Stapler; born the first of Nouember being tuesday.

Richard Baines, the younger, was, on this evidence, the eldest of a family of four, and was his father's only son

---

[1] Mark Eccles, op. cit., p. 110.
[2] See Appendix X to his *Life* of Marlowe.

and heir. He appears to have had the education suitable
to his position and prospects. Brooke quotes from the
Minutes of Parliament of the Middle Temple (i. 251, ed.
C. T. Martin) the admission entry on 21 May 1582, of
'Mr Richard, son and heir of Richard Baynes of Shrewsbury, gent., *specially;* fine £5.' The elder Baines had
presumably property in Shrewsbury as well as elsewhere
in the county of Salop, for this 'Mr Richard' is evidently
the same as the 'Richard Baynes of the Middle Temple',
son of the merchant of the Staple, deceased, the subject
of the Privy Council's Orders on 31 December 1588, and
2 February 1588–9, quoted below. There is only one
Richard Baines in the Middle Temple admission lists.
But if he was born late in October 1566, he must have
been admitted at the unusually early age of fifteen and
a half. It seems, however, to have been at this time a *pro
formâ* admission (members of the Inns of Court themselves
sometimes entered their children in infancy). For it was
usual then, as now, for law students to proceed to the
Inns of Court after residence at the university. Witness
the dialogue between Justice Shallow and his cousin
Silence in *King Henry IV*, Part II, Act III, sc. ii:

Shallow. I daresay my cousin William is become a good scholar.
       He is at Oxford still, is he not?
Silence. Indeed, sir, to my cost.
Shallow. He must then to the Inns of Court shortly.

Joseph Foster had therefore reason in his *Alumni Oxoni-
enses* for identifying the Mr. Richard Baynes of the
Middle Temple with 'Richard Baynes of London, gent.',
aged seventeen, who matriculated at Oxford, as a member
of St. John's College, on 8 February 1583, but who had
come into residence at St. John's in the Michaelmas Term,
1582. For in the college Buttery books his name appears
in the list of receipts for that term '*pro Batellis convic-
torum*'—i.e. for the batells or board of commoners (as distinguished from '*socii*', or fellows). The entry is repeated
in the three later terms of the academical year 1582–3, in

the four terms of 1583-4, and in the first and last terms of 1584-5. Thus Baines completed the greater part of his academical course, though the interruption of his studies during half of his last year at Oxford may help to account for the fact that, so far as the records show, he did not take a degree.

His father, who, according to Elizabethan standards of age, was now growing old, may well have wished, as some of the documents quoted later suggest, to initiate his son and heir into some of his complicated financial affairs. Any such association can have lasted little more than three years. For we can now determine within a few days the date of the death of Richard Baines, the elder. The burial register of St. Peter's, Cornhill, for 1588 contains the following entry:

Decem 3 Tuesday Mr Richard Baynes Merchant of the Staple, pit in ye south Chapell   yers 56.

Two days later, on 5 December, a commission granted 'Richardo Baynes filio naturali et legitimo Richardi Baynes nuper dum vixit parochie omnium Sanctorum maior in Themstreate Civitatis London defuncti' to administer the goods of the same, 'cum consensu Gracie Baynes relicte dicti defuncti'. There can be no doubt, as the name of Grace Baines, the widow, proves, that the reference here is to the merchant of the Staple and his son Richard. But as his chief connexion in London was with the parish of St. Peter's, Cornhill, it is curious to find him described as of the parish of All Hallows the Great. Presumably he had some property there; every new document adds to the extent of his holdings.

As the younger Richard was only twenty-two when his father died intestate (as is stated in a letter of the Privy Council, 31 December 1588), he was scarcely equal to the responsibility of administering a considerable estate, and he soon got into trouble. The Privy Council's letter, quoted by Tucker Brooke, states that the elder Richard Baines, merchant of the Staple, had borrowed of John

St. Leger, merchant stranger, the sum of £338. 15*s*., and was, when he died, 'of sufficient wealth and ability to discharge the said debt'; but that his son Richard 'seeketh by deceitful and subtle means to defraud the said St. Leger'. He was therefore to pay him within some reasonable time, or to be bound 'to answer the same before their Lordships with convenient speed'. The sequel is recorded in a minute of the Privy Council, 2 February 1588–9:

Richard Baynes of the Middle Temple in London, gentleman, being bound to make his appearance before the Lords of her Majesty's most honourable Privy Council, this day made his said appearance, which for his indemnity for the said bond is entered into this Register of Council, and he thereupon enjoined to give his attendance daily on their Lordships till by their order he shall be dismissed.

The formula, with the substitute of bond for warrant, is practically the same as in the Privy Council minute of 20 May 1593, concerning Christopher Marlowe himself. Nor was this an isolated instance of corrupt practice on the part of the younger Richard in the administration of his father's estate. An application against him for fraudulent dealing was brought in the Court of Requests by Thomas Gell of Hopton in Derbyshire in November 1590, and he was ordered to appear to answer the complaint under a penalty of £100. The sequel is unknown.

Thus the character and situation of Richard Baines the younger suit the part of an informer. He belonged to a family that had an aptitude for being mixed up with the shadier sides of legal affairs. His father had been a troublesome, clamorous, and wilful vexer of divers of Her Majesty's subjects (Star Chamber, B. 28/14); his uncle, Roger Woodrup, was suspected by Sir Francis Walsingham of 'synyster practyzes'. He himself had been in trouble with the authorities and was familiar with Privy Council procedure. When they summoned the 'atheist' Marlowe before them, he may well have seen an opportunity of fishing in troubled waters and turning the affair to his own advantage. He speaks as one whose identity is known, 'as I Richard Baines will justify and approve both by mine oth and the testimony of many honest men'.

It is uncertain when exactly Baines handed in his Note. The original document, presumably in his own hand, is undated.[1] But a copy 'as sent to her Highness',[2] the Queen—a proof of the importance attached to it by the authorities—after reproducing, with a slight variant, the heading in the Note, scores it through and substitutes, 'A Note deliuered on Whitsun eve last of the most horrible blasphemes vtteryd by Cristofer Marly who within iii dayes after came to a soden and fearfull end of his life.' As Whitsun Eve in 1593 was on 2 June and as Marlowe was killed on 30 May, he did not die three days after the delivery of the Note. If the scribe meant this he was mistaken either as to the date of delivery or of the dramatist's death. The words might mean that Marlowe died within three days of uttering the blasphemies. But Baines is evidently not referring to his utterances on only one occasion. If he really delivered the Note on 2 June he cannot have known of Marlowe's death on 30 May, and in that case must have been sorely disappointed to find later that his labours as an informer were wasted and presumably unrewarded.

Yet the biographers of Marlowe owe him a debt for enabling his charges to be compared with those of Kyd and for supplying links with other figures in the dramatist's circle. There is nothing in the Note to indicate that Baines knew Marlowe personally. The accusations are such as might be made by any one moving in London Bohemian circles and collecting the gossip current there. They are jotted down in confused order, but they may be grouped under various heads.

There is the general charge that he is a propagandist of atheistic views: 'almost into every Company he cometh he perswades men to Atheism willing them not to be afeard of bugbears and hobgoblins'; and asserting 'that the first beginning of Religion was only to keep men in awe'.

[1] Harl. MSS. 6848, ff. 185-6.   [2] Harl. MSS. 6853, ff. 307-8.

The opening and closing sections of Richard Baines's Note denouncing Marlowe's opinions on religion

Then come his sceptical views about the Old Testament and Moses, beginning with the heresy 'that the Indians and many Authors of antiquity have assuredly written of aboue 16 thousand yeares agone wheras Adam is proued to haue lived within 6 thowsand yeeres'. This view, as has been seen,[1] originated with Harriot, and it is noticeable that the Note continues: 'He affirmeth that Moyses was but a Jugler and that one Heriots being Sir W. Raleigh's man[2] Can do more then he.' Then follow instances of the crafty ways in which Moses imposed upon the Jews.

But the attack on the Old Testament is mild compared with that on the New, which is 'all . . . filthily written' and with the revolting allegations against Christ and St. John, where Baines develops with brutal frankness what had been more briefly and hesitatingly set forth by Kyd. There is attributed to Marlowe, as in Kyd's second letter, a gibe at St. Paul who alone among the apostles 'had wit, but he was a timerous fellow in bidding men to be subiect to magistrates against his conscience'.

Here Baines adroitly mingles religious and political heterodoxy as also implicitly in the item among the dramatist's opinions:

'That if there be any god or any good Religion then it is in the papistes because the service of god is performed with more Ceremonies, as Elevation of the mass, organs, singing men, Shaven Crownes & etc. That all protestantes are Hypocriticall asses.'

And he passes to a purely political and treasonable charge when he puts into Marlowe's mouth the statement:

'That he had as good right to coine as the Queen of England, and that he was acquainted with one Poole a prisoner in Newgate who hath greate skill in mixture of metalls and hauing learned some thinges of him he ment through help of a Cunninge stamp maker to Coin ffrench Crownes pistoletes and English shillinges.'

[1] See above, pp. 114.
[2] The words 'being Sir W. Raleighs man' are omitted in the copy sent to the Queen, to spare her susceptibilities.

This 'one Poole', it has been seen,[1] was John Poole, a coiner whose acquaintance Marlowe had made in Newgate during his fortnight's imprisonment after the fatal Bradley affray. Here at any rate Baines was partly speaking by the book, and we cannot therefore dismiss his whole Note as a mere set of malicious fabrications. But before discussing further the question of Marlowe's 'atheism', there are two other names mentioned by Baines that have to be taken into consideration. One is Richard Chomley who 'hath Confessed that he was perswaded by Marloe's Reasons to become an Atheist'. The other is Sir Walter Raleigh who is named in the Note only as Thomas Harriot's employer but who, on the authority of Robert Parsons, was known as the head of a school of atheism that held its meetings in his house.

[1] See above, p. 104.

XV

THE 'ATHEISM' OF CHOMLEY, RALEIGH, AND MARLOWE

IN his Note Baines spoke vaguely of one Richard
Chomley, but the Government knew well who was
meant. It is significant that against his name in the copy
made for the Queen there is a marginal note in another
hand, 'he is layd for', i.e. steps are being taken to arrest
him. From 'Remembraunces of wordes and matter against
Richard Cholmeley' (Harl. MSS. 6848, f. 190) it is clear
that he had been in the service of the Crown, for it is
alleged that 'being imployed by some of her Maiesties
prevy Counsaile for the apprehenson of Papistes, and
other daungerous men, hee vsed, as he saieth, to take
money of them and would lett them pass in spighte of
the Counsell'. He is probably the Chomley twice mentioned, though unfortunately without his Christian name,
in the proceedings of the Privy Council in 1591. On 13
May a warrant was issued to John Slater, one of the
Messengers of Her Majesty's Chamber 'to repaire vnto
the dwelling places of Mr. Thomas Drurie,—Roen, one
of the Messaungers of her Majesties Chamber, & of Mr.
— Chomley, companions of the said Drurie, or to anie
other place or places whersoever, for the apprehending
and bringing them before their Lordships without delay,
al excuses set apart, to answeare to such things as shalbe
objected against them'. On 29 July there was another
warrant 'to paie to one Burrage and Chomeley that apprehended Thomas Drewry, vi^{li}'. The combination of the
names in the two warrants can scarcely be a mere coincidence. It looks as if Chomley had turned against Drury,
and helped the Privy Council to secure his arrest. Then,
perhaps dissatisfied by the reward for this or later services,
he had proved false to his employers. It is declared in the
'Remembraunces' that 'he speaketh in generall all euill of

the Counsell; saying that they are all Athiestes and Machiavillians'; and that 'he hath certain men corrupted by his persuasions, who wilbe ready at all times and for all causes to swear whatsoever seemeth good to him. Amonge whom is one Henry Younge and Jasper Borage and others.' This Borage must be the 'Burrage' of the warrant of 29 July. He, too, seems to have turned against the Government for in an endorsement he is labelled 'dangerous', while Young is described as 'taken and made an instrument to take the rest', i.e. had turned Queen's evidence. He was the son of a Kentish gentleman, and had offered to kill Elizabeth.[1]

In another document (Harl. MSS. 6848, f. 191) a Government informer, who was acting as an *agent-provo-cateur*, goes into more detail about a treasonable conspiracy that Chomley was organizing:

'Yesterday hee sente two of his companions to mee to knowe if I would ioyne with him in familiaritie, and bee one of their dampn-able crue. I sothed the villaynes with faire wordes in their follies because I would thereby dive into the secretes of their develishe hartes, that I mighte the better bewray their purposes to drawe her Maiesties subiectes to bee Athiestes. Their practise is after her Maiesties decease to make a Kinge amonge themselues and liue accordinge to their owne lawes, and this saieth Cholmeley willbee done easely, because they bee and shortely wilbe by his and his felowes persuasions as many of their opynion as of any other religion.'

He then proceeds to accuse Chomley of blasphemies similar to those attributed by Baines to Marlowe, as that 'Moyses was a Jugler & Aaron a Cosener'. Treason and 'atheism' were, as usual, linked by the informer.

Both these documents are undated, but at the Privy Council held on 19 March 1593 a warrant was issued to George Cobham, one of the Messengers of Her Majesty's Chamber, 'to apprehende Richarde Chomeley and Richarde Stronge and to bringe them before their Lordships'. The Government were warned by their agent that the arrest

[1] Ethel Seaton, 'Marlowe, Poley, and The Tippings' (*R.E.S.*, July 1929).

would be no easy matter. 'This cursed Cholmeley hath 60 of his company and hee is seldome from his felowes and therefore I beeseech your worship haue a special care of your selfe in apprehending him, for they be resolute murdering myndes.' This may explain the fact that it was more than three months before he was apprehended, and then not by Cobham. On 29 June Justice Young wrote to Sir John Puckering (Harl. MSS. 7002, f. 10) to 'advartise' him 'that yestar night, at ix of the cloke, Mr. Wilbrom came to me and brought Richard Chomley with him; he did submet hym selfe to hym'. Young further states that he has committed Chomley to prison, and that 'Chomley sayd vnto my men as he was goyng to preson, that he did kno the Law, that when it came to pase, he cold shefte will ynowgh'.

But as Danchin has shown, he appears to have been saved by the intervention of the Earl of Essex, who on 13 November wrote to Sir E. Littleton, Sir E. Aston, and R. Bagot, thanking them for their trouble in the matter of his servant Chomley, and asking for its continuance that his innocency may be established.[1]

Chomley's ultimate fate is uncertain, but his chief importance to Marlovian biography lies in the fact that through him we get the only direct contemporary testimony to the dramatist's personal association with Raleigh. Both Kyd and Baines had borne witness to Marlowe's intimacy with Harriot, but to know the 'man' of an Elizabethan nobleman was not necessarily to be familiar with his 'lord'. Kyd had asserted that his own lord could not endure Marlowe's name or sight. But one of the charges against Chomley in 'the Remembraunces of words and matter' is that

'Hee saieth & verely beleueth that one Marlowe is able to shewe more sounde reasons for Atheisme then any devine in Englande is able to geue to prove devinitie & that Marloe tolde him that hee hath read the Atheist lecture to Sr Walter Raliegh & others.'

[1] Historical MSS. Commission, 4th Report, p. 330, quoted by Danchin, *Revue Germanique*, Jan.–Feb. 1914.

This 'lecture' can scarcely have been the treatise by 'the late Arrian', part of which was found in Kyd's possession. This was, as we now know, a transcript of a document dating back nearly half a century, and it had not been in Marlowe's hands for about two years. The lecture may have been part of the unprintable book which, according to Simon Aldrich, Marlowe wrote against the Scriptures.[1] Baines may have been referring to it when he alleged that Marlowe 'hath quoted a number of contrarieties oute of the Scriptures which he hath given to some great men who in convenient time shalbe named.' Unfortunately for us the 'convenient time' was never to come, and thus Chomley remains our only witness to personal intercourse between Sir Walter and the dramatist. We are not warranted on this slender basis to assume that there was such a familiarity between them as the dedication of *Lucrece* suggests between Southampton and Shakespeare. Yet there can be little doubt that when Baines spoke of 'some great men' he had Raleigh chiefly in mind. And it has been aptly pointed out that Sir Walter himself wrote, 'To believe what all men say of the same thing is not possible; for then we shall believe contrarieties'.[2]

In any case when on 'one Wednesdaye sevenight before the Assizes', in the summer of 1593, probably within a month or two after Marlowe's death on 30 May, Sir Walter Raleigh, his half-brother Carew Raleigh, Sir Ralph Horsey, Ralph Ironside, minister of Winterbottom, and others, met at the tables of Sir George Trenchard, at Wolverton, and when towards the end of supper a disputation arose on theological matters, there was no reference to 'the Atheist lecture' or to Marlowe's opinions. The question of what the soul is having been posed by Carew, Sir Walter asked Ironside to answer it for the benefit of the company:

'I have benn (sayeth he) a scholler some tyme in Oxeforde, I have

---

[1] See above, p. 110.
[2] M. C. Bradbrook, *The School of Night*, p. 18.

aunswered vnder a Bachelor of Arte & had taulke with diuines, yet heithervnto in this pointe (to witt what the reasonable soule of man is) have I not by anye benne resolved. They tell vs it is *primus motor* the first mover in a man &c.'

Ironside sought to satisfy Raleigh by quoting 'the generall definicion of Anima out of Aristotle 2° de Anima cap: 1°', and thence deducing 'the speciall definicion of the soule reasonable'. But Sir Walter, in this respect no true 'Clerk of Oxenford', repudiated the Aristotelian definition 'as obscure & intricate'. Similarly, at a later stage of the discussion, he was dissatisfied with the Aristotelian definition of God as 'Ens Entium', for 'neither coulde I lerne heitherto what god is'.

We have the best warrant for the accuracy of Ironside's account of this 'disputation'. Not only was he giving his testimony on oath before a Commission on Atheism held at Cerne Abbas in March 1594, but one of the Commissioners, Sir Ralph Horsey, had been among the company at Sir George Trenchard's table and was thus in a position to check the truth of his story. It was a grave scholastic discussion with nothing of the iconoclastic and ribald elements of the opinions attributed to Marlowe by Kyd and Baines. It is significant of Raleigh's conventional practice, whatever his speculative opinions, that he ended the dialogue by asking 'that grace might be sayed; for that, quoth he, is better then this disputacion'.

In other depositions, however, before the Commission we hear of a member of Sir Walter's 'retinew', Thomas Allen, Lieutenant of Portland Castle, who evidently had something of the mocking humour of Marlowe. Different witnesses declared that 'he is greate blasphemer & leight esteemer of Religion; and thereaboutes cometh not to Devine service or sermons'; that he 'did teare twoe Leaves out of a Bible to drye Tobacco on'; that 'when he was like to dye, being perswaded to make himselfe reddye to God for his soule' he answered, 'he woulde carrye his soule vp to the topp of an hill, and runne god, runne devill, fetch it that will have it'.

Like master, like man, Allen had a servant, Oliver, who walking home from church scandalized two ladies of the congregation by coarse jeers against the morals of Moses, whom he compared with Solomon.

Harriot's heresies are mentioned by several of the deponents, one of whom 'hath harde that one Herriott attendant on Sir Walter Rawleigh hath been convented before the Lordes of the Counsell for denyinge the resurrecion of the bodye'. There is no record of such an appearance of Harriot before the Privy Council. Nor, as far as is known, were the examinations at Cerne followed by any action against Raleigh or his friends.

Yet the depositions before the Commissioners may furnish a clue to at any rate a partial solution of the puzzling discrepancy between the sinister notoriety of the 'School of Atheism' in popular opinion and the writings of two of its leading members, Raleigh and Marlowe. It is evident that what had above all outraged contemporary orthodoxy was the attack by members of the School on the verbal inspiration of the Bible, on what is now known as 'fundamentalism'. Protestantism having rejected an infallible Church in favour of an infallible Book was horrified and alarmed by what seemed to be a concerted attack on what it had thought to be an impregnable Maginot line of defence. Nor was it only Protestantism that took up its guard. It was a Jesuit that accused the School of jesting at the Old and New Testaments, at Moses and at Christ, in the meetings at Sir Walter's house.[1] So at Cerne, as has been seen, Allen, one of his followers, is charged with the sacrilege of tearing leaves out of a Bible, to dry the weed imported by his chief, which was in no good repute; and Allen's servant makes the matter worse with scandal about Moses and Solomon. Harriot, who had become a by-word for his heterodox views of Biblical chronology, has now to answer for a reported denial of the Scriptural doctrine of the resurrection of the body. One of the counts against Richard Chomley was

[1] See above, p. 113.

that he made a jest of Scripture and that he called Moses a juggler and Aaron a cosener.

It is evident that all this is in line with the details of the indictment of Marlowe's 'atheism' by Kyd and Baines and doubtless by Greene before Chettle bowdlerized his manuscript. He, too, is accused of jesting at the divine Scriptures, and of mocking at prophets and apostles as jugglers, who maintained by their arts an 'everlastinge superstition' in the minds of the people. Marlowe's genius, it has been seen, was strangely compounded of analytic and imaginative elements. To the former the 'contrarieties' involved in the literal methods of Biblical interpretation offered a challenge which he was quick to accept. His method was one of sap and mine. Wherever he went, as his accusers aver, in his 'common speeches', his table talk, and otherwise he let loose his mordant wit upon sacred subjects. In this respect he was a provocative, propagandist, explosive force.

Did Marlowe's 'atheism' culminate in the repulsive blasphemies against Christ which Baines, in part supported by Kyd, attributed to him? It is, of course, impossible to say what may have dropped from the dramatist's lips in a ribald mood. But there is nothing in his writings that can be matched with the coarse obscenities placed in his mouth by the informers. These may have been a vulgarized and poisoned version of Marlowe's denial of the divinity of Christ. The venomous exaggerations of Baines seem to rest upon this as their basis, and the disputation which passed from Marlowe to Kyd was a Socinian treatise. It has indeed been argued that in *Doctor Faustus* 'the divinity of Christ is no longer in question',[1] when Faustus is found at the end aspiring not after knowledge, but salvation:

O, I'll leap up to my God!—Who pulls me down?
See, see where Christ's blood streams i' the firmament!
One drop would save my soul, half a drop: Ah, my Christ!

But the lines are, as I think, too dramatically appro-

[1] M. C. Bradbrook, op. cit., p. 110.

priate on the lips of the agonized Doctor on the brink of his doom to be pressed into the service of biography.

But on its negative side Marlowe's revolt from ortho- doxy went far beyond an assault on Biblical literalism and denial of the Incarnation. While individual passages in the plays must be taken in their particular context, the general impression left by *Tamburlaine, Part II*, and *The Jew of Malta* is that the dramatist was hostile to all forms of institutional religion. The followers of Christ, of Mahomet, and of Moses are in turn pilloried and held up to scorn. And as between Catholicism and Protestantism there seems little left to choose. Marlowe's aesthetic sensibilities may, as Baines alleged, have biased him in favour of the ceremonial pomp of the orthodox ritual. But the invective against the Papacy in almost identical terms by the English king in *Edward II* and by Henry III of France in *The Massacre at Paris* seems to have some- thing of a personal ring, and in the latter play it is the Huguenot leader, Henry of Navarre, who shows to most advantage.

So much for the destructive results of Marlowe's rationa- lizing intelligence. But neither he nor Raleigh, each in his different way, of true Renaissance temper, could rest in negatives alone. In the discussion round Sir George Trenchard's table on 30 May 1593 Sir Walter, though he takes up a critical position towards the Aristotelian definitions of the soul and of God, is as far as possible from a ribald or flippant attitude. The more constructive and positive side of his doctrine is to be found in his writings, especially his two treatises, *The Soul* and *The Sceptic*. These have recently been acutely discussed and analysed in some detail.[1] What is important to emphasize here is that the 'atheist' Raleigh, while recognizing the limita- tions of human knowledge, affirms that the Soul is divine in its origin and its aspiration:

'Is it not a manifest argument that it cometh from God, seeing

[1] M. C. Bradbrook, op. cit., pp. 53–63. See also Miss Ellis-Fermor, *Christopher Marlowe*, pp. 163–5.

in all things it resteth not till it come to God? The mind in searching causes is never quiet till it come to God, and the will never is satisfied with any good till it come to the immortal goodness.'[1]

This immortal goodness is elsewhere termed 'an eternal and infinite being', and as all the rivers in the world after 'divers risings and divers runnings' fall at last into the great ocean, 'so after all the searches that human capacity hath and after all philosophical contemplation and curiosity, in the necessity of this infinite power, all the reason of man ends and dissolves itself.'[2]

In the opening words of his *History of the World* the attributes of Deity are majestically set forth:

'God, whom the wisest men acknowledge to be a power ineffable and virtue infinite: a light by abundant clarity invisible; an understanding which only itself can comprehend: an essence eternal and spiritual, of absolute pureness and simplicity: was and is pleased to make himself known by the work of the world.'

The soul created by such a power must be immortal, and to this belief he clings in his last verse written on the brink of 'the dark and silent grave':

And from which Earth and Grave, and Dust,
The Lord shall raise me up I trust.

From a dramatist no such explicit statement can be expected. But, as has been seen,[3] there are passages in *Tamburlaine, Part II*, which define the Godhead in terms strikingly akin to those used by Raleigh (ii. ii. 49–54):

That he that sits on high and never sleeps,
Nor in one place is circumscriptible,
But everywhere fills every continent
With strange infusion of his sacred vigour,
May, in his endless power and purity,
Behold . . .

In these lines the Deity is conceived as both transcen-

[1] *A Treatise of the Soul* in *Sir W. Raleigh's Works* (Oxford, 1829), viii. 582.
[2] Preface to *History of the World*, op. cit., ii. xvii.
[3] See above, p. 90.

dent and immanent; it is the former aspect that is dwelt on in v. i. 199–201:

> Seek out another Godhead to adore,
> The God that sits in heaven, if any God,
> For he is God alone, and none but he.

And banishment from his presence, as Mephistophilis tells Faustus (I. iii. 79–82), is in itself damnation:

> Think'st thou that I who saw the face of God,
> And tasted the eternal joys of heaven,
> Am not tormented with ten thousand hells
> In being depriv'd of everlasting bliss?

Here the 'atheist' Marlowe's conception of heaven and hell is more spiritual than that of the Puritan Milton in *Paradise Lost*. Yet when Milton in *Lycidas* takes as his standard the 'perfect witness of all-judging Jove', we know that under the Olympian title he envisages the Biblical deity. It is otherwise with Marlowe. When he invokes God as Jupiter, the title is as significant to him as any Scriptural designation. The cry, 'Great Pan is dead', had never rung in his ears. He is like a visitor to Rome in these days to whom the memorials of the Republic and the Empire speak more eloquently than the glories of medieval and Renaissance churches. It was through Rome, as has been seen, and not through Greece, through Virgil and Ovid, not through Homer and the Attic stage, that the vision of the classical world had been opened to Marlowe. Yet by nature he was less 'an antique Roman' than a Greek. Divinity was primarily revealed to him in neither its Old nor its New Testament manifestations, as the All-Righteous or the All-Loving, but under its Hellenic aspects of ideal beauty and 'knowledge infinite'. Faustus 'confounds hell in Elysium' and craves that after death 'his ghost be with the old philosophers'. But of Marlowe himself it may be said that during his lifetime his 'ghost' or spirit kept company with the old philosophers, including among them the myth-makers of the ancient world, and that what his contemporaries called his atheism was largely a legacy from them.

Love's Labour's Lost, Willobie his Avisa, and 'The School of Atheism'

IF credit is to be given to recent critical theories,[1] the assailants of the 'School of Atheism' included the youthful dramatist, William Shakespeare. His early play, *Love's Labour's Lost*, ridiculing the attempt to establish an 'Academe' in defiance of the natural relation of the sexes, is full of references to blackness and to night, including the lines (IV. iii. 250–1):

> O paradox! Black is the badge of hell
> The hue of dungeons and the School of Night.

'The School of Night', it has been urged, is to be identified with Raleigh's 'School of Atheism'. It was to Matthew Roydon, the associate of Marlowe and of Harriot, and his own 'dear and most worthy friend', that Chapman dedicated in 1594 his work *The Shadow of the Night*, which included a *Hymnus in Noctem*. Two lines in the *Hymnus*:

> No pen can anything eternal write
> That is not steeped in humour of the Night

find a ' retorting challenge ' in Berowne's cry:

> Never durst poet touch a pen to write
> Until his ink were temper'd with Love's sighs.

Love's Labour's Lost, it is contended, is a satire upon Raleigh's 'School', and it is further suggested that it was written in 1593 for a private performance in the house of some grandee who had opposed Raleigh and Raleigh's men—possibly the Earl of Southampton's. If, however, this is the date of *Love's Labour's Lost*, Shakespeare could have seen *The Shadow of the Night* only in manuscript.

On the other hand, it has been maintained[2] that a counterblast came from the 'School' in the enigmatic poem, *Willobie his Avisa*, published in 1594. G. B. Harrison takes the view that both Henry Willobie, the reputed author, and Hadrian Dorrell, who signs the preface, are fictitious, and that the work is from the pen of Matthew Roydon, to whose *Astrophell* it has points of close simi-

---

[1] See the introduction to the New Cambridge edition of *Love's Labour's Lost* (1923).

[2] G. B. Harrison in the essay appended to his edition of *Willobie, his Avisa* (1926), supported by M. C. Bradbrook (op. cit., pp. 168–71).

larity. Harrison argues that Avisa, the heroine of the poem, was born at Cerne Abbas and was the hostess of an inn in the neighbouring town of Sherborne, where Raleigh had the lease of the Abbey from January 1592. Avisa's rejected suitor H. W. is to be identified with Henry Wriothesley, Earl of Southampton, and his friend W. S. with William Shakespeare. Moreover, from the mention of *Lucrece* in the prefatory verses to *Willobie his Avisa*, signed 'Vigilantius: Dormitanus', and the line 'Let *Lucres-Auis* be thy name', Harrison concludes that the author intended *'Willobie his Avisa* to be coupled in the reader's mind with Shakespeare's *Lucrece'*.

This whole interpretation, except for the identification of W. S. with Shakespeare, has been directly challenged by Leslie Hotson.[1] He holds that the author was indeed the Henry Willobie (or Willoughby) of West Knoyle, Wiltshire, who matriculated, as a member of St. John's College, Oxford, on 10 December 1591, at the age of sixteen. A link has been found between him and Shakespeare, for his elder brother, William, married a sister of Katherine Bamfield, wife of Thomas Russell, whom the dramatist was to appoint as one of the overseers of his will.

'Vigilantius' and 'Dormitanus' have also been given an Oxford background. Hotson has ingeniously identified them with two Balliol undergraduates, Robert Wakeman and Edward Napper, aged eighteen and sixteen in 1594. It would be gratifying to find in my own college one of the earliest allusions to Shakespeare as a poet. But if Hotson's interpretation is correct, any association between *Willobie his Avisa* and Raleigh's 'School' must be given up.

[1] See *I, William Shakespeare Do Appoint Thomas Russell Esquire* (1937), pp. 53–70.

30 MAY 1593 AT DEPTFORD STRAND

AS Marlowe was at Deptford Strand by the tenth hour
before noon on 30 May 1593, it looks as if he had not
returned to take up residence again at Scadbury after his
interview with the Privy Council. But it is remarkable
that of the four actors in the tragic event of that day the
three most important, Marlowe, Poley, and Ingram
Frizer, had been in intimate relation in different ways
with Thomas Walsingham. He had recently been Marlowe's host. Poley had been in close touch with him
during the Babington plot and later.[1] Frizer was in his
employ, and Nicholas Skeres, the fourth of the quartet,
had been in intimate association with Frizer and had
probably come into connexion with Poley at an earlier
date.[2]

Things seem to have gone well with Poley since his
release from the Tower in the autumn of 1588. He had
been taken back regularly into the Government service
from the last part of that year, and the Declared Accounts
of the Treasurer of the Chamber contain a series of payments to him 'as an accredited messenger to and from
English ambassadors, state agents, and courts abroad.[3]
The first entry is as follows:

To Robert Poolye gent vppon a warrant signed by Mr Secretary
Walsingham dated at the Courte xxvij^{mo} December 1588 for
bringinge lettres in poste for her majesties affaires from the King
of Denmark to the Courte at Richmonde—xv^{li}.

The second entry is of a payment on 8 July 1589, again
on Walsingham's warrant, for the carrying of letters to
several places in Holland 'and retourninge with like lettres

---

[1] See above, pp. 125 and 127.   [2] See above, p. 125.
[3] *Robert Poley's Movements as a Messenger of the Court, 1558 to 1601*,
by Eugénie de Kalb (*R.E.S.*, Jan. 1933, pp. 13–18).

to the Courte againe—xij^{li}'. Thenceforth for a number of years the warrants for payment are signed by 'Mr vice-chamberlane', Sir Thomas Heneage. Four of them, on 23 February 1589/90, 20 May 1591, 20 December 1591, and 23 June 1592 are to Poley for acting as messenger with letters to and from the town of Berwick. Others on 23 July 1590, 22 December 1590, 1 March 1591/2, 3 September 1592, and 12 February 1592/3 are for similar errands to various places in the Low Countries. One dated at Oxford, 25 September 1592, shows that Poley took letters to Dover and brought the answers to Oxford while the Queen was being entertained by the University at Christ Church.[1]

Another detailed entry is as follows:

'To Roberte Poolye uppon a warrant signed by Mr vicechamber-layne dated at Hampton Courte xvij^{mo} December 1592 for his chardges & paynes in carryinge of lettres in poste for her heighnes speciall service of greate importance from Hampton Courte into Scotlande to the Courte there, and for his attendaunce in that place and service, and rydinge in sundrye places within that province by the space of two whole monethes and for his retourne in the like poste with lettres of aunswere to Hampton Courte agayne the xiijth of December laste—xliij^{li}.'

Poley was no stranger to Scotland. In 1586 Morgan had written to Mary that he 'hath bene heretofore to Scotland & knoweth the best wayes to passe into Scot-lande'.[2] The Government were now making full use of his familiarity with that country, for after this two months' excursion he soon paid two further visits to the court there, for which he received payment on 6 January and 23 March 1592/3, the March visit being described as 'for her heighnes speciall and secret affayres of great importaunce'.

It was about this time, according to Kyd, that Marlowe had intended to resort to the King of Scots. But it is the

---

[1] Boas, *University Drama in the Tudor Age*, pp. 254 ff.
[2] See above, p. 120.

next of the entries concerning Poley that is of special importance for the dramatist's biography:

'To Robert Poolye upon a warrant signed by Mr vicechamber-layne dated at the Courte xij^{mo} die Junij 1593 for carryinge of lettres in poste for her Majesties speciall and secrete afaires of great ymportaunce from the Courte at Croyden the viijth of Maye 1593 into the Lowe Countryes to the towne of the Hage in Hollande, and for retourninge backe againe with lettres of aunswere to the Courte at Nonesuche the viijth of June 1593 being in her majesties service all the aforesaid tyme—xxx^{s}.'

It will be seen that Poley's period of service covered by the warrant, from 8 May to 8 June, includes 30 May and 1 June. The significance of this will be discussed below.

Additional evidence of Poley's official employment after his release from the Tower is furnished by his ciphers used in correspondence with the authorities. Three sets of these (two of them in duplicate) have been identified by Ethel Seaton.[1] One is of uncertain date, another belongs to 1596–7, and a third has been assigned to 1590–1. The inclusion in the heading of this set of some Flemish names and addresses in Antwerp fits in with the evidence from payment warrants of Poley's activities during these years in the Low Countries.

There is further evidence in the deposition of one Robert Rutkin, broker, dated probably April 1591, which is obscure in some of its references, but which shows Poley as an agent for Sir Thomas Heneage in affairs relating to the Low Countries:

'Robert Rutkin broker saieth that the party who wrote the lettres vnto him by the name of Bar[nard] Riche is Michaell Moody who liveth either at Brussels or Antwerpe. . . . The said Rutkin saieth that his neighbour mencioned in the letter is one Poolye & that he deliuereth him letters for Sir Thomas Henneage & sendeth letters to him from Sir Thomas Henneage . . . the said Robert Poolye lyveth in Shorditch.

[1] *Robert Poley's Ciphers* in *R.E.S.*, April 1931. Miss Seaton gives the references to these ciphers in *State Papers* 106, vol. ii, in P.R.O., with lists and a facsimile of one cipher.

'He was at the poste this time to loke for lettres from him but
had none & recyueth no lettres from him but that hee ac-
quanteth Sir Thomas Henneage withall. Hee was sent over by
Sir Thomas Henneage with letters to diuers persons about a yeare
past.'

About a year later Sir Robert Cecil, writing to Sir
Thomas, refers to an interview with Poley:

'I haue receauyd your lettre & I will shew it as occasion may
serue. I have spoken with Poly & find him no Foole. I do suspend
all tyll our meeting which I wish may be shortly.'

Nicholas Skeres, if the identification of him with
'Skyrres' is correct,[1] has already been seen in the company
of Poley on 2 August 1586, during the Babington plot.
He seems to have been the younger son of Nicholas Skeres,
senior, citizen and merchant-tailor, and a parishioner of
Allhallows the Less, who by his will, 9 September 1566,
left to his wife one-third of his estate, and to his sons,
Jerome and Nicholas, still in their minority, another
third.[2] It was evidently the same Jerome 'Skyers' of the
City of London, and Nicholas 'Skyers' of Furnival's Inn
who, with Matthew Roydon of Thavies Inn, entered on
6 January 1581/2 into a bond to pay a London goldsmith,
Henry Banyster, £40 by the Feast of the Purification
(2 February) following. As Roydon's name appears first,
Moore Smith, who discovered the document, suggests
that he was the debtor and the others his securities.[3] In
any case it is of interest to find a Nicholas Skeres associated
as early as 1581/2 with Marlowe's friend, Roydon. But
it is almost impossible to identify this man of some substance with the 'Nicholas Skeeres' whom William Fleetwood, writing to Lord Burleigh on 7 July 1585, mentions
amongst a number of 'maisterles men & cut-purses, whose
practice is to robbe Gentlemen's chambers and Artificers'
shoppes in and about London'. Even if this is a different

---

[1] See above, p. 125.
[2] E. Vine Hall, *Testamentary Papers*, iii (1937), p. 25.
[3] *M.L.R.*, Jan. 1914.

man, it is probably the more respectable Nicholas Skeres of Furnival's Inn who was mixed up in the Babington plot. The conspirators were, in different ways, men of standing and, if he was a spy, the Government would not have employed a man branded in the previous year by the Recorder as a cut-purse. It is in favour of the spy theory that in 1589 Nicholas Skeres was paid by the Government for carrying important post between the Court and the Earl of Essex.

It is in the same year that, through the investigations of Leslie Hotson, we get our first information about Ingram Frizer.

On 9 October 1589 he bought the Angel Inn, Basingstoke, for £120, but sold it again within two months. One of the vendors of the 'Angel' entered at the same time into an obligation to him for £240, but failed to discharge the debt, and Frizer obtained a judgement against him in Easter Term 1592. Here Frizer, styled 'of London, yeoman' was the complainant, but another case, in which he was defendant, is more informative. At a date not earlier than June 1598 Anne Woodleff of Aylesbury, Bucks., and her son Drew complained to the Lord Keeper concerning proceedings of Frizer 'abut fyve years now past'. Drew Woodleff had appealed to Nicholas Skeres for financial help, as Roydon appears to have done in 1581/2. Skeres had in turn approached Frizer, who promised Drew assistance in return for a signed bond for £60. But instead of ready money Frizer could only offer 'a commoditie' for which Drew 'mighte have threescore pounds (which was a certayne number of gunnes or greate Iron peeces)'. Drew, who must have been a simpleton, then asked Frizer to sell the guns on his behalf, and Frizer came back with 'only Thirtie pounds protestinge that that was all that he coulde at that tyme gett', but 'in truthe the saide peeces or gunnes were his owne & the xxx^{li} he broughte his owne and never offered them to be soulde at all but lett them remayne uppon Tower Hill'.

Moreover Drew alleged further chicanery. It was

arranged that 'Skeres shoulde contrarie to the truthe affirme that he oughte to the said Fryser xx^tie marks in money & so procure your saide Orator to enter into Bonde lykewyse . . . to paie vnto him the saide twentie marks protesting that when he the saide Fryser should Receive the same at your Orators hand he would paie it vnto the saide Skeres'.

This bond was duly sealed and delivered. Then as Drew had not 'of his and mothers estate' enough to make up the two sums of £60 and 20 marks he was induced 'in his then unwarie age' to enter 'into a statute of cc^li vnto a gentleman of good worshipp . . . the saide Fryser his then Maister'.

The entry of this 'statute' Hotson discovered among the Lord Chamberlain's papers at the Record Office. On 29 June 1593 'Drew Woodlef of Peterley, Bucks., gentleman', was bound to Thomas Walsingham of Chislehurst, Kent, Esquire, in the sum of £200 to be paid by 25 July 1593. Thus the gentleman of good worship, Frizer's master, is proved to be Thomas Walsingham of Scadbury, with whom Marlowe had been staying in the middle of May.

If Frizer did not know Marlowe before, he then had the opportunity of making his acquaintance. According to the best informed of the contemporary narrators it was he who asked the dramatist to the fateful meeting at Eleanor Bull's tavern in Deptford Strand on 30 May 1593. 'One named Ingram . . . had inuited him thither to a feast'.[1] Research has hitherto failed to identify this Eleanor Bull, a widow, or the name of her tavern where Marlowe, Frizer, Skeres, and Poley were together from the tenth hour before noon.

What followed from that hour is told in the inquisition on 1 June, returned by William Danby, Coroner of the Household:

'Prandebant & post prandium ibidem quieto modo insimul fuerunt & ambulaverunt in gardinum pertinentem domui prae-

---

[1] William Vaughan in *Golden Grove* (1600).

Inquisition taken at Deptford Strand, on 1 June 1593, concerning the death of Chris

Marlowe and returned into Chancery by William Danby, Coroner of the Household

dicto vsque horam sextam post meridiem eiusdem diei & tunc recesserunt a gardino praedicto in cameram praedictam & ibidem insimul & pariter cenabant.'

After supper a quarrel arose about the payment of 'le recknynge' between Frizer and 'Morley'. The latter was lying on a bed, and the former was sitting near it, with his back towards it and with the front part of his body towards the table. Poley and Skeres were sitting so close to Frizer on either side of him that he could not take flight. Whereupon 'Morley' 'ex subito & ex malicia sua' drew Frizer's dagger, which he was wearing at his back, and gave him two wounds in his head, two inches long and a quarter deep. Frizer, pinned between Skeres and Poley, 'in sua defensione & saluacione vite sue', struggled to get back his own dagger, with which he inflicted on his assailant

'vnam plagam mortalem super dexterum oculum suum profunditatis duorum policium & latitudinis vnius policis de qua quidem plaga mortali praedictus Cristoferus Morley adtunc & ibidem instanter obijt.'

Such was the account that was accepted by the Coroner's jury of sixteen men when the inquest was held on 1 June, 'super visum corporis Cristoferis Morley ibidem iacentis mortui & interfecti'. The body must have been buried immediately after the inquest, for the Register of St. Nicholas Church, Deptford, contains the entry under *Anno Dom.* 1593, 'Christopher Marlow, slaine by ffrancis ffrezer; the ·1· of June'. A fortnight later, on 15 June, a writ of *certiorari* was issued to summon the case into Chancery. The Coroner Danby made his return, and a Pardon was issued to Frizer on 28 June on the ground that he slew Christopher Morley 'in defensione ac saluacione vite sue'.

Such, on the face of it, is the tale contained in the legal records. Are we justified in going behind them, and questioning the truth of the jury's verdict?

Since Hotson's discovery in 1925 of the inquest

documents considerable fresh light has been thrown upon the composition of the jury, especially from testamentary sources.[1] Two of them, Nicholas Draper and Wolstan Randall are distinguished in the inquest list as 'generosi'. Of Draper nothing further is known, but Randall in his will of 18 February 1602/3 left among other bequests to his wife the lease of a house, and of a stable belonging to the Lord Admiral who had a house in Deptford. William Curry, the third in the list, is not there called 'generosus' but he is ' of Deptford Strand, gentleman,' in his will, 16 April 1612, and he leaves to his wife his house, wharf, and garden besides £100, and to his son 200 marks. John Barber is called 'of Chatham, carpenter', in his will of 4 April 1608, but he seems to have lived previously in Deptford, where he had houses and freelands which he left to his son. Among the other jurors were Robert Baldwyn, yeoman, of East Greenwich; Giles Field, grocer, of Deptford; George Halfpenny, baker, of Limehouse; James Batt, husbandman, of Lewisham; Thomas Batt, senior, yeoman, of Bromley, Kent. All these left substantial legacies in houses, goods, or farm animals. Two other jurors, Henry Awger and Henry Dabyns (Dobbins) have been identified[2] as a manorial tenant and a baker.

It is a varied picture. The jury was evidently not packed from men in any one class, but included persons of substance in various stations of life. They were, it would appear, capable of judging evidence and not likely to be browbeaten. And from the inquisition it would appear that they did not perform their duty perfunctorily. They viewed the body and took measurements of the fatal wound over the right eye as also of the wounds in Frizer's head. They inquired into the proceedings of the whole day—the meeting at ten o'clock, the dinner, the subsequent quiet conference and the walk, and the supper at six in the afternoon. They reconstructed in detail the fatal affray that followed.

[1] Specially by E. Vine Hall, op. cit., pp. 5–14.
[2] By J. W. Kirby in *T.L.S.*, 17 July 1930.

But were they prejudiced against a playwright notorious as an atheist, and recently arrested by order of the Privy Council, or were they misled by false evidence? It would be easier to answer if we had the individual depositions as in the examinations before the Recorder concerning Poley and Mistress Yeomans. There not only Yeomans and Ede gave evidence but household servants. Did the Coroner ask for testimony from Eleanor Bull or any of the tavern tapsters? And by which of the principal witnesses were he and the jury most influenced? Here, I think, we are now in a position to make things somewhat clearer than when Hotson made his discoveries.

Frizer appears to have been a man of some substance, and his shady relations with the Woodleffs were probably not known at this time. But he does not seem to have held any public position before June 1593, and appearing in the Coroner's Court, with his unhealed two-day-old wounds, he was virtually himself on trial for murder. Skeres seems to have had an equivocal career and played subordinate parts. Poley, as has been seen, had spent much time in prison, but he was no ordinary rogue. He had been mixed up in great affairs, and had been on familiar terms with political personages and men of high station. He had been in the confidence of Christopher Blunt and the Sidneys; he had talked with Morgan through the windows of the Bastille; he had supped with Anthony Babington before the break-up of the conspiracy; he had (according to his own account) made Mr. Secretary look out of his window and grin like a dog. And we have his own avowal, reported by Yeomans at an earlier date, 'I will sweare and forsweare my selfe rather then I will accuse my selffe to doe me any harme'. It is, I think, a safe inference that (whatever the actual facts may have been) it was mainly the evidence of Poley that got Frizer off and branded Marlowe as the criminal.

The position of the participants in the affray, as described in the Coroner's 'return', has been sharply

T

criticized, particularly by Miss de Kalb (*T.L.S.*, 21 May 1925):

'Marlowe (says the evidence) snatches a dagger from the rear of Friser's belt and deals him two futile flesh-wounds on the head: such insignificant cuts (on the evidence) as might be self-inflicted to corroborate a put-up story; or such as a man, fighting for his life against heavy odds, might get in, slashing wildly, before he was overpowered. But is it conceivable that any man in mortal earnest would recline on a bed to hack at an antagonist who is sitting upright and certain to retaliate? Friser, though seated between Poley and Skeres "so that he could not in any wise get away", is able to grapple with Marlowe, who is behind him on the bed, to struggle with him for the dagger, and to give him a mortal wound—and this without interference from the two other men who (apparently) waited passive. These two inactive observers were exceedingly competent to keep Friser within the reach of Marlowe; but as for separating them no such reasonable effort is recorded.'

In the same number of *T.L.S.* William Poel dealt, to the same effect, with a special aspect of the struggle:

'Marlowe could not have inflicted two wounds on Frizer's head "of the length of two inches and of the depth of a quarter of an inch" with either the point or edge of a dagger. Captain Hutton in his book on "Elizabethan Combats" has shown that when quarrels arose it was not unusual for a man to draw his dagger and with the handle pummel the head or shoulders of his adversary in order to hurt him without danger to his life. Frizer's scalp-wounds can only be explained in this way. But the blow that slew Marlowe must have been given with terrific force by a man intent on killing his victim, because the blade, where it was one inch wide, penetrated Marlowe's brain to a depth of two inches! Yet Frizer declares that when he gave his blow he was seated between Skeres and Poley "and that he could not in any wise *get away* in his own defence". But what his companions had to say on this matter we are not told, and these men seem to have been the associates of Frizer.'

Another point has been pressed from the medical angle by Samuel Tannenbaum:

'One who knows the anatomy and pathology of the human brain knows that it is impossible for death to follow immediately upon the infliction of [a two-inch wound above the eye.] . . . . To have caused instant death, the assassin would have had to thrust his dagger horizontally into Marlowe's brain to a depth of six or seven inches—and that could not have happened if Frizer and Marlowe had been wrestling as the witnesses described.'[1]

On grounds such as these it has been argued that the story told to the Coroner and jury, and accepted by them, was faked, and that Marlowe, instead of being the aggressor in the affray, was the victim of a deliberately planned political murder. The length and privacy of the conference between the quartet savour of something weightier than an ordinary 'feast' in a tavern. And there is a suspicious similarity between the setting of the Deptford episodes and an incident in the Babington conspiracy when a number of the plotters, including Skeres, might have been taken 'at supper in Poley's garden', probably the Garden Inn near Fleet Street. 'It was evidently unhealthy', as Miss Seaton caustically remarks, 'to frequent an inn or to walk in its garden in Poley's company, as Marlowe was to know too late'.[2]

And there is documentary proof that as in August 1586 so in May 1593 Poley was in the service of Elizabeth's government. The warrant of 12 June 1593, quoted above, shows that on 8 May he had left Croydon for The Hague with official dispatches and that on 8 June he had brought the answers to the Court at Nonesuch, 'being in her majesties service all the aforesaid tyme'. This unusual formula, as Miss de Kalb has noted,[3] was intended to cover his employment during the whole month between 8 May and 8 June, when instead of carrying back the answering dispatches of the States-General straight to the Court, he had broken his return journey to meet Marlowe at Deptford. The Government was at any rate determined that he should not suffer in any way as a consequence of the fatality of 30 May.

[1] *The Assassination of Christopher Marlowe*, pp. 41–2.
[2] 'Marlowe, Robert Poley, and the Tippings' in *R.E.S.*, p. 280.
[3] Loc. cit., in *R.E.S.*, pp. 13–14.

But does this mean that he was acting as their agent in luring Marlowe to his doom? Poley would have had no scruples about playing such a part. But why should the Privy Council have taken such a roundabout way of getting rid of the atheist playwright? He had been arrested and bound over, and they could have dealt with him judicially as they had already done with his fellow dramatist, Thomas Kyd. Still less probable is the theory that the trio at Deptford were tools of Raleigh who was afraid that Marlowe would make revelations to the Council that would incriminate him and his school of atheism.[1] Poley would certainly not have risked the loss of his government employment by loitering on his way to Nonesuch in order to carry out a criminal plot of Sir Walter's. And if Frizer had been the actual instrument of such a design, could he have remained for years afterwards in the service of Thomas Walsingham, Marlowe's friend?

While, therefore, the theory of a political murder cannot be ruled out, it is difficult to find an adequate motive for it or to trace a convincing origin for it in any special quarter. On the other hand, sudden and violent quarrels over the settlement of accounts have been familiar in all periods. And as in the record of the Bradley homicide,[2] so here the introduction of an English phrase into the legal Latin seems to come from the very lips of one of the deponents:

'post cenam praedicti Ingramus & Cristoferus Morley locati fuerunt & publicauerunt vnus eorum alteri diuersa maliciosa verba pro eo quod concordare & agreare non potuerunt circa solucionem denariorum summe vocatum le recknynge.'

Moreover, the condemnatory phrases in the Coroner's return, 'ira motus versus praefatum Ingramum ffrysar' ... 'ex subito & ex malicia sua ... pugionem maliciose adtunc & ibidem evaginabat' tally remarkably with the description of Marlowe by Kyd in his letters to Puckering: 'As I & many others in regard of his other rashnes in attempt-

---

[1] Samuel Tannenbaum, op. cit., pp. 48 ff.   [2] See above, p. 102.

Extract from the Register of the Church of St. Nicholas, Deptford, including, among the burial entries for 1593, 'Christopher Marlow slaine by ffrancis ffrezer; the ·1· of June'

ing soden pryvie iniuries to men did ouerslypp though often reprehend him for it.' Was the assault on Frizer, without warning and from behind, the crowning and final instance of Marlowe's 'rashness in attempting soden pryvie iniuries to men'? There are so many complicating factors in the whole affair that we do best to suspend judgement, remembering that coroners' findings have given cause for criticism ever since the Elsinore grave-diggers discussed the rights and wrongs of Ophelia's Christian burial.

> *2nd Clown.* But is this law?
> *1st Clown.* Ay, marry is't; crowner's quest law.

There is evidence, as will appear in the next chapter, that the three companions of Marlowe on the day of his death survived into the next century, and one of them at least, Ingram Frizer, into the reign of Charles I. The circumstances of the affair, in the official version, must have been known to a considerable body of people—the Coroner and the sixteen jurymen, the officials of the Court of Chancery through whose hands the legal documents concerning the inquest and the pardon passed, the households of Eleanor Bull and the Walsinghams. It is therefore surprising that the references to the event in the years immediately following should be so comparatively scanty and so curiously vague or misleading. Mistakes began on the very day of the inquest, when the entry of Marlowe's burial in the St. Nicholas Church Register gives the Christian name of his slayer, 'ffrezer', as 'ffrancis' instead of Ingram. Nor is there any indication in the churchyard of the place of the grave.

In the copy of Richard Baines's Note concerning Marlowe's blasphemies sent to the Queen, as has been mentioned above,[1] the original title is scored through and altered to 'A Note deliuered on Whitson eve last of the most horrible blasphemes vtteryd by Cristofer Marly who within iii days after came to a soden & fearfull end of his

---

[1] See p. 250.

life'. Apart from the difficulty of dates already discussed, the official scribe here is tantalizingly vague; his phrase would cover any form of accidental death.

Thomas Kyd's letters to Sir John Puckering were written after (probably soon after) Marlowe had met his fate, for he says, 'It is not to be nombred amongst the best conditions of men, to taxe or to opbraide the deade'. Kyd paints Marlowe in the darkest colours, but he gives no hint that he had brought on his own doom by an unprovoked assault, though, as has been seen, the words 'his other rashnes in attempting soden pryvie iniuries to men' might well cover the Deptford stabbing affair. Another contemporary playwright and poet, George Peele, uses common form when in the *Prologue to the Honour of the Garter*, published in 1593, he apostrophizes 'Marley' as 'unhappy in thine end'.

And strangest of all, the only contemporary who appears to allude in the same year with any particularity to the playwright's death is completely misleading. Gabriel Harvey had come up to London in August 1592 to attend to legal affairs concerning the estate of his brother John who had died in July. He stayed in London, apparently at the house of his printer John Wolf in St. Paul's Churchyard till towards the end of July 1593. Marlowe's tragic fate must have caused consternation in 'Paul's', where, as Kyd tells us, he had friends. Moreover, another brother of Gabriel Harvey, Richard, had been Rector of Chislehurst since 1586[1] and therefore in touch with the Walsingham household. Gabriel Harvey was thus in a position to get accurate information from more than one source. Yet, to all appearance, he labours, for edifying purposes, the circumstance that Marlowe died of the Plague, which was rife in 1593! A poetical epilogue to *A New Letter of Notable Contents*, addressed to Wolf and

---

[1] He had been collated on 1 Oct. 1586, and again on 6 Dec. He was licensed to preach on 18 Sept. 1587. Marlowe would appear to have heard him on a visit to Scadbury, for he is reported to have called him an ass, fit to preach about nothing but the iron age.

dated from Saffron Walden, 18 September 1593, begins
with a sonnet on '*Gorgon*, or the Wonderfull yeare'. This
records leading events of 'the fatall yeare of yeares . . .
Ninety Three', and ends the recital with 'Weepe Powles,
thy *Tamberlaine* voutsafes to dye'. The Tamberlaine of
'Powles' who died in 1593 seems to be Marlowe. What then
is to be made of the last section of the Epilogue, the
'Glosse'?

> Is it a Dreame?   or is the *Highest minde*
> That euer haunted Powles or hunted winde,
> Bereaft of that same sky-surmounting breath,
> That breath that taught the Tempany to swell.
> He & the *Plague* contended for the game.
> The hawty man extolles his hideous thoughtes,
> And gloriously insultes upon poore soules,
> That plague themsealves: *for faint harts plague themselves*
>
> .   .   .   .
>
> The graund Dissease disdain'd his toade Conceit
> And smiling at his tamberlaine contempt,
> Sternely struck-home the peremptory stroke,
> He that nor feared God, nor dreaded Diu'll,
> Nor ought admired but his wondrous selfe . . .
> Alas! but Babell Pride must kisse the pitt.

It might be possible to wrest some other meaning out
of part of this, but 'The graund Dissease . . . sternely
struck-home the peremptory stroke' apparently implies
Marlowe's death from the plague. Yet the real fact of his
instantaneous death-wound from Frizer's dagger would
have been far more impressive, as a moral warning, than
his demise from the pestilence that carried off its thousands
without discrimination. The more Harvey's references are
considered the more enigmatic they become.[1]

Not so with the next known account of the event, by
Thomas Beard, in his *Theatre of Gods Judgements*, chap.
xxv (1597). The work is a translation from the French,

---

[1] Hale Moore in an article on 'Gabriel Harvey's References to Marlowe'
(*Studies in Philology*, July 1926) throws light on incidental points, but
does not help to solve the basic problem. See however p. 283.

illustrating 'the admirable Iudgements of God upon the transgressours of his commandements'. Among the three hundred additional examples with which Beard augmented his version was the divine punishment of 'one of our own nation, of fresh and late memory, called *Marlin*', of whose atheism he gives the conventional account, and then continues:

'It so fell out that in London streets as he purposed to stab one whome hee ought a grudge vnto with his dagger, the other party perceiuing so auoided the stroke, that withall catching hold of his wrest, he stabbed his owne dagger into his owne head, in such sort, that notwithstanding all the meanes of surgerie that could be wrought, hee shortly after died thereof . . . and together with his breath an oath flew out of his mouth.[1] . . . But herein did the iustice of God most notably appeare, in that he compelled his owne hand which had written those blasphemies to be the instrument to punish him, and that in his braine, which had deuised the same.'

This is, at any rate, an effective piece of 'tendencious' narrative. It was necessary for Beard's purpose that Marlowe's own hand should be the instrument of his death, without it being a case of suicide. And though he thus gives a twist to the facts he knew not only that Marlowe was killed in a brawl, but that the two combatants made use of the same dagger—a very unusual circumstance. And if Hotson is right in his ingenious conjecture that 'London streets' is a printer's error for 'London streete', a thoroughfare in East Greenwich (Deptford being West Greenwich), Beard got within 'a few hundred yards' of the actual scene of Marlowe's death.

But in the next year, 1598, Francis Meres in his *Palladis Tamia* supplemented Beard's account, to which he refers his readers, with highly coloured details:

'As the poet *Lycophron* was shot to death by a certain riual of his: so *Christopher Marlow* was stabd to death by a bawdy seruing man, a riuall of his in his lewde love.'

[1] Aldrich was probably echoing Beard's account when he told Oxinden that Marlowe 'was stabd with a dagger and dyed swearing'. Other versions derived from Beard are quoted by Bakeless, op. cit., pp. 235–6.

Here Meres's obsession with parallels, which dominates his tractate, works more mischief than Beard's theological fanaticism. Frizer, though in the service of Thomas Walsingham, was not a 'seruing man', and 'le recknynge', not 'lewde love', was the accepted cause of the affray. The further flourishes that Anthony Wood and later writers have added to the rodomontade of Meres are well known.[1] But in 1600 William Vaughan, drawing evidently upon independent information, gave in his *Golden Grove* an account that in many respects hit the mark:

'It so hapned that at Detford, a little village about three miles distant from London, as he meant to stab with his ponyard one named Ingram, that had inuited him thither to a feast, and was then playing at tables, he quickly perceyuing it, so auoyded the thrust, that withall drawing out his dagger for his defence hee stabd this Marlow into the eye, in such sort, that his braines comming out at the daggers point, hee shortlie after dyed.'

Vaughan, of course, goes wrong in stating that two weapons were used, but this proves that his account is not based upon the Coroner's inquisition, and that it therefore has independent value. Hence it is important that he should be right about the place of the affray and the identity of Marlowe's slayer—whom he calls, after a fashion of the time, by his Christian name only. The two details that Ingram Frizer was the host at the entertainment, and that he was playing at tables [i.e. backgammon] are not inconsistent with the legal record, and may be correct. At any rate there was no need to insert them to point the moral, which Vaughan, like Beard, was anxious to enforce: 'Thus did God, the true executioner of diuine iustice, worke the ende of impious Atheists.'

But those who were making theological capital out of the playwright's death did not have it all their own way. In the light of the facts, as we now know them, of the fatal affray on 30 May 1593, Blount's dedication of his

---

[1] An entertaining summary of them is given by Philip Henderson, in "*And Morning in his Eyes*", pp. 197-9.

1598 edition of *Hero and Leander* to Sir Thomas Walsingham is a remarkable document:

'Sir, wee thinke not our selues discharged of the dutie wee owe
to our friend, when wee haue brought the breathlesse bodie to
the earth: for albeit the eye there taketh his euer farwell of that
beloued obiect, yet the impression of the man, that hath beene
deare vnto us, liuing an after life in our memory, there putteth vs
in mind of farther obsequies due vnto the deceased. And namely
[i.e. especially] of the performance of whatsoeuer we may iudge
shal make to his liuing credit, and to the effecting of his determinations preuented by the stroke of death. By these meditations (as
by an intellectual will) I suppose my selfe executor to the vnhappily deceased author of this Poem, vpon whom knowing that
in his life time you bestowed many kind fauors, entertaining the
parts of reckoning and woorth which you found in him, with good
countenance and liberall affection: I cannot but see so far into the
will of him dead, that whatsoeuer issue of his brain should chance
to come abroad, that the first breath it should take might be the
gentle aire of your liking: for since his selfe had been accustomed
thervnto, it would prooue more agreeable & thriuing to his right
children, than any other foster countenance whatsoeuer.'

Who would dream that behind the bland and unctuous
phrases of this dedication there lay the story of Marlowe's
sudden blow from behind at Frizer, the fatal affray and
the viewing of 'the breathlesse bodie' by the Coroner's
jury before it was 'brought to the earth'? And what did
Sir Thomas Walsingham, with whose family Frizer retained his connexion for at least ten years after the Deptford homicide, think of such expressions as the 'vnhappily
deceased author of this Poem' and 'the effecting of his
determinations preuented by the stroke of death'? To
one who had had first-hand information about the tragedy
of 30 May 1593 these conventional flourishes must have
sounded strangely unreal. Had Blount in view not so
much Sir Thomas as the general reading public, and is
this indirect *apologia* a counterblast to the fulminations
of Beard and Meres?

There is no need to assume, as has been done, that
Blount's 'impression of the man, that hath beene deare

vnto us, living an after life in our memory' was shared
by Shakespeare in his invocation, through the lips of
Phebe (*As You Like It*, III. v. 80–1),[1] of the poet from
whose *Hero and Leander* he quotes a pregnant line:

> Dead Shepherd, now I find thy saw of might:
> 'Who ever lov'd, that lov'd not at first sight?'

But it is to say the least, a remarkable coincidence, that
in the same Act of the same play (III. iii. 9 ff.) Touchstone
should use enigmatic words to which the statement about
'le recknynge' in the Coroner's inquisition gives for the
first time a possible clue:

> 'When a man's verses cannot be understood nor a man's good
> wit seconded with the forward child Understanding, it strikes a
> man more dead than a great reckoning in a little room.'[2]

The parallel here may be merely fortuitous. In any case
the echoes of the tragedy, within the lifetime of the
survivors, are, as has been seen, so divergent that the
lesson of caution in taking at its face value even contemporary evidence is driven home anew.

[1] See above, p. 230

[2] Since Oliver F. W. Lodge first suggested that Shakespeare was here
referring to Marlowe's death (in *T.L.S.*, 14 May 1925) he has been supported by W. Poel, *T.L.S.*, 21 May, Paul Reyher, 9 July 1925, and by
Dover Wilson in the 'New Cambridge' edition of *As You Like It* (1926).
The reviewer of this edition in *T.L.S.*, 30 Dec. 1926, maintained that this
imputed 'brutality of sentiment' to Shakespeare 'who could joke in public
on the sordid tragedy of the greatest of his fellow poets'. In *T.L.S.*,
6 Jan. 1927, Wilson and Lodge disavow this imputation. Bakeless, op. cit.,
p. 297, also accepts the topical interpretation of the passage.

Addition to Note 1 on p. 279

In *The Times Lit. Supp.*, 18 Jan. 1941, T. W. Baldwin plausibly suggests
that G. Harvey's puzzling line, 'Weepe Powles, thy *Tamberlaine* voutsafes to dye', refers not to Marlowe but to a swaggering frequenter of
Paul's, Peter Shakerley.

THE SURVIVORS

THE story of Marlowe's last days may be rounded off by tracing the subsequent fortunes of the chief figures associated with it.

Thomas Kyd did not long survive his fellow dramatist. How long he remained in prison after 12 May 1593 we do not know, but his imploring letters to Puckering after his release do not seem to have procured his reinstatement in the service of his 'lord' or to have otherwise bettered his fortunes. He apparently lost his market on the London stage and devoted a winter's week at the close of 1593 or the beginning of 1594 to translating Robert Garnier's neo-classic play *Cornelie*, which was published in 1594 with a dedication to the Countess of Sussex who had translated his *Marc Antonie*. It was praised by the intellectuals, but the reading public let 'poore *Cornelia* stand naked vpon euery poste'. This was probably Kyd's last venture, for before the end of the year he was dead, and on 30 December his parents took the strong step of renouncing the administration of his goods.[1] It would seem that they wished to disassociate themselves entirely from a son whose career had ended in disgrace. If Kyd by his accusations had wronged Marlowe, he appears to have paid the penalty.

And there are grounds for the belief that in the same month of December 1594 Marlowe's other chief accuser, Richard Baines, met a yet worse fate. In the Stationers' Register on 6 December (Arber ii. 316) there is entered to Thomas Gosson and William Blackwell 'a ballad intituled *the wofull lamentacon of* RICHARD BAYNES executed at *Tyborne* the 6. of December 1594'. No copy of the 'lamentacon' which would have helped to identify the culprit and his crime seems to have survived. But Cooper

---

[1] Boas, *Works of Kyd*, pp. lxxvi–vii.

in *Athenae Cantab.* ii. 174 (followed by Peile and by Venn), had no warrant except the name for stating that this Richard Baines was the member of Christ's College there mentioned, of whose career nothing whatsoever is known. With regard to Richard Baines of the Middle Temple, his record, so far as it is known, is not inconsistent, under Elizabethan conditions, with such a calamitous end. And it is notable that, so far as we are aware, there is in any case no further mention of him in any contemporary document. Of special significance is the omission of his name from his mother's will, made on 17 August 1597. Her death took place within eight days, as is shown by this entry in the burial register of St. Peter's, Cornhill:

1597 August 25 Thursday: Mrs Grace Banes widow, her pit in the South Chappell 50.

The main provisions of the will are as follow :

... I most hartelie desire that my bodie maie be laied and placed in Sainct Peters church where my late deare husband Richard Baynes lyeth And I doe by this my last will and Testament give and bequeath to my daughter ffrauncis Baynes the somme of three hundred and fiftie poundes of lawfull monie of England Also I give and bequeath her the lease of my house which I now dwell in scituat in Sainct Peters parishe I give to my good brother Sir Nicholas Woodrofe for a remembrance of me a ringe of fortie shillinges price and the like to my brother Mr Robert Woodrofe Also I give to my welbeloved sisters M^{ris} Kingsmill my Ladie Woodrofe Mistris Grevell and M^{ris} Woodroofe everie of them·one ringe of twentie shillinges price for a remembrance of me I give to my goddaughter Grace Reve twenty shillinges Item I give to my cosen Kente twentie shillinges To my cosin Allin twentie shillinges in monie and some of my olde apparrell at the discretion of my Executrix. ... I give and bequeath betwixt my two daughters, that is Marie Smith and ffrauncis Baynes all my lynnen whatsoever my beddinge and whatsoever belonges theirto except bedstedes Also my carpettes and cushions brasse and pewter to be equallie devided betwixt them by the discretion of some of my honest neighbours or frendes. I give my daughter Smith my Rubie ringe my Ale cuppe and two spoones of sylver and guilt Item I give to my sonne in lawe Robert Smithe my Saphire Ringe my guilt standinge cuppe with a cover. . . . I give to Ursula Katherin Robert and Marie Smith my daughters children everie of them tenne poundes to be paide them by my Executrix at theire ages of eightene yeeres if they or anie of them so longe live. Item I give to my brother Robert Woodrofe his children to be devided amongest them fortie poundes of lawfull monie of England I doe ordaine and appoint my daughter ffrauncis Baynes my full and sole Executrix of this my last will and testament.

This will, with its detailed dispositions to relatives of different grades in three generations, besides minor and charitable bequests, makes the impression of having been very carefully drawn up by the testatrix. But two names are conspicuously absent, those of her son Richard and her youngest daughter Ursula. The latter must have died in childhood. Richard, too, must have been dead. He had either not married or his wife and offspring were passed over in his mother's will. Grace Baines speaks affectionately of her 'late deare husband'; her silence about her late only son is easily understood, if he died a felon's death at Tyburn.

Of the three companions of Marlowe in Eleanor Bull's tavern on 30 May 1593 Nicholas Skeres is the most difficult to follow in his later life, partly because the references, as has been seen, may not be all to the same man. 'Nicholas Kyrse, alias Skeers, servant to the Earl of Essex' was arrested on 13 March 1594/5 by Sir Richard Martin, Alderman, 'in a very dangerous company' at the house of one Williamson. This was probably Nicholas Williamson, who on 7 April 1595, when he was a prisoner in the Gatehouse, made a deposition about Poley. Skeres after his arrest was imprisoned in the Counter in Wood Street to await examination. Nothing further is known of him till 31 July 1601 when the Privy Council issued warrants to the Keeper of the prison of Newgate for the removal of Nicholas Skiers and — Farmer, prisoners in his custodie, unto Bridewell.

If this Nicholas Skeres, who was lodged in one London gaol after another, was the associate of Ingram Frizer in the Woodleff litigation and the Deptford Strand affray, their paths afterwards must have diverged widely. For the slayer of Marlowe seems to have shared the good fortunes of his master, Thomas Walsingham, who in July 1597 was visited by Elizabeth at Scadbury and was knighted, and was a member of Parliament in her reign and in that of James I, whose queen made a favourite of Lady Walsingham.

A year after the Deptford Strand fatality, in June 1594, Frizer took over from Thomas Smyth a house in the parish of St. Saviour's, Southwark, with possession for three years. But he was driven out by Edmund Ballard, against whom he brought a suit on 17 October for recovery of possession, which was granted to him with £5 damages and 6d. costs. The suit against him by the Woodleffs, probably in 1598, has already been described. At a later date he moved to Eltham, where he appears to have spent the rest of his life. In a deed of sale, discovered by Hotson, dated in June 1602, he is described as 'late of London, yoman and nowe dwelling at Eltham in the Countye of Kente'. Eltham is near to Chislehurst, and he still kept up his connexion with the Walsingham family. In December 1603, after a delay which required the intervention of Sir John Fortescue, a lease in reversion of some lands belonging to the Duchy of Lancaster, at a rent of £42. 6s. 3d., was granted to Ingram Frizer for the benefit of Lady Walsingham, the wife of Sir Thomas.

In 1611 he appears on the Subsidy Roll as one of the two certified assessors of the parish of Eltham, being taxed one and fourpence on a holding of land valued at 20 shillings. An inquisition was taken by a commission at East Greenwich[1] on 16 July concerning certain charities by the oaths of sixteen 'good and lawful men of the County' among who was 'Ingram Frezer'. Among the Commissioners were the Bishop of Rochester, the Vicar of St. Nicholas Church, Deptford, and Sir Thomas Walsingham. Miss de Kalb has further ascertained that

[1] J. W. Kirby in *T.L.S.*, 17 July 1930.

he had a married daughter, Alice Dixon, and a grandson, John Bankes; that he had sufficient means to keep a maid-servant; that he held a position of respect in Eltham, and was churchwarden from 1605 till his death in August 1627, when he was buried in the church.

Documents at Somerset House show further that after his death his daughter Alice propounded a 'nuncupative' or oral will and claimed to be his executrix. The will was contested by the grandson, John Bankes, suing through his father of the same name, and the Prerogative Court declared that Frizer had died intestate. The final result of the litigation is not known. But in any case Frizer had died in the odour of sanctity, and evidently 'lived down' any disrepute attaching to his transactions with the Woodleffs or any suspicion of ill-fame as a homicide.

With Robert Poley also things seem to have gone on prosperously enough till the close of the century. There is documentary evidence that he continued to be em-ployed as a government messenger.[1] Six weeks after Marlowe's death, on 14 July 1593, he was paid for carrying letters to France and bringing back replies. Further pay-ments followed on 19 August 1594 and the first of April 1595 for similar errands to Brussels and Antwerp. About the time of the Antwerp visit Nicholas Williamson, a prisoner in the Gatehouse, was deposing, on 7 April, that 'if Pooly or Barnard Maude shall come again into the lowe countryes they are threatened to be apprehended'.[2] Whatever may have been the foundation for this state-ment, Poley was again receiving payments on 1 August 1595 for carrying letters to and from Brussels, and on 7 March 1596/7 for the same service to and from The Hague. It was presumably after this visit to The Hague

---

[1] E. de Kalb, loc. cit. in *R.E.S.*, pp. 17–18.

[2] Williamson also alleged that 'Creichton chargeth Pooley to haue poysoned the Bishop of Diuelinge' (Dublin). I know nothing of the cir-cumstances or the grounds of this accusation unless it is a confused reference to a suspicion mentioned by J. H. Pollen (*Mary Queen of Scots and the Babington Plot*, p. cxxv) that in 1585 Poley poisoned in the Tower Richard Creagh, Archbishop of Armagh.

that he wrote the letter dated 5 March from Hogesden[1] in which he states, 'Being evene now retou^rned, I thought good to send this inclosde, before I came my sellfe', and forwards at the same time 'a booke in sheets, one of the firste I thinke came out of the presse: the subiects cheefly intended againste the religion and goue^rme[n]t of Englande'.[1]

The Declared Accounts of the Treasurer of the Chamber do not record all the payments to Poley for his services as a messenger abroad. On one of the copies (Item 105 A) of his 1596-7 cipher Miss Seaton has found a memorandum[2] of 'A note of mony delivered to Robert Pooley imployed in Flande^{rs}', and entry of a payment to him on 3 December 1596 of £20 'by y Steward as appeareth by an acquittance'. There are also memoranda of two further payments to him of the same sum on 25 March and 23 July 1597.

The payment on 23 July was made at the Court at Greenwich. Poley was therefore at home in the summer of 1597, and he could therefore have been one of the 'two damn'd Villans', who, as Ben Jonson told Drummond, were placed during his close imprisonment 'to catch advantage' of him. Mark Eccles has recently argued[3] that Jonson was referring to his imprisonment in the Marshalsea from early in August till 8 October 1597 for his part in *The Isle of Dogs*, and that there is an echo of his gaol experiences in his *Epigram*, ci, 'Inviting a Friend to Supper', when he declares:

> And we will haue no *Pooly*' or *Parrot* by.

Parrot (or Parratt) is accused by a Newgate prisoner of being a spy and extortioner, and the coupling of his name with that of 'Pooly' here is highly suggestive. Poley would indeed be raised to a bad eminence if not only Marlowe but Jonson came within his baneful orbit.

However this may have been, by the end of 1598 he was again being employed on foreign service. By a warrant of

---

[1] 'Robert Poley's Ciphers', *R.E.S.*, April 1931, p. 150.   [2] Loc. cit., p. 139.
[3] 'Jonson and the Spies', *R.E.S.*, Oct. 1937, pp. 385 ff.

19 December he was being paid for bringing letters to and fro from the Governor of Bayonne, and by a warrant of 10 July and 21 December 1600 for similar missions to Elizabeth's agent at The Hague and Sir John de Laye in France. These three warrants were all signed by 'Mr Secretary'. Yet by the close of 1600 Poley had fallen out of favour with that great official. A long letter to Sir Robert Cecil dated 17 December 1600 begins, 'Since it pleasde your Honor to sequester mee from your seruice and bountye'. He seeks to regain Cecil's favour by promising to 'search out and discover the obscure Arte & cunynge which the Jesuits vse'.

'I find the pollyticke Jesuite to be the most dangerous personne that anye commonwealth can nourishe or suffer beeing continvallye whisperinge & busye in seacrett & peremptorye oppositions & devices procedinge from theyr proude ambityous and violent humors, for the most parte very dangerous or preiudicyall to the Prince & State wher they lyve favour'd or forbydden; which maye to the purpose be fytlyeste examyned and vnderstoode by theyr manifoulde procurements and practises againste oure Cuntrye.'

He describes their methods in some detail, and warns Cecil of their hostility to him personally and to the English Queen and State. He then undertakes to provide an effective counterblast to their machinations:

'Howe agreeable & needfull itt is also in some generall volume exactly to examyne aunswer & controule [i.e. contradict] the particular abuses of their sedicyous and pestilent Bookes, I humblye refer to your honorable Consyderation: confidentlye assuringe you that if it shall please your Honor to accepte the offer & give supportaunce & means needfull to the performance of so importante a businesse as this discoverye wyll bee: that then with learninge & knowledge sufficyent a Booke shal be wrytten & sett forthe, much more substancyall to the effects afore specyfyde then any hath beene heretofore publishde in that kinde.'

As he had previously done on 5 March 1596/7, Poley sent with his letter an example of the type of literature that he was eager to expose and confute:

'The Booke inclosde was (as I thinke your Honor knowes) 5 years

since disperste in wrytten Coppyes by the Author R. Suthwell.
And lately by Garrett, Garnett and Blackwell putt in printe
though foreadvisde by good discretion nott to do itt. Wher the
leafe is putt in your Honour maye readylye finde howe they deale
with Sir Fra[ncis] Walsingham, I proteste most falcelye slandringe
him and wyckedlye abusing him.'

The book was evidently the pamphlet by Robert Southwell, the Jesuit poet and controversialist, entitled *An
Humble Supplication to Her Maiestie*. It was printed
anonymously, and is dated at the end 14 December 1595
as well as 1595 on the title-page.[1] It is an eloquent, un-
compromising *apologia* for the Jesuits as propagandists of
what in Southwell's eyes is the only saving faith:

'The whole and onely intent of our comminge into this Realme
is no other, but to labour for the saluation of soules, and in peace-
able and quiet sort to confirm them in the ancient Catholike faith,
in the which theyr forefathers liued & died, these thousand foure
hundred yeares, out of which we undoubtedly beleeue it is impossible that any soule should be saved.'

Poley probably chose this particular work to send to
Cecil because in the attack upon the memory of Sir Francis
Walsingham Southwell magnified the part played by
Poley himself in the Babington plot. He states in its
most explicit and extreme form the contemporary Roman
Catholic thesis that Babington and his accomplices were
dupes drawn into a net by Poley as the chief *agent-
provocateur*. Cecil was the last man to believe this, but
it might help to impress him with a sense of Poley's
importance.

'As for the action of *Babington*, that was [in truthe][2] rather a
snare to intrap them, then any deuise of their owne, sith it was
both plotted, furthered, & finished, by S[ir] *Francis Walsingham*,
& his other complices, who laied & hatched al the particulers
thereof, as they thought it wold best fall out to the discredit of
Catholiks, & cutting of the Queene of Scots; for first it is to be

---

[1] The copy in the British Museum, one of the very few extant, has a
large number of MS. corrections in a contemporary hand.
[2] Added in MS.

known to all, that *Poolie* being Sir *F. Walsinghams* man, and throughly seasoned to his Maisters tooth, was the chiefe instrument to contriue & prosecute the matter, to draw into the net such greene wittes, as (fearing the generall oppression, and partly angled with golden hookes) might easilie be ouer wrought by M. Secr. subtile & sifting wit. . . . And though none were so deepe in the very bottome of that conspiracy as *Poolie* himselfe, yet was hee not so much as indited of any crime, but after a little large imprisonment (more for pollicy then for any punishment) set at liberty, & is in more credit then euer he was before.'

Southwell's crowning indictment is contained in the following passage:

'It is further knowen that the coppie of that letter which *Babbington* sent to the Queene of Scots, was brought ready penned by *Poolie*, from M. Secretary: the answere whereof, was the principal grounds of the Queenes condemnation. There was also found in Sir *Frauncis Walsinghams* accountes after his decease, a note of 7000 pounds bestowed vpon [*Nawe*][1] & *Curlie*, who being the Queenes Secretaries, framed such an answere as might best serue for a bloody time, & fit his intention that rewarded them with so liberall a fee.'

It may reasonably be conjectured that it was here that Poley put in a leaf to draw Cecil's special attention. For Southwell here asserts that Babington's letter of 12 July 1586 to Mary Queen of Scots, in which he offered to murder Elizabeth, was composed by Sir Francis Walsingham and brought to Babington 'ready penned' by Poley; and that Mary's answer on 17 July, agreeing to the proposal, was the work of her secretaries influenced by an enormous bribe.

It is sufficient to say that the authenticity of both Babington's and Mary's letters has been overwhelmingly demonstrated for all who do not follow in the tradition of Southwell's partisanship. But what I am more concerned with here is the curiously similar and sinister association of Poley with the tragedies of the Queen of Scots on the one hand and of Marlowe on the other. The

[1] Substituted in MS. for the printed *Nato*.

partisans of Mary in the sixteenth century accused Poley
of being privy to the fabrication of a letter, which led up
to what they considered the political murder at Fotherin-
gay. The partisans of Marlowe in the twentieth century,
who dispute the verdict at the inquest, implicate Poley
in the fabrication of evidence to conceal what was presumably a political murder at Deptford.

Whether or not it was a result of this petition to Cecil
in December 1600, Poley was employed twice in the
following year as messenger to and from the English ambassador in Paris. Warrants for payments to him were
issued by Mr. Secretary on 4 August and 5 September.
It would seem to have been in connexion with the former
of these visits that in July 1601 he tried to smuggle into
England a young cousin, George Cotton, who had been
for two years a student at St. Omer, but who was stopped
at Dover by the Warden of the Cinque Ports. On 18 July
1602 he again wrote to Cecil about the Jesuits, sending him
information derived from Robert Barrois, a priest. He
avers that Cecil's low estimate of his previous services 'is
the cause that I haue not since presented myself with offer
of my duty, although I much desire my endeavours might
please you, my necessities needing your favour'.[1]

So in the ebb-tide of his fortunes he disappears from
view. But whatever were his crimes and follies, the ad-
venturer was born under no ordinary star who crossed the
paths of Christopher Blunt and Anthony Babington, of
Francis and Thomas Walsingham, of Philip and Frances
Sidney, of Mary Stuart and Christopher Marlowe. He is
the very genius of the Elizabethan underworld.

[1] See references by Sir Edmund Chambers in a review of Leslie Hotson's
The Death of Christopher Marlowe (*Mod. Lang. Rev.*, Jan. 1926). His
quotations are from Hatfield MSS. xi. 216, 278, 302, and xii. 230.

In view of Cecil's attitude I think it unlikely that Poley was 'our well-
beloved Subiect R.P.' to whom in or about 1600 the next vacant place
of yeoman waiter in the Tower was granted (Ethel Seaton in *R.E.S.*,
April 1931, p. 150). And much more improbably was he the Robert
Pooley, 'citizen and haberdasher of London', who made a will in 1626
(E. Vine Hall, *Testamentary Papers*, iii. 22).

MARLOWE THROUGH THE CENTURIES

FROM THE JACOBEAN AGE TILL TO-DAY

IT is one of the many paradoxes confronting us in relation to Marlowe's career that the popularity of his plays with theatre-goers, so rapidly achieved, seems to have ended almost as rapidly. Though, as will be seen, the plays were revived from time to time in the seventeenth century their vogue ended with Elizabeth's reign. Even to the reading public, if we may judge by the number of editions called for, they made less appeal than *Hero and Leander*, to say nothing of the translation of Ovid's *Amores*. Exception must be made of *Doctor Faustus*, but this was in a version which included much that was not from Marlowe's pen.

It is possible that the dramatist's tragic end, with the legendary embellishments pointing the moral of the fate of the 'atheist', may have helped to affect the fortunes of his plays in the theatre. But, apart from this, there was a more general cause. In the Jacobean period the established popularity of Shakespeare, and in still greater measure that of Ben Jonson and Beaumont and Fletcher, rapidly out-moded the stage-fashions of the era typified by Marlowe and Kyd. The fact that Henslowe found it expedient to pay considerable sums to Jonson for two sets of additions to *The Spanish Tragedy* in 1601 and 1602 and to William Birde and Samuel Rowley for additions to *Doctor Faustus* in 1602 before his revival of these two plays is in itself significant that this shrewd commercial manager realized a change in theatrical tastes. Caustic evidence to the same effect is supplied abundantly from a more highbrow quarter by Ben Jonson. Even before the sixteenth century was out he was guying *The Spanish Tragedy* by making the coxcomb Bobadill and the Town Gull, Master

Mathew sing its praises (*Every Man in his Humour* I. v. 46–51 (1598)):

> *Bob.* What new book have you there? What! *Go by, Hieronymo?*
> *Math.* Ay, did you ever see it acted? Is't not well penned?
> *Bob.* Well penned! I would fain see all the poets of these times pen such another play as that was.

So in the Introduction to *Cythia's Revels* 1600 it is some one 'with more beard than brain' who vociferates that 'the old *Hieronimo*, as it was first acted, was the very best and judiciously penn'd play of Europe'; and in the Introduction to *Bartholomew Fair* (1614), 'whoever will swear *Ieronimo* or *Andronicus* are the best plays yet shall pass unexcepted at here as a man whose judgment shows it is constant and hath stood still these five and twenty or thirty years'. Ironical depreciation gives place to downright invective when Jonson attacks the author of *Tamburlaine* in *Discoveries*:[1]

> 'The true artificer will not run away from nature, as he were afraid of her; or depart from life and the likeness of truth; but speak to the capacity of his hearers. And though his language differ from the vulgar somewhat, it shall not fly from all humanity with the Tamerlanes and Tamer-Chams of the late age, which had nothing in them but the scenical strutting, and furious vociferation to warrant them to the ignorant gapers.'

It is a classic instance of the havoc wrought by the violent swing of the pendulum in theatrical taste that so fine a wit as Jonson should have been able to see nothing but 'scenical strutting and furious vociferation' in *Tamburlaine*. There was more excuse for Thomas Heywood's apology to Charles I and his Queen for daring to present before them at Whitehall in 1633 a play so out of the fashion as *The Jew of Malta*. Even so its revival by such a theatrical connoisseur as Heywood proves that he believed that it could still be an attraction on the stage.

There are other occasional references to performances of

---

[1] *Ingeniorum discrimina. Not. 10.*

some of the plays in the reigns of James I and Charles I. The most striking is that by John Melton in *The Astrologaster, or the Figure Caster* (1620):

'Another will fore-tell of Lightning and Thunder that shall happen such a day, when there are no such Inflammations seene, except men goe to the *Fortune* in *Golding-Lane*, to see the Tragedie of Doctor *Faustus*. There in deede a man may behold shagge-hayr'd Deuils runne roaring ouer the Stage with Squibs in their mouthes, while Drummers make Thunder in the Tyring-house, and the twelve-penny Hirelings make artificiale Lightning in their Heauens.'

Edward II (as the title-page of the 1622 quarto states) was acted by Queen Anne's men at the Red Bull theatre. This was probably between 1612, when the previous quarto had appeared, and 1619 when the Queen died. *Tamburlaine* was performed at the same theatre, apparently about 1640. In Cowley's *The Guardian* (Act III. vi), acted at Cambridge on 12 March 1641/2, two of the characters have a furious altercation:

Blade. First, leave your raging, Sir: for though you should roar like *Tamerlin* at the Bull, 'twould do no good with me.

Truman. I, *Tamerlin*, I scorn him, as much as you do, for your ears. I have an action of slander against you, Captain. . . . I'll not be call'd *Tamerlin* by any man.

Considering how few these definite references to performances in the first half of the seventeenth century are, it is surprising to find Edmund Gayton's statement in *Festivous Notes on Don Quixote* (1654):

'I have known, upon one of these festivals . . . where the players have been appointed, notwithstanding their bills to the contrary, to act what the major part of the company had a mind to; sometimes *Tamburlaine*, sometimes *Jugurth*,[1] sometimes *The Jew of Malta*, and sometimes parts of all these.'

The last words might almost apply to the 1663 edition of *Doctor Faustus*, 'as it is now acted', which omits the two longest additions, in Act III. i and ii, of the 1616

---

[1] A lost play by Will Boyle mentioned by Henslowe in 1599–1600.

quarto, and substitutes, besides a new scene at the Court
of the Soldan, echoes of the siege episodes in *The Jew of
Malta*. The complete elimination from this text of
references to the Deity and religious matters has suggested that it may have been acted in this form by strolling
companies during the Commonwealth period.[1]

How far the innumerable references to, and burlesques
of, episodes and lines in the plays,[2] especially *Tamburlaine*
and *Doctor Faustus* are reminiscences of performances seen
rather than of texts read, it is impossible to say. But if
one may judge from these allusions in plays, poems, and
pamphlets between 1603 and 1660, where Marlowe continued to hold the stage it was by virtue of the cruder and
more melodramatic features in his dramas. Tamburlaine's
'roaring' at his pampered jades, the devils and the
squibs in *Doctor Faustus*, the artificial nose of the Jew—
it was these that caught the ears or eyes of theatre-goers
and stayed in their memories. Of the unique qualities of
his genius as a poetic dramatist there is but the faintest
recognition. An exception would have to be made if
Michael Drayton was thinking of him as a playwright
when he wrote the exquisitely apt lines on him in the
elegy to his friend Henry Reynolds, *Of Poets and Poetry*
(1627):

> Next Marlowe, bathed in the Thespian Springs,
> Had in him those brave translunary things
> That your first poets had; his raptures were
> All air and fire, which made his verses clear,
> For that fine madness still he did retain,
> Which rightly should possess a poets brain.

But it is to be noted that Marlowe is introduced between Warner and Nashe, and that there is no allusion
here to the stage or to the theatre as when Drayton passes
on to speak of Shakespeare and Jonson. He was probably

---

[1] Tucker Brooke, *Works of Marlowe*, p. 141.
[2] These are admirably summarized by Tucker Brooke in 'The Reputation of Christopher Marlowe' (*Trans. of Connecticut Acad. of Arts and
Sciences*, vol. xxv, 1922).

here recalling the raptures of air and fire in *Hero and Leander*. It was by this poem, in Heywood's view, that Marlowe gained 'a lasting memory', while in *Tamburlaine* and the *Jew* it was the actor, Edward Alleyn, who won a peerless name.[1] Even Ben Jonson, so contemptuous of 'the Tamerlanes and the Tamer-Chams' was often heard to say of the lines in *Hero and Leander* that 'they were Examples fitter for admiration than for parallel'.[2] And the waves of the Thames echoed to the romance of the Hellespont as Taylor, the water-poet, rowed his boat, 'Repeating lines of *Hero and Leander*'.

Of Marlowe's uncompleted poem only Blount's 1598 edition is known, and this in a single copy. It was superseded for contemporary readers in the same year by Linley's edition with Chapman's continuation, and the popularity of the composite work was attested by the rapid succession of further editions in 1600, 1606, 1609, 1613, 1617, 1622, 1629, and 1637.

There was a sustained demand also for the translation of the *Amores*, though none of the editions has a date or a printer's name, and 'at Middleborough' is almost certainly a blind. Four editions can be distinguished of the complete three Books of the *Elegies*, and two of these editions, it has been claimed on typographical grounds, can hardly have been printed earlier than 1640.[3] There are also two editions of selections, surviving respectively in one and two copies. On the other hand, the 1600 issue of the Lucan translation seems to have satisfied the demand.

On turning from the poems to the plays it is surprising, after the resounding triumph of *Tamburlaine*, to find that only one edition of either Part was called for in the seventeenth century, Part I in 1605 and Part II in 1606. Of *Edward II* two Jacobean editions appeared in 1612

[1] The Prologue to *The Jew of Malta* at the Cockpit.
[2] R. C.'s Preface to William Bosworth's *Chast and Lost Lovers* (1651). Quoted by Tucker Brooke, op. cit., p. 364.
[3] Tucker Brooke, *Works of Marlowe*, p. 553.

and 1622. *The Jew of Malta* survives only in the 1633 quarto.

It was *Doctor Faustus* that alone among the plays rivalled with the reading public the popularity of *Hero and Leander*. The 1604 quarto was reprinted in 1609 and 1611, and the 1616 version 'with new additions' reappeared in 1619, 1620, 1624, 1628, 1631, while even after the Restoration there was, as has been seen, a public for the 1663 mutilated version. Indeed, the booksellers of this period still thought that there was a reading public for all Marlowe's dramas for they all appear in the successive playlists of Rogers and Ley (1656), Edward Archer (1656), and Francis Kirkman (1661 and 1671).[1] Archer and Kirkman explicitly state that all the plays in their lists can be bought. Among the purchasers we may probably count Milton's nephew, Edward Phillips, who in *Theatrum Poetarum* (1675) called Marlowe 'a kind of a second *Shakespeare* . . . though inferior both in Fame and Merit'. Though Phillips based this claim chiefly on *Hero and Leander*, and went wrong about the authorship of *Tamburlaine*,[2] yet he could declare: 'of all that he hath written for the Stage his *Dr. Faustus* hath made the greatest noise, with its Devils and such-like Tragical sport, nor are his other 2 Tragedies to be forgotten, namely his *Edw. the II* and *Massacre at Paris*, besides his *Jew of Malta* a tragic comedie,[3] and his Tragedy of *Dido* in which he was joyned with *Nash*'. The 'Tragical sport', as Phillips calls it, was degraded by the actor William Mountford into the farcical medley of *The Life and Death of Doctor Faustus* with the *Humours of Harlequin and Scaramouche* (1697); and by a dancing-master, John Thurmond, into the still lower buffoonery of *Harlequin Dr. Faustus* (1724).[4]

---

[1] See Appendix II to W. W. Greg's *A List of Masques, Pageants, &c.*

[2] See above, p. 70.

[3] The booksellers were evidently puzzled how to classify *The Jew of Malta*. Archer lists it as H (History); Kirkman in 1661 as T (Tragedy) and in 1671 as TC (Tragicomedy).

[4] See *Doctor Faustus*, ed. F. S. Boas, pp. 50–1.

An affront, of a different kind, to Marlovian tragedy was offered by Charles Saunders, author of *Tamerlane the Great* (1681), which was said by its critics to be 'only an Old Play transcrib'd'. Saunders protested that

'I never heard of any Play on the same Subject, untill my own was Acted, neither have I since seen it, though it hath been told me, there is a Cock Pit Play going under the name of the *Scythian Shepherd*, or *Tamberlain the Great*, which how good it is, anyone may judge by its obscurity, being a thing, not a Bookseller in London, or scarce the Players themselves, who Acted it formerly cou'd call to remembrance.'[1]

It is evident that Saunders had not troubled himself to look at Kirkman's catalogues.

The ignorance of Saunders and, what is more significant, the silence of Dryden, herald the almost complete eclipse of Marlowe during the first half of the eighteenth century. Except for Thurmond's travesty of *Doctor Faustus*, and the inclusion of *Edward II* in Dodsley's *Old Plays*, 1st edition (1744), followed by that of *The Jew of Malta* in the 2nd edition (1780), there is little to record. But from about the middle of the century the actors, Garrick and J. P. Kemble, and the scholars, Isaac Reed, George Steevens, and Edmund Malone begin the search for copies of the early editions of the plays and poems for which we owe them an incalculable debt.

The beginnings, too, are laid of Marlovian biography, which made it henceforth impossible to say with Aubrey that he had been killed by Ben Jonson or with Oldys that he was born early in Edward VI's reign, though as late as August 1819 an anonymous writer in *The Monthly Review* raises the astounding query, 'Can Christopher Marlowe be a *nom de guerre* assumed for a time by Shakespeare?' Meanwhile, Thomas Warton had anticipated the modern interpretation of Marlowe's atheism,[2] and had thereby provoked Joseph Ritson into printing for the first

---

[1] Tucker Brooke, *Reputation of Christopher Marlowe*, p. 384.
[2] *History of English Poetry*, 1774–81.

time Richard Baines's 'Note' of his blasphemies.¹ Malone
in his made-up volume of Marlowe's works inserted
manuscript annotations showing knowledge of the dramatist's academic career and disposing of the legend that he
was an actor before he became a playwright.

It is somewhat puzzling why suddenly in the early
decades of the nineteenth century there came something
like a spate of reprints of Marlowe's plays and poems.
It began, paradoxically enough, with the inclusion of his
translation of Lucan in *Poems in Blank Verse (not Dramatique) prior to Milton's Paradise Lost*, edited by Bishop
Percy and George Steevens (1807).² In 1810 *The Jew of
Malta* and *Edward II*, already included in Dodsley's *Old
Plays*, were reprinted in Scott's *The Ancient British
Drama*. In 1814 *Doctor Faustus* appeared in vol. i of
C. W. Dilke's *Old English Plays* where *Edward II* was
again reprinted. *Hero and Leander* was included in Sir
Egerton Brydges's *Restitution* (1815), Chapple's *Old English Poets* (1820), and Singer's *Select English Poets* (1821).
Dido followed in vol. ii of Hurst, Robinson & Co.'s *Old
English Drama* (1825).

The comedian, William Oxberry, edited in 1818 separate texts of *The Jew of Malta, Edward II, Doctor Faustus,
The Massacre at Paris*, and the apocryphal *Lust's Dominion*, followed by *Tamburlaine*, Parts I and II, in 1820.
All of these, together with *Dido*, were reissued by him in
1827 in a single volume, *The Dramatic Works of Christopher Marlowe*. A unique publication of 1818 was the text
of *The Jew of Malta* as prepared by S. Penley for Edmund
Kean's revival of the play at Drury Lane on 24 April
1818. This included beside Penley's own additions and
changes a number of excerpts from *Edward II*.

In 1826 from the house of Pickering came the first
collected edition of Marlowe's works in three volumes.
The anonymous editor, apparently George Robinson,
performed his task so carelessly that his successor,

¹ *Observations on Warton*, 1782, pp. 39 ff.
² See Tucker Brooke, loc. cit., p. 389.

Alexander Dyce, could convict him of 'the grossest errors'. Yet it is important as the first of the collected editions, and a British Museum copy contains valuable manuscript annotations by James Broughton, who also contributed two important articles chiefly relating to Marlowe to *The Gentleman's Magazine*, 1830. On the other hand, the great critical trio of the Romantic movement did less than might have been expected for the recognition of Marlowe's genius. If Lamb praised the death-scene in *Edward II* almost extravagantly in his *Specimens* (1808), yet he could speak of the 'difficulty' in culling a few sane lines from *Tamburlaine*. Coleridge says very little about him. Hazlitt, in his 1820 Lectures on *The Literature of the Age of Elizabeth*, includes him among a set of writers, 'whose names are now little known, and their writings nearly obsolete', though he states that 'Marlowe is a name that stands high, and almost first in this list of dramatic worthies'. He shows real appreciation of *Doctor Faustus* but underestimates *Edward II*. And his illustrations of the 'mighty line' are drawn not from *Tamburlaine* which he does not mention, but from the apocryphal *Lust's Dominion'*.

With Alexander Dyce's three-volume edition (1850) the period of critical editing of Marlowe's Works begins. Dyce modernized the spelling and his collation of the original texts may be criticized in some of its aspects. But his remarkable knowledge of Elizabethan literature and his scholarly acumen give his edition (reissued in one volume in 1858) a permanent value. Francis Cunningham's one-volume edition (1870) added little to Dyce. A. H. Bullen's in three volumes (1885) is specially notable for its Introduction, where his fine aesthetic sensibility produced the most adequate interpretation of Marlowe's genius that had yet appeared. Bullen's edition, like Dyce's, was in modernized spelling, but in the same year 1885, there appeared at Heilbronn the first volume of a 'historisch-kritische Ausgabe' of Marlowe's works in the original spelling. This was *Tamburlaine*, edited by Albrecht Wag-

ner, with a collation of the known original texts. It was
followed in 1889 by an edition of *Doctor Faustus* by Her-
mann Breymann, with the 1604 and 1616 texts in parallel
form. An edition of *The Jew of Malta* in the same year
by Wagner brought this scholarly venture to a premature
end.

About the same time a number of the plays were being
made accessible to readers in general through the first
volume of the Mermaid series (1887), the Clarendon Press
editions of *Edward II* and *Doctor Faustus*, and of the same
plays in the Temple Dramatists series.

In 1910, exactly sixty years after Dyce's edition and
a quarter of a century after Bullen's, C. F. Tucker Brooke
brought out the one-volume Oxford edition of Marlowe's
Works, in the original spelling, with a full collation of the
early texts, and with facsimiles of their title-pages. To
the present time Brooke's edition remains the only one
in Elizabethan spelling.

Side by side with the editorial labours on Marlowe's
writings had gone intensified research into his personal
career. An obstacle from the very first had been placed
in the way of his biographers by the inaccurate entry in
the Deptford Church register of the name of his slayer
as 'ffrancis', instead of Ingram, 'ffrizer'. Confusion was
worse confounded when an inquiry by James Broughton
in 1820 elicited the following reply:

Extract from the Register of Burials in the Parish of St. Nicholas,
Deptford.
    1st June 1593. Christopher Marlow slain by Francis Archer.
A True Copy.—D. Jones, Minister.

This 'true copy' sent many investigators in search of a
phantom 'Archer', though there were others who got as
near as 'Frezer' or as 'Frazer', and Sidney Lee in his
article on Marlowe in the *Dictionary of National Biography*, vol. xxxvi (1893), thought it well to hedge on the
matter. Here the question rested for over thirty years.

Meanwhile, however, new light was being thrown upon

other phases of Marlowe's career. In 1894 Lee drew attention to the appearance of the two sureties in October 1589 on his behalf before the Recorder. A reference in Lee's article on Thomas Kyd in the *Dictionary of National Biography* put me in 1898 on the track of Kyd's letter to Puckering accusing Marlowe of atheism, supplemented in 1921 by Ford K. Brown's discovery of Kyd's second, unsigned, letter. In 1904 J. H. Ingram included in his *Christopher Marlowe and his Associates* facsimiles of important documents relating to the dramatist's Canterbury and Cambridge years. In 1909 G. C. Moore Smith threw fresh light on the Cambridge period from the Corpus Christi Account Books.

A new stage in Marlovian biography was opened by Leslie Hotson's discovery in 1925 of the documents relating to the inquest on Marlowe proving the identity of his slayer and of his two other companions on the day of his death. The spelling of his name as Morley in these documents led Hotson also to conclude that he was the Christopher Morley to further whose graduation the Privy Council had intervened in June 1587.

Hotson's discoveries have opened up new lines of investigation, especially concerning the dramatist's associates. Miss E. de Kalb in *The Times Literary Supplement*, 21 May 1925, gave particulars of Frizer's later life from the Eltham Parish registers; and in the *Review of English Studies*, January 1933, she printed the documentary records of Poley's activities as a Messenger of the Court, 1588 to 1601. In *Marlowe and his Circle* (1929) I gave fresh particulars of Poley's career from documentary sources, and in *The Review of English Studies*, April 1931, Miss Seaton explained and illustrated his system of ciphers.

In an Appendix to his *Life* of Marlowe (1931) Tucker Brooke threw fresh light on the informer Richard Baines and his relatives, and this was supplemented, especially from testamentary evidence, by E. Vine Hall and myself in *The Nineteenth Century and After*, December 1932. Vine

Hall also in 1937 from similar evidence was able to show the status of a number of the jurymen at the inquest.

Mark Eccles in 1934, from researches at the Middlesex Guild Hall, discovered that the charge in 1589 which obliged Marlowe to find sureties was in connexion with the killing of William Bradley in which the dramatist was involved with Thomas Watson, and for which they both were imprisoned in Newgate. He also in 1592 had to enter into a recognizance to keep the peace towards two constables in Holywell Street.

The most recent additions to the dramatist's biography have been made by John Bakeless in his *Christopher Marlowe* (1938). He has thrown new light on the Marlowe family from the Canterbury city archives, and has supplemented Moore Smith's data from the Corpus Christi Account-Books by the investigation of the College Buttery Book, with its more detailed record.

Some of the other contributions to the study of individual plays, or of special phases of Marlowe's work, have been by Knutowski on *Dido*, Fraulein Thimme on *The Jew of Malta*, Percy Simpson in his two English Association essays on *Doctor Faustus*, Miss Seaton and F. Danchin on sources of *Tamburlaine*, and Tucker Brooke on Marlowe's Reputation. Miss Ellis-Fermor in 1927 made a brilliant attempt on a shaky chronological foundation to trace the development of his ideas in the plays and poems. Philip Henderson produced a vigorous study of the dramatist and his environment from a left-wing point of view in 1937. He took his title 'And Morning in his Eyes' from Swinburne, who wrote a poem in honour of William Poel's revival of *Doctor Faustus* by the Elizabethan Stage Society in 1896. Further revivals of this and other of the plays have followed on both sides of the Atlantic, usually before academic or festival audiences.

A piece by C. E. Lawrence, *The Reckoning*, based on the inquest story, was acted at the Royal Academy of Dramatic Art on the occasion of the Elizabethan Literary Society's Jubilee (1934). Mainly on the initiative of this

Society, a Memorial to Marlowe was erected in Canterbury. It was unveiled in 1891, with the design not completed, by Sir Henry Irving, and in its completed state in 1928 by Sir Hugh Walpole, who, like the dramatist, was a pupil at the King's School.

A memorial of a different kind was begun in 1930 by the publication of the first two volumes, under the general editorship of R. H. Case, of a six-volume edition of *The Life and Works of Christopher Marlowe*. Each volume, in modernized spelling, had a separate editor, and aimed at embodying the latest results of Marlovian scholarship. The edition was completed in 1933.

II

AN ATTEMPT AT A SUMMING-UP

I HAVE thus traced in outline the chequered fortunes of Marlowe's reputation as a man and a writer during the three centuries and a half since 30 May 1593, when he died by the hand of Ingram Frizer. Is it now possible to form a clear picture of his personality and his achievement?

So far as his biography is concerned, we are met with the curious paradox that the more we learn about his life the more puzzling are many of the aspects that it presents. It makes the impression of a series of kaleidoscopic views following upon one another without any apparent relation. At every succeeding period of his career Marlowe seems to have an entirely different set of associates. Canterbury gives him a respectable family connexion, and sends him from its King's School to Corpus Christi College with a scholarship. But when he has once bidden farewell to the place of his nativity, the city, the family, and the school all appear to drop completely out of his life. He spends six years at Cambridge in close association with Archbishop Parker's other scholars from the King's School and from Norwich, and goes through the regular academic routine before graduating B.A. Yet none of his

Corpus Christi contemporaries is afterwards mentioned among his friends. Though his B.A. certificate is signed by his College tutor and he continues afterwards to hold his scholarship, pressure has to be put on the academic authorities by the Privy Council, on the score of his having rendered some unspecified good service to her Majesty, before he is allowed to proceed to his M.A. degree.

Immediately afterwards this young man of twenty-three years, who has been dividing his time between his studies in preparation for taking Holy Orders and some form of Government employment bursts upon the London world as a playwright acclaimed by theatre-goers and assailed by envious rivals. Two years later he is suddenly revealed in company with Thomas Watson in a fatal street affray with its sequel of his arrest and imprisonment in Newgate. From this confinement he is soon released on the bond of two sureties, Richard Kitchen and Humphrey Rowland, with whom he has no other apparent connexion. Watson was probably known to him through Thomas Walsingham, but he is not mentioned by Kyd in the list of Marlowe's friends. Of these the most prominent is Thomas Harriot, but in all the mathematician's voluminous writings there is no reference to Marlowe. And though Harriot was in Raleigh's service, it is not from him but from the obscure Richard Chomley that we hear of any personal contact between the dramatist and Sir Walter.

Kyd is tantalizingly silent as to the name of the lord for whose players Marlowe wrote, and the glimpse that he gives of the meeting between the two dramatists in one room on some occasion in or about 1591 throws no light upon the nature of their association, tempting though it be to assume that this was for professional purposes. Nashe's memorial verses which might have told us more than we know of the relations between himself and Marlowe have disappeared. Most important of all, there is not a jot of evidence pointing to personal intercourse between

Marlowe and Shakespeare, though conjecture has run riot on the subject.

Nor have we any details of Marlowe's previous association with Thomas Walsingham before the Privy Council's order on 18 May 1593 to have him arrested at Scadbury. What a glaring contrast between this order and the certificate of good service given to him by the Council six years before! The arrest was probably occasioned by Kyd's charges, but why does Richard Baines, who apparently had no connexion with either of the dramatists, suddenly now come forward with his incriminatory 'Note'? Strangest of all, why is Marlowe found on 30 May 1593 in a Deptford tavern with three associates, most unfitted by their previous records to be in the company of a poet-playwright of genius? And though the most prominent of the trio, Robert Poley, has left a series of confessions and letters and ciphers, Marlowe's name is nowhere to be found in any of them. And, as the final enigma, though the entry of his burial is extant in the Register of the Church of St. Nicholas, Deptford, his grave has disappeared, and he has vanished as completely from earthly view as if his name were writ in water.

Thus viewed his life-record forms a drama as absorbing as any of his own tragedies but with the strange inconsequence of one of those modern Russian plays where characters wander in and out without any apparent relevance to the action. Yet somehow in the end they do fit in, and so with Marlowe there must have been causal links between the seemingly unrelated episodes in his career. Some have been suggested in the course of the present study. Whether these are accepted or not, I feel convinced that Marlovian research in recent years has provided striking examples of how increasing knowledge, however welcome, reveals also new depths of ignorance and raises problems hitherto unforeseen. 'Alps on Alps arise.'

But in the light of what we do now know it seems to me that we cannot accept without qualification the epigrammatic summing-up of the dramatist's career in *The Return from Parnassus*, Part II. i. ii:

> Marlowe was happy in his buskined Muse,
> Alas, unhappy in his life and end.

There is no sufficient reason to believe that Marlowe was 'unhappy in his life'. Indeed at various turning-points in it, as I have tried to show, he seems to have been favoured by fortune and even in serious crises to have fared better than Watson or Kyd. And though doubtless he was unhappy in his end, it might even be urged that it was better for him to find sudden death at the hand of Ingram Frizer than to suffer, if the Government acted on Kyd's and Baines's charges, the dread Elizabethan penalties for atheism and treason.

The question of Marlowe's atheism has been already examined. That of his treason is more puzzling. How is it that within a few years of earning the Privy Council's certificate of good service he fell under its ban? No fully satisfactory answer can be given. But Kyd's allegation of Marlowe's intended flight to the Scottish Court; Baines's charge of counterfeit coining; the association with a revolutionary desperado like Chomley and an *agent-provocateur* like Poley, point in different ways to equivocal political practices or intentions. And we now know that in the fatal Bradley affray and in the affair with the constables Marlowe had been in collision with the representatives of the law.

All this is a reminder of what we are apt to forget, that no one can hope to understand the Elizabethans who does not realize that they 'lived dangerously'. To test them by modern standards of morality or maxims of worldly prudence is to go astray. Men who were constantly face to face with violent revolutions of fortune, who were surrounded by a network of espionage and intrigue, whose words or actions might bring them at any moment to the Tower or Newgate, to the block, or the stake, were not predestined to be patterns of scrupulous rectitude. Not only men of the underworld like Poley, Chomley, and Frizer, but statesmen and persons of quality, Christopher Blunt, Francis Walsingham, Walter Raleigh, are far from complying with the codes that would be binding on them to-day. Even a Philip Sidney in *Astrophel and Stella* gives voice to his passion, idealized and transfigured though it be, for the woman who had become the wife of a rival. And as to the writer of the greatest of all Elizabethan sonnet-series, can we really credit the suggestion that Shakespeare 'probably returned to his native town and home every summer or autumn for months at a time, and there prepared for the coming Christmas season, writing happily and swiftly in the midst of his family and friends'?[1] The triangular drama of the poet, the noble patron, and the dark lady comes between us and this rose-coloured idyll of domestic bliss.

And this brings us up against another strange aspect of Marlowe's career. In it there is no record of any figure corresponding to the dark lady or even to Stella. Baines accuses him of loving boys. But neither he nor Kyd nor any one else, till Meres invented the tale of the fatal duel with a rival in his lewd love, charged him with being an ordinary profligate. Baines also accused him of being fond of tobacco. But though he died in a tavern, his enemies do not denounce him as a drunkard, and the legal documents give no support to the theory that Marlowe was 'probably more than a little drunk'[2] when he attacked Frizer.

Kyd was, of course, not thinking of intoxication when he arraigned Marlowe as 'intemperate and of a cruel heart'. What he had in mind was his 'rashnes in attempting soden pryuie iniuries to men'. There rises before us a figure of passionate impulse and restless intellect, quick at word and blow, equally ready with the dagger-point and the no less piercing edge of a ruthless dialectic. This mordant temper was conjoined with a soaring and radiant imaginative faculty. It is a fusion peculiar to the Renaissance and

[1] From the Preface to E. J. Fripp's *Master Richard Quyney*.
[2] Bakeless, op. cit., p. 226.

it leaves Christopher Marlowe, when all is said and done, something of an enigma. William Shakespeare of Stratford-on-Avon we recognize, and Ben Jonson of Westminster, but this son of Canterbury and Cambridge has in him a quality aloof from the English country-side or the banks of the Thames. He would have breathed more congenial air sauntering beside the Arno or swimming in a gondola along the Grand Canal.

But if the man, Kit Marlowe, seems still to evade us, we can determine more clearly the place of Christopher Marlowe, the playwright. Lamb was not well inspired when he called him 'the true (though imperfect) Father of our tragedy'.[1] In a sense the title might be given to Thomas Sackville, for in the Inner Temple play *Gorboduc*, of which he was the chief author, Senecan machinery and rhetoric, and five-act divisions were united with a theme drawn from British history. Blank verse for the first time became the instrument of the English tragic Muse, and though it was end-stopped and stereotyped in form it showed at its best (as has been insufficiently recognized) the quality of melodious rhythm which distinguishes Sackville's *Induction to A Mirror for Magistrates*.

But it was Kyd who, so far as we know, acclimatized neo-Senecan drama on the boards of the public theatre, and who has thus a fuller claim than Sackville to be called 'the true (though imperfect) Father of our tragedy'. He united the Senecan apparatus, including Ghost, Messenger, and Chorus to a realism and constructive power that were new to the English stage and ensured the triumph of *The Spanish Tragedy*. Hence sprang that long line of 'revenge' plays which reach their apotheosis in *Hamlet*.

Marlowe, as has been seen, came under loftier influences than those of the Roman world of Nero. In his six years at Cambridge he drank deep of the spirit of the Augustan age enshrined in the poetry of Virgil and Ovid. He 'learnt

---

[1] *Extracts from the Garrick Plays*, in *Works of Charles and Mary Lamb*, ed. E. V. Lucas, IV. p. 426.

[their] great language, caught [their] clear accents'. He thus felt himself free from the first to dispense with the traditional machinery and types of the Cordoban stage, though he retained the five-act structure, and, in glorified form, the instrument of blank verse.

His method, as investigation in recent years has made increasingly evident, was to choose a subject congenial to his temper and then to follow his sources with close fidelity. It was part of his technique to capture at once the eyes and ears of the theatre audience with an arresting opening and to send them home at the close enthralled by an elaborately worked up *finale*. In the intervening scenes he paid relatively little attention to the articulation of the plot, though he showed skill and discrimination in choosing from his materials the episodes that best suited his purpose, and, when he wished, he could manage terse and economical dialogue. He had not the prodigal creative faculty that is the supreme attribute of the world's master-dramatists, though the minor figures in his plays are often firmly enough outlined within a brief compass. His distinctive achievement was to endowe the protagonists in his dramas with his own elemental vitality so that they stormed their way into the imagination of gallants and groundlings alike. And, as has been seen throughout the course of this study, he enlisted in the service of Melpomene not only the 'new learning' which was the old transformed, but also the science of his day in its various branches—physiology, cosmography, astronomy, and the rest. And in a theatre open to the air how must the constant invocations by Marlowe's characters of celestial powers have gone home to the hearers, whose fortune it was thus to hear voiced

> The high that proved too high, the heroic for earth too hard,
> The passion that left the ground to lose itself in the sky.

But Marlowe, with the strong realist element in his complex personality, was aware that the air and fire of his raptures could not alone win and keep the favour of an

Elizabethan theatre crowd. The old view that he was without humour has been disproved by the examples quoted from his table-talk, and echoes of such talk, with its acid flavour, have been traced in the plays. But far more effective, to judge by the mass of contemporary allusions, were the episodes of crude sensationalism and barbaric violence which mingled so incongruously with the loftier flights of his tragic muse. And, as has been seen, it was not long before these baser elements were taken to be representative of his art not only by the groundlings but by the intelligentsia.

That helps to explain why revivals of Marlowe's plays on the amateur or professional stage to-day do not fully realize expectations. Some of the features that made for their contemporary triumph now leave us cold or even antagonized. Even the alliterative attraction of Ben Jonson's tribute to 'Marlowe's mighty line' may have done him some disservice. It has fastened attention unduly on the more sonorous and declamatory aspects of his verse and diction. These no doubt served their purpose well, especially when he was a newcomer to the London stage. But 'might' is not the crowning virtue of Marlowe's poetic dialogue. It lies rather in a perfect lucidity and precision which translate thoughts and emotions into rhythmical speech with felicitous exactness. This is in the deepest sense the 'classical' element in Marlowe's genius. It was instinctive with him. It was polished in the Augustan school of Latin poetry. It lifts him, regarded purely as a master of dramatic utterance, into the company of the highest. In the loftiest reaches of *Tamburlaine* and *Doctor Faustus* he was the first of Englishmen, perhaps of modern Europeans, to make the theatre echo to accents that were not unworthy to vie with those of Sophocles or Euripides

> Presenting Thebes, or Pelops' line,
> Or the tale of Troy divine.

But with Marlowe this classical diction was the

interpreter and instrument of a restlessly moving and questing spirit ever in pursuit of the illimitable ideals of beauty and knowledge and power, ever in search of

> One thought, one grace, one wonder at the least
> Which into words no virtue can digest.

To the more rarefied atmosphere of the Stuart age this exaltation of spirit was alien, or it passed from poets and playwrights to philosophers and scientists. Thus the quintessential element in Marlowe's genius was incommunicable and it died with him. He founded no school. The prose of Lyly's *Campaspe* and *Endymion* lives on, transfigured, in *As You Like It* and *Much Ado about Nothing*. Kyd's Hieronimo and Shakespeare's Hamlet are unmistakably akin. But even if *The Merchant of Venice* and *Richard II* are indebted to *The Jew of Malta* and *Edward II*, the obligation does not go deep. The measure of the division between Marlowe and Shakespeare may be seen in the contrast between Faustus and Prospero. It was of the creator of the latter that Dryden wrote

> But Shakespeare's magic could not copied be:
> Within that circle none durst walk but he.

Of Jonson and Fletcher he has also much to say; of Marlowe not a word. It has been left to later generations increasingly to realize that Marlowe's 'magic', within its narrower circle, is as potent and inimitable as Shakespeare's, and still wields its enchanting spell. When he died by violence before his time can we wonder that the tragic Muse was inconsolable and exacted retribution by breaking the mould wherein he had been cast?

APPENDIX

[*A List of Principal Documents and Early Editions*]

CHAPTER I

1. Roll of the Freemen of the City of Canterbury from A.D. 1392 to 1800.

   [Transcribed, in alphabetical arrangement, from the City Chamberlains' Accounts by Joseph Meadows Cowper (1903).]

2. Archdeaconry Register in Public Record Office, Canterbury.

   [Contains the wills of Christopher Marley (5 March 1539/40), vol. 21, fol. 258 f.; Dorothy Arthur, vol. 50, fol. 361; John Marlowe, vol. 52, fol. 373, and Katherine Marlowe, vol. 54, fol. 267, printed by Tucker Brooke, *Life of Marlowe* (1930), pp. 89–96.]

3. The Register Booke of the Parish of St. George the Martyr within the Citie of Canterburie.

   [Printed from the original Registers by J. M. Cowper, 1891. Facsimile of the entry of Christopher Marlowe's baptism in J. H. Ingram's *Christopher Marlowe and his Associates* (1904).]

4. MS. Register of St. Andrew's Church, Canterbury.

5. MS. Register of St. Mary Bredman, Canterbury.

6. City of Canterbury MSS. Accounts, in the Beaney Institute.

   [References by John Bakeless in *Christopher Marlowe* (1937), pp. 333–5.]

7. Canterbury Marriage Licences, 1568–1618.

   [Printed by J. M. Cowper, in alphabetical arrangement, from 'Liber Licentiarum', in the Archdeaconry archives (1892).]

8. MS. Accounts of the King's School, Canterbury, in the Cathedral Library.

   [Facsimile of Treasurer's accounts of payments made in 1578–9 to King's School Scholars, including Marlowe, in Ingram, op. cit., p. 33.]

CHAPTER II

1. MS. Cambridge Matriculation Lists in the University Registry.

2. MS. Grace Books of the University of Cambridge.

   [Facsimiles of entries of Marlowe's admission to B.A. and M.A. degrees in Ingram, op. cit., pp. 81 and 93.]

3. Indenture between John Parker and Corpus Christi College concerning Archbishop Parker's scholarships.

 [Discovered by John Bakeless in a manuscript book of C.C.C. 'Statuta', &c.]

4. MS. Corpus Christi College Admission Book (Registrum Parvum).

 [Facsimile of entry of Marlowe's admission among the Pensioners, in Ingram, op. cit., p. 47.]

5. MS. Corpus Christi College Buttery Books.

 [Containing entries of weekly payments by Marlowe between tenth week of Michaelmas term, 1580, and third week of Michaelmas term, 1586.]

6. MS. Corpus Christi College Order Book.

7. MS. Corpus Christi College Accounts (Audits, &c., 1575–90).

 [Extracts relating to payments of Marlowe's scholarship 1580–5 and 1586–7, given by G. C. Moore Smith in 'Marlowe at Cambridge', *Modern Language Review*, January, 1909.]

8. The Privy Council MS. Register, 29 June 1587. Entry 'Whereas as it was reported that Christopher Morley', &c.

 [Printed in *Acts of the Privy Council*, ed. Dasent, vol. xv, pp. 140–1, and in J. Leslie Hotson's *The Death of Christopher Marlowe* (1925), pp. 58–9, as 'A Certificate from the Privy Council in favour of Marlowe'.]

9. Historical MSS. Comm., Salisbury MSS. xii. 211–12. Letter from William Vaughan from Pisa, 14 July 1602, to Privy Council concerning 'one Christopher Marlow'.

 [Reprinted in Hotson, op. cit., pp. 60–1.]

10. MS. Bills of Keepers of the Gatehouse Prison, Westminster, 1596–1606. Entry in sheet from 25 June to 23 September 1604 *re* 'Christopher Marlowe *alias* Mathews, a seminary preist'.

 [Quoted by Sir Israel Gollancz in *The Times*, 23 June 1925, 'The Other Marlowe'.]

11. MS. Records of the English College at Valladolid. Entries *re* John Matthew (Mathews) *alias* Christopher Marler, 1599–1603.

 [Quoted by J. B. Whitmore in *The Times*, 24 July 1925, 'The Other Marlowe: Fresh Evidence for Identity'. See also Sir I. Gollancz 'The Other Marlowe', ibid. 25 July.]

12. Calendar of State Papers relating to English Affairs preserved principally at Rome, vol. ii, 1572–8, ed. J. M. Rigg (1926).

CHAPTERS III–IV

(Where copies are unique, the library or owner is mentioned.)

1. Epigrammes | and | Elegies. | By I. D. and | C. M. | *At* Middleborugh. [*Second title-page.*] Certaine | of Ovids | Elegies. | By C Marlow, | *At* Midleborugh. 12ᵐᵒ. n.d.

2. Epigrammes | and | Elegies. | By I. D. and | C. M. *At* Middleborough. [*Second title-page.*] Certaine of Ovids | Elegies. | By C. Marlow. *At* Middleborough. 12ᵐᵒ. n.d. (Huntington.)

3. Ouids Elegies: | Three Bookes. | By C. M. | Epigrammes by I. D. | *At* Middlebourgh. 8ᵛᵒ. n.d. (Bodleian Douce 031.)

4. All | Ovids Elegies: | 3. Bookes. | By C. M. | Epigrams by J. D. *At* Middlebourgh. 8ᵛᵒ. n.d.

5. Title-page as in 4, but with different ornaments.

6. Title-page as in 4, but with different ornaments.

7. Lucans | First Booke | Translated Line | for Line by Chr. | Marlow. | *At* London. | Printed by *P. Short*, and are to be sold by *Walter* | *Burre* at the Signe of the Flower de Luce in | Paules Churchyard. 1600. 4ᵗᵒ.

8. The | Tragedie of Dido | Queene of Carthage: | Played by the Children of her | Maiesties Chappell. | Written by Christopher Marlowe, and | Thomas Nashe Gent. | [Names of 'Actors', i.e. Dramatis Personae.] At London, | Printed by *the Widdowe Orwin, for Thomas Woodcocke*, and | are to be solde at his shop, in Paules Church-yard, at | the signe of the Blacke Beare. 1594. 4ᵗᵒ.

   [No copy containing the elegy by Nashe on Marlowe 'inserted immediately after the title-page', vouched for by Tanner and Warton (see p. 50, above), has been traced.]

CHAPTERS V–VI

1. Tamburlaine | the Great. | Who, from a Scythian Shephearde, | by his rare and wonderfull Conquests, | became a most puissant and migh | -tye Monarque. | And (for his tyranny, and terrour in | Warre) was tearmed, | The Scourge of God. | Devided into two Tragicall Dis- | courses, as they were sundrie times | shewed vpon Stages in the Citie | of London. | By the right honorable the Lord | Admyrall his seruantes. | Now first, and newlie published. | London. | Printed by *Richard*

Ihones: at the signe | of the Rose and Crowne neere Hol- | borne Bridge. 1590. 8ᵛᵒ.

[*Half-title.*] The second part of | The bloody Conquests | of mighty Tamburlaine. | With his impassionate fury, for the death of | his Lady and loue, faire Zenocrate: his fourme of exhortation and discipline to his three | sons and the maner of his own death.

2. Tamburlaine | the Great. | Who, from a Scythian Shepheard, | by his rare and wonderfull Conquestes, be- | came a most puissant and mightie | Monarch: | And (for his tyrannie, and terrour in warre) | was tearmed, | The Scourge of God. | The first part of the two Tragicall dis- | courses, as they were sundrie times most | stately shewed vpon Stages in the | Citie of London. | By the right honorable the Lord Admirall, | his seruantes. | Now newly published. | Printed by *Richard Iones*, dwelling at the signe of | the Rose and Crowne neare Holborne | Bridge. 1592. 8ᵛᵒ. (British Museum.)

    [The head-title to Part II is, with some variants of spelling, similar to the half-title in the 1590 edition.]

3. Tamburlaine | the Great. | Who, from the state of | a shepheard in Scythia, by his | rare and wonderful Conquests, be- | came a most puissant and mightie Monarque. | As it was acted: by the right Ho- | norable, the Lord Admyrall | his servantes. Printed at London by *Richard Iohnes*: at the Rose | and Crowne, next above St. Andrewes | Church in Holborne. 1597. 8ᵛᵒ. (Huntington.)

    [Head-title to Part II as in 1592 edition.]

4. Tamburlaine | the Greate. | Who, from the state of a Shep- | heard | in Scythia, by his rare and | wonderfull Conquests, became | a most puissant and mighty | Monarque. | London. | Printed for *Edward White*, and are to be solde | at the little North doore of Saint Paules | Church, at the signe of the Gunne. | 1605. 8ᵛᵒ.

5. Tamburlaine the | Greate. With his impassionate furie, for the | death of his Lady and Loue faire Zenocra- | te: his forme of exhortation and discipline | to his three Sonnes, and the manner of | his owne death. | The second part. | London. | Printed by *E. A. for Ed. White*, and are to be solde | at his Shop neere the little North doore of Saint Paules | Church at the Signe of the Gunne | 1606. 8ᵛᵒ.

CHAPTER VII

1. Middlesex Sessions Roll 284, No. 1. Recognizance of Christopher Marlowe, 1 October 1589.

   [Noted by J. C. Jeaffreson in *Middlesex County Records*, vol. i, p. 257. Facsimile by J. H. Ingram, op. cit. Printed by Tucker Brooke, op. cit., pp. 96–7, and marginal note interpreted by Mark Eccles, *Christopher Marlowe in London*, p. 33.]

2. Middlesex Sessions Roll 284, No. 12. List of persons committed to Newgate from 9 Sept. to 2 Oct. 1589.

   [Entry relating to Thomas Watson and Christopher Marlowe printed by Eccles, op. cit., p. 34.]

3. Chancery Miscellanea 68, file 12, no. 362. Writ and return into Chancery of a Gaol Delivery at Newgate reciting the Coroner's inquest on William Bradley killed in an affray with Watson and 'Morley'.

   [The return printed by Eccles, op. cit., pp. 22–4.]

4. Patent Roll C 66/1340, membrane 34. / Enrolment of the pardon of Thomas Watson.

   [Printed by Eccles, op. cit., pp. 25–6.]

5. Star Chamber 5 A 1/29.

   [Evidence of Richard Kitchen, 1 June 1600, on behalf of W. Williamson, host of the Mermaid. Printed by Eccles, op. cit. p. 87.]

6. Registers of St. Botolph's Church, East Smithfield.

   [Extracts relating to Humphrey Rowland, 1577–93, printed by J. Leslie Hotson in 'Marlowe Among the Churchwardens', in the *Atlantic Monthly*, July 1926.]

7. King's Bench Controlment Roll 29/222, m. 12/. Summons to Humphrey Rowland.

   [Printed by Hotson, *Atlantic Monthly*, July 1926, and Eccles, op. cit., p. 95.]

8. Henry Oxiden's Common-place Books, in British Museum (Add. MSS. 28012) and Folger Shakespeare Library.

   [Extracts by Eccles in 'Marlowe in Kentish Tradition', *N. & Q.*, 13, 20, 27 July, 24 Aug. 1935.]

9. Thomas Kyd's signed letter to Sir John Puckering, the Lord Keeper. Harl. MSS. 6849, f. 218.

   [Transcribed, with facsimile, in *Works of Thomas Kyd*, ed. F. S. Boas, 1901; transcribed by F. C. Danchin, *Revue Germanique*, Nov.–Dec. 1913, and Tucker Brooke, op. cit., pp. 103–6.]

10. MS. Fragments of a Socinian treatise quoted in John Proctor's *The Fal of the Late Arrian* (1549). Harl. MSS. 6848, ff. 187–9 (formerly 172–4).

> [Transcribed, with facsimile of f. 189, by Boas, op. cit., and by F. C. Danchin, loc. cit. W. Dinsmore Briggs (*Studies in Philology*, April 1923) has identified the printed source of the fragments, and has shown what is their right order in 'the Late Arrian's' treatise.]

CHAPTER VIII

1. State Papers (Domestic), vol. ccxxii, no. 13, 7 Jan. 1588/9. Examinations of William Yeomans and others before William Fleetwood, Recorder of London.

2. Ibid., no. 14. Deposition by Richard Ede.

> [Short abstract of both documents in *Calendar of State Papers, Domestic, 1581–90*, p. 573.]

3. State Papers relating to Scotland and Mary, Queen of Scots.
   C.S.P., vol. xvi, 10 July 1585 (Thomas Morgan to Mary, Queen of Scots).

4. „ vol. xvi, 15 July 1585 (Charles Paget to Mary).

5. „ vol. xvii, 18 January 1585/6 (Thomas Morgan to Mary and Curll).

6. „ „ 21 March 1585/6 (Thomas Morgan to Mary).

7. „ „ 31 March 1586 (Charles Paget to Mary).

8. „ vol. xviii, 27 July 1586 (Mary to Thomas Morgan).

9. „ vol. xix, [Aug.] 1586 (Charges against Poley).

10. „ „ [Aug.] 1586 (Confession of Poley).

> [Printed in slightly abbreviated form, in modernized spelling, in *Calendar of State Papers relating to Scotland and Mary, Queen of Scots, 1547–1603*, vol. viii, edited by William K. Boyd.]

11. Lansdowne MSS. 49, f. 63. Letter of Babington to Poley. Other copies in Bodleian, Rawlinson MSS. D 264/1, and B.M. Addit. MSS. 33938, no. 22.

12. Bills of the Lieutenant of the Tower in P.R.O.

> [Nos. E 407/56; nos. 44, 47, 50 printed by Eugénie de Kab in *Nineteenth Century and After*, Nov. 1927.]

13. State Papers (France), xvii, 26. Letter to the Earl of Leicester from Poley, Feb. 1587 (?).

> [Transcript slightly abbreviated in *Cal. of State Papers, Foreign, June 1586–June 1588*, pp. 228–9.]

CHAPTERS IX–XI

1. The Famous | Tragedy | of | The Rich Iew of Malta. | As It Was Playd | Before The King And | Queene, In His Majesties | Theatre at White Hall, by her Majesties | Servants at the Cock-pit. | Written by Christopher Marlo. | London; | Printed by *I. B. for Nicholas Vavasour*, and are to be sold | at his Shop in the Inner-Temple, neere the | Church. 1633. 4to.

2. The | Massacre | At Paris: | With the Death of the Duke | of Guise. | As it was plaide by the right honourable the | Lord high Admirall his Seruants. | Written by Christopher Marlow. |At London | Printed by *E. A. for Edward White*, dwelling neere | the little North doore of S. Paules | Church, at the signe of | The Gun. 8vo.

3. MS. expanded version of ll. 812–27 of Tucker Brooke's text of *The Massacre at Paris.*

> [Transcripts by J. P. Collier in Dodsley's *Old Plays*, vol. viii (1825), and in *History of English Dramatic Poetry* (1831). The leaf, now in the Folger Shakespeare Library, is reproduced in facsimile with a transcript in modernized spelling and punctuation by J. Quincy Adams in *The Library*, March 1934. W. W. Greg adds an unedited transcript.]

4. MS. title-page of *Edward the Second*, dated 1593, and first seventy lines.

> [Prefixed to imperfect copy of the 1598 quarto of the play in South Kensington Museum. Facsimile in Malone Society's reprint of the play, ed. by Greg.]

5. The troublesome | raigne and lamentable death of | Edward the second, King of | England: with the tragicall | fall of proud Mortimer: | As it was sundrie times publiquely acted | in the honourable Citie of London by the | right honourable the Earle of Pem- | brooke his seruants. | Written by Chri. Marlow Gent. | Imprinted at London *for William Iones*, | dwelling neere Holbourne conduit at the | signe of the Gunne, 1594. 8vo.

6. The troublesome | raigne and lamentable death of | Edward the second, King of | England: with the tragicall | fall of proud Mortimer: And also the life and death of Piers Gaueston | the great Earle of Cornewall and mighty | fauorite of King Edward the second, as it was | publiquely acted by the right honorable | the Earl of Pembrooke his | seruantes. | Written by Chri. Marlow Gent. | Imprinted at London by *Richard Bradocke,* | *for William Iones* dwelling neere Holbourne conduit, | at the signe of the Gunne, 1598. 4to.

7. The troublesome raigne and lamentable death of Edward the second, King of England, &c. . . . *for Roger Barnes.* 1612. 4to.

   [Two issues, in one of which a page is duplicated. Unique copy of corrected issue in B.M. (644 b. 68).]

8. The troublesome raigne and lamentable death of Edward the second, King of England, &c. . . . *for Henry Bell.* 1622. 4to.

   [Two issues, one repeating the statement of the earlier editors that the play was acted by the Earl of Pembroke's servants, the other altering this to 'As it was publiquely acted by the late Queenes [Anne's] Maiesties Servants at the Red Bull in S. Iohns streete'.]

9. The First Part of the Contention betwixt the two famous Houses of Yorke and Lancaster. . . . *Thomas Creede,* for *Thomas Millington.* 1594. 4to.

   [Another edition, Valentine Simmes for Millington, 1600.]

10. The True Tragedie of Richard Duke of York . . . as it was sundrie times acted by the Right Honourable the Earle of Pembrooke his seruants. *P.S.* for *Thomas Millington.* 1595. 4to.

    [Another edition; *W. W. for Millington,* 1600.]

11. The Whole Contention betweene the two Famous Houses, Lancaster and Yorke. . . . Divided into two Parts: And newly corrected and enlarged. Written by William Shakespeare, Gent. *for T[homas] P[avier].* 1619. 4to.

12. [In the Shakespeare First Folio.] The Second Part of Henry Sixt, with the death of the Good Duke Humfrey. The Third Part of Henry the Sixt, with the death of the Duke of Yorke. 1623.

13. The Lamentable and True Tragedie of M. Arden of Feuersham in Kent . . . for *Edward White.* 1592. 4to.

    [Other editions, *I. Roberts for White.* 1599; *Eliz. Allde.* 1633.]

14. The Tragedye of Solyman and Perseda . . . *Edward Allde for Edward White*. n.d. 8vo.

[Another edition, *Allde for White*, 1599.]

CHAPTER XII

1. A Pleasant Conceited Historie, called the taming of a Shrew . . . *Peter Short*, sold by *Cuthbert Burley*. 1594 and 1596. 4to.

   [These editions of *The Taming of a Shrew* contain (in addition to about thirty lines from both Parts of *Tamburlaine*) several passages from *Doctor Faustus* in their earliest known form.]

2. The | Tragicall | History of D. Faustus. | As it hath been Acted by the Right | Honorable the Earle of Nottingham his seruants. | Written by Ch. Marl. | London | Printed by | *V[alentine] S[immes] for Thomas Bushell*. 1604. 4to. (Bodleian.)

3. The | Tragicall | History of the horrible | Life and death | of | Doctor Faustus. | Written by Ch. Marl. | Imprinted at London by *G[eorge] E[ld] for Iohn | Wright*, and are to be sold at Christ-Church gate. 1609. 4to.

4. Another edition with similar title, by *Eld for Wright*. 1611. 4to. (Huntington.)

5. Henslowe's Diary, f. 108^v:
   'Lent vnto the companye the 22 of novmbr 1602 ⎫
   to paye vnto w^m Bvrde & Samwell Rowle   ⎬ iiij^{li}.'
   for ther adicyones in doctor fostes the some of ⎭

6. The Tragicall History | of the Life and Death | of Doctor Favstus. | Written by Ch. Mar. | London | Printed *for Iohn Wright*, and are to be sold at his shop | without Newgate, at the signe of the | Bible, 1616. 4to. (British Museum.)

   [The first edition with the Additions, and with the woodcut on the title-page of Dr. Faustus with his conjurer's gown, book, and wand, and with a dragon at his feet.]

7. The Tragicall History | of the Life and Death | of Doctor Favstus. | With new additions. | Written by Ch. Mar. | Printed at London *for Iohn Wright*, and are to be sold at his | shop without Newgate. 1619. 4to. (Robert Garrett, Baltimore.)

8. Another edition with similar title. 1620. 4to. (British Museum.)

9. Another edition with similar title. 1624. 4to. (British Museum.)

10. Another edition with similar title. 1628. 4to.

11. Another edition with similar title. 1631. 4to.

12. The Tragicall History | of the Life and Death of | Doctor Faustus | Printed with New Additions as it is now Acted. With several | New Scenes, together with the Actors Names | Written by Ch. Mar. | Printed for *W. Gilbertson* at the Bible without Newgate 1663. 4to.

CHAPTER XIII

1. The Passionate Shepherd to his Love.

   [Different versions in *The Passionate Pilgrim* (1599), *England's Helicon* (1600), John Thornborough's commonplace-book, and *The Compleat Angler* (1653 and 1655).]

2. Sir W. Raleigh's *Reply*.

   [Different versions in *England's Helicon* and *The Compleat Angler*.]

3. 'I walked along a Stream', &c.

   [Lines, signed 'Ch. Marlowe', in the section of *England's Parnassus* (1600) entitled 'Description of Seas, Waters, Rivers, &c.']

4. Hero | And | Leander. | By Christopher Marloe. | London, | Printed by *Adam Islip,* | *for Edward Blunt.* | 1598. 4to. (Folger Shakespeare Library.)

5. Hero And | Leander: | Begun by Christopher Marloe; and | finished by George Chapman. | Vt Nectar, Ingenium. | At London | Printed by *Felix Kingston, for Paule Linley,* and | are to be solde in Paules Church-yard, at the | signe of the Blacke-beare. | 1598. 4to.

6. Hero And | Leander: | Begunne by Christopher Marloe: | Where-unto is added the first booke of | Lucan translated line for line by | the same Author. | Vt Nectar, Ingenium. | At London | Printed for *John Flasket* | and are to be solde | in Paules Church-yard, at the signe | of the Blacke-beare. | 1600. 4to.

   [Includes, without mention on the title-page, Chapman's additional Sestiads; mentions, but does not include, the translation of Lucan.]

7. Hero And | Leander: | Begunne by Christopher Marloe, | and finished by George Chapman. | Vt Nectar, Ingenium. | At London | Imprinted for *John Flasket,* and are to be | sold in Paules Church-yard, at the signe | of the black Beare. 1606. 4to.

8. Another edition, *for E. Blunt and W. Barrett,* 1609. 4to.

9. Another edition, *W. Stansby for E. Blunt and W. Barrett,* 1613. 4to.

10. Another edition, *G. P[urslowe] for E. Blount.* 1607. 4to.

11. Another edition, *G. P[urslowe] for E. Blount,* 1622. 4to.

12. Another edition, *A. M[athews] for R. Hawkins,* 1629. 4to.

13. Another edition, *N. Okes for W. Leake,* 1637. 4to.

CHAPTERS XIV–XV

1. Thomas Kyd's signed letter to Sir John Puckering. Harl. MSS. 6849, f. 218 (see above, chap. VII, no. 8).

2. Thomas Kyd's unsigned letter to Puckering. Harl. MSS. 6848, f. 154.

   [Transcribed by Ford K. Brown, with some misreadings, in *T.L.S.*, 2 June 1921; by Tucker Brooke in *Life*; and with facsimile, in *English Literary Autographs, 1550–1650: Part I. Dramatists,* ed. W. W. Greg (1925), no. xv (b).]

3. The Privy Council's warrant to Henry Maunder for the arrest of Marlowe, 18 May 1593.

4. Entry in the Privy Council's Register of Marlowe's appearance before their Lordships, 20 May 1593.

5. Registers of St. Peter's Church, Cornhill.

   [Transcribed in Harleian Society's Registers, vol. i. Contains dates of the christenings of the children of Richard Baines, senior, and of his own burial.]

6. Minutes of Parliament of the Middle Temple.

   [Edited by C. T. Martin. Contains admission entry of Richard Baines.]

7. St. John's College, Oxford, Buttery books, 1582–3, 1583–4, 1584–5.

   [Containing the receipts of the 'batells' of Richard Baines.]

8. Entry in the Privy Council Register of Richard Baines's appearance before their Lordships, 2 February 1588/9.

9. Charges of Richard Baines against Marlowe. Harl. MSS. 6848, ff. 185–6 (formerly 170–1) (original Note). Harl. MSS. 6853, ff. 307–8 (formerly 320–1) (copy sent to Queen Elizabeth).

   [Original transcribed with a few omissions by Boas, op. cit. and in full by Tucker Brooke, op. cit. Original and copy transcribed in full by Danchin, loc. cit.]

10. ⌠'Remembraunces of wordes and matter againste Ric[hard] Cholmeley.' Harl. MSS. 6848, ff. 190 (formerly 175).

11. ⎸Charges against Chomley by an anonymous informer. Harl. MSS. 6848, f. 191 (formerly 176).

12. ⌡Letter of Justice Young announcing Chomley's arrest. Harl. MSS. 7002, f. 10.

[Chief parts of these three documents printed by F. S. Boas in *Fortnightly Review*, Feb. 1899, pp. 223–4. Printed in full by Danchin, loc. cit.; 10 and 11 printed by G. B. Harrison, in *Shakespeare's Fellows*, pp. 71–4 (1923).]

13. The Privy Council MS. Register, 13 May and 29 July 1591, and 19 March 1592/3. Warrants mentioning Chomley.

[Printed in *Acts of the Privy Council*, ed. Dasent, vols. xxi and xxiv.]

14. Letter of Earl of Essex concerning Chomley, 13 Nov. 1593.

[Summarized in Historical MSS. Commission, Fourth Report, p. 330, and by Danchin, op. cit., p. 63.]

15. Depositions of witnesses before the Commission held at Cerne Abbas in Dorset on 21 March 1594, in answer to interrogatories concerning Atheism or Apostacy. Harl. MSS. 6849, ff. 183–90.

[Extensive extracts printed by J. M. Stone, *The Month*, June 1894, and by F. S. Boas in *Literature*, nos. 147 and 148. Full transcript by Danchin, loc. cit., and by G. B. Harrison in Appendix to his edition of *Willobie His Avisa* (1926).]

CHAPTER XVI

1. Declared Accounts of the Treasurer of the Chamber.

[Contain payments to Poley, 1588–93, transcribed by Eugénie de Kalb in *R.E.S.*, Jan. 1933.]

2. State Papers, 106, vol. ii.

[Contain Poley's ciphers. Described, with a facsimile, by Ethel Seaton in *R.E.S.*, March 1931.]

3. State Papers (Dom.), Elizabeth, vol. ccxxxviii, no. 140. Deposition of Robert Rutkin, broker, concerning Poley as an agent of Sir Thomas Heneage, April (?) 1591.

[Summary in *C.S.P. (Dom.)*, *1591–4*, p. 35.]

4. State Papers (Dom.), Elizabeth, vol. ccxlii, no. 25. Letter of
   Sir Robert Cecil to Sir T. Heneage, 25 May 1592, concerning
   interview with Poley.

   [Summary, op. cit., p. 223.]

5. {Close Rolls 1339.
6. {Exchequer Plea Rolls 381, 394, and 396.

   [Concerning financial transactions by Ingram Frizer, 1589–95.
   Summaries by J. Leslie Hotson, *The Death of Christopher Marlowe*,
   pp. 42–57.]

7. Chancery Proceedings, Elizabeth, bundle W. 25, no. 43. Suit
   of Woodleff *versus* Frizer.

   [Printed from the imperfect original document by Hotson, op. cit.,
   pp. 69–71.]

8. Lord Chamberlain, 4/192, p. 267. Bond of Drew Woodleff to
   Thomas Walsingham, 29 June 1593.

   [Summary by Hotson, op. cit., p. 48.]

9. Lansdowne MSS. 44, no. 38. Letter of William Fleetwood to
   Lord Burleigh, 7 July 1585, mentioning Skeres.

   [Mentioned by Sir E. Chambers, *T.L.S.*, 21 May 1925.]

10. Chancery Miscellanea, bundle 64, file 8, nos. 241 a and 241 b.
    Writ of *certiorari* to summon the case of Ingram Frizer into
    Chancery.

11. Inquisition returned by William Danby, Coroner of the House-
    hold, in obedience to the writ.

    [Both documents printed in full, with English translation, by
    Hotson, op. cit., pp. 26–34.]

12. Patent Rolls 1401. Enrolment of the Pardon of Ingram Frizer.

    [Printed with facsimile by Hotson, op. cit., pp. 34–7 and frontis-
    piece; printed by Tucker Brooke, op. cit., pp. 108–10.]

13. Wills of jurymen who served at the inquest on Marlowe.

    [Extracts from the original documents at Somerset House in
    E. Vine Hall's *Testamentary Papers*, III (1937).]

14. Register of the Church of St. Nicholas, Deptford. Entry of
    Marlowe's burial, 1 June 1593.

    [Facsimile of part of the page containing the entry in J. H. Ingram's
    Christopher Marlowe and his Associates, with an erroneous transcrip-
    tion. See Hotson, op. cit., pp. 21–2.]

CHAPTER XVII

1. Will of Grace Baines, 17 August 1597 (Prerog. Court Cant. Cobham 83).

   [Main sections printed by F. S. Boas and E. Vine Hall in *Nineteenth Century and After*, Dec. 1932.]

2. Privy Council MS. Register, 31 July 1601. Warrant for the removal of 'Skiers' and Farmer from Newgate to Bridewell.

   [Printed by Dasent, op. cit., xxxii, p. 130.]

3. {Signet Office Docquets: Warrant, 5 Sept. 1603.
4. {State Papers (Dom.), Addenda, James I, xl. 46.
5. {P.R.O. Index 6801.

   [Three documents relating to lease of reversion of lands belonging to the Duchy of Lancaster to Frizer on behalf of Lady Audrey Walsingham. Printed by Hotson, op. cit., pp. 49–50.]

6. Subsidies 127/566. Entry concerning Frizer as an assessor of the parish of Eltham.

   [Summarized by Hotson, op. cit., p. 51.]

7. Eltham Parish Registers. Entries *re* Frizer in Eltham to August 1627.

   [Summarized by Eugénie de Kalb, *T.L.S.*, 21 May 1925.]

8. Declared Accounts of the Treasurer of the Chamber.

   [Contains payments to Poley, 1594–1600. See chap. xvi, no. 1.]

9. State Papers (Dom.), Elizabeth, vol. cclxxv, no. 141. Letter of Poley to Sir R. Cecil, 17 Dec. 1600, concerning Jesuits.

   [Transcribed, in abridged form, and in modernized spelling, in *C.S.P. (Dom.), 1598–1601.*]

10. Hatfield MSS. xi. 216, 278, 301, and xii. 230. Poley in July 1601 and July 1602.

    [Summarized by Sir E. Chambers, *Mod. Lang. Rev.*, Jan. 1926.]

INDEX

Adams, J. Quincy, 169–71.
Ailesbury, Thomas, 114.
Alasco, Albertus, 52.
Aldrich, Simon, 19, 35, 110, 256, 280 n.
Alexander, Peter, 192–3, 195–7.
Allde, Edward, 151.
Allen, John, 102.
Allen, Thomas, 257–8.
Allen, William, 26.
Alleyn, Edward, 66, 69, 168.
Alleyn, Richard, 106.
Amor Constans, 223.
Archer, Edward, 70, 299, 300.
Arden of Feversham, 66 n., 198–200.
Ardern, Alice, 200.
Ariosto, *Orlando Furioso*, 95, 100.
Aristotle, 231, 260; *Analytics*, 16; *de Anima*, 257; *Organon*, 16, 160.
Arnall, William, 246.
Arthur, Christopher, 3.
Arthur (Marlowe), Catherine, 3, 5, 6.
Ashe, Eve, 107.
Assheton, John, 112.
Aston, Sir E., 255.
Audley, Thomas, 127.
Awger, Henry, 272.

Babington, Anthony, 124–5, 259, 268, 273, 291–3.
Bagot, R., 255.
Baines, Fraunces, 246, 285–6.
Baines, Grace, 248, 285–6.
Ba(i)nes (Smith), Mary, 246, 285–6.
Baines, Richard (merchant of the Staple), 246–9, 285.
Baines, Richard (of the Middle Temple), 104, 113–14, 212, 245–52, 254–60, 277, 284–6, 301, 304, 308–10.
Bai(y)nes, Ursula, 246, 286.
Bakeless, John, 4 n., 5 n., 9 n., 10 n., 12 n., 17 n., 114 n., 147 n., 152, 154 n., 168 n., 283 n., 305.
Baldwyn, Robert, 272.
Ballard, John, 124.
Bamfield, Katherine, 264.
Banes, Richard, 246.
Bankes, John, 288.

Banyster, Henry, 268.
Barber, John, 272.
Barrois, Robert, 293.
Batt, James, 272.
Batt, Thomas, 272.
Baynes, Richard (Christ's College, Cambridge), 245.
Baynes, Richard (of Whaddon), 246.
Baynes, Thomas, 246.
Beard, Thomas, 279–82.
Beaumont, Francis, 294.
Belleforest, François de, *Cosmographie Universelle*, 19, 95, 100, 131.
Bennett, H. S., 138 n., 142 n., 153, 158 n., 168–9.
Birde (Borne), William, 167, 205–6, 294.
Blackwell, William, 284.
Blount, Edward, 42–3, 112, 224–5, 281–2, 298.
Blunt (Blount), Charles, 118, 122.
Blunt (Blount), Christopher, 118–22, 127, 273, 293, 310.
Blunt, William (Lord Mountjoy), 118.
Boas, F. S., 37 n., 55 n., 193 n., 204 n., 205 n., 206 n., 211 n., 216 n., 266 n., 241 n., 242 n.; *Marlowe and his Circle*, 304.
Bonfinius, A., 88–90, 100.
Borage, Jasper, 253–4.
Boswell, E., 204 n.
Bosworth, W., *Chast and Lost Lovers* 298 n.
Boyle, Will, *Jugurth*, 296 n.
Bradbrook, C. M., 90, 113 n., 259 n., 263 n.
Bradley, William, 102, 108, 117, 236, 252, 305, 309.
Bradocke, Richard, 173.
Breton, Nicholas, 70.
Breymann, H., 303.
Bridgman, James, 21.
Brooke, C. F. Tucker, 4 n., 5 n., 13, 43, 49, 105, 132, 154, 168, 192–8, 206, 242 n., 244, 246, 248, 297 n., 298 n., 303–4.

PRINTED IN GREAT BRITAIN AT THE UNIVERSITY PRESS, OXFORD
BY VIVIAN RIDLER, PRINTER TO THE UNIVERSITY